The Pathan U

MW00558892

The Pathan Unarmed

Opposition & Memory in the North West Frontier

Mukulika Banerjee

James Currey
OXFORD

School of American Research Press
SANTA FE

Oxford University Press
KARACHI & NEW DELHI

Oxford University Press
5-Bangalore Town
Sharae Faisal
Karachi- 75350 Pakistan

Oxford University Press
YMCA Library Building
Jai Singh Road
New Delhi 110601 India

James Currey
73 Botley Road
Oxford OX2 OBS

School of American Research Press
Post Office Box 2188
Santa Fe, New Mexico 87504-2188

Copyright © Mukulika Banerjee 2000
First published 2000
1 2 3 4 5 033 02 01 00

British Library Cataloguing in Publication Data

Banerjee, Mukulika
The Pathan unarmed: opposition & memory in the North West Frontier
1. Pushtuns – Pakistan – History   2. Pakistan – History
3. Pakistan – Politics and government
I. Title
305.8'91593

ISBN 0-85255-273-4 (James Currey paper)
ISBN 0-85255-272-6 (James Currey cloth)

Library of Congress Cataloging-in-Publication Data
is available on request

ISBN 0-933452-69-1 (SAR Press paper)
ISBN 0-933452-68-3 (SAR Press cloth)

ISBN 0-19579-388-9 (OUP Karachi cloth)

Typeset in 10/12 pt Monotype Photina
by Saxon Graphics Ltd, Derby, UK
Printed and bound in Great Britain
by Woolnough, Irthlingborough

Dedicated To the Khudai Khidmatgars

They themselves would not wish me to claim perfection for them, yet surely the virtues indicated here by definite illustrations cannot fail to earn our humble respect and affection.

(Mary Barr, *A Red Shirt Camp*, 1942)

Contents

Acknowledgements

This book was originally intended to be a short newspaper article. That was twelve years ago. Over the years many people have provided encouragement and help. Jit Uberoi of the Delhi School of Economics helped broaden my initial vision by suggesting I investigate the Khudai Khidmatgars for a doctoral thesis and he has followed the project closely throughout. At Oxford, it was my supervisor John Davis who urged me on at a time when the chances of my getting into Pakistan seemed remote, and who always shared with me his healthy scepticism of modish theory, and profound understanding of the twin ventures of anthropological explanation and ethnographic writing. Ramchandra Guha, Ramchandra Gandhi, Subhash Malik, Kapila Vatsyayan, Mohammed Yunus all encouraged a seemingly impossible idea in its early stages. I am particularly grateful to Shafqat Kakakhel, who gave me my first visa to Pakistan while he was Acting High Commissioner in New Delhi.

It would have been impossible for me to do months of fieldwork in Pakistan without Wali Khan's hospitality, and his wonderful family made me feel one of them, especially Bibi, Nazo, Nasreen, Parveen and Gulalai. Habibullah accompanied me on my travels in search of ageing Khudai Khidmatgars as chaperon, guide and committed son of a Khudai Khidmatgar himself, and my research in Pakistan would not have been possible without him. I thank him for his untiring enthusiasm and friendship, and also his family, who provided me with a second home in the field at Peshwar.

Financial support was provided by the Radhakrishnan Bequest, Bagby Trust, Beit Commonwealth Fund, Indira Gandhi Trust and a Junior Research Fellowship at Wolfson College. The staff at the India Office Library, School of Oriental and African Studies in London, National Archives and Nehru Memorial Museum and Library in New Delhi, and at the Tylor and Bodleian Libraries in Oxford were always most helpful and efficient.

Veena Das, Paul Dresch, Michael Gilsenan, Ashis Nandy, Lydia Sciama, Jit Uberoi and the late Ernest Gellner each read the doctoral thesis and gave me detailed comments. I have presented parts of this material at the universities of Cambridge, Delhi, Edinburgh, London, Manchester, Oxford, the Collège de France in Paris and the Centre for the Study of Social Sciences in Calcutta. My thanks to participants at those seminars for their feedback and especially to Chris Bayly, Ravinder Kumar, T. N. Madan, Amit Kumar Grupta, Deepak Mehta, Manoranjan Mohanty, Yogendra Yadav, Phil Burnham, Chris Fuller, Jonathan Parry, Pnina Werbner, Roger Ballard, Tapan Raichaudhari, David Page, David Washbrook, Judith Brown, Abner Cohen, Edouard Conte, Gautam Bhadra and the late Anthony Hyman. Particular thanks go to Douglas Johnson for being a most supportive publisher, but also for his inspiring ethnographic histories of the Nuer.

Jonathan Spencer provided detailed and insightful comments on the draft of this book and his suggestions have helped improve the final product enormously. Thanks also to an anonymous reviewer at OUP for a most helpful report. At the Institute of Social and Cultural Anthropology at Oxford, where I was based as a doctoral student,

I would like to thank Nick Allen, Marcus Banks, Bob Barnes, Paul Dresch, Wendy James and Peter Riviere whose work and teaching set high standards of ethnographic enquiry and theoretical analysis. For their friendship and collegiality at Oxford I thank Jairus Banaji, Iftikar Malik, Richard Murphy, Peter Parkes, Mahesh Rangarajan, Pritam Singh, Wiqar Shah and Mohammed Wasseem.

My students and colleagues at the University College London have provided a lively and congenial environment during the last three years and my special thanks go to Murray Last for provoking me to think of new ideas and always sharing his own, and to Danny Miller for his encouragement and helpful comments on the manuscript.

My friends Charles and Primila Lewis, Susan Manly, Audrey Maxwell, Pratima Mitchell, Christa Salamandra, Gail and Manavendra Thakur have shared with me innumerable chats, meals and ideas. Shirley Daniels and Jacquie Watson generously provided me a home in London which facilitated archival research for this project.

Margaret and John Watts have made me welcome in my new family in England and have tolerated with good humour a daughter-in-law preoccupied with deadlines. My parents, Roma and Akshay Banerjee, have believed in this project from the day I read fateful the newspapers which was to change the course of my life. They have always been there with their love, unstinting faith and encouragement, even when it meant letting go. I offer this book as a vindication of their trust. My sisters Madhulika and Krittika have always been there for me and through our daily emails and late-night chats have shared all the agonies and stories linked to this project and brought a fresh and balanced perspective to work and life.

I thank my husband Julian Watts at the end, partly out of convention but also because his contribution has been the greatest. He has given unselfishly of his time and energy as if the book were his own, and done so out of love and companionship, and perhaps a little post-colonial guilt. To all the above people my warmest deep-felt thanks. I take responsibility for the shortcomings which remain.

Khan Abdul Gaffar Khan
(sketch by Nandalal Bose)

Khan Abdul Gaffar Khan
(Badshah Khan) in his forties

A large-scale gathering of Khudai Khidmatgar activists in the 1930s

Youthful Khudai Khidmatgar guard of honour for Gandhi's visit to N.W.F.P.

Abdul Gaffar Khan at All India Congress Meeting with Maulana Abul Kalam Azad (left), Jawaharlal Nehru (centre), Rajendra Prasad (far right)

Nehru & Badshah Khan spinning the charkha

Badshah Khan & Gandhi flanked by Khudai Khidmatgar generals

Badshah Khan arriving in Delhi airport (with Indian president Snajiva Reddy on left)
his baggage as ever confined to one small bundle

Badshah Khan
in old age

The author with three Khudai Khidmatgar veterans and friends.
Note the black trunk in the far right which contained carefully preserved memorabilia

Hati Sarfaraz Nazim
(interviewee 1)

Waris Khan
(interviewee 2)

'Jarnail' (General) Hazrat Gul
(interviewee 24)
in the Awami National Party Office
in Peshawar.
Note the poster
with picture of Badshah Khan
on the wall behind him and
the picture of Afghan President Najibullah

Grana (interviewee 17) demonstrating how she swept
during Khudai Khidmatgar village cleanliness drives

Contemporary representation (1992) of Badshah Khan as non-violent solider of Islam, clothed for the struggle but unarmed.

Typical example of ubiquitious representation of Badshah Khan in the 1990s in N.W.F.P., Pakistan

Introduction

Pursuing the Riddle of the Non-violent Pathans

In the winter of 1988 an elderly Pathan, Khan Abdul Gaffar Khan, died aged 98. Growing up in Delhi I had witnessed a long succession of obituaries and funerals as more or less celebrated veterans of the independence struggle passed on to their final reward. Yet none had seemed to provoke either the genuine sentiment or the wave of media coverage which accompanied Gaffar Khan's final illness and death. Editorials eulogised him without fear of contradiction as the 'greatest non-violent soldier of Islam' and 'one of the greatest nationalist leaders who claimed the loyalty of thousands of non-violent Pathans'. We were told that to his followers, far away in the North West Frontier, he had come to be known as 'Badshah' Khan, meaning emperor or khan of khans. For the rest of India his status had been signified by the honoured nickname of 'Frontier Gandhi'.

At the time I was a graduate student in Sociology at the Delhi School of Economics and happened to be reading the classic anthropological literature on the Pathans. I followed with interest the media's tale of the Khudai Khidmatgar, or 'Servants of God' movement, a predominantly Pathan and Muslim movement which had practised non-violent methods in its anti-colonial struggle against the British and been the ally of the mainly Hindu Indian National Congress. Television documentaries showed the scratchy films of the nationalist period, in which a lean muscular man well over six feet tall with jet black hair and beard strode along next to Gandhi in the mountains of the Frontier. Newspapers printed similar snapshots of Badshah Khan standing next to the Mahatma, towering above him in stature but wholly attentive in demeanour.

The Khudai Khidmatgars had supported an unpartitioned India but in 1947 Congress had agreed to Muslim League demands for a referendum in the Frontier province. Boycotted by the tens of thousands of Khudai Khidmatgars, the referendum's low turn-out gave a result in favour of joining Pakistan. Badshah Khan had then asked the Pakistan government to allow the creation of 'Pakhtunistan', a semi-autonomous region for the Pathans within the new nation, but the request was refused. For this impertinence, along with their apparently Gandhian method and close and continuing links with Congress, the Khudai Khidmatgars were branded traitors and Indian sympathisers, and were punished by successive Pakistani governments with imprisonment and the confiscation of their land. Badshah Khan himself spent many years in jail before, in old age, finally entering exile among his fellow Pathans across the border in Afghanistan.

I recalled earlier coverage of his occasional visits to India for political discussions or medical treatment, when senior Congress leaders had seemed to be genuinely solicitous about his welfare but also slightly fearful, as of a strict older brother. Badshah Khan retained his stern moral and physical presence to the end and had no truck with the later populism which Gandhi's grandson, the philosopher Ramchandra

1

Gandhi, has dubbed in a delightful pun the 'grin revolution'. As the Indian prime minister Narasimha Rao noted in an address to mark the centenary of Badshah Khan's birth, he was of that generation of leaders who did not smile and wave to the crowds but rather scolded them for their lapses, yet was all the more adored and applauded for it. Badshah Khan had continued to criticise the policies and habits of governments in both India and Pakistan, but more than anything his survival into extreme old age was itself a living reminder of the austere ethos and self-dedication of that earlier generation of leaders, a tacit shaming of younger politicians grown fat with power.

As he lay ailing in Delhi the government of India offered him a future resting place next to Gandhi's mausoleum, an unprecedented offer indicative of his prestige and stature. But characteristically Badshah Khan expressed his desire to be buried in the garden of his house in Jalalabad in Afghanistan, where he had spent most of his later life. He was transferred from Delhi to Peshawar where he died among his family and followers a few days later. In an exception to protocol his funeral was attended by several national leaders, including the Prime Minister of India, Rajiv Gandhi, thereby implicitly attributing to him the status of a head of state.

The burial in Jalalabad caused other unprecedented events. A one-day ceasefire was declared in the Soviet–Afghan war so that mourners could safely traverse the distance between Peshawar and Jalalabad, the two cities at either end of the Khyber Pass, which marks the official boundary between Afghanistan and Pakistan. Furthermore, the visa requirements were waived and for that day alone thousands crossed freely to join the funeral procession as it inched along the winding roads of the majestic Pass. In his death, Badshah Khan thus bore witness to the possibility of a closed boundary becoming an open frontier, restoring to the North West Frontier its open character of past centuries and eliminating the artificial barriers between the Pathans who lived on either side.

But, for all the drama and acclaim surrounding his death, much of Badshah Khan's story remained mysterious to me. Well versed in the deeds of Gandhi, Nehru, Patel and Bose, my generation had not been taught much about him or his movement. While most older people in Delhi knew his followers were called the 'Red Shirts' because of the uniforms they wore and used this label (or its Urdu translation, *Surkh Posh*) when referring to the movement, no one seemed to know quite why they had worn uniforms, or why red ones, or why they called themselves the Servants of God.[1] It seemed that the passing of the years, along with the distancing caused by Indo-Pakistan tensions, had made the Frontier even more remote and enigmatic to Indians and obscured this episode of our shared history.

The North West Frontier has almost as alien and exotic a place in the Indian imagination as it does in the British. Like many Indians, particularly Bengalis, my image of the Pathans and the Frontier was mainly derived from Tagore's moving short story *Kabuliwallah*, in which a friendship between a gentle Pathan peddler and a little Bengali girl is tragically broken when the Pathan is sent to jail for murdering a debtor in a lapse of temper. Its successful cinematic adaptation was frequently shown on

---

[1] This is true in Pakistan as well, as I realised later. I constantly meet even reasonably well-educated people who have no idea who the Khudai khidmatgars were.

television and always moved me to tears. And, as in so much of North India, we had stories in our family of similarly itinerant 'Kabuliwallahs' – men 'from Kabul' – who had come around each year selling dried fruits and perfumes from the Afghan mountains to my father's family when he was a child. Above all, for many in India as in Britain, Pathans were like the brave and fierce but also wild Mahbub Ali in Kipling's *Kim*.

The classic anthropological literature on the Pathans seemed not too discordant with these literary images, providing more methodical but still colourful accounts of the system of blood feuds and vendettas and the overwhelming codes of honour and hospitality among seemingly ungovernable tribes. And yet now in 1988 I had suddenly learnt that between 1930 and 1947 the Pathans, quite against their wild and martial reputation, had employed not rifles and guerilla tactics but rather the method of disciplined non-violent civil disobedience against the British. Moreover, belying their reputation for feuding and factionalism, they had remained united for almost two decades. How had it come about that the same 'hot-headed' Pathans I had read about as a child and studied as a graduate student were transformed into a successful non-violent protest movement?

This compelling puzzle appeared unresolved, even unconsidered, in the academic literature. The anthropology I was reading at the time provided no answers. Frederik Barth wrote his famous monograph on the Swat Pathans in 1959 but did not mention the Red Shirts, nor indeed any colonial past of political struggle among the Pathans. Akbar Ahmed has also written extensively on the Pathans but again makes no mention of the Red Shirts. Nor had the Red Shirts received any coverage in the otherwise richly detailed and localised historiography on the Indian nationalist movement (a genre which Sunil Khilnani has wittily characterised as 'pointillist'). There are several good accounts focusing on the party political manoeuvring in the Frontier by the Congress and the Muslim League between 1937 and 1947, but their focus is very much on the details of high-level politicking and the nature of the Khudai Khidmatgar (KK) movement remains obscure.

Warming to the subject I found several biographies of Badshah Khan, the most definitive being by Tendulkar, who had previously written an eight-volume biography of Gandhi. This was full of interesting anecdotes about Badshah Khan, his numerous stays with Gandhi in Wardha and his sense of betrayal at the time of partition, but overall he is presented as a mere appendage to Gandhi, as very much the ninth volume. Other books had interesting sketches by his contemporaries, but again the spotlight was on Badshah Khan and his profound friendship with Gandhi, with the mass following figuring only as a shadowy backdrop.[2] I thus remained in the dark about the masses of Pathans who had made up the rank and file of the Khudai Khitmatgars. Was their adoption of non-violence really so inexplicable, no more than a bizarre cultural joke? It was this question which drove my research.

I soon determined the locations of the various relevant archival materials: fortnightly reports between the provincial government in Peshawar, the government of India in New Delhi and the British government in Whitehall were kept in the India Office Library at Waterloo, London. Correspondence between the central and

---

[2] See Tendulkar 1967; Desai 1935; Easwaran 1985; Korejo 1994.

provincial committees of Congress were housed in Delhi's National Archives and the Nehru Memorial Museum Library. Police Special Branch reports on the activities of Badshah Khan and Khudai Khidmatgars (KK) were to be found in Peshawar. I felt that to answer the questions I considered important, however, it was vital to try to find and speak with surviving Pathan members of the KK in order to discuss what it was that had made ordinary Pathans adopt non-violence. Answering this question seemed vital both to understanding this unusual strand of the Indian nationalist struggle and to providing some important historical depth to ethnographic representation[3] of the Pathans.

The Delhi School of Economics turned down my research proposal on the grounds that it was unfeasible for an Indian to do prolonged fieldwork within such a strategically sensitive part of Pakistan and I therefore relocated to Oxford to begin my doctorate. The Frontier still has a powerful hold on the British imagination and my proposed research was greeted with enthusiasm and encouragement, although the fact remained that securing a visa would be far from easy.[4] In addition, there was the challenge of arranging to live and work as a single woman in an area where a rigorous *purdah* continues to be observed. Shortly before leaving for Oxford, however, I was fortunate enough to meet Badshah Khan's son, Khan Abdul Wali Khan, in Delhi. He was visiting his cousin Mohammed Yunus, a Pathan who had chosen to move to Delhi at Partition and become a well-known figure in the Congress regime. I had met Mohammed Yunus soon after Badshah Khan's death in my quest for information about the Khudai Khidmatgars. He had been very happy to hear of my interest in his uncle's movement but wasn't hopeful of my chances of visiting the Frontier. Two years later, however, he persuaded Wali Khan to fit me in to his busy schedule and I went to meet the still imposing seventy-year-old Wali Khan on a cold November morning, suitably chaperoned by my father. Wali Khan is a senior politician in his own right and the undisputed leader of Pakistan's Awami National Party, the political heirs of the Khudai Khidmatgars. The promised five-minute meeting lasted two hours, at the end of which Wali Khan seemed convinced that my academic interest in the movement was genuine and enthusiastic. In his inimitable way he gave me a traditional Pathan kiss on both cheeks and invited me to stay with his family in the Frontier for the entire duration of my study; he also assured my father that I would be well looked after by his wife and daughters. This outcome, far beyond my expectations, was a fitting prelude to the months which followed when I benefited from the generosity of Wali Khan and all the other people I came to know in the Frontier. He insisted, however, that procuring the necessary visa was my job – he would exercise no clout there, 'though once you are in Peshawar, you are my responsibility'. After some prolonged and intensive persuasion on my part, the Pakistan High Commission in Delhi kindly granted me a visa and I set off for the Frontier.

In the winter of 1992, four years to the day since I had first started to think about the Khudai Khidmatgar movement, I had my first break in the field. I had spent

[3] As the Comaroffs have said, 'A historical ethnography must begin by constructing its own archive' (Comaroff and Comaroff 1992: 34).
[4] Indians were rarely allowed to visit it, especially if they wished to do so for long periods of time, and, after three wars, the only Indians who could visit Pakistan easily were those with families or religious shrines they wanted to visit. I had no such excuses, which made my application for a visa easily dismissable.

months getting to know Wali Khan's family, refusing offers of marriage from acquaintances eager to help me out of the misery of spinsterdom, learning Pathan recipes from the cook and in the process getting to hang around the outdoor kitchen, making friends with the numerous servants and generally practising my Pashto: in other words, doing all the things anthropologists do when trying to find their feet and participate in their host societies. But I had yet to meet a Khudai Khidmatgar. All my polite enquiries among Wali Khan's friends and visitors had revealed remembered names but also sighs of regret and tales of their recent death – 'If only you had been here six months ago ... two years ago ... twenty years ago!' were the rueful replies. This was not entirely unexpected, since the young revolutionaries of the 1930s and 1940s had to be at least 75 years old. But what I had not been prepared for was the total lack of records concerning KK activists, who had been denied the priviliges and state pensions extended to other nationalist freedom fighters in India and Pakistan. The significance of the stigmatisation of the Khudai Khidmatgars as 'traitors' was slowly dawning on me.

On 20 January 1992, however, there was great excitement as it was the fourth anniversary of Badshah Khan's death and there was to be a big political rally in Shahi Bagh in Peshawar. Both Wali Khan and his wife, Naseem Bibi, herself a member of the provincial assembly, were to address the rally and this was my first chance to attend an important political event linked directly to my work. Arriving early at the grounds, my heart leapt at the sight of ranks of political workers clothed in bright red, keeping order among the enthusiastic masses. But when the dust settled I saw that they wore red *shalwar kameez*, the standard male dress in contemporary Pakistan, whereas I knew from the few black and white pictures I had seen of KK uniforms that they had looked distinctly like those of the colonial army, right down to their Sam Browne belts. In any case these men were all far too young to be the Red Shirts I was looking for. As I scanned the horizon from the window of the car which was serving as our mobile *zenana* (women's quarters), however, I saw a familiar face. I had met Habibullah earlier when he had visited Wali Khan's home in the company of Haji Sarfaraz Nazim, who had been Badshah Khan's long-time secretary. Habibullah had shown great interest in my project, since his father had been a dedicated Khudai Khidmatgar and died just six months before my arrival. We greeted each other as old friends and I begged Habibullah to chaperon me around the rally so that I could look for old Red Shirts.

We wandered through crowds buzzing with that familiar festive atmosphere which arises in the subcontinent regardless of the precise occasion, somehow combining elements of the religious festival, the political gathering and the school sports day. Amid the dust, the music on the public address system, the makeshift food stalls and the excited chattering of gaily dressed people, enthusiastic vendors were selling calendars, trinkets, badges and banners which carried Badshah Khan's unmistakable face imposed on a lantern, the symbol of the Awami National Party (ANP). I scanned the scene anxiously. When we had almost covered the entire length of the grounds, we came across two old men, sitting very still amidst the bustle in the winter sun. One of them wore a faded red shirt. Habibullah hesitated and then seemed to recognise them. There was much hugging and handshaking as they ascertained that Habibullah really was Israr Khan's son – after all these years! I waited patiently, thrilled that finally two Khudai Khidmatgars stood before me. A long conversation was impossible at that moment: the speeches were starting and I had to report back to my *zenana*. But I took down the names of their villages and promised to visit as soon as I could.

This initial contact provided other possible names and villages. Over the next few months, generously accompanied by Habibullah, I managed to track down and interview some 75 KK veterans. When I arrived at the villages we always had to decide where to sit. It was not really proper for me to enter their homes, nor could I enter the *hujra* (men's guest house). They, meanwhile, could not sit in the women's *zenana*. Usually therefore, a neutral space was found outdoors in the sun and a few string cots from the *hujra* were dragged out to serve as seating. I quickly learnt that as the guest I was expected to sit at the comfortable end of the cot, with the less comfortable end being occupied by my host, and if I offered my seat as a mark of respect to my elder I was blessed profusely but firmly overruled.

These conversations invariably attracted audiences of between twenty and fifty villagers. They came to take a break between chores and were curious about my interest in their grandfathers' stories. At times I could sense their incredulity that I had gone through such logistical problems simply to chat with the oldest and often most eccentric man in the village, whom they at best dimly respected for some now obscure sacrifice in the past. Initially my every action was scrutinised as they watched this strange Hindu travelling alone in Pakistan, a young woman who wanted to write a book and who knew life in the land of the English. After a few minutes, however, they too became caught up in the old men's stories. Some seemed to be hearing them for the first time, while many more seemed to be listening with new ears, the stories transformed by my presence and note taking from old men's ramblings into revolutionary history.

My informants seemed satisfied with my somewhat gauche efforts to maintain a suitable modesty, and they were much more concerned to make sure that I recorded their accounts carefully, waiting patiently as I wrote it all down. They were always pleased by the fact that I was from India, the land where they long ago made friends and allies and for whose independence they had fought. They usually assumed I was Muslim, though if asked directly I admitted to being a Bengali Hindu. However, this was also all right – since, as Mohammed Hamdulah Jan happily noted, in the past the kingdom ruled by the Pathans had reached as far as Bengal, and so our ancestors might well have met already.

The conversations we had were at best semi-structured interviews; while I was looking for answers to some specific questions and raised particular themes, the chronology and direction of the conversation was guided entirely by the informant. Because of the difference in our world views I could not immediately understand some of the ways in which they reckoned time. For instance, if I asked someone his age he would ask me in turn, 'How old are you? ... I had spun twenty sets of clothes by the time you were born!' Since I came from the land of Gandhi he expected me to know how long it took to spin and wear out *khadi* clothes. I expected our conversations to reach back to the events of half a century ago, but in practice we usually went back far further, since most found it impossible to tell me about the KK movement and Badshah Khan without describing their own life histories, too. They thus drifted from one story to another, guided by their memories, and while I made occasional interventions to clarify or pursue, my general attitude was respectful and attentive rather than interrogative. Even then, they did not always respond to these interventions or, if they did, it was often in a highly indirect or elliptical way. Sometimes they became impatient, usually when I had produced my file of notes from the British archives to compare facts, since they felt it was *their* story that had to be heard and believed above all others. Often their otherwise disparate narratives made reference to shared episodes or threw up recurring tropes and seemed thereby to hint at an emergent oral tradition about the KK movement and its achievements.

It often happened that at the end of our conversation I would ask if they knew of any other surviving members. The initial response was always a sad shaking of heads – they could name individuals but they must surely be dead; it had been so long, after all. I would then invite them to join Habibullah and me on our search and after many wrong turnings amid the dusty tracks of the North West Frontier we would find the village and sometimes, after further searching, the old comrade in question. My questions would then have to wait as these Khudai Khidmatgars who had marched together sixty years earlier now met again as old, old men. News of children, illnesses and deaths were exchanged amidst laughter, tears, embraces and commiserations; it was a most moving sight and a great privilege to be present. Our subsequent conversations were never straightforward interviews as they interrupted each other's stories, clarified opinions, filled in details and shared old jokes. By the end of the day our pick-up truck would be full of an excited group of elderly Pathans who were eagerly catching up on news and sharing a long-remembered, much-cherished camaraderie in the precious moments before we dropped each one home in time for evening prayers.

Most of these Khudai Khidmatgars had not had many previous opportunities to tell their stories of struggle and heroism. They described to me with passion what it was like to be swept up in the revolutionary anti-British fervour and to follow an utterly charismatic leader, and they vividly conveyed the exhilaration of self-sacrifice. But from their own grandchildren and great grandchildren they seemed distant, unable to communicate with the fast-changing younger generation who are swept up by the stern rhetoric of Islamic fundamentalism or the easy virtue of entrepreneurship and foreign goods. It is not easy to explain non-violence to youths who are surrounded by cheap weapons and who have seen at first hand both ruthless military governments and heroic Afghan freedom fighters. Although most have a vague respect for the old Khudai Khidmatgars as men who fought for the independence of their country, it is not well-informed and few have much idea about the political life of the old men or the precise role they played in the liberation struggle.

It is important to stress, however, that these differences are not the natural result of age differences or the fact that the veterans are now very old and speak slowly and quietly, their thoughts occasionally wandering. In fact, there is an inherent respect for anybody of such advanced age. Rather, such hazy awareness reflects the systematic efforts the Pakistani state has made to promote its own vision of the nationalist struggle, a vision which criticises and marginalises the Khudai Khidmatgars. After Partition nearly all activists had their homes raided and all personal papers were removed and burnt (including those of Badshah Khan himself) in a clear attempt to destroy any source which might provide an alternative conception of the historical events. Most other artefacts pertaining to the KK movement were similarly destroyed. The KK headquarters was demolished in 1948, destroying its own records along with Badshah Khan's lovingly tended vegetable gardens. The old red uniforms and pictures of Badshah Khan which I sometimes encountered in people's homes had been preserved in great secrecy and at some peril.

In India, although Gandhi remains pre-eminent, other nationalist leaders are also represented in official history, especially where they had a regional following, such as Subash Bose in Bengal, Bhagat Singh in Punjab or Tilak in Maharashtra. In Pakistan, by contrast, the official credit for independence is attributed solely to Jinnah, whose image remains omnipresent, prefacing the nightly news programme on TV. There have been neither memorials nor museums to Badshah Khan. The KK movement also receives no mention in school history text books, where the emphasis is very much upon Pakistan as a Muslim state whose precursors run directly from the Prophet Mohammed to Jinnah, a portrayal which leaves no place for the KK alliance with the Hindu-dominated Congress or their opposition to the Muslim League's call for a partitioned India. Similarly, the official emphasis on the unity of the contemporary nation leaves no room for the KK's subsequent calls for an autonomous Pathan homeland. Censorship has been very extensive and no biographies of Badshah Khan were allowed in Pakistan until recently. I was questioned sternly by customs officials at Lahore airport about my copy of Badshah Khan's autobiography, published in Kabul. I had to feign indifference, saying it was a casual acquisition in a bazaar to help me learn Urdu.

In all these ways the state has denied to subsequent generations any access to the historical truth of the KK movement and presented a very critical and partial picture of it. State-sponsored history has intervened forcefully to suppress an emotive episode from the past which it fears would arouse feelings of Pathan pride and autonomy. Thus younger people have been cut adrift from their activist forebears. The picture has improved somewhat, however, in the recent part, which has demonstrated the continued potency of historical images and their counter-hegemonic use. The dominant position of the Muslim League ruling party has been undermined by the military rule of General Zia al-Haq and by the rise of the Bhuttoist Pakistan People's Party. Gradually the senior followers of Badshah Khan have been released from prison and allowed to establish the ANP under the leadership of Wali Khan. The ANP soon won elections in the Frontier Province and also became a player on the national stage as a third-party power broker and then ironically as a coalition partner of the Muslim League itself from 1991.

The first thing the ANP did on assuming office was to begin naming streets and squares and buildings in Peshawar after Badshah Khan and other prominent KK leaders. They put up Badshah Khan's image throughout the province on large and colourful posters and billboards. I saw one freshly painted portrait which depicted him as a chivalrous *mujahid* wearing a shirt of mail, astride a white stallion, and carrying a non-violent red flag rather than a sword. Commemorative meetings were held in his honour on the anniversaries of his death and birth, and plans were drawn up to establish a Badshah Khan memorial centre and archive.

To some extent such initiatives reflected the continuing respect and affection which many Pathans had for Badshah Khan, and they were also an assertion of Pathan dignity and pride after the long decades during which their role in the nationalist struggle had been suppressed. However, there was also a deliberate attempt to construct a cult of memory around Badshah Khan. Much of the ANP's support in the Frontier rests on its claim to be the true heir of the KK movement, and such media representations and special events are clearly designed to re-emphasise and legitimate this claim.

We should also note, however, that the use of Badshah Khan's name is not monopolised by the ANP. The new political alliance with the old enemies in the Muslim League brought fresh reflections and a revaluation of the old struggles. Some of my informants invoked Badshah Khan specifically to criticise the current generation of ANP politicians by contrasting their moral standards and political principles with his.[5] Thus, as many scholars working with oral history have noted, stories about the past are often told as a critical commentary on the present.

The Analytical Significance of the Khudai Khidmatgar movement

As I have noted, I was first attracted to researching the KK movement by the historical riddle of the notoriously violent Pathans' embrace of non-violent protest. From a more analytical perspective, however, I would suggest that the movement and its study shed some light on a number of key topics and themes in modern social anthropology, notably those of colonial ethnography, the place of élites and subalterns in popular political movements, the relationship of tribal society and the modern state, the relationship between religion and political protest, and also issues of cultural and social creativity, and the relationships between history, ethnography and memory.

The political events in the Frontier in the two decades before independence are fascinating. In a province with a 92 per cent Muslim presence the Congress Party dominated politics for 20 years, winning a clear electoral victory in 1946 on a manifesto that urged a non-partitioned India. Barely a year later, however, the Muslim League won a referendum which took the province into Pakistan. The challenge of analysing why this dramatic turn-around occurred has attracted several scholars, notably the historians Jansson and Shah and the political scientist Rittenberg, all of whom have written accounts detailing the workings of Congress and Muslim League politics in the Frontier and the interventions of the colonial government (Jansson 1988, Rittenberg 1992, Shah 1999). For the most part, however, they concentrate on the high-level party manoeuvring during the years 1937 to 1947, when the Congress and the KK were already firmly entrenched in parliamentary politics in the Frontier. In the accounts of Jansson and Rittenberg, the rather surprising fact that Congress actually had such mass support in the first place is taken largely as a given. There is little investigation of the way in which this

---

[5] They think of the ANP in Weberian terms: 'after coming to power the following of a crusader usually degenerates very easily into a quite common stratum of spoilsmen' (Weber 1946 (1919): 125).

support was created by the work of the KK movement between 1930 and 1937. This partly reflects their methods, which focused on official archive documents; where interviews were conducted, it was with the ideologues and *khans* of the Congress and Muslim League. They did not consult any of the 'mass members' about their perceptions of and support for the KK movement. The consequence of this is such unhelpful assertions as that: 'they [the KK] had a programme of social and economic reform, which although very vague, had strong appeal among the rural poor' (Jansson 1988: 240). This gives the historiographical stereotype of ignorant peasants following prominent leaders for obscure reasons – a view which inevitably limits the ability of these writers to explain the rise of the Congress in the Frontier and, equally, its eventual defeat, since they can have only a partial view of the dynamics of activism before and during Partition. If the programme and appeal of the KK were really so vague, then the mass of people who gave political parties their support must perforce be portrayed as passively manipulated by decisions and manoeuvres made in the remote echelons of the party hierarchy.

The account by Sayed Wiqar Ali Shah, himself a Pathan, sets out with some care the way in which these political events took place in a context of ongoing concern among the Pathan intelligentsia about the social and cultural circumstances of the Pathans and the need to defend their condition and political position as an ethnic group. In his introductory chapters Shah stresses the importance of the KK movement, sets out something of its social and political programme, and praises its achievements in forging Pathan unity and adopting non-violent methods of protest. Shah's main interests lie elsewhere, however, and the remainder of his book is a very thorough and helpful archive-based account of the political contestations between the colonial regime, Congress and the Muslim League. As a result of this emphasis, his account of how unity and non-violence were achieved by the Pathans is necessarily very brief, amounting to an assertion that it stemmed from the Pathans' own fatigue with the debilitating effects of feud and division, and their response to Badshah Khan's use of traditional images of fraternity and peace from Islam and Pathan culture. While both these statements are certainly valid, we may assume the process was more complex than this in practice. Accordingly I have sought to give a more extensive and nuanced account of the ideology and activities of the KK. In particular I have sought to present the views of its mass membership, since I regard their motivations and thinking as a vital part of an adequate description of the movement, and of the events leading up to the Partition of 1947.

To that extent the approach taken in this study seeks to move away from the more conventional historiographical accounts mentioned above and is closer to the work of the Subaltern Studies movement which has so revolutionarised Indian historiography over the last twenty years through its polemical attacks on élitist 'history from above' and, more importantly, by its painstaking attempts to retrieve and explore the the 'mass' or subaltern view from amidst local archives. Ranajit Guha's introduction to the groundbreaking first volume of *Subaltern Studies* made several key critiques of the extant historiography of modern India, which typically assigns sole credit for the nationalist achievement and forging of the nation to the leadership of the bourgeoisie as embodied in the Congress and Muslim League parties (Guha 1982). Peasants had too often been portrayed by this historiography as innately volatile elements whose occasional forays into mass demonstration or other forms of protest reflected at best a response to colourful leaders, and at worst an unwelcome diversion from the processes of high politics grinding on in the government and party apparatus. Guha also criticised the implicit use of a kind of behaviourist model in which the masses simply respond in unthinking ways to the stimuli of want or charismatic words. In such élitist historiography, political mobilisation was thus seen to be achieved along 'vertical lines': masses responding directly to leaders, with no importance being attached to recruitment along horizontal linkages of workplace, community or caste. More generally, Guha argued that insufficient attention has been paid to the lives of the lower and intermediate social strata and the ways in which they adjusted to the conditions of the Raj and developed new social and political forms in response. This realm of 'politics of the people', he argues, should really be treated as an autonomous domain, but 'élite historiography fails to acknowledge, far less interpret, the contribution made by the people *on their own*, that is *independently of the élite*, to the making and development of this nationalism' (Guha 1982: 3; original emphasis).

In my analysis of the KK movement I do try to 'assess the mass articulation of nationalism' through the testimonies of ordinary KKs. The reasons why the Pathans boycotted British institutions, went to jail, suffered *lathi* charges or even simply joined the movement are complex and they were not mere puppets in the hands of manipulating leaders. Rank-and-file members carefully thought about the aims and methods of their movement and the subtle ideology on which it was based. I also show how Pathans, belying their stereotype, exhibited strikingly 'non-volatile' behaviour, and in particular how their organisation was recruited, forged and maintained via horizontal networks of kin, lineage and village.

Among the many excellent studies conducted under the rubric of *Subaltern Studies* (Volumes I–XI 1982–99) my work perhaps has closest parallels with that of the historian Shahid Amin (Amin 1995). His key interest is an incident which took place on 4 February 1922 at a town in North India called Chauri Chaura when a 'mob' attacked a police station and burnt twelve policemen inside in retaliation for earlier humiliations and oppression. This has passed into the folklore of Indian nationalist history as an episode of shame which made Gandhi call off his nation-wide civil disobedience movement. Roundly condemned from all quarters, it is cited in school history lessons as an instance of an otherwise passive rural population suddenly losing control and 'going mad' in an action counter-productive to the wider struggle. But Amin seeks to explore the background and undercurrents of the event more carefully and shows how it had a logic of its own which grew out of a complex amalgam of picketing, the 'politics and religiosity of vegetarianism', 'the demiurgic presence of Gandhi, local elaborations of his teachings', and 'the self-empowerment of the volunteers' (Amin 1995: 193–4). We thus gain a picture of the 'internal face of popular nationalism' as well as a sophisticated retelling of the past.

Amin's central riddle is a perfect inversion of my own. While he explores an instance of violence within a larger non-violent campaign of civil disobedience, my task is to explain the long period of non-violence which 'broke out' within a society notorious for its violence. But the approach and methodology are very similar, with Amin conducting what he calls 'historical fieldwork', talking to elderly participants in the event and their relatives, as well as drawing on archive sources. One can only

regret that such utilisation of oral sources remains something of a rarity in the field of
Subaltern Studies. While their ongoing excavation of local archives in India remains
valuable, the current generation of historians will be the last to have the opportunity
to seek out oral accounts from the elderly participants in the nationalist struggle.[6]

One conceptual difficulty arising out of the subaltern approach is its excessive
emphasis, partly polemical no doubt, on the fundamental separateness of the
domains of élite and subaltern politics. Conceptually, this sometimes leads to the
subaltern realm being defined rather relationally, as that which is not of the élite, and
this somewhat undermines the intrinsic value the subaltern scholars seek to
attribute to it. Practically, such a view can lead to an extreme 'non-élite' picture in
which we see only leaderless masses. I would argue, however, that it would be quite
unrealistic to ignore in this way the role of charismatic leaders in local political movements. To do so in the case of the KK would certainly be in breach not only of the facts
as I understand them but of the memories of the KKs themselves, who always
emphasise the vital role of their leader. There is thus a need to problematise and
understand the overwhelming importance which my informants placed on the role
of Badshah Khan himself in achieving the transformation of their own behaviour
and the success of the KK movement.

I would argue that social anthropology has been rather good at resolving this kind
of analytical tension between the roles of the masses and the élite. Political anthropology in general conceptualises the realm of the political primarily in terms of power
and culture, and it therefore attempts to analyse the symbolism, ideology and
everyday practice of politics. From this perspective, Jean and John Comaroff, while
noting that anthropology naturally tends to the subaltern in so far as its practitioners
rarely focus on the 'chronicles of courts, kings ... and embassies', warn against the
assumption that anthropologists can rest content with merely uncovering histories
from below and giving voice to the underdogs of a civilisation. The Comaroffs argue
that the stories of the repressed do not in themselves provide revelation: '[T]o become
something more, these partial "hidden-histories" have to be situated in the wider
worlds of power and meaning that gave them life. ... [F]or historiography, as for
ethnography, it is the relations between fragments and fields that pose the greatest
analytic challenge' (Comaroff and Comaroff 1992: 17). From this perspective both
élite and subaltern 'stories' must be situated within a wider structure of culture and
power: only then do they have the potential to give insights into the contexts and
processes of which they were a part. As Escobar comments, 'What is crucial ... is that
social movements be seen as cultural struggles in a fundamental sense, that is, as
struggles over meanings as much as over socio-economic conditions' (Escobar 1992;
my emphasis).

Accordingly, rather than privileging either leadership or rank and file, political
anthropology strives to describe the ways in which the two share organic links and

[6] See the work of the Oral History Workshop in Britain, pioneered by Paul Thompson and others, as one
model for such an exercise (Thompson 1988). In Indian historiography, the notable exception has been
work conducted on the violence during Partition. See for instance Butalia 1998 and the writings of Veena
Das and Ashis Nandy. In this context the move of many Subaltern Studies writers into the elaborate
deconstruction of literary texts and philosphical scrutiny seems even more wasteful – one answer to the
much debated question 'Can the subaltern speak?' is surely 'If they're asked'.

exert dialectical influences which are played out within a shared cultural framework. In doing this, it also unearths the multivocality, and range of motivations, meanings and interpretations which both ordinary participants and leaders bring to a struggle. Hence, in my discussion of the KK movement I do attend to the vital role of Badshah Khan, but I seek to explain his charisma by showing the ways in which his practice and rhetoric were grounded carefully in the 'mass culture'. Equally, I explore the organisational structure of the movement and show how it was designed specifically to manage any potential tension or separation between the leadership and mass membership, and to avoid any undue reliance of the latter on the former.

If Subaltern Studies radically altered what could be taken for granted in the writing of colonial historiography, then a still greater impact was made by the more or less contemporary emergence of the concept and critique of Orientalism (Said 1978). Subsequently historians and other scholars have had to pay far closer attention to the nature of the representations of the Other purveyed in the archival materials from which they build their accounts, since such sources reflect more or less explicitly the perspective of the colonial élite, and present essentialist and condescending depictions of indigenous political actors. There is thus a clear congruence between the orientalist and subaltern critiques.[7] From this perspective the Khudai Khidmatgars suffered from a particularly acute double subalternity: not only were they an undervalued mass peasantry who were deemed incapable of constructive political action by their own (or at least the Indian) bourgeoisie; they were also, as Pathans, the victims of particularly extreme orientalist repesentations, which portrayed them as far more hotheaded and unpredictable than even the average Indian peasant. Moreover, this 'orientalist' view of the Pathans was held equally by their fellow Indians, not least those within the nationalist movement. In the present study, I thus seek to explore the ways in which such stereotypes intervened in events and influenced both the actions of the KK movement and the official responses to them.

While the critique of Orientalism has indeed been a valuable one, however, embraced with enthusiasm by literary scholars and historians alike, it has also fostered mushrooming debates of wilful obscurity and sometimes doubtful value. Although anthropologists have not been immune from such agonising about the Other, generally they have been rather better at keeping close to the details and nuance of such representations. Recently there have been some particularly clear cautions about the need to handle Orientalism with care. Nicholas Dirks has expressed his concern that 'if we accord totalising power to such entities as the West, or the Orientalists, we will misunderstand and misrecognise the spaces of resistance' (Dirks 1995: 10). He therefore stresses the need to break down the idea of either a monolithic Other or a monolithic colonial regime. In similar vein, Nicholas Thomas has argued for the need to examine carefully the heterogeneity of the colonial record by analysing not only the reports filed by district officers but also materials as diverse as missionary archives, travellers' accounts, museum displays,

---

[7] See Prakash 1990 for a useful navigation through these debates, plus the responses by O'Hanlon and Washbrook 1992 and Prakash 1992.

and art and photography, each of which may be read as revelatory 'texts' of colonial discourse(s). In their variety and inconsistency, such texts when taken together substantially weaken the image of the 'totalising' nature of the colonial project which the orientalist critique tends to purvey. An excellent standard for such endeavour was set long ago by Bernard Cohn's work on the Indian colonial period, which carried out meticulous and original work describing and analysing the varied institutions and technologies of control deployed by the colonial state in areas as diverse as language, censuses, museums and law (collected together in Cohn 1997). Unhampered by post-colonial literary theory, he lucidly draws from his sources the complex activities, processes and contradictions operating within British colonial power.

By also making the colonialists the object of investigation in this way, we come to recognise their own multivocality and refine our view of colonial authority. In turn we then have to become more sensitive and nuanced in describing indigenous resistance to that power, thereby advancing the wider project of de-essentialising our portrayals of the colonised. Through my discussion of the furious British riposte to the emergence of the KK movement, I try to make a contribution to this kind of work. Although in some respects British representations of the Pathans were stubbornly unitary and enduring, and their actions relentlessly harsh, none the less, by reading between the lines (sometimes literally, as in the case of handwritten marginalia), it is possible to hear the hesitations and confusions in the minds of ostensibly single-minded administrators. More broadly, the non-violent approach adopted by the KK movement was clearly intended to play upon such hesitations and ambiguities by laying down a challenge to the colonial regime's image of itself. Thus we gain a clearer view of a small part of the 'culture of colonialism' (Thomas 1994).

This interest in colonialism has reinforced the growing awareness within social anthropology of the need to ground its more structuralist and synchronic descriptions of culture and social structure within the diachrony of historical events, and few ethnographies today remain unaware of the long past underpinning the ethnographic present. In this respect, however, the relative lack of recent work on the Pathans of the Frontier (due largely to the difficulties of access) has meant that the literature is still dominated by older classics which are less sensitive to important aspects of Pathan history. From Barth's work, for instance, it is hard to guess that Swat society was ever colonised or that it existed within a larger state system.[8] Yet the centralised structures imposed by the colonial administration directly determined the problems of land distribution and feuding that Barth discusses. As a consequence, his rightly celebrated account of both the Pathan code of honour – *Pukhtunwali* – and their factionalism and feuding gives a misleading impression of immutability, time-lessness and inevitability. Akbar Ahmed discusses at length the 'martial tribal tradition' of the Pathans and their appetitie for *jihad*, and refers in evidence to the violent uprising in Swat in 1897 and to the prominent role of the Pathans in the wars in Kashmir in 1947–8 – but he does not take into account the period 1930–47

---

[8] This failing is not confined to the North West Frontier Province. Bourdieu, for instance, does not mention the French in his account of Kabyle society in *Outline of a Theory of Practice* (1997). See Spencer 1997 for a critique of synchronic studies in political anthropology.

(Ahmed 1976). The Khudai Khidmatgar movement was a quite different nationalist (and religious) response from those he describes, but was far more a genuinely Pathan phenomenon than the wars that followed.

If one were to draw one's understanding of Pathan society from such accounts, the birth of a widespread non-violent grassroots political movement would indeed remain inexplicable. In contrast, in my reading of *Pukhtunwali* I seek to show how its key institutions underwent significant redefinition during the colonial period, particularly as the KK movement gradually drew a segmentary-feudal society into provincial and national politics. I try to give a sense of the experience of the Pathans who took this process forward as they modified their own taken-for-granted ideas on feud, honour, violence, hierarchy and even Islam, in the course of committing to the new movement and its struggle. Although the changes were in some ways temporary, it is none the less of great interest and significance that the Pathans who lived through the experience of the KK movement bear little resemblance to those described hitherto in the anthropological literature. This is not to challenge the veracity of earlier anthropological accounts, but simply to emphasise the importance of recognising the mutability of cultural practice.

My approach is thus much closer to more recent scholars who have worked on the Pathans, notably Jon Anderson, Charles Lindholm and David Edwards. Reacting against the presentation of Pathan culture and identity as fundamentally the enactment of a static code – what Barth calls 'doing Pukhtu' – Edwards presents a far more dynamic ethnographic model of Pathan society on the basis of his own research among the Pathans during the war with the Soviet Union (Edwards 1986). He stresses the need to take into account the ways in which the inherited code, or 'model of appropriate action', is transformed by Pathans into *particular responses* to present and future predicaments.[9] Notions of Pukhtunness therefore are not static but rather the subject of negotiation and innovation.

Similarly, much of the discussion of Pathan society, *Pukhtunwali* and 'what it means to be a Pukhtun' must at the very least be helpfully enlarged by the twenty years of Pathan history that is the subject of this book. By considering the crucial history of the Pathan in their struggle against the British, a far more nuanced picture of Pukhtun society emerges as one not predicated on blind adherence to an inherited 'code'. I would argue instead that we should think of *Pukhtunwali* as providing for the Pathans what Bourdieu has famously called the habitus – 'a system of lasting, transposable dispositions' that function 'as a matrix of perceptions, appreciations and actions' (Bourdieu 1977: 82–3). The practices that it generates vary and are 'emergent and unfinished', and the habitus does not determine actions so much as set a basic framework and logic within which actions can be taken in response to the predicaments thrown up by life. Certainly this is how I conceive of the way in which the KK movement pieced together and propagated a non-violent ideology that was at once quite remote from existing behavioural codes, yet also fully consistent with

---

[9] He does this in the second part of his thesis by studying *mujahiddin* poetry of the Afghan–Soviet war, in order to demonstrate the appropriation and transformation of the model. His textual and content analysis of this poetry reveals that 'the *landai* [poem] symbolises to the individual self the presence of the social other and compels the transformation of the ancestral "model of" into a futural "model for" action' (Edwards 1986: 192).

them. In this respect, I would argue, it is a valuable and enlightening example of profound social creativity.

I have stressed the temporal dimension of cultural change, of ebbs and flows in practice over time which must be tracked by the ethnographer. I also wish to highlight, albeit more speculatively, the spatial dimension. While the KK ideology was certainly grounded in *Pukhtunwali* and Islam, it was also an extraordinary *bricolage* of ideological influences, bearing traces of Christianity, Gandhist Hinduism, European militarism, and even Gandharan Buddhism. Such processes of influence, synthesis and cooption take place in every culture, but it seems to me unarguable that they take place with particular rapidity, clarity and general panache in frontier settings. By considering both the Frontier and frontiers through the prism of the KK movement, we thus receive a particularly vivid reminder that cultures and our descriptions of them can no more be bound by the space of our fieldwork site than they can by the time of our stay.

I greatly hope, therefore, that our thinking about colonialism, mass political action, tribal society, social creativity, memory, and above all Pathan culture will each benefit in some small way from this book's account of a period in Pathan history when 'doing Pukhtu' was 'done different'.

Plan of the Book

This is a work of social anthropological analysis rather than historiography and for the most part the discussion is broadly thematic rather than chronological. The course of events in the Frontier are both compelling and vital to a proper understanding of the movement, however, and so I bracket the main analytical account with two more narrative chapters on how the movement emerged out of and subsequently returned into Pathan society.

Chapter 1 sketches the geography and history of the Frontier, describing the classical elements of Pathan culture and social structure and their deformation under British colonial rule. It also reviews the British stereotypes of the Pathans and shows their influence on the draconian system of rule which the British established in the early twentieth century. Chapter 2 describes the various formative political events and experiments which fed into Badshah Khan's distinctive ideology and led to the eventual birth of the KK movement in 1930. It discusses in some detail my informants' discussions of their motivations for joining the movement.

Chapter 3 gives what I believe to be the first detailed account in English of the organisational structure and social and political activities of the movement. It discusses the various ways in which Pathans were trained to undertake non-violent protest and shows how the movement rendered significant changes in traditional features of Pathan life, most notably through the widespread resolution of feuds. Chapter 4 explores the British response to the KK movement, which embraced both sophisticated political counter-propaganda and a sustained brutality unprecedented in the Raj. Chapter 5 discusses the nature of the leadership of the KK movement and shows it to be a highly successful combination of charismatic and bureaucratic elements which together helped sustain the movement's activism over seventeen long years. It also shows the way in which the movement's organisational structure both respected and modified traditional social status, and reconciled the hierarchical and egalitarian elements in Pathan culture.

Chapter 6 discusses in more detail the ideology of the movement, and in particular explores the way in which Badshah Khan drew not on Gandhian thought, but rather on elements of Islam and *Pukhtunwali* in order to persuade his followers of the rightness of non-violence. Chapter 7 explores the various tensions between the KK movement, their Congress allies and Muslim League critics. It also discusses the KK's struggle to remain aloof from violence and communalism as religious tensions intensified throughout the subcontinent, and their final shattering disappointment when they learnt that the Frontier was to be part of Pakistan. Chapter 8 briefly considers the testimonies of my informants from a slightly more formal perspective in the context of recent anthropological discussions of memory and narrative. The Conclusion then draws together the main themes of the book before arguing that the KK's non-violence was quite different in its philosophical provenance from that of Gandhi, but that it was equally successful in achieving what Weber had considered impossible, namely the successful application of ethics to politics.

A Note on Sources

This book relies heavily on oral data gathered from rank-and-file Khudai Khidmatgars, and as I hope I have made clear in this introduction I see these data as its primary virtue. They were complemented by extensive work in the colonial archives, however, and there is no statement in respect of specific events, dates or facts which relies only on an oral source. This was not a particularly onerous constraint given the fullness of the records, and the fact that my primary interest was the opinions and practice of the rank-and-file members themselves. Social anthropologists will probably be willing to take my extensive use of oral material on trust and move straight to Chapter 1, but I perhaps owe it to historians to say a further brief word on my sources.

There are a growing number of rich and profoundly historical works which use oral methods and data, many of them concerning Africa (for excellent examples see Johnson 1994 and Feierman 1992). In the Frontier, Shah (1999) conducted interviews with high-ranking KK and their descendants and indicates his willingness to use oral testimony when prudent to do so. Earlier writers on the KK movement, however, expressed their suspicion of oral sources: Jansson, for example, stresses the unreliable and selective nature of memories, and his own willingness to use such evidence 'only under special circumstances and with reservations' and 'only when supported by written sources' (Jansson 1988: 22). Conversely, he declares his confidence that official documents *had* to be accurate, since their utility for administrators lay precisely in providing a reliable guide to action. Baldly stated, this looks a rather odd assumption, for, if their intended utility was the facilitation of efficient colonial governance, the documents were highly likely to encode a very particular, and usually pejorative, reading of a particular set of circumstances. In the case of the KK movement, for instance, the reports constantly describe it as a movement of 'rowdies'. Still stranger is the assumption that the colonial administration was in fact efficient. Often it was not, and precisely because its officers and their reports were *not* accurate and reliable. For example, the frequent likening of the KK to 'Bolsheviks' in internal reports was so preposterously inaccurate that it could hardly constitute a rational 'guide to action' in the way Jansson assumes. Lastly, the one kind of oral data in which he does have some confidence – information concerning family, genealogy and similar matters, 'on which people's memories are generally extremely reliable in that part of the world' (Jansson 1988: 22) – is precisely the area which anthropologists long ago showed to be full of creative and innovative 'recollections'.

A common concern about oral narratives is that they are influenced by emotion and self-presentation, the expectations of the audience or listener, and the tendency of human memory to revert to stock narrative patterns and cognitive schema. In her excellent work on oral tradition among Persian-speaking Afghans, Margaret Mills elegantly describes the influence of such narrativity: 'acts of narration ... are acts of interpretation, assigning causal and other relationships and relative emphasis to clusters of propositions (e.g. actions, objects and persons, and qualities)' (Mills 1991: 341). But such influences of narrative form or genre expectation apply equally to written records. Although the British colonial reports are contemporary with the events discussed, they were written under very specific narrative expectations. In particular, for those charged with keeping order, the expected narrative form is: problems arose, I intervened, now all is well. Thus there are strong incentives to play up the scale of the initial problem if the report is finalised, or to play down a current problem if the report is an interim one and the remedial measures have yet to be taken. This has most obvious implications for estimates of the size of crowds or the energy or violence of their activities. Such a narrative form is seen even more clearly if the problem can be blamed on some other administrator. Douglas Johnson shows the substantial errors and erratic policies in Nuerland which resulted from the tendency of each incoming governor to suggest in his assessments that his predecessor had made a botch of the job and left things in a state of disorder, necessitating the vigorous use of his own new broom. Here then we see the influences of genre expectation and the psychology of self-presentation intimately entwining in the colonial written records (Johnson 1981, 1994). I would also suggest that the concerns historians express about the adverse influence of subjectivity on memory are less a concern about oral sources specifically than a despair about the messiness of human beings in general. Henige points out that 'it is rare to to find any really substantial similarity between an oral testimony and a written account since the two sources generally evoke two different points of view' (Henige 1982: 71). Yet instead of probing and articulating the roots of these divergences, as I try to do throughout this study, many historians seem to favour either agreeing with the written sources or else suspending their judgement entirely.

There are of course serious points at issue, both methodological and epistemological, in debates over oral historiography. Generally I have tried to follow the advice of Jan Vansina, one of the great pioneers of Africanist oral history. He begins on a sceptical note, advising us that most people claim to remember opinions, both their own and those of others, and that all such claims are suspect. Remembered motivations are even worse, since they are 'even more difficult to observe, easy to falsely attribute, often unconscious, and usually more complex'. Such information must be distrusted, he warns, unless there are strong indications to the contrary. Such indications include 'concrete action resulting from standing on an opinion, as when a person is jailed for his beliefs, such factors as a particularly strong emotion followed by action as a result of public expression of it, or even a particularly pithy expression of the opinion itself' (Vansina 1980: 269). In response to this I would simply note that these criteria *were* met by the oral testimonies I gathered. My informants were well able to summarise pithily both their own opinions and the movement's ideas; most had indeed been to jail for their beliefs and had the scars to prove it; and in the course of their narratives most were aroused into displays of emotion and enthusiasm.

Such is the basic defence of my material. I return in Chapter 8 to consider these oral testimonies in the light of some more recent anthropological discussions of memory.

A Note on Naming

I will use the term 'Pathan' throughout (as both noun and adjective) to refer to the main ethnic group and culture of the Frontier, since the Anglophone reader is generally more familiar with it than the other versions used in the literature and in the Frontier itself, such as Pukhtun, Pakhtun and Pashtun. The only exception to this is where I quote from others' written sources. The Pathans' language, however, I refer to conventionally as 'Pashto'.

1

The Frontier, the Pathans & the British in the Early Twentieth Century

Invoking the Frontier and Frontiers

The North West Frontier Province lies in the north of Pakistan, with Afghanistan to its west, Punjab and Kashmir to its east, and Baluchistan to its south.[1] It is about four hundred miles long and for much of its length little more than a hundred miles across. The Province is bound to its north and west by the mighty Hindu Kush mountains and in the south by the Sulaiman range. Flanking the Province on the east is the Indus river, which constitutes something of a geographical and cultural dividing line between the Frontier Province and the rest of the subcontinent, and arguably between the cultures of the Middle East and South Asia more generally. Rolling hills cross the Province, enclosing between them valleys made fertile by the subsidiary channels of the Kabul river which bring waters from the mountains of Afghanistan. Other rivers like the Swat and Kurram have been diverted during the last hundred years through thousands of irrigation canals to meet the increased needs of agriculture. The main crops are much as they were a hundred years ago – maize, millet, wheat and barley are the staples, but sugar cane, cotton and tobacco are more valuable. A quarter of the cultivated land is irrigated by canals, since the climate is a dry, continental one, with harsh cold winters and long scorching summers which end only with the dramatic monsoon rains.

There are various theories about the ancestry and language of the Pathans. One school considers them descendants of Aryan nomads from Central Asia who settled four thousand years ago in the plains and hills of eastern and southern Afghanistan. On this view their language, Pashto, is probably derived from Saka, a Central Asian language, and belongs to the East Iranian language family, though heavily influenced by Indo-Aryan (Ghani 1988). Another school thinks they are Semitic. Either way, contemporary vocabulary is replete with loan words from Arabic and Persian. For their own part, the key point for the Pathans of the Frontier is that they came into contact with the Muslims during the life of the Prophet, whom their original ancestor, Qais, sought out at Medina. He embraced the faith and was awarded the name Abdur Rashid, and his people thereafter were known as 'Pathans'. Later, the Pathans became subjects of the Hindu kings of

[1] It lies between the latitudes 31°N and 36°N and the longitudes 69°E and 74° E.

21

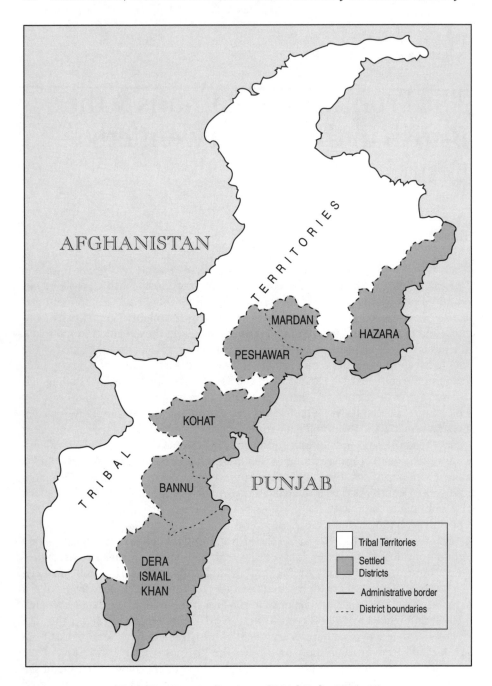

North West Frontier Province of British India 1902–47

Kabul, but in the tenth century an independent Muslim Turkic principality invaded and drove the Hindus out, settling and intermarrying and bringing the mass of Pathans into Islam. The Pathan tribes helped the new regime win further battles in India and Central Asia.

From the medieval period to the nineteenth century the Pathans remained part of the great Muslim empires of North India, and in the late sixteenth and seventeenth centuries they were caught up in the conflicts between the Afghan and Mughal emperors, siding with the former. During this time of strife some of the tribes left Afghanistan, crossing the Hindu Kush to seize land and settle in the fertile plains of the Kabul and Indus river basins, and the Pathans have straddled the great range ever since. There are few tractable passes through the mountains and the most famous of them, the Khyber, is the main route of communication between Afghanistan and India, Central Asia and South Asia. As such it has always borne rich trade and traffic, from which the Afridi and Shinwari tribes in particular have long profited through tolls and plunder (Singer 1984). Thus while the treacherous mountains of the Hindu Kush provide a broad geographical barrier – the name literally means 'Hindu Killer' – the Khyber Pass also provides a narrow and rugged but well-trodden thoroughfare. As such, its control has been indispensable to any power in the region and the frontier city of Peshawar, ten miles to its east, has been a key stronghold for kingdoms that ruled from east or west.

The British were no exception and the status of the Khyber continually concerned them. The first official British contact with the region took place during Europe's Napoleonic wars when Mountstuart Elphinstone was sent as an envoy by the East India Company to establish diplomatic links with the Persian-speaking Durrani dynasty of the Kingdom of Kabul, which ruled as far east as the Indus and whose court was then in its winter capital of Peshawar: 'In the year 1808, when, from the embassy of General Gardanne in Persia, and other circumstances, it appeared as if the French intended to carry the war into Asia, it was thought expedient by the British government in India to send a mission to the King of Caubul, and I was ordered on that duty' (Elphinstone 1839: 1). The 27-year-old Elphinstone displayed remarkable initiative and verve in his courting of the regime, and all subsequent writers on Pathan society and history remain in his debt for the two-volume *An Account of the Kingdom of Caubul*, a remarkably early piece of authentic ethnographic description. But in the years following Elphinstone's departure the Kingdom of Kabul was weakened by dynastic rivalry and warring among the Pathan tribes, and in 1823 it was decisively defeated at the Battle at Nowshera by the Sikhs, who then extended their own Kingdom of the Punjab westwards to Peshawar.

The British, meanwhile, grew increasingly anxious about Russia's ongoing expansion in Central Asia and the possible threat it posed to India, and they fretted over how best to control and defend the Frontier. Some officials advocated a 'close border' policy, which accepted the existence of the Sikh kingdom and regarded it as a kind of buffer. Others, however, feared that this left a largely ungoverned zone between Peshawar and Kabul which was populated by Pathan tribes with no declared loyalties who might be vulnerable to Russian blandishments. Proponents of this view proposed a 'forward' policy which would advance direct British control and influence beyond the Indus and all the way to Kabul. Actual policy vacillated between the two positions. The First Anglo-Afghan War in 1837 arose out of the heavy-handed promotion by the British of their favoured candidates within the Kabul court, but ended in their sound defeat. Chastened, they reverted to the 'close border' option, signing a tripartite treaty in 1838 with both the Sikh and Kabul kingdoms. The treaty was soon annulled, however, and the British reverted to the forward policy, fighting two wars with the Sikhs in 1846 and 1848 and annexing the whole of the Punjab and the Pathan lands as far as Peshawar into their own empire in 1849. The Second Anglo-Afghan War broke out in 1878 when the Kingdom of Kabul again resisted British efforts to control its court, and again the British were defeated amid the brutal mountains. In each Anglo-Afghan War (there was a third in 1919) the Pathans in the Frontier fought in support of their fellow tribesmen across the Hindu Kush.

In 1893 the so-called Durand Line was negotiated with the Amir of Afghanistan and drawn up as a formal boundary separating his territory from that of the British. It was drawn to coincide with the Khyber, with the British hoping they could thereby control strategic access to the narrow pass. Gradually the old caravan route for mules and camels was joined by railways, tunnels and zigzagging roads thrust through the rock to facilitate the rapid movement of troops to defend the border. The amazing railway line rising right through the Khyber Pass itself was finally completed in 1925, an impressive if ultimately eccentric feat of engineering. Thus the British went to great effort and expense to seal off the area, and to construct a rock and iron curtain on the fringe of their Raj.

From an Anglophone perspective, therefore, nurtured in the tradition of Kipling, *Kim* and *The Man Who Would Be King* (not to mention *Carry on up the Khyber*), it is rather natural to conceive of the North West Frontier Province as a front line, a periphery, a point of termination. Certainly the British tried to make it such, and the very name they assigned it, drily cartographical, suggests a geographical marginality and no man's land (something which continues to irk the Pathans today).[2] Yet such a marginalised characterisation is quite inappropriate given the Frontier's actual role and experience over a longer history. Having journeyed around North India and Afghanistan, the historian Arnold Toynbee wrote that it was necessary to draw a distinction between two kinds of geographical limits: 'culs-de-sac are regions on the fringe ... that have received successive influences from the centre but have not been able to pass them further afield. Roundabouts are regions on which routes converge from all quarters of the compass and from which routes radiate to all quarters of the compass again' (Toynbee 1961: 2). The British viewed the Frontier very much as a cul-de-sac, controlled from the centre and usefully denying entry to undesirable Russian neighbours. For Toynbee, however, the real historical character of the region was as a roundabout, a centre of communication receiving and spinning off influences among South, West and Central Asia, India and the West. Lying on a highway of conquest, it had witnessed successive waves of invaders: Persians, Greeks, Bactrians, Scythians, Kushanas, White Huns and Mughals, to name but a few.

---

[2] The persistence of the British name in modern Pakistan irritates contemporary Pathan leaders, who point out that the Sindis have Sind, the Baluchis Baluchistan, the Punjabis Punjab, and hence that the Frontier Province should be given a 'proper name' which better reflects the ethnicity and culture of the people living there – 'Puktunistan', for instance, or 'Pukhtunkhwa'.

Toynbee's view is supported in detail by Uberoi's sparkling discussion of the multi-ethnic, multicultural composition of the later Mughal nobility. Uberoi argues that the only way to understand the otherwise bewildering array of facts – the seemingly endless and disconnected comings and goings of armies, dynasties and peoples, of things, traits and ideas – is to conduct a structuralist analysis which highlights the marriages and trade taking place across the various binary oppositions of Muslim and non-Muslim India, inner and outer Asia, highlands and lowlands, an exchange of men and women which provided the unifying links for the entire far-flung Mughal nobility:

> The Hindu Kush not only divided the Oxus from the Indus, Central from South Asia, but also simultaneously interconnected the two parts of inner Asia and outer Asia into a system of inter-relations. By Frontier logic the wall is also a corridor and to divide is also to inter-connect. Thus the Hindu Kush by analogy is to be compared less to an open and shut gate than to a kind of a revolving door whose equal functions in history were to separate, mutually attract and interchange the currents of inner and outer Asia. It was a periodic historical process of separation, encounter and exchange in different spheres of life. (Uberoi 1978: 73)

While images of roundabouts and revolving doors are certainly more illuminating than those of borders or cul de sacs, even they do not fully capture the fluidity of frontiers, or their essence as contested zones. As a crucial area for expeditions and empires through three millennia the Frontier's revolving door has moved and changed its nature continually under the influence of its most recent watchmen. Far from being the no man's land which the British tried to make of it, and which is the typical fate of areas abutting lineal borders (the Indo-Pakistan border zone, ten kilometres wide, in nearby Punjab being a bleak example), the Frontier has for the most part been an 'everyman's land', a frequent scene of civilisational clashes and encounters. Reflecting on this past, Uberoi suggests that 'it is the essential nature and diachronic rhythm of the frontier to change in time, alternating from a firm dividing line into its opposite, a meeting point, and back again. In that historical process the frontier renews itself as well as those either side of it' (Uberoi 1978: 75).

The most extraordinary example of such renewal is the great lost civilisation of Gandhara, which William Dalrymple has recently described in evocative terms (1999). Gandhara was a mountain kingdom established in the Frontier by Alexander's Greeks, who, having crossed the Hindu Kush to conquer Persia's remotest province, found themselves stranded by their leader's untimely death in Babylon. They settled, married and mingled, adopting Buddhism in combination with their own Greek philosophy and classical ideas. Over the centuries they sculpted Buddhas wearing togas, the figures bearing the grace of India, the proportion of Greece. The kingdom's coins tell of Diomedes of Punjab, Menander of Kabul. New cities were built on classical grids, yet with Buddhist shrines at every intersection. Acropolises were still being built in the seventh century long after the demise of classical Greece and traders came from all over the world – Rome, Egypt, China – to do business in the capital city of Pushkalavati. Gandhara survived a thousand years and after its collapse left a legacy of finely constructed *stupas*, Indo-Hellenic Buddhist monasteries, some still perfectly preserved in remote locations in the Frontier with classical Grecian porticos, pillars and pediments. In appreciating the fantastic scene around him Dalrymple writes that it is 'difficult at first to understand how the warlike Pathans of the NWFP [North West Frontier Province] could be descended from the gentle Greek philosophers who created the notably peaceful civilisation of Buddhist Gandhara'.

I had a different sense when I stood before the monasteries in the early days of my fieldwork. Might not some of the inspiration for the non-violence of the Khudai Khitmatgars during their freedom struggle came from this awareness of the area's earlier Buddhist inhabitants, the ruined *stupas* serving as a distant reminder of a different philosophy? Their occasional visibility is much like their contemporary ideological presence, for local people dimly but persistently remember the Buddhists as a 'peaceful people'. Was not Pushkalavati, in its modern incarnation as Charsadda, the final home of Badshah Khan? Might not the Pathans have drawn upon what Wendy James has called 'the long-accumulated cultural deposit of unremembered events' (James 1988: 2)? If such a linkage is ultimately fanciful, one can at least say with confidence that the ideology of the Khudai Khidmatgar movement was in its own way a rather wonderful cultural bricolage and synthesis worthy of the Frontier kingdom of Gandhara. The only sadness is that the suppression the movement suffered after Partition means that, unlike Gandhara, it has left little mark on the horizon.

The journey down from Swat on to Peshawar brings one's thoughts back to earth. Few of the subsequent rulers in the region managed the longevity and artistry of the Gandharans. Peshawar today is dominated by its fort, built by the Sikhs in the last century, but otherwise suffers a lack of imposing architecture surprising in a place of its age and significance.[3] It thus has the slightly transient air of a town where ancient rulers have long since been usurped and newer ones have not set down deep roots, leaving it as an entrepôt and outpost for modern kingdoms based elsewhere. As other anthropologists have written:

> There is often a stirring if perhaps superficial resemblance between border towns everywhere; thus Newry [on the Eire/Ulster border], for example has some of the characteristics of Peshawar in Pakistan's North West Frontier: the money changers, the lorries lined up for customs, the rush to buy consumer durables (some of which are smuggled), even down to the sporadic bomb blast and violent death. (Donnan and Wilson 1994: 9)

Peshawar's famous Kissa Khani bazaar continues in its time-honoured role as a venue not merely for trade but for the exchange of amazing tales and sad stories by itinerants and visitors, though now the tellers and listeners are more often Afghan refugees and Western 'aid personnel' than the travelling silk merchants and highland pastoral nomads of the past.

Thus, as many before me have realised, researching the history and culture of the Frontier is a more complex and elusive task than for other, less turbulent areas. It is very hard to find any local written records more than a century old – if ever written at all, they seem to have been irrevocably lost or destroyed amid the many raids and expeditions that sought to subdue the area before moving on. The Frontier's location

---

[3] This fort was built on the ruins of an earlier Mughal one. The present structure, we are told by contemporary observers, is no match for the beauty of the earlier structure.

and history have thus left it with an abundance of events but a paucity of records. This complex story of comings and goings seems almost to have shaped the views of the Pathans themselves, who in everyday conversation eschewed any cumulative or teleological narrative of the region in favour of vivid historical vignettes, grounded in landscape. As I have mentioned, on the road to Swat the ruins of Takht Bai, a Buddhist monastery, were described by my travelling companions as having been constructed by 'a peaceful people'. A few miles later as we went through the Malakand Pass they reminded me that we were retreading the great warrior Alexander's route to India. When driving through the Khyber Pass, my companions always pointed to the Britishers' Durand Line at a particular bend on the road. Such was their sureness and precision it took me three visits, each time peeking round my veil, to realise the line was entirely imaginary and not chalked high up on the rock. Alexander, the Gandharans and the British were referred to almost as old friends, as if they had been passing through only the day before, more as fellow residents of the Frontier's domain than as awe-inspiring precursors. Veena Das, in another context, calls this phenomenon the 'creation of contemporaneity in non-contemporaneous events' (Das 1995: 134).

I am conscious that I have relied here on merely figurative and allusive comments, and I am certainly not trying to assign to the Pathans some particularly distinctive historical mode of thought. I am, however, trying to hint at the distinctive cultural processes operating in frontiers, and in the Frontier. In their introduction to *Border Approaches* (1994) Donnan and Wilson make a plea for an anthropology of frontiers which recognises that the people who live within this kind of frontier 'cultural land-scape' have a special relationship to the states and other peoples which surround them, and that frontier regions are 'often major magnets of change in socio-political processes of significance to many people beyond their locality and even beyond the state' (Donnan and Wilson 1994: 2). An anthropology of frontiers is thus an anthro-pology of 'political negotiation and contest' (*ibid.*: 7).[4]

In trying to fence off the Frontier province by establishing the Durand Line, the British had, in the manner of modern nation states, sought to establish a definite boundary line. As Richard Muir (quoted by Benedict Anderson) suggests: 'Located at the interfaces between adjacent state territories, international boundaries have a special significance in determining the limits of sovereign authority and defining the spatial form of the contained political regions. ... Boundaries ... occur where the vertical interfaces between state sovereignties intersect the surface of the earth ... . As vertical interfaces, boundaries have no horizontal extent.'[5] Such politically demar-cated boundary lines of vanishing breadth are by definition peripheral. They are static, fixed, and serve to separate. Passage through them comes only after a complex secular rite of passage of 'Immigration', 'Customs' and 'Passport Control'. By keeping human inhabitants out of such zones, the attempt is made physically to create difference through distance, an imperative requirement for neighbouring societies which risk dilution through proximity. The emptiness and cultural void of these

---

[4] Donham and James 1986 similarly look at the varied nature of the historical relationships between the centres and peripheries of Ethiopia and Sudan.
[5] Richard Muir, quoted in Benedict Anderson 1991: 172.

areas are meant to obliterate the traces of civilisation, of identity, and the transition from one culture to the next is sudden and stark.

Frontiers, in contrast, are fluid and mobile and serve to connect and exchange elements of the areas they bridge. They are not peripheral, but central to civilisational processes. Genuine frontiers are spatially extended regions with their own cultural processes and imperatives which tend toward the syncretic and dialectic. Gandhara was born out of just such a process, a prolonged and extraordinary fusion of civilisations, and all achieved some 1,500 years before Kipling stated that east and west would never meet, and the British sought with gun and bunker to turn a frontier into a border.[6]

Fundamentals of Pathan Culture

Pathan culture is itself a good instance of the syncretic processes typical of frontiers – maturing at a crossroads of civilisations, it bears the marks of many. I have argued at length elsewhere (Banerjee 1990) that the Indus river constitutes a decisive break in terms of cultural patterns. To the West the climate is predominantly of Mediterranean type and societies share characteristics of language, segmentary structure and acephalous organisation, endogamous marriage rules, notably parallel-cousin marriage, and egalitarian ideas about leadership and power that are similar to the social formations of the Middle East. East of the Indus, the climate revolves around the tropical monsoon; social structures are dominated by caste organisation, hierarchy and centralised authority, and, in marriage rules, parallel-cousin marriage is rare.

The North West Frontier, lying as it does on the west bank of the Indus, displays transitional features of these two broad types of social formation. The basic framework of the Pathan social structure is its segmentary lineage system. The basic mechanisms of this will be familiar from Evans-Pritchard's classic account of the Nuer of the Sudan (and see Dresch 1986 for a more recent exposition in the context of Yemen). The population is split into a hierarchy of social groups of diminishing size and extent – typically tribes, clans, sub-clans, lineages, sections and families. Each group defines its membership by shared descent through the patriline from a common male ancestor. (This strict patrilineal descent is accompanied by a preference for marriage to the father's brother's daughter – that is, patrilateral parallel-cousin marriage.) The larger the group, the further back in time this common ancestor lies: thus a section may consist of men sharing a common patrilateral grandfather or great grandfather, whereas a clan will trace shared ancestry back through potentially a dozen or more generations. Among the Pathans, the suffix *zai* or *khel* after the name of the ancestor indicates the name of the clan to which a person belongs – thus Yusufzai is the clan of the descendants of Yusuf. In the event of social conflict, depending upon the kin relationship of the protagonists, groupings of various levels of the hierarchy may come together to support one another and fight together. Thus first cousins, descended from a shared grand-

---

[6] Thanks to William Dalrymple for the Kipling conceit.

father, would often fight each over land or inheritance, but they would join together as members of the same segment to fight more distant relatives from another segment. Equally both segments would join together to oppose members of another lineage. These related lineages would join to fight people from another sub-clan and so on. This is the basic principle of segmentary opposition, or, as the Pathans have traditionally described it, *parajamba*, meaning 'taking sides'. The logic of the system is also seen in another specific term, *tarburwali*, meaning enmity between first cousins, regarded by the Pathans as one of the most frequent causes of strife.

Amidst the Pathans' segmentary structure, however, there are also clear elements of caste-like social stratification. Barth argues that intersecting the lineages are social groups called *quom*, which differ greatly in prestige and power and together embody a hierarchical ideology which looks very similar to the caste system in India. Dumont has argued famously that the Indian caste system centres on Hindu notions of purity and pollution. The Pathans, however, are Muslims (mostly Sunni), and the language and symbols of religion have a prominent role and importance in everyday life, with religious observance considered to be an integral part of being a Pathan. Barth argues, therefore, that the foundation of the quasi-caste hierarchy in the Frontier is not purity, but rather ideas of honour and shame (Barth 1959).

Honour also lies at the heart of Pathan custom, which is encoded in *Pukhtunwali*. According to the literature, *Pukhtunwali* is a highly distinctive code of ethics and behaviour, dating back more than a thousand years, which is founded on several interrelated institutions and concepts.[7] Most famous is *Badal*, usually translated as 'revenge, feud or vendetta', which refers to the exchange of challenge and violence in the face of insult or injury. Conversely, *Nanawatai* literally means 'coming in' but is best translated as 'sanctuary'. A Pathan is custom-bound to offer sanctuary to anyone who requests it, even his most bitter enemy.[8] *Melmastia* is both the offering of generous hospitality and the honourable use of material goods. Again, extending such hospitality is obligatory even if the guest is one's enemy. *Purdah* in its narrow sense refers to the seclusion of women, but its broader meaning is the honourable organisation of domestic life. Similarly, *jirga* has the broad meaning of the honourable arrangement of public affairs, but has the more specific reference of

> an assembly of elders who are called to decide specific issues and whose decisions are binding on parties in conflict ... . The *jirga* regulates life through decisions ranging from the location of a mosque ... to larger issues such as regulating foreign relations with other tribes and even conveying decisions of the tribe to government. Decisions are based on a combination of Islamic law and Pukhto custom. (Ahmed 1980: 90)

In Akbar Ahmed's analysis, at the core of all of the aforementioned institutions and concepts is *nang*, which can be glossed as 'the condition of integrity' (Edwards 1986: 99). The issuing and acceptance of challenge in the face of insult, the extension of sanctuary and hospitality, and the respect for the rules of *purdah* and

---

[7] In modern times several social anthropologists have written about the nature of Pathan societies in Afghanistan and Pakistan, the best-known studies being those of Fredrik Barth and Akbar Ahmed, with more recent scholars such as Meeker, Anderson and Edwards providing excellent added detail and nuance.

[8] Though such a request may in turn mean lessened prestige for the appellant if used as a means of not returning a challenge.

jirga are each instances of 'honourable activity' expressing *nang*. Hence Ahmed sees *Puktunwali* as essentially a code of honour (Ahmed 1980: 91). Barth suggests that when a man strives to live in accordance with this exacting code he is 'doing' Pashto (Barth 1981: 105). For Barth, 'doing Pashto' is of more profound significance for Pathan identity than merely speaking Pashto, and *Pukthunwali* is the 'native model' which provides the Pathans with their self-image: 'This Code is the idiom through which the Pukhtun expresses his Pukhtunness' (Ahmed 1980: 89, 91).

In past centuries this cultural superstructure of Puktunwali had been supported by a distinctive economic base. When the Pathans first crossed over the Hindu Kush the newly conquered tracts of land were allocated among the tribes, their clans and subsections (Baha 1978: 132). The land assigned to a tribe was called *daftar* and the individual shareholder a *daftari*. A man who ceased to be a *daftari* lost not only land but the right to be called a Pathan at all, becoming instead a *faqir*, labouring for other people and without a voice in the village or the tribal councils. Thus, besides full tribal members, Pathan villages consisted of such dependent cultivators, village servants, menials and artisans, some of whom would be of non-Pathan ethnicity, brought home as prisoners from wars and raids. It is these various groups who feature prominently in the caste-like stratification Barth discusses.

Tribal land continued to be periodically reapportioned according to the principles of an elaborate system known as *wesh*. Under *wesh*, the tribe was obliged to redistribute its *daftar* lands on a cycle of between five and thirty years. This redistribution involved not merely the shares of individual *daftari*, but those of whole lineages and segments, thereby entailing the movement of entire groups to new lands. Michael Meeker has made the appealing suggestion that such redistribution was a regular re-enactment and reminder of the heroic conquests and settlement which first brought the Pathans to the region (Meeker 1980). Be this as it may, *wesh* did ensure some semblance of equitable distribution by preventing particular groups or individuals from benefiting from the best land in perpetuity. To that extent *wesh* underpinned and reflected the ideology of egalitarianism and honour which was central to the ideas of *Pukhtunwali*. All *daftari* were to be guaranteed sufficient land for them to be able to live up to the material and non-material demands of the *Pukhtunwali* code. As Edwards defines it: '*Namus* ... comprises all those things with which a Pakhtun man surrounds himself – rifles, land, women – and that collectively constitute his sense of honor. Without women in his home, without land to his name, without a rifle to shoulder, a man is weightless and naked (*luchak*)' (Edwards 1986: 75).

In the same egalitarian vein, while decisions affecting the tribe were taken by the *jirga* (council) of senior men, the composition of the *jirga* was decided by the votes cast by all the *daftari* of the tribe. *Jirgas* were mostly convened to discuss issues on a case-by-case basis, and did not have permanent powers. As in most segmentary societies, the traditional figure of chief or *khan* emerged as an individual of authority and particular honour only in specific contexts and situations, rather than having any permanently ascribed status or power, and no *daftari* paid tribute or revenue to individual leaders.

However, the region's later history began to disrupt this social and economic structure. From the eighteenth century the Pathan lands became subject to increasingly centralised rule by the Mughal and then the Kabul kingdoms. These regimes developed refined systems for the collection of tribute and revenue,

coopting influential senior men to collect revenues and undertake other administrative tasks in return for grace and favour rights over areas of land and exemption
from paying revenue themselves (Jansson 1988: 39). Such intervention by the
state in questions of land created increasingly substantial landholdings for some of
these men and began to put a strain on the ideal of redistributionism enshrined in
wesh.

Having annexed the Frontier, the British continued and widened this network of
revenue collection. They brought a further refinement, however, which was the
replacement of mere grace and favour rights with the allocation of full legal
ownership of tracts of land to favoured *khans*.[9] This decisively undermined the
already declining *wesh* system, the spirit of which was quite at odds with fixed tenure
ownership. Thus, as Janssen notes:

> The most important innovation introduced by the British land policy in India was the
> concept of ownership itself. Previous arrangements had given people different rights in the
> land and to its produce. But when the British idea of ownership was enforced, someone
> came to own the land more or less to the exclusion of everybody else. A prominent feature of
> these reforms was that the British wanted to create a landlord class in their own image.
> (Jansson 1988: 43)

The primary motivation for creating such a class was the desire to establish the classical colonial framework of indirect rule, employing members of the landed élite to
secure political control and carry out services of a judicial, administrative and fiscal
nature. If this local landed élite did not exist it had to be invented and between 1868
and 1880 the British administration in the Frontier set out detailed rules concerning
land ownership, rents and tax, and this codification in effect reified several strata
(Janssen 1988: 41–6; Shah 1999: 6–8).

At the top were the 'big *khans*'. These were the substantial landed aristocracy who
had been designated by the colonial authorities as 'natural leaders' of the people and
given extensive privileges, such that they typically owned thousands of acres, had
substantial wealth and status and exercised great influence over the villages in their
domain. The big *khans* would remain throughout the loyalist linchpins of British rule
in the Frontier. They were assisted operationally by thousands of *lambardaris*, semi-
hereditary revenue and tax collectors. Many *lambardaris* also acted as village
headmen and performed police duties, taking as payment a percentage of the
village's land revenue and water rate.

Also part of the landed élite were the 'small *khans*'. They were far more numerous
than the big *khans* and their landholdings could vary considerably in size, some being
very substantial, others quite small. Their main defining feature was that they were
landowners who were not favoured by the government and not directly employed in
its service. As a result, the small *khans*' informal influence at the local level was often
considerable, however, since their relative independence of the state and smaller
lands meant they had far closer direct contacts with peasants and ordinary cultivators than the remote big *khans* who were so obviously complicitous with the
British. In the twentieth century such influence was further boosted by the small

[9] See Jon Anderson's 'There Are No Khans Anymore' (1980) for an account of recent incursions of development on Pathan social structure.

khans' growing role in lending credit to the peasantry.[10] Until the early twentieth century the small *khans* were not as a group opposed to the British administration and were more concerned to gain its recognition and favours. Subsequently, however, they became significant political actors in the belief that they would only gain greater political influence in the absence of the British. Many of them became involved in various ways with the nationalist movements, most notably Badshah Khan himself, the son of a prosperous small *khan*.

Neither group of *khans* cultivated land themselves. By the turn of the twentieth century much of their land operated in a quasi-feudal manner, with men who essentially had lost their independence cultivating the *khan's* land and giving him allegiance. A large minority of Pathan peasants were in such a position. The narrow majority of peasants formed what the British categorised as 'peasant proprietors', small cultivators who still had notionally independent social status and who held land from the *khans* by paying rent in kind, typically a specified share of their own crop. Despite their notional status, however, in so far as they were tenants at will and had no permanent rights to the land, their tenure was dependent on the quality of their personal relationship with their landlords, and so in practice they too were hard-pressed to avoid doing his bidding.

The rent of the tenants at will was usually paid in kind, but in the somewhat more urbanised Peshawar and Mardan districts cash payments became increasingly common at the end of the nineteenth century, largely as a result of the extension of irrigation, which allowed thirstier cash crops to be cultivated. The increasing monetarisation in these districts also led to the emergence of middlemen who leased land from the *khans* and then sub-let it to others for cultivation, thus sparing the *khans* the trouble of land and estate management. This gave rise to a low-status stratum who were renting land for a fixed term at a fixed cash rate. These were often men who had had to leave other land because they had fallen into debt and been compelled to sell or mortgage it. Together the rise of cash cropping, money rents and a competitive market in sub-tenancy led to increases in both rents and the price of land. This trend was reinforced by the growth of population and the improvement of markets and communications, which caused a general rise in prices for produce. Thus, between 1864 and 1900, rent levels steadily increased.

By the early twentieth century, therefore, little more than fifty years after the dawn of British rule in the Frontier, their efforts and legal provisions had caused the landlord class as a whole to gain in strength and influence. The Pathan peasantry were at best in the position of tenants at will, their tenure dependent on the quality of their personal relationship with their landlords, and at worst in thrall to semi-feudal masters or increasingly demanding rentiers. Thus, their social position had diminished significantly from the traditional ideals of the proud and independent *daftari* sharing as an equal member in his tribe's land.

Meanwhile the big *khans'* relationship with the British became ever more symbiotic. In 1889–90 the Deputy Commissioner Robert Bruce launched a more

---

[10] This was helped by their growing control over credit facilities. Legislation of 1904 forbade the further sale of land from cultivators to non-cultivators and, as intended, the result of this Act was the drastic curtailment of the activities of Hindu moneylenders.

formal system in which leading landlords were selected and graded according to their supposed power and influence and paid proportionate allowances by the government to cement their loyalty. These grants continued to grow into the twentieth century under the comprehensive term 'political pensions', and included payments in cash, property and other forms. In addition, posts in the administration were given to big *khans* and their relatives, along with honorific titles, such as Khan Sahib, Khan Bahadur and Nawab, and even, for a few, knighthoods. In return, they were required to render a range of services such as providing men for military service and controlling the tribe and clans as corporate bodies (Baha 1978: 34).

Particularly crucial for the life of the Frontier were the changes made by the authorities to the traditional *jirga* structure. Traditionally, a tribal *jirga* had to perform simultaneously the roles and duties of police, magistrate and judge. It sought to maintain or restore peace and order in times of trouble but was also an authority for settling disputes and dispensing justice. It would review cases including breaches of contract, disputes about tribal boundaries, distribution of water rights, claims to land and pasture, infringement of custom, enmity between cousins, and the frequent questions of inheritance. The *jirga's* members were elected by the whole body of the tribe, mostly from among elders, men of experience and integrity, and the memories of the elders would serve as a record of decisions and precedent.

After the British annexation the entire tribal system was abolished within the Settled Districts. The British were keen to utilise the idea of the *jirgas* as part of their apparatus of indirect colonial rule, however, and so officials reconstituted them and gave them responsibility for adjudicating on criminal cases according to the newly introduced colonial laws. Traditional *jirga* decisions were consensual and often ambiguous, with the focus on limiting conflicts rather than locating blame, and sentences of a restitutive rather than penal nature. The new role, however, obliged the *jirgas* to make clear-cut decisions on guilt and levy fines, now paid of course not to the victims but to the state. Things becames still worse after 1904, when Deputy Commissioners were empowered to refer the whole panoply of civil cases to the *jirgas* as well. The government appointed its loyal landlords to the *jirgas* and expected them to exert firm control over its decisions, and the *jirgas* thus functioned as glorified magistrates who took an increasing role in dealing harshly with any political activism or nationalist opposition. The 1904 legislation also gave the *jirgas* extended powers of arrest and imprisonment without right of appeal.

Since the *jirga* members were no longer elected but appointed, and since there was no mechanism of appeal against its decisions, there was no safeguard to stop the *khans* taking action through the *jirga* against their own enemies or those of their clients by implicating them in fictitious 'feuds' or accusing them of seditious activities. Furthermore, the Frontier Crimes Regulation of 1904 allowed for collective punishments when no individual culprit could be found and hence such enmity could be levelled against entire families or lineages (Baha 1978: 30). Given the prevailing values of honour and challenge, such decisions, whether malicious or not, frequently resulted in retaliatory actions by the maligned defendant and his kin and escalating exchanges of violence.

By the early twentieth century, therefore, two major changes brought about by colonial rule had combined to produce substantial and increasing levels of violence.

First, the shift from the principles of tribal *wesh* to a system of powerful landlord estates meant that tenants were increasingly obliged to turn out in support of their *khan* in the event of a dispute – even if, for example, this meant opposing one's own relatives who worked for some other landlord. Hence the traditional Pathan term of *parajamba* – taking sides – in practice shifted its sense (*ibid.*: 40–1). Whereas in the past it was the units within the segmentary framework which constitued the basis of political mobilisation – men taking sides with their brothers, segment, lineage, clan – now, instead, factions or political blocs were increasingly formed through 'vertical mobilisation' by *khans* of their dependants (much as Fredrik Barth described the process for Swat in the 1950s). Such estate-based factionalism had a pernicious effect on the levels of conflict and violence in Pathan society. Where previously feuds and disputes had for the most part occurred between relatively limited numbers of people and at a low intensity of violence, disagreements were now more likely to escalate into full-blown fights between larger numbers of increasingly well-armed clients.

Second, the increasingly arbitrary and vindictive decision making of the new-style *jirgas* both raised the frequency of grievances and conflicts and weakened the traditional means for resolving them. All this took place, meanwhile, against a background in which the erosion of landholdings, growing poverty and social weakness meant that many Pathans felt increasingly unable to live up to the classical demands of honour and *Pukhtunwali*. Many ended up living habitually beyond their means to sustain the appropriate status and levels of hospitality which were necessary for prestige and marriage negotiations, and eventually ended up in chronic debt, dropping irrevocably down the rural social hierarchy. The associated frustrations and heightened pride and sensitivity that such difficulties brought contributed further to social tensions and division. Thus levels of feud and conflict in the Frontier had reached unprecedented levels by the first decades of the twentieth century, with hundreds of murders a year in the Settled Districts, extensive fighting and countless cases of kidnapping and arson.

Violence was not confined within the Pathan communities, however, and the Frontier witnessed a number of armed uprisings against the British. The Anglo-Afghan wars in which the tribal Pathans fought on behalf of their Afghan brothers were the most important instances of such mobilisation, but there were many others, usually originating in the tribal areas and led by charismatic religious leaders in the name of an Islamic *jihad* against the infidel. The senior Muslim clerics, the *ulema* (pl. of *alim*), enjoyed high status in Pathan life. Qualified in theology and *sharia* law, they would give opinions on religious matters but also on social and personal issues, and hence by their decisions influenced all areas of life (Shah 1999: 10–11). Traditionally the *ulema* exercised judicial and executive powers among the tribes and even assumed political authority during periods of crisis. Of lesser status were the *imams* or *mullahs*, who led public prayers at the mosque but did not give sermons, and who were appointed by the local congregation.

In India as a whole many *ulema* enjoyed a tradition of playing a close supporting role to Muslim rulers and their affairs of state, and they made a similar accommodation with the new colonial rulers. Shah argues, however, that the *ulema* of the Frontier had a long pedigree of anti-establishment sentiment, remaining remote from rulers and state patronage. In the colonial period this translated into fierce opposition to the British, whom they saw as infidels striving to impose slavery on the free Islamic community of Pathans, and throughout the 1890s in particular they inspired the tribes of the Tribal Area to strike back. The most successful and significant of these campaigns was the 1897 uprising led by Hadda Mullah in Swat, who won concessions of land and relative autonomy from the British and thereby established the mini-state of the Walidom of Swat. But there were many others, and the battles waged by Mullah Shami in Waziristan and by Powindah Mullah – to name but two – inflicted heavy casualties on the colonial forces, the tribesmen fighting with great valour and commitment. In each case, however, the severely punitive immediate response by the colonial regime was followed by yet further accumulation of armed resources in the Frontier. By the turn of the twentieth century, therefore, to the increasingly exasperated British the North West Frontier appeared a hotbed of endemic violence and lawlessness, and of erratic but fierce resistance.

British Images of the Pathans

It is now a common observation within colonial studies that the British imperialists' imagery and evaluation of the colonial Other shifted significantly through the nineteenth century. As the empire spread, took on a moralising fervour and became increasingly formalised, the relative curiosity and open-mindedness about other cultures shown at the start of the century hardened into a bitterly judgemental and negative view by the time of the empire's ideological highpoint at Victoria's diamond jubilee of 1897. This shift was particularly striking in the case of the Pathans. The accounts of the Pathans written by British observers in the first decades of the nineteenth century, notably Elphinstone, were often positive, and the Pathans were compared favourably to the other peoples of India:

> All communication with the Afghauns is rendered agreeable by the dependence which can be placed on what they say. [T]hey have not that indifference to truth, and that style of habitual and gratuitous falsehood, which astonishes an European in natives of India and Persia. A man of the first nation seems incapable of observing anything accurately; and one of the second, of describing it truly: but unless ... some motive is apparent for misrepresenting the truth, one may generally rely on the Afghauns both for correctness and fidelity. (Elphinstone 1839 (1815): 326)

> An English traveller from India would view them with a more favourable eye ... the cold climate ... people not fluttering in white muslins while half their bodies are naked, but soberly and decently attired in dark-coloured woollen clothes ... . He would admire their fair complexions and European features, their industry and enterprise, the hospitality, sobriety, and contempt of pleasure which appear in all their habits; and above all, the independence and energy of their character. (*Ibid.*: 198)

Such relatively positive views partly reflected the intellectual currents in Europe at the time. Elphinstone was very much a product of the Scottish Enlightenment and sympathetic to republican ideas, and at the time of his visit the British monarchy was at a particularly low ebb. He and his contemporaries, with their thorough classical educations, enjoyed the sense of being in a land that had been fought over by

Alexander, and ruminated on the similarities between the Pathan *jirgas* and Athenian republicanism. He similarly admired the egalitarianism inherent in the *wesh* system of land distribution, which he described in detail. This was also a time of romantic views of the open-heartedness and integrity of the 'noble savage', of Hiawatha and the Celtic Ossian. Further, the fun-loving society of the late Georgian and Regency periods also took a relaxed view of the more exotic habits it encountered around the world, whether sexual, familial or narcotic. This is a period, as Ashish Nandy has pointed out, before the Orient became typecast as a place which was merely 'not Europe'. Most fundamentally, there was at that time no direct military confrontation between the British and the Pathans, and so the early writers could afford a certain generosity of representation.

This soon changed. In 1839 a large British army marched on Kabul. Demonstrating the technique of domination practised throughout the empire, it overthrew the ruler and installed a puppet; the bulk of the army then withdrew, assuming the country had been quashed. The Pathan tribesmen carried out constant sniping and skirmishing, however, and in 1840 Kabul rose in a revolt so ferocious that the remaining British accepted a truce and promised to withdraw under guarantee of safe passage. So it was that 16,500 people set off over the mountains back toward India: 700 British soldiers, 4,000 sepoy infantry and numerous campfollowers. For ten days they came under constant attack. Some were offered safe conduct and removed to an Afghan fort, where they were found still alive a year later. Gradually, however, the rest were killed. Only one survivor made it back, Surgeon William Brydon, half dead, an image immortalised in the celebrated painting 'The Remnants of an Army' by Lady Elizabeth Butler, which was later hung in the Tate Gallery. Angry and humiliated, a year later the British invaded the adjacent province of Sind, a response which Mountstuart Elphinstone, in retirement in England, bitterly criticised as the action of 'a bully who has been kicked in the streets and goes home to beat his wife in revenge' (quoted in Moorhouse 1983).

As the nineteenth century wore on, the classical and romantic models of polity gradually gave way to the bleaker world of utilitarianism, religous prurience, Social Darwinism and racial theory. Under the gaze of growing British imperial arrogance, blinkered by its sense of manifest destiny, the colonised peoples found themselves increasingly deprecated as backward and uncivilised. In the case of the Pathans, however, such images gained extra density and luridness from the fear and suspicion that grew out of the repeated bloody defeats the British had suffered at their hands in the Afghan wars. The potency of these images was enhanced in the strange twilight world of the 'Great Game', with British nervousness about Russian ambition continually exacerbating their perception of the apparent ungovernability of the Pathans on their border. As in other colonial situations, the British blamed the rising violence on the natural character of the indigenes, failing to see how they themselves had prompted it through their destruction of the traditional mechanisms of governance and destabilisation of the old socio-economic order.

These circumstances together eroded the earlier positive views of the Pathans, and by the end of the nineteenth century any ethnographic sensitivity and insight of the kind Elphinstone had displayed were all but lost. From this later period there survive numerous accounts by British men and women who lived, worked and travelled in the Frontier; doctors, nurses, political agents, travellers and soldiers all generated various forms of written account which contributed to the hardening of the classic British stereotype of the 'violent and duplicitous' Pathan:

> In the presence of strangers they are proud of their nationality and especially of the 'Nang-i-Pukhtuna' or 'Pukhtun honour' and assume an air of dignity and integrity which is but ill-supported by the other traits of their character. The Afghan is vain, bigoted in religious matters and national or tribal prejudices, revengeful of real or imaginary injuries, avaricious and penurious in the extreme, prone to deception which they fail to conceal, and wanting in courage and perseverance. But withal they assume a frankness and affability of manner, which coupled with their apparent hospitality, is very apt to deceive and disarm the unwary. They are, moreover, by nature and profession a race of robbers, and never fail to practice this peculiarly national calling on any and every available opportunity. Among themselves, finally, the Afghans are quarrelsome, intriguing, and distrustful of each other, and by neighbouring nations they are considered faithless and intractable. (Bellew 1862: 25)

> We have judged the Afghan as we have found him and we have found him very wanting. He has his virtues and he has his vices, and to our mind the latter overbalance the former very heavily. He is not fit to govern either himself or others, and sadly wants a master. If we don't take up that role, Russia will. For a master the Afghans want, and a master they must have sooner or later. Which is it to be? (Bellew 1880: 55)

Such accounts and memoirs were avidly read in Britian and helped convince public opinion of the reasonableness and acceptability of using force in suppressing colonial rebellion in the Frontier.

If in an absolute sense the depictions of the Pathans became increasingly negative, however, they retained some positive features when compared to the even more negative depictions of other Indians, notably Bengalis. In the later colonial period British discourse used notions of effeminisation to delegitimise, discredit and disempower colonised men, and colonial rule came to be seen as a manly prerogative with an aggressive, muscular chivalric model of white manliness taken as indicative of racial, national, cultural and moral superiority (Krishnaswamy 1998: 3). In contrast 'effeminate' was systematically used as a derogatory label applied to élite Hindu Bengali males to suggest they were physically, intellectually and morally soft, frail, weak and cowardly, reflecting their fertile but debilitating climate (*ibid.*: 20). In an influential discussion, the author and administrator Macaulay noted: 'There never perhaps existed a people so thoroughly fitted for a foreign yoke.' Effeminacy was thus put forward as both explanation and justification for India's loss of independence. As political consciousness and aspirations among Indians began to grow, the label of effeminacy was rapidly extended from the Bengali 'babus' to the discontented Indian middle classes as a whole, and by the end of the nineteenth century effeminacy had become the most powerful signifier of India's cultural decline and moral shortcomings.

These images had direct implications for the Frontier. Terrified by the ferocity of the Indian insurgency in 1857 and disillusioned by the demands of the Indian middle class, the colonial adminstrators found the restless urban centres increasingly distasteful and focused their attention on the Punjab and North West Frontier. There, remote from the argumentative Indian middle class, they could exercise a more rugged and paternalistic style of imperialism. Far from conventional adminis-trative controls and regulations, the Frontier could still provide 'a refuge for romance, exoticism and adventure but also a place of real business where struggle to maintain and expand the empire took place' (Krishnaswamy 1998).

As such, it was precisely the kind of setting and example which Baden-Powell wished to draw upon in his Boy Scout movement. As Robert MacDonald shows, the idea of frontier life exerted a great influence on the nation's idea of itself at the turn of the century, and upon the founding of the Boy Scout movement in particular. For Baden-Powell and others, the Edwardian Englishman appeared physically and morally weak, spoiled by the home comforts of urban living, and bullied by his suffragette women, and he did not inspire confidence ahead of the great war everyone was expecting. Looking around the empire, however, the men of the Australian outback, Canadian North West and South African veldt seemed in far better shape, strong and self-sufficient, accustomed to life in the open, altogether 'real men', men as God intended them to be according to Baden-Powell. To revive English manhood, therefore, its men needed a simpler, more disciplined life, preferably in the open air, with fewer temptations and more real challenges. They needed constant adventure and red-blooded action, and general separation from the debilitating influence of mothers and wives, thereby developing the pure masculine character required. As Macdonald concludes: 'The frontier provided British society at the begining of the century with an alternative ethic, answering this general fear about the condition of the nation's virility. [T]he idea of frontier was still potent and romantic to many Edwardians and it came to symbolise an attractive solution to a set of increasingly complex problems at home' (MacDonald 1993: 5).

Although the NWFP was not a colonial frontier in the process of being settled in the same way as Canada and South Africa were, in most other respects life there perfectly fitted the bill. Life for officers was a constant but disciplined round of healthy outdoor activities – riding, sports, big game hunting and pig sticking, mountain climbing and, best of all, fighting the Pathans, which brought not only exhilaration but also the duty and occasional sacrifice necessary to dignify the whole enterprise. Thus service on the North West Frontier was seen by many observers and partici-pants as not merely personally enjoyable, but as the perfect crucible for forging a new generation of hardy Englishmen.

As a result, despite their gloomy views of Pathan morality and behaviour, many of those who spent time in the Frontier, particularly in the military, came to view it as a wonderful place for a man to live, and developed a more than sneaking regard for the Pathan as a worthy and sporting adversary. Following the Second Afghan War of 1878 there was little large-scale fighting, and military activities were largely confined to 'regular skirmishing with tribesmen on the frontier, seen by both sides more as blood sport than warfare ... . [T]he frontier engagements provided the most gripping tales in the huge mythology of British arms in India' (Moorhouse 1983: 137). There is an endless supply of such tales from old soldiers. It was said that Pathans sometimes applied to the nearest British political agent for medals after particularly exciting scraps with the troops he had ordered against them. One engagement led to a stalemate with a prolonged sniping bout; eventually a Pathan, bored by the British force's hopelessly inaccurate shooting, stood up to advise them that their sights were set too low. On another occasion a long sortie in the foothills of the Hindu Kush finally resulted in the capture of some tribesmen, whose leader asked the British commander whether the Pathans had fought well. The officer replied: 'Of course – I would not have shaken hands with you unless you had!' As Moorhouse concludes, such 'swashbuckling yarns, full of honour and treachery, bravery and comradeship, danger and dash, were all calculated to make adolescent hearts run wild'. Similarly, Krishnaswamy argues that for the British the North West Frontier allowed 'unrestrained expression of aggression, and rationalised, reproduced and reinforced the values and attitudes of a Victorian public school' (Krishnaswamy 1998: 129).

The imagery of the Pathans was influenced by their place within this 'schooling' and the elaborate distinction between martial and non-martial races in India which the British drew up and elaborated in the wake of the 1857 mutiny was posed in its purest and most conventional form between the sturdy, wild and pure-bred Pathan and the intelligent, educated, mongrelised Bengali, whose rootless cosmopolitanism and elaborate Hinduism contrasted with the traditionalism and austere Islam of the Pathans. Although the British denounced the ferocity of the Pathans and their utter disregard for restraint, they admired the rebellious spirit, since it could always be crushed with force and had no threatening political consequences, unlike the politicised and restless Bengali middle class (*ibid.*: 68).

There was a further layer of complexity in British attitudes to the Pathans, however, namely the inter-racial homosexuality that took place in the Frontier. Some of the very men who would have been regarded as an acute symptom of the crisis of manhood found in the Frontier a place not of moral and physical improvement but of irresistible temptation and vice. The place of male homosexuality in Pathan life is a sensitive topic, but it did have a traditional place among youths and young men. Sexual frustrations had to be carefully discharged, given the strict controls on women and the extreme risks of liaising with unmarried women in the context of honour and revenge. As among the ancient Greeks and Persians, the heavy cultural emphasis on masculinity and manly pursuits probably also played some role.

Homosexual liaisons with Pathans thus had a significant place in the burgeoning corpus of late Victorian and Edwardian erotica, as Ronald Hyam discusses in his study of the British experience of sexuality and empire (Hyam 1990). Hyam relates the experiences of one young officer called Searight, who had struggled to find carefree opportunities for homosexual acts in England, aside from juvenile experiments at his public school. In Bengal he found things somewhat easier: 'India acted as the safe and effective catalyst or displacement channel for the pursuit of his dangerous interests in a way that had never been possible in Britain itself.' It was his regiment's move to the Frontier, however, that gave him free rein. Hyam states: 'The Pathans took him to a problem-free paradise where all problems were dissolved.' In his unabashed account of his pederastic and often frankly paedophiliac activity, Searight recorded having frequent sex with over 100 boys between 1911 and 1917, mostly Pathans who came to his bungalow for money. Most were around fourteen or fifteen, but some were as young as nine. A would-be writer – E. M. Forster had begun work on his novel *Maurice* soon after encountering Searight in India – he celebrated his sorry record in verse:

And now the scene shifted and I passed
From sensuous Bengal to fierce Peshawar
An Asiatic stronghold where each flower
Of boyhood planted in its restless soil
Is – *ipso facto* – ready to despoil
(Or be despoiled by) someone else; the yarn
Indeed so has it that the young Pathan
Thinks it peculiar if you would pass
Him by without some reference to his arse.
Each boy of certain age will let on hire
His charms to indiscriminate desire,
To wholesale buggery and perverse letches.
To get a boy was easier than to pick
The flowers by the wayside; for as quick
As one went out, another one came in.
Scarce passed a night but I in rapturous joy
Indulged in mutual sodomy with a boy,
Fierce eyed and entrancing.

The remainder becomes increasingly pornographic (see Hyam 1990: 131).

As many modern commentators have noted, there was an intimate bond between the British and the Indian men they ruled, subjugated and controlled. Ashish Nandy has noted that this compelled Anglo-Indian women to regard thesmelves as 'sexual competitors of Indian men, with whom their men had established an unconscious homoeroticised bonding' (Nandy 1983: 10). Indian women too were caught in this homosocial crossfire between colonising and colonised men (Krishnaswamy 1998: 51). As we have seen from our discussion of Baden-Powell above, the British had acute concerns about their own effeminacy. They thus affected to despise what they saw as the physical and moral effeminacy of (Hindu) Indians. Yet they also found it compellingly seductive. This led, Krishnaswamy argues, to what she calls the 'complex homosocial dynamics of colonial desire' (*ibid.*: 32).

In respect of the Pathans, however, the situation was still more complex. On the one hand they were continually celebrated for their manliness and explicitly contrasted with the 'down country' effeminate Hindus who would never look you in the eye like a man. On the other hand, despite this manly virility, or more accurately precisely because of it, numerous British men in the Frontier matched Searight's example in their lust for Pathan flesh. A 1932 book quoted by Krishnaswamy, *The Underworld of India*, suggests something of the reason for this. Alluding directly to the Pathans, it states that 'while in the West homosexuality or pederasty is the sign of the degenerate or mentally unstable and accompanies the disappearance of manliness and self-respect, in Asia it is often the vice of the most resolute characters ... the last word in daring and reckless courage' (in Krishnaswamy 1998: 32). In other words the Pathans provided an altogether more manly kind of homosexual.

Ultimately, then, the Pathan's apparent combination of 'real manhood' and effeminate sexuality weirdly resonated with the British colonial officers, steeped as they were in both acute anxiety over their own masculinity and intense misogynistic and homosocial contexts of friendship, work and leisure. In this sense the analogy between the Frontier and public school was even more accurate since it 'provided a predominantly male place in which it was relatively safe for men to explore the crucial terrain of masculine desire' (*ibid.*: 129). As Kipling wrote, east and west may meet, but only when two strong men stand face to face, though they come from the ends of the earth.

The significance of this was not the fact that many were thus able to indulge a previously repressed side of their personalities through exploiting young boys, but that the associated underlying anxieties would sometimes resurface in the course of colonial administration and decisions. Krishnaswamy's description of Indian men in general applies doubly to the Pathans' influence on the British: 'homosexual yet manly, heterosexual yet effeminate, Indian masculinity injects a fearful indeterminacy into the economy of colonial desire' (*ibid.*: 32), with the homosocial space of the Raj 'constituted by contending male fears, frustrations and fascinations' (*ibid.*: 18, 32). Such tensions were visible, I would suggest, in the often seemingly hysterical response to events of disorder, and most specifically in the quite perverse use of homo-erotic punishments of KK political activists (which I discuss in Chapter 4).

There were thus deep undercurrents in the British attitude to the Pathans, with the critical accounts tempered by warmer sentiments including soldierly and fraternal admiration for their courage and manliness, and even for some an intense homo-erotic desire. The official portrayals of the Pathan, however, were far more focused and less ambivalent, and it was they that were meant to guide colonial rule and administration. Jon Anderson has drawn our attention to the 'information technology' of colonial rule and the way it affected the production of writings on the Pathans: 'Generalised and categorical assessments by educated bureaucrats who limited their contacts [with Pathans] to official business extended a recognition of common human nature that becomes explicit in British writing on Pakhtuns as "worthy opponents" in the beginning, [but] "treacherous" and "changeable" at the height of empire' (Anderson 1992). At the height of empire this apparatus produced generalised summaries of the Pathan 'character' to be reproduced and widely distributed for induction purposes among officers serving in the North West Frontier Province:

> The East is the country of contradictions, and the Afghan character is a strange medley of contradictory qualities, in which courage blends with the most touching fidelity, intense religious fanaticism with an avarice which will even induce him to play false to his faith, and a lavish hospitality with an irresistible propensity for thieving. (Pennel 1909: 17)

Such advice on how to handle the Pathans was even distributed in verse form to make it more memorable; an officer had only to recall the following lines to remind him of the nature of the enemy he was dealing with:

> Tender hearted grasp a nettle,
> It will sting you for your pains
> Grasp it like a man of mettle
> Soft as silk it then remains. (*Ibid.*: 19)

Thus in the early decades of the twentieth century Frontier policy remained a continual effort to prove British mettle and manliness through grasping the nettle of the 'wild tribes'.

Governing the North West Frontier

In the prolonged shadow boxing of the Great Game, Britain and Russia came closest to war on the Frontier at the time of the Penjdeh incident in 1885. Thereafter, the likelihood of a Russian expedition against India was highly remote. None the less, throughout Lord Kitchener's tenure as Commander-in-Chief of the Indian Army from 1902 to 1909, the Indian Army was reformed and designed to facilitate the rapid deployment of a field army in the Frontier in the shortest possible time. This remained the case up to the Great War, despite the Anglo-Russian entente of 1907 (Jeffery 1981: 370).

These continuing fears of Russian ambition further enhanced the importance of controlling the Pathans as the vital 'Gate Keepers of the Indian empire'.[11] By the turn of the twentieth century it was a basic datum of British policy in the Frontier that the Pathans were violent, duplicitous and barely governable. Moreover, the British were increasingly aware of specific weaknesses in the control framework they had tried to establish. By drawing the Durand Line in 1894 the British had hoped to create a border which would seal off their empire hermetically from the acquisitive interest of the Russians. The Line, however, arbitrarily divided the Pathans on either side of the Hindu Kush.[12] Although the Khyber itself could be defended reasonably well, other more difficult passes were largely unpoliceable and the ever-resourceful Pathans managed to sustain significant levels of exchange of goods, news and women. The tribes did not sever their links with those on the Afghan side, or abandon their interest in Afghan affairs. For its part, Afghanistan continued to regard the tribes in the Frontier as being within the Afghan zone of influence and paid them subsidies (Jansson 1988: 27). The border thus remained porous, maintaining a liminal quality which made the British almost irrationally anxious, and led them to create a regime of control in the Frontier which was substantially harsher than elsewhere in the subcontinent.

In 1901 the Viceroy, Lord Curzon, reviewed the Frontier's administrative structure in the light of the recent tribal uprisings in Swat, the fragility of the Durand Line and the putative strategic designs of the Russians.[13] After the British defeat of the Sikh kingdom in 1848, the territory had been divided into two kinds of zones: the Tribal Areas (roughly the mountains) and the Settled Districts (the plains). The former were left as semi-autonomous units over which the British exerted little day-to-day governance. They were not taxed, being seen as too volatile, and indeed received quite generous subsidies in return for their loyalty to the empire (which of course did not always prevent them launching *jihads*). The

[11] Telegram No. 2/W dated 2 June 1930, NWFP to Home Department Simla NAI.
[12] See Pettigrew 1994 for a discussion of the Punjab frontier as created in 1947.
[13] Curzon's Minute, 27 August 1900, C.C. vol. 319, p. 2, in Baha 1978: 13–15.

Settled Areas, in contrast, had their tribal structure and *jirgas* dismantled and were fully incorporated into the administrative and legal framework of the Governor of Punjab. It should be noted, however, that the distinction between Tribal and Settled Districts was never as clear as the labels suggested, and embodied some rather wishful thinking on the part of the authorities. The supposedly wild tribes had a relationship with the state which was often symbiotic, not least through the subsidies they received, while, as we have seen, the supposedly Settled Districts had very high rates of feuding and violence and were to be the hotbed of nationalist protest in the 1930s. (See Ahmed 1980 and Lindholm 1993 for discussion of the Settled and Tribal Districts' precise relationship with the modern Pakistan state, and debate over whether one or other area demonstrates *Pukhtunwali* and Pathan tradition in 'purer' form than the other.)

Curzon's review concluded that the Frontier required 'more prompt, more imperative and more direct' imperial control and he thus removed what he called the obstacle of the 'elaborate organisation' of the Punjab government, added the six Settled Districts to the Tribal Area to constitute a full province in its own right, and named it the North West Frontier Province. The new province incorporated some two dozen tribes and nearly five million people, just under two-thirds of them in the Settled Districts, and it was launched with a grand festive durbar in 1902. The explicit intention of this change was that it would make it easier 'to tailor policies and measures best suited for the peculiar circumstances of the Frontier'. Such 'tailored policies' were not slow in coming. First there was the introduction of the Frontiers Crimes Regulations, which provided for the suppression of crime in the Settled Districts. Police were granted powers of demolition over buildings and premises used by anti-state elements. There was also the associated Tranquillity Act, which severely curtailed rights of assembly and contained wide-ranging rules and definitions in respect of 'seditious activities'. Further measures in 1904 approved increased expenditure on railways and roads to ensure a more mobile military presence, and the permanent stationing of the élite Guides Cavalry at Mardan exclusively for the defence of the Frontier. In addition, the police and military invested heavily in a sophisticated wireless system and elaborate surveillance and intelligence networks. All of these measures were designed to prevent the circulation of political ideas and were far more repressive than in other parts of the Raj, reflecting the authorities' concerns about both external and internal threats in the area. In Settled and Tribal Districts alike security was tight, with strict surveillance of any political activities and rewards for clerics and landowners if they helped to curb anti-British sentiment.

Despite the elaborate system of tax and rent collection, the NWFP was a deficit province from its very inception, with its subsidy from the Government of India being nearly double its own revenue. This was hardly surprising given the substantial security forces stationed in the Frontier and the extensive infrastructure they required. In addition, since the 40 per cent of the population who lived in the Tribal Areas paid no taxes, the entire burden lay on the Settled Districts. The provincial economy generally was poorly developed, with much small-scale agriculture, underdeveloped cottage industry and almost no modern manufacturing.

To pay for the oppressive apparatus of police and army, the government attempted to raise the level of taxation in 1908/9. Conditions, they argued, had been so revolutionised by better prices, communications, methods of cultivation and the growth of supplementary sources of income that the abandoning of the old rates of assessment was in order. The revenue demand was substantially increased in the Settled Districts: by 65 per cent in Bannu, 44 per cent in Kohat, 180 per cent in Kurram and 500 per cent in the Daur valley. Roos-Keppel, the second Chief Commissioner of the NWFP, raised objections to the increases and expressed the view that popular discontent had not yet erupted into the open only because there were no permissible means of conveying it: 'no press, no bar and no public opinion; and not even rioting, since the people know that the Province is crammed full of troops' (in Baha 1978: 149).[14] In response to his concerns the Government of India subsequently decided, somewhat arbitrarily, to afford relief ('enhancement') in cases of excessive tax bills in the Bannu and Hazara districts, and to follow a somewhat 'liberal' policy in granting remissions in Kohat. This left the remaining districts of Mardan and Peshawar to bear the bulk of the increased taxes; in the 1930s these were to be the central strongholds of Khudai Khidmatgar support.

The taxation burden was further aggravated by the extensive irrigation projects undertaken with both financial and political aims. Proposing yet another irrigation canal, the Provincial Governor wrote to the Viceroy's office saying that: 'A work of this sort which necessarily assists in settling down and bringing prosperity to a restless people, must have a good political effect.'[15] The canals, however, appear not to have lived up to the expectations of policy makers. While the Lower Swat and Kabul river canals irrigated a larger area than originally expected, the areas irrigated by the Upper Swat and Paharpur canals fell far short of their targets, and brought heavy and increasing operational expenses: the Irrigation Department was losing hundreds of thousands of rupees per year by the early 1920s. Such operational costs inevitably added further to the province's tax bill and continued to divert money away from other areas of the provincial budget.

As a result of its weak fiscal position and the heavy focus on policing, military infrastructure and irrigation, the Frontier also suffered from lower expenditure on social facilities, education and sanitation than other areas of the Raj. There were very few schools and literacy rates were very low even by the standards of the rest of India, with rates of only 25 out of 1000 males literate in 1911, and negligible numbers among women.

The Frontier was also subject to a quite different political structure from the other provinces of India. Key officials serving in the NWFP were recruited from the almost exclusively British-manned Indian Political Service and not from the more Indianised Indian Civil Service. As late as 1947, of 124 administrative officers in the province only 17 were Indian. Further, Indian Political Service officers employed in the Political Secratariat were under the direct charge of the Viceroy, putting them in a similar position to officers conducting quasi-diplomatic and consular representation to the princely states or in other sensitive posts like those at Aden and Kabul (Jansson 1988). This showed yet again that the regime still thought of the Frontier as neither a core nor a normal part of its imperial domain.

---

[14] Roos-Keppel to Secretary, Government of India, 10 August 1908, in Baha 1978.
[15] Deane to Secretary, Government of India, 27 November 1907, in Baha 1978: 185.

Even more significantly, concerned about the Frontier's volatility and the potential for discontent given the harsh conditions prevailing there, the colonial government deliberately retarded its democratic development. The Montague-Chelmsford Reforms presented in 1918 proposed to introduce a basic democratic structure of elections throughout India and was duly enacted in the Government of India Act of 1919. Such an expression of popular opinion was considered undesirable in the NWFP, however, and the measures were not applied there. Even in 1929, the Simon Commission on constitutional reform reiterated the unsuitability of the NWFP for democratic institutions that were acceptable elsewhere in India. As a consequence, the Frontier was kept under the direct charge of a Chief Commissioner and was denied the governance mechanisms of Governor and elected Legislative Assembly which were introduced elsewhere.

Conclusion

In comparison with other areas of India, the North West Frontier Province was heavily militarised, oppressively policed, in possession of fewer civil liberties and democratic concessions, weighted with a particularly large taxation burden, and had fewer schools and sanitary facilities. In addition, the Pathans had been doubly divided by the British, who in the classic manner of 'divide and rule' had sought to transform an open frontier into a closed border. The Durand Line sought to prevent communication between the Frontier Pathans and the Pathans in Afghanistan. Further restrictions sought to prevent communication between the Pathans of the Settled Districts and their brethren in the Tribal Areas. In general the Pathans were closely watched over by a colonial regime which was simultaneously scared, dismissive and admiring of them, and occasionally even desirous.

The tensions arising from such a repressive framework were played out within a cultural framework quite unlike the rest of India, based around a segmentary society and a powerful code of honour, lineage and revenge. But changes to the traditional system of land ownership and social structure had brought growing class tensions and given rise to increasingly acute contradictions between the values of the *Pukhtunwali* code and the newly feudalised economic structure. These contradictions were manifested in high levels of intra-Pathan violence, high levels of factionalism and low levels of social cooperation, and hence the Pathans were in no position to offer concerted resistance to the British.

Such, then, was the catalogue of ills which Badshah Khan would ultimately seek to address through the Khudai Khidmatgar movement.

2
Origins & Birth of the Khudai Khidmatgar Movement

Badshah Khan's Early Years and Emergence as a Political Leader

The man who would one day be honoured by his followers as Badshah Khan, '*khan* of *khans*', was born somewhat more modestly in 1890 as Khan Abdul Gaffar Khan, the son of a prosperous *khan* who owned the largest estate in the village of Utmanzai in the Peshawar district (Khan 1983: 11).[1] Within the social and administrative framework of the Frontier discussed in the previous chapter, his father was a 'small *khan*'. After a few years in his local village school the young Gaffar was sent at the age of eleven to the English-medium Edwardes College in Peshawar, which was run by Christian missionaries, and there he received daily instruction in the Bible, mathematics, geometry and history, at all of which he shone. To have received such a broad and advanced education put him in a tiny minority of Pathans, the vast majority of whom were illiterate, and his subsequent near obsessive emphasis on education for all seems to have stemmed at least partly from an appreciation of his own good fortune.

While still a pupil he successfully applied for a commission into the élite Guides Cavalry, but, when an encounter in Kissa Khani bazaar made him realise that as a native officer he would have to salute British soldiers of lower rank, he decided he could not be part of such a discriminatory and unjust system.[2] Having turned his back on the army, he decided to follow his older brother Khan Sahib to university in England, but after all necessary arrangements had been made his mother voiced her apprehensions about losing her remaining son to the West and its influence, and he promised to remain in the Frontier.[3]

Aged 20, he rejected the life of leisure of a young *khan* and instead started opening village schools. There were very few government-aided schools of any kind in the Province and government rules specified that they had to use Urdu as the medium of instruction, a disincentive to Pashto speakers. In 1910 Badshah Khan opened a school in his own village, and started touring other villages to encourage them to do likewise. Progress was slow, however, with many parents expressing doubts about the value of education. Partly this reflected the general difficulty of persuading a mostly

---

[1] All the citations here are from this autobiography and are my own translations from the Urdu translation (Khan 1983) of the original Pashto text. There is also an abridged English translation available entitled *My Life and Struggle* (Khan 1969).
[2] Khan 1983: 48.
[3] *Ibid.*: 49.

illiterate peasantry of the value of schooling, especially given the non-vocational courses on offer. However, there were also factors more specific to the Pathans. Government-aided schools were secular, which put off the deeply religious Pathans – not without the encouragement of their *mullahs,* who often feared that improved literacy would undermine their own monopoly on interpretation of scripture and hence their authority in the community.[4] More generally, many Pathans, even wealthy ones, attached little importance to education, seeing it as an unmanly activity. Lastly, the chronic factional rivalries afflicting Pathan society tended to prevent effective cooperation in establishing and managing schools. With great persistence over the next few years Badshah Khan did manage to establish several village schools, usually with the financial support of other small *khans,* but touring the villages he became increasingly aware of the poor living standards and social tensions afflicting the Pathans and also brushed up against the interference of the colonial authorities, ever suspicious of indigenous initiatives.

Perceiving the malign influence of the British on Pathan life he drew closer to the nationalist cause and started to read as much nationalist literature as he could obtain amid the tight censorship prevailing in the Province, and sought out like-minded intelligentsia for discussion.[5] However, there was little scope for formal political activity in the Frontier at that time. A branch of the All India National Congress founded in Peshawar in 1905 was dissolved and banned in 1907, and its leaders detained under the Frontier Crimes Regulation. In 1912 a branch of the Muslim League was established at Peshawar, but soon after it called on Pathans to volunteer to fight the anti-Muslim forces in the Balkan Wars and was branded 'extremist' by the authorities, who banned it and arrested its leaders. As Shah notes, the suppression of politics among the small urban intelligentsia in Peshawar meant that the centre of politics shifted to the rural areas (Shah 1999: 17).

Badshah Khan continued with his educational activities, latterly in cooperation with the Haji of Turangzai, a charismatic religious elder. Waris Khan recalled:

> When I was very young, I met the Haji of Turangzai as he sought the help of the people in the matter. He consulted the elders in the village about the idea of the school and they all liked the idea. The people of the village welcomed him and carried the Haji into their village on a *charpoy.* This spread from village to village. The Haji invited Badshah Khan to inspect the schools that had been opened and to join him on the tours and in the movement. People sent their children to these schools and paid fees in kind. They gave grain, milk and so on. (I.2)

Badshah Khan subsequently found out that the authorities intended to arrest them for their activities and he advised the Haji to leave for his own safety, but the Haji was persuaded by some local *mullahs* to make a stand and call a *jihad* (Khan 1969: 96).[6] Badshah Khan was against the *jihad* for pragmatic reasons:

---

[4] *Ibid.*: 32.

[5] *Ibid.*: 32. He made contact with the Dar-ul-Ulm Islamic seminary in Gudar, where he talked politics with new friends, notably the poet Fazl Mahmood Mukhfi, who brought contemporary political themes into traditional Pashto romantic poetic forms.

[6] The Haji was from a saintly family who came from the the village next to Badshah Khan's. He had participated in the 1897 armed uprising which had established the Walidom of Swat but had subsequently turned to a more contemplative life, urging Pathans to give up their feuds and resolve their disputes through *sharia,* not English law.

I thought that we did not have the necessary wherewithal for it and that we would lose badly. I suggested that we first tour the villages as we needed to organise the people of Buner who had no weapons like people in the other tribal areas and were certain to lose any war on their own. (*Ibid.*: 97)

His protestations did not prevail, however, and after a few violent encounters with the colonial forces the revolt fizzled out and the Haji fled to the Tribal Areas. Badshah Khan was arrested.

He was put in fetters, and asked to walk to Peshawar, which you know is about 40 miles from there. They arrested him for a three-year imprisonment. On the way he was given nothing to eat save for some wild mulberries. People in the villages saw him being led along on the main road in the scorching heat, and they asked who this man was and why he had been arrested. They were told that he was a big *khan* from Utmanzai and his offence was that he had opened schools for the people. People brought him food and sat him down in the shade of trees. (I.2)

Badshah Khan recalled more tersely: 'All our schools were closed down and the teachers were arrested along with their supporters' (Khan 1969: 98). He also noted the disappointment this caused among local people and the extent to which it discouraged them from participating in such self-help projects

This was a small-scale *jihad*, but the conclusions Badshah Khan drew applied equally well to the many other such eruptions which sporadically lit up the Frontier. He felt that violent uprisings could not be sustained due to the limited supplies of ammunition and material available and hence were always vulnerable to attrition by the better-resourced colonial forces. Further, such *jihads* only aggravated British anxieties about their vulnerable Frontier and provoked them into using heightened violence and ruthlessness themselves, and in the face of such lethal counter-measures popular support inevitably melted away in disillusionment and help-lessness, no matter how charismatic the leader. As he concluded: 'Earlier, violence had seemed to me the best way to revolution ... but experience taught me that it was futile to dig a well after the house was on fire.' That is, he felt the British presence in the Frontier was by this time too strong and well encamped to be ousted by violent rebellion.

Following this setback he sought to increase his awareness of wider nationalist politics by establishing links with some of the major nationalist seminaries in the rest of the subcontinent, notably the famous Deoband school.[7] He visited Deoband every six months between 1916 and 1919 to discuss strategies for opposing British rule and undertook undercover political work on its behalf. Like most of the Frontier's political activists he then participated in the nation-wide Khilafat agitation, which initially was a Muslim protest against British post-war policy in Turkey and its bullying of the Caliph, but which took on a wider anti-British resonance and drew Hindu involvement. Khilafat committees and district branches were opened throughout India, including in the Frontier, to plan protest activities. As a grand gesture of protest, in 1920 the national leadership ordered a *hijrat*, that is, a migration out of land controlled by infidels (*dar-ul harb*) into one of Islam (*dar-ul*

---

[7] For more on the Deobandis see Barbara Metcalf 1982.

Islam). The only feasible place for this was the North West Frontier and the Emperor of Afghanistan offered to receive and support any Pathans who actually managed to get through the tight British security. Badshah Khan went on the *hijrat* as one of its leaders but had to watch its rapid disintegration into farce as the British, after initial nervousness, simply allowed the protesters to cross, until some sixty thousand had overwhelmed their hosts in Afghanistan. Some of the radical *ulema* unsuccessfully begged the reluctant emperor to invade the Raj as he had done the year before, to liberate the Pathans in the Frontier, and tensions were further encouraged by British informers and provocateurs. Eventually the Frontier Pathans were transferred forlornly back across the Khyber, and Badshah Khan and others were arrested and imprisoned.

Though the engagement with the *hijrat* had raised the profile of the nationalist struggle among the people of the Frontier, Badshah Khan reflected on its short-comings. Leaving the battleground was clearly not the solution and any struggle the Pathans waged would have to be from their own soil.[8] The grand gesture, moreover, had set back the more concrete work he had been doing in setting up schools and trying to establish a covert nationalist centre in the tribal areas. The *hijrat* also further confirmed his feeling that religious leaders tended to be unreliable and erratic influences in the political arena. Jarnail ('General') Abdul Aziz's testimony to me took up this point:

> Before the Khudai Khidmatgar movement there had been a *hijrat* movement. But people had to return eventually after having migrated to Afghanistan. Badshah Khan used to say that in his movement there would be no *mullahs*. He said this because earlier it was the *mullahs* who had goaded people into fleeing and migrating to an Islamic state. People had been disappointed in them .... (I.25)

Thus, as we shall see in detail in due course, when he later launched the Khudai Khidmatgars he took pains to avoid both the religious dogmatism of such figures and the trappings of their charismatic but naive leadership.[9] Lastly, he became determined that Pathans should do more to guide their own actions and protest strategies, rather than simply respond to the calls of ideologues in the rest of India who knew little of the Frontier's circumstances.

By the early 1920s, therefore, Badshah Khan had concluded that taking advantage of mere emotive enthusiasm to call people to participation in either violent *jihad* or grand dramatic gestures such as the *hijrat* was counter-productive in the long run, doomed as it was to bring eventual disappointment and loss of faith. Instead, to be effective the struggle would have to possess a more long-lasting and overtly political nature which could sustain people through the inevitable disappointments along the way: 'I realised that revolution could not be done in a hurry

---

[8] See Murray Last's discussion of the anti-*hijra* party in Sokoto, Northern Nigeria. He argues that by rejecting *hijra* (migration) a new manifestation of *dar-ul-Islam* was achieved, what Last calls imaginatively the 'colonial caliphate'. By virtue of doing this, 'a distinct coherent northern Nigerian culture' was moulded which was 'distinct from white colonials, Christians or indeed other Muslims in Nigeria or West Africa' (Last 1997: 70).

[9] While the KK movement was based on ethical and spiritual principles which he proclaimed to be at one with the Quran, the KK never proclaimed itself to be specifically Islamic and its membership included Sikhs and Hindus.

and that it was no easy task ... it needed sensible and intelligent people ... people needed to be politically educated and needed a certain dedication.' In particular, to protest effectively the Pathans would need to establish sufficient unity to sustain their political struggle even in the face of the continual British efforts to play upon traditional divisions between tribes and lineages. Badshah Khan therefore said at a political gathering some years later:

> Be cautious and let not the *firangi* ['foreigner'] have an opportunity. He is planning to send his spies to us, just as he did during the *Hijrat*. These very spies spoiled the *Hijrat* movement. Be careful about his tactics. Today he is planning that through his spies, he will create split among us, will get the youths provoked and then arrest them. (Ramu 1992: 107)

Achieving such improved solidarity, however, in turn implied the need to reform traditional Pathan social practices, particularly those surrounding honour and violent feuds. Pathans would have to be persuaded to become either slower to take insult or more willing to seek out a peaceful resolution.

The outcome of these reflections was the decision to undertake a wider programme of reform among the Pathans: 'I decided to go back to my village and adopt the path of non-violence. I decided that I would open *madrasahs* (seminaries) for education, for the reform (*islah*) of the bad customs among Pathans and to stop them from violence, to inspire a love for their country.' In 1921, in concert with some members of the Pathan intelligentsia and small *khans*, Badshah Khan launched the Anjuman i Islah ul Afaghina (Society for the Reform of Afghans) to pursue social and educational work in the Settled Districts. The small group of activists toured villages to discuss key themes, such as the importance of education, the beauty of Pashto language and poetry, the need to avoid feuds and factionalism, and the need to avoid excessive spending on hospitality and social events which could be spent investing in the community, not least on schools.

Gradually a network of schools was established, mostly located in Peshawar district. Secretary Wahidullah from Shava told me how this was done:

> Badshah Khan came to our village for the first time I think in 1923. This was after the Khilafat movement. His emphasis then was on education. In Masjid Ghulam khel a school was set up. Children were given proper desks to work at, and so on. Soon a local level organ- isation of this Afghan reform movement was set up in our village. A Secretary was elected. I was one of the children who studied in that school. Funds came from *zakat*. That was the 10 per cent of his property that every Muslim has to pay to the community. This institution was organised in every village. One in every 10 or 12 villages was chosen as a site for a Middle school for older children [the 10–14 age-group], to cater for the surrounding villages. There was one here in Noakhali. (I.26)

Waris Khan and others praised the fact that the *zakat* tithe was now being distributed to the benefit of the village children:

> In Badshah Khan's reform movement collections were distributed among schoolchildren, not among mullahs' (I.2).

> At the beginning Badshah Khan tried to open Azad Islamia High Schools all over the Province, in every village for the education of Pukhtun children. I joined the school when I

was 10/11 years old. The admission fee was one rupee and all facilities including stationery were provided for. (I.52)

Deputy Tamash said:

> My house was next to Badshah Khan's in Utmanzai. So I heard about his idea right from the time that it was initiated. He said that he wanted to open schools in the Frontier in order to remove illiteracy; so he had the idea of the Azad schools. The revenue for running these schools relied entirely on relatives and village folk for collecting donations, revenue in kind and so on. (I.54)

Eventually hundreds of pupils were attending some 70 such independent schools (Shah 1999: 23), learning Pashto, history, mathematics, the Quran and Hadith, plus some vocational skills like carpentry, weaving and tailoring. Badshah Khan sent his own son, my fieldwork host Wali Khan, to one such school. Much of the funding was donated by the Society's members, many of whom also taught, and the education was free and open to all religions and castes. The curriculum in these schools was somewhat similar to the *Swatantra Pathshalas* elsewhere in India, which were similarly independent of the government and which set their own agenda and included spinning the *charkha* as a part of the curriculum (see Amin 1984: 12).

Badshah Khan felt such schooling was of great political importance in the longer term. He hoped that improved literacy and numeracy would help the peasantry better grasp the detailed mechanisms of tax and rent and thereby avoid the worst excesses of cheating and exploitation perpetrated by the *khans* and their *lambardars* (collectors). Equally, to boost Pathan standards of living such skills were vital if Pathans were to become more active in business and trade, hitherto the speciality of Hindus in the province. The schooling he designed explicitly included readings and discussions of verses from the Quran, in the hope that people would start to think more independently and question the fatalist and passive interpretation of Islam which he felt most *mullahs* purveyed, discouraging the community from helping and improving itself. Such teaching inevitably resulted in further heated arguments with the *mullahs*. Gul Rahman of Pdang told me: 'You know that Badshah Khan tried to first start by educating the Pukhtuns. But there was a lot of anti-propaganda against education by some *mullahs* at the time. They used to recite these verses ... which meant that if we educated ourselves we would go to hell' (I.40). The 85-year-old Haji Chairman Meherban Shah added:

> Most of the mullahs opposed the *madrasah*. The school taught Urdu and gave an Islamic education ... . The mullahs used to educate their children but used to deny education to the general public. They wanted us to stay ignorant and used to rationalise it by saying that if we wanted education it implied our love for money. Therefore for this crime we would burn in this life and in hell after ... . (I.36)

By offering Pathans education in their mother tongue, rather than the Urdu preferred by the government, people were encouraged to take pride in their own language and culture.

The education drive and the emphasis on social reform more generally gave ordinary villagers the opportunity to tackle problems that were immediately relevant and understandable to them, as they were encouraged to channel their energies into building and materially supporting the running of the schools. Sanitation work was similarly concrete and Jarnail Hazrat Gul remembered that 'Badshah Khan had started a programme of reform. He said that we needed to start by cleaning our villages' (I.24). Badshah Khan and his fellow activists in the Society urged villagers to sweep clean their villages, and to dig latrines and drainage trenches. This emphasis on the need to uplift the social standards of Pathan society through improved sanitation and education would remain a constant through the rest of Badshah Khan's political activities, even at the height of the non-cooperation struggle against the British. He always saw such activities as an essential part of raising social awareness and political consciousness. By involving villagers in building and supporting schools Badshah Khan aimed to help them gain a sense of empowerment over their lives. Moreover, in the context of the colonial regime's acute neglect of educational and social infrastructure, such activity was a clear statement of Pathan self-assertion, of a defiant refusal to continue to submit meekly to such neglect.

Such activities, however, and particularly the schools, were also part of a long-term strategy to raise political and nationalist consciousness sufficiently to support a robust and sustained agitation against British rule. Waris Khan said (and others echoed him):

> Badshah Khan opened schools in the North West Frontier to increase social consciousness. (I.2)

> Badshah Khan said that without education it will be impossible to oppose the British. (I.54)

> Every Thursday, the children used to have a meeting where they were told about the independence movement, the current world affairs, the world war and so on. (I.52)

As Haji Sarfaraz Nazim, an ideologue of the KK movement, explained, 'The reform movement was called Anjuman Islah ul Afaghina ... . It was only after the reform movement was well established that the political struggle began' (I.1).

Unfortunately the colonial authorities were equally sensitive to the potentially radical political implications of such mobilised self-help, and Badshah Khan was arrested under the Frontier Crimes Regulations on charges of subversion for his activities with the Society for Afghan Reform, and his ongoing links with the Khilafat committees which he had been asked to lead. 'Initially people did not understand his ideas about schools ... but when Badshah Khan was jailed in Charsadda for his activities, people were very upset and up in arms to rescue him' (I.54). Sentenced to three years 'rigorous imprisonment' he was kept for many months in very poor conditions in a Frontier prison among ordinary criminals. Eventually, however, with his health declining, he was transferred to Dera Ghazi Khan prison in the Punjab, which contained other political prisoners, and it was there that he first encountered radical non-violent protest methods.

The majority of the prisoners were Sikhs arrested for their membership of the Akali movement, at its height in these years, which used non-violent agitation to struggle for religious reform. The main motivation behind the Akali or Gurdwara agitation was its desire to wrest control of hundreds of Sikh shrines or *gurdwaras* from the priests – who managed their finances and lands and determined their pattern of worship –

since many priests were appointees of the British government, which required them to defend colonial rule and allowed them to divert communal funds for their personal gain (see Fox 1985 for a full account). Wresting control of the symbolic and financial capital of the *gurdwaras* would allow the Akalis to promote more effectively their vision of religious and community reform and nationalist protest.

In Dera Ghazi Khan jail, the political prisoners from the Akali movement refused to take off their black turbans in the prison as instructed by the guards; when forcibly stripped of them, they protested by removing the rest of their clothes down to their loin cloths and chanting *Sar jave, ta jave, mera Sikh dharam na jave* ('I may lose my head but not my Sikh faith').[10] They then greeted the visit of the Deputy Commissioner with a renewed barrage of chanting – *Sat Sri Akal! Jo bole so nihal!* ('God is Great! He who says this is devout!') – whereupon they were threatened with additional sentences unless they abandoned the protest. The issue of headgear was not personally significant for Badshah Khan as a Pathan Muslim, but out of solidarity he joined with the Hindus and Sikhs in their protest and they were all duly taken to court and sentenced to an additional nine months, after which they were given a further ultimatum, which many continued to ignore.

After some three years of this Badshah Khan was left alone in the protest with Baba Kharak Singh: 'He was a very powerful man, firm and immovable as a mountain. Nobody could order him about.' When the Inspector General revisited the prison, he said: 'Well, Singh?' And Kharak Singh replied: 'Yes, Wade?'. He was put in solitary imprisonment for this impertinence and his supply of milk, recommended by the doctor on health grounds, was stopped. In a poignant account, Badshah Khan describes how the two men could then only see each other through a hole in the door: 'The Sardar soon became very weak and I did my best to give him some food through the hole in the door as often as I could manage. Sardar Kharak Singh was a fine man. In spite of all his miseries he never lost his courage and determination.'[11] The long months alone with Baba Kharak Singh were spent discussing religion, nationalist politics generally and, in particular, the principles and methods of effectively organising mass movements in largely rural areas. That the colonial government too noticed similarities between the movements is borne out in the following report and the use of the Punjabi word *jatha*, associated with bands of Akalis, for the KKs. The Deputy Commissioner observed on 11 March 1932 that 'The most disquieting feature of the demonstration is the fact that large parties of villagers have been organised into "jathas" and brought into the city to join in the gaiety.'[12] As Badshah Khan recalled in his autobiography,

> Never, in any other prison, has it been my good fortune to spend such happy days in the congenial company of learned religious and political leaders. It was of the greatest benefit to me. The discussions we had there left a deep impression on me and can never be blotted out.

[10] This was specially ironical given that it was colonial policy which had made the turban inextricably linked to Sikh identity. This was largely the result of the standardised turban which was introduced for Khalsa Sikhs, the favoured recruits into the Indian Army, to distinguish clearly from the turban of Punjabi Muslims and Hindu Dogras. See Cohn 1997: 106–11.
[11] From Khan 1969: 69–104. Eventually Badshah Khan was transferred to Mianwali prison to make room for a new intake of prisoners from the second Khilafat and Guru-ka-Bagh agitations.
[12] L/P&J/12/32 IOLR.

In addition to the vivid introduction to civil disobedience techniques, Badshah Khan was particularly impressed by the steadfastness, determination and devotion to the cause of the Akali prisoners. This firmness of purpose, he felt, seemed to reflect both each individual's firm understanding of what they were fighting for, and the mutual bolstering brought about by the high *esprit de corps*, and he would eventually seek to take both these features into the design of the Khudai Khidmatgar movement.

Upon his release Badshah Khan returned home to find that in his absence the 70 Azad schools had shrunk to a handful on account of lack of funds and qualified teachers. The excitement of the prison struggle had further radicalised his nationalist commitment, however, and he determined to revitalise the Society for Reform of the Afghans and to combine its social projects with more outspoken political agitation. The Society resumed a wide range of activities and in 1927 Badshah Khan started a sugar depot at his village of Utmanzai and urged peasants to join him in the business, so that they could sell their combined crops directly in a cooperative fashion and bypass the middlemen traders. This was part of his effort to boost Pathan living standards and make trade and commerce more respectable in the eyes of the Pathans. Waris Khan and others recalled that

> Before, the *gur mandi* in Charsadda was controlled by Hindus. Badshah Khan established a new one in which the commissioning could be done by Muslims. (I.2)

> The other *khans* had no ideas about independence ... therefore they opposed Badshah Khan and called him a Hindu because he started a sugar factory in Utmanzai. He did this because at the time no *khans* and Muslims were involved in business, but business brought prosperity for people and they no longer had to rely on moneylenders. (I.54)

The Society continued to promote Pashto language and literature and arranged regular oral poetry contests, which encouraged a large number of new poets and contributed to the development of modern Pashto literature. In May 1928 they launched the first political journal in Pashto, *Pashtun,* which contained literature, political essays, dramas and religious writings, official and non-official news. Circulation eventually rose to 3,000 in subsequent years, although publication was frequently interrupted for long periods by lengthy bans imposed by the authorities. The Society's small number of activists worked hard touring the various districts and urging villagers to abandon their feuds and unite in a struggle against both the social evils afflicting them and the alien rule that had been imposed on them.

In 1929, however, the Frontier political activists were thrown into turmoil by events in Afghanistan, where, with the help of British agents, the reformist king Amanullah had been overthrown by Habibullah, a Tajik warlord, plunging the country into civil war. The members of the Society for the Reform of the Afghans protested against the British interference and agitated on behalf of Amanullah, asking the Khilafat committees throughout India to contribute to a fund for aiding the Afghans. The Khilafat and Congress Committees remained aloof, however, and the Society noted bitterly that, while the Pathans had sacrificed much in embarking on the *hijrat* during the Khilafat movement, such political support was evidently not reciprocated. They thus set out to design a political movement which would undertake radical political agitation purely in the interests of the Frontier. Badshah Khan presided over the decision to launch the Zalmo Jirga, or Youth League, to recruit literate young men into the struggle through peaceful means for India's independence. To complement this movement by accommodating illiterate and older nationalist sympathisers, another organisation was launched soon after in November 1929. This was the Khudai Khidmatgars, or Servants of God.

The Launch of the Khudai Khidmatgar Movement

Recalling the launch of the KK, Badshah Khan said that he had become aware that the Society for the Reform of Afghans in particular had achieved only a very partial and limited degree of success in mobilising mass interest in either social reform or nationalist struggle. More specifically, Badshah Khan had come to the conclusion that their activities so far had not 'bred a sufficient sense of self-sacrifice' that was needed for a fully committed nationalist struggle (Khan 1983: 52). Reflecting on the experiences of his earlier life, he felt that the solution to both his current political problem of promoting a unified nationalist struggle in the Frontier and his ongoing practical concerns about improving education and living standards lay in the cultivation of a greater sense of *service* in Pathan society. He drew an unfavourable comparison between the values of his Christian schoolmasters and those of his fellow Pathans, who, he argued, valued generosity but not selfless service: 'The Wigram brothers served people with indescribable love and good intentions. I learnt humanity, helping one's fellow brothers, pride in one's nation and the service of God's creation from Mr. Wigram. We Pukhtuns not only failed to serve our fellow beings, we fought with them instead ... .' As we shall see in the following chapters, the meaning of this notion of service was a complex and subtle one, but at its heart was the notion that Pathans should be willing to put aside the egocentricism of personal feuding in order to give up their time and energy, and even their lives, in the struggle to secure improved living conditions and political freedom for their brethren. Thus he envisaged the KK movement as a vehicle for embarking on a far more committed and intensive programme of social activism and directly confrontational political protest.

He began to tour the Settled Districts to promote the new organisation. One innovation was a network of training camps to prepare and induct new members. In addition to being the site for further agitation on the familiar topics of schooling, sanitation and the need for unity, the camps undertook physical training to prepare volunteers for the physical demands of lengthy marches and orderly demonstrations. Another important innovation was the suggestion that volunteers should dip a set of clothes in coloured dye. Fazle Rahim Saqi recalled: 'There was a lot of discussion about the colour of the uniforms ... people suggested white, khaki ...' (I.53). Eventually, however, brown or chocolate colouring was selected, since it was cheap and easily available (Shah 1999: 28). It was true that while the movement acquired the popular name of Red Shirts the actual colouring varied between brown and scarlet, especially in the early days, as people dyed their *khadi* as well as they could with the colourings to hand. Initially these shirts had the simple rationale of aiding mutual recognition on marches and at mass events, but they rapidly took on a significance of their own. By early 1930, the KK strength was around 1,000 volunteers.

In December 1929, at a decisive All India National Congress conference in Lahore, Jawarhalal Nehru pledged Congress to the attainment of complete independence for India and announced the launch of a mass campaign of civil disobedience to achieve it. Badshah Khan, as vice president of the Frontier Congress Committee (which had been re-established in 1922), attended, along with other activists from the Frontier.[13] He endorsed the Congress programme completely and in early 1930 the Peshawar Congress Committee named Abdul Gaffar Khan and his Khudai Khidmatgar followers as their ally in a forthcoming civil disobedience campaign.[14] Badshah Khan undertook a whirlwind tour of the Province, asking villagers to join the KK and participate in the Congress civil disobedience campaign. He urged Pathans not to pay taxes or rent and said that village officials working for the state as collectors or in other roles should resign, or be socially boycotted if they did not. Dr Waris of Gharader, Mardan, recalled listening to such a speech: 'Badshah Khan explained to us that the only way in which we would be able to change the situation of foreign rule would be by civil disobedience, by picketing their offices and ... by the need to boycott foreign cloth ... because the profits that the English made from their goods were used for arms against us' (I.66). A British report stated: 'The chief points made in the speeches and resolutions have been a refusal to pay revenue, [call for] resignation of village officials, the [social] boycott of Government servants and the settlement of criminal and civil cases by village councils ... . Frequent references to the boycott of foreign cloth and the use of *khaddar*.'[15] In addition, a full-scale boycott of all the liquor stores in Peshawar was planned as a blow against anti-Islamic habits and foreign-made goods.

The watershed event in the politics of the Frontier was the Kissa Khani Bazaar massacre of 23 April 1930.[16] A Congress Committee of Enquiry was due to arrive from Delhi to begin an investigation into the grievances of the NWFP, in particular the Frontier Crimes Regulation and other repressive measures. A huge crowd, including several hundred Red Shirts, gathered at Peshawar station to welcome the Committee, but were told that it had been stopped in Punjab and refused permission to enter the Province. The local Congress leaders then held a mass rally and resolved to start the picketing programme of liquor shops immediately in protest at the Committee's detention. The authorities decided to arrest Badshah Khan and some of his supporters on charges of sedition and wrongful assembly under Section 144 of the Frontier Crimes Regulation. There then followed a sequence of arrests and commotion, with government vehicles colliding with one another, fire breaking out, panic, and then troops firing on the crowd. The disturbances continued on and off for about three hours and some 200 demonstrators were killed in total.[17] The troops

[13] Many of them were dual members of Congress and Khilafat committees. Nehru's line was too radical for some of them, and on their return to Peshawar the Provincial Khilafat committee split, the majority affiliating to Congress, the rest remaining loyal to the Central Khilafat and in due course joining the revived branch of the Muslim League.

[14] Chief Commissioner's Report 1930, L/P&J/12/9 IOLR.

[15] Chief Secretary's Report 1929, L/P&J/12/9 IOLR.

[16] It is worth noting that this was a month after Gandhi's famous and celebrated 'Salt March' to Dandi, flouting repressive colonial salt laws.

[17] Report [With Evidence] of the Peshawar Enquiry Committee (appointed by the Working Committee of the Indian National Congress), Allahabad, 1930, pp. 6–28.

then withdrew and the city was in effect held by the crowds for four days until enlarged government forces re-entered. Sir Herbert Thompson recalled laconically that the loss of the provincial capital had rather unnerved the Governor, but that, since the coup was unplanned, the city was soon brought back under the control of the administration: 'A child astonished by its own tantrum, returning to the security of the nanny's hand.'[18]

The fall-out from the massacre was considerable, however. The government commissioned a report by an enquiry committee which set itself up at the Queen Victoria Memorial Hall in Peshawar and invited eye-witnesses to give evidence. At the same time it strove to suppress all non-official communication about the events and the news took some time to filter out of the Frontier. When it did, the All India Congress Committee sent Sardar Vithalbhai Patel to carry out its own investigation, but he too was denied entrance into the Province and had to base himself in distant Rawalpindi in the Punjab. The Frontier government proscribed local newspapers from mentioning the Patel review under Section 99A of the Frontier Crimes Regulations.[19] It also used the provision of Section 15 of the Emergency Powers Ordinance to stop the entry of pro-Congress newspapers into the Province and to intercept messages coming from Congress leaders in Delhi and Calcutta. Activists were denied access to the interior of the Province.[20] Behind this black-out the author-ities took vigorous and often brutal repressive measures against the nationalists throughout the Settled Districts.

The violence of the British actions in Kissa Khani, the news black-out and the Patel Committee's subsequent revelations about the brutal methods routinely used in disciplining the Frontier population shocked even the most seasoned Congress workers. It became clear to Congress HQ that in seeking to control the Frontier the authorities were using very different standards of force and political repression than in the rest of India. As 85-year-old Muhammadi Shah put it, 'the British had started to use violence here in the Frontier – they justified it by saying this Province is a rebel-lious one' (I.47). None the less, in the course of the Kissa Khani events the Pathans had demonstrated genuine non-violence in the face of the severest provocation. The Patel report declared that:

> News of the Peshawar incidents was withheld by the Government and only garbled versions were given to the public. Part of the truth leaked out, however, which electrified the whole country. The courage, the patriotism, the non-violent spirit of the war-like Peshawaris became famous and earned for the whole province a unique place in the history of the struggle. Peshawar day was celebrated all over the country to commemorate the heroic deeds of that city.[21]

Thus, from being a minor sideshow, the Pathans became nationalist heroes overnight.

The massacre and its aftermath led to a huge upsurge in popular interest in the KK, and growing financial support and technical advice from the rest of the Congress

[18] Roland Hunt and John Harrison, 1980: 190
[19] Home/Pol. 30/3/31 1931 NAI.
[20] Girdhari Kripalani's Report File No. P-16/1932 AICC Papers NMML.
[21] File No. P-16 (1932) AICC Papers NMML.

movement. Increased attention was devoted to the enrolment of new volunteers and a pyramidal structure linking village-level KK committees to higher-level ones was developed. Government reports noted with concern the movement's growing momentum. Soon after the massacre, one of the first reports to mention the red shirts stated that: 'Abdul Gaffar Khan's organisation of the "red coated volunteers" ... are now to be found in almost every village of the Charsadda *tahsil* [sub-district] and the eastern portion of the Mardan *tahsil*, where they have indulged in open defiance of the Seditious Meetings Act.'[22] In the same report it is reported, 'A society known as the Khudai Khidmatgaran have appeared in large numbers wearing red clothes and have been setting up red stands over villages in the Charsadda tehsil.' This is the first mention of the KKs in the official record.[23] The British also noted specifically as 'a serious feature' that a large number of volunteers attending such meetings were from other villages, 'often at a considerable distance from the scene of the meetings, [and] in some sort of military formation'.[24] In short, the movement appeared to be taking the Pathans beyond their more usual parochial concerns and activities as they began to be mobilised at places far away from their own localities, and this revealed a growing unity among them which greatly disturbed the authorities. A report told of a meeting held in honour of Badshah Khan at Tahkal Bala held in June 1931 in which the audience numbered about 7,000–8,000 and included 1,000–1,500 Red Shirts and 500–600 women.[25]

The authorities quickly sought to disrupt the KK's communications in an attempt to 'paralyse the Red Shirt movement' and they met with some success when they arrested '[an] agent near Batagram in possession of 13 letters addressed to "Red Captains" in the villages of Doaba. [The] Letters urged the holding of weekly meetings, preparations for picketting and that money should be obtained if required, from the so-called "Government Chest".'[26] The authorities also resorted to more lethal methods, however (Shah 1999: 33). On 16 May troops attacked Badshah Khan's home village of Utmanzai, looting property and setting homes ablaze, and other villages suffered a similar fate, with KK sympathisers being incarcerated. Through the long hot summer brutal *lathi* charges on KK demonstrators became routine and on 16 August Martial Law was declared in the Province, completely severing communication with the rest of India. Both the Congress and KK organisations were banned and Badshah Khan and others were arrested and sent to the Punjab for three years of imprisonment. Government brutality intensified still further and on 24 August police fired on a protest meeting at Hathi Khel in Bannu district, killing seventy people. The government also urged its loyalist *khans* to help restore order by any means, and their henchmen further added to the violence.

Such measures seemed only to provoke further enthusiasm and enrolment, however, and it was apparent that the KKs had captured the imagination of the Pathans. In 1931 government reports stated:

[22] Chief Secretary's Report, 1930, L/P&J/12/9 IOLR.
[23] Note the spelling: the plural of khidmatgar is indicated correctly in the Persian style. This was dropped later for the English convention of adding the letter 's' at the end to indicate the plural version.
[24] Chief Commissioner's Report, 1930, L/P&J/12/9 IOLR.
[25] Confidential Police Special Diary dated 26 June 1931, No. 130/Sdr/S.B. (NAI).
[26] Chief Secretary's Report, August 1930, L/P&J/12/9 IOLR.

Abdul Gaffar Khan's appeal for the recruitment of the 'Red Shirts' has met with an enthusiastic and ready response ... .[27]

Recruitment has been proceeding briskly in the Charsadda sub-division, where drilling has been taking place daily, watched by a small crowd of spectators. Funds are again being collected to provide uniforms for those who cannot afford to buy them, and 'recruiting officers' are busy touring the principal villages. At a big meeting held in Badragga village in Sam Ranizai (Malakand Agency) it was decided to launch the movement in that area; reports received from the Mardan sub-division show that the use of red clothes is noticeably more general and that with the absence of control the tone of the agitators is becoming less restrained.[28]

Having been little more than 1,000 at the start of 1930, KK membership was estimated at some 25,000 by the end of 1931. How did this recruitment and growth take place?

Motivations for Joining the Khudai Khidmatgars

Badshah Khan was convinced that in order to anchor the movement securely at the grassroots level he had to raise the understanding and consciousness of his audiences *before* calling upon them to make sacrifices, since only such a firm understanding would help them overcome the inevitable disappointments and setbacks. His approach was quite different, therefore, from the sudden call to arms of a charismatic leader. As Sarfaraz Nazim said: 'Badshah Khan first told the people the facts of British rule and explained the situation to them. Then he led them. It was not the other way around. He did not expect them to follow automatically' (I.1). As he had done throughout the late 1920s Badshah Khan toured the villages of the Settled Districts, talking to the people in gatherings in mosques or in the *hujra* (mens' guest rooms) of a sympathetic and influential person of the village. In the hundreds of speeches he delivered he continually pointed out the government's neglect of its responsibilities in respect of basic social infrastructure and its misuse of ordinary Pathans' taxes to support the very police and army which oppressed them.[29] The following extract is typical of the kinds of speeches he was making, using concrete examples to make people aware of the injustices of the colonial regime:

> Fifty per cent of the children in our country are ill. The hospitals are meant for the English. The country is ours, the money is ours, everything belongs to us, but we are hungry and naked in it. We have not got anything to eat, no houses. He has made *pukka* roads because he needs them for himself. These roads were built with our money. Their roads are in London. These are our roads but we are not allowed to walk on them. He excites the Hindus to fight the Muslims and the ... Sikhs to fight the Muslims. Today these three are the sufferers. Who is the oppressor and who has been sucking our blood? The English. (Ramu 1992: 61)

---

[27] Chief Secretary's Report, 1931, L/P&J/12/32 IOLR.
[28] Chief Commissioner's Report, 1931, L/P&J/12/32 IOLR.
[29] For example, see the November issue of *Pakhtun*, article entitled, 'Responsibility of the Government and Disturbances in the Country', 1930.

Muffariq Shah recalled this message vividly: 'Badshah Khan spoke at great length about British oppression in our land. He used to say, "the buffaloes are yours, the children of the British eat *ghee* (butter) and your children have nothing"' (I.20).

Drawing the attention of individuals to the unjust features of British rule was the relatively easy part, however. Far harder was forging sufficient sense of unity among the Pathans to allow them to come together in effective mass protest. Looking back, Badshah Khan recalled that the British had introduced 'a treacherous form of an unfair and partial *jirga* system' in which innocent folk could get implicated in any crime. This in turn led to further resentment, insults and feud, and as a result 'society was torn by *parajamba* [factionalism], murder and fighting'. Thus Badshah Khan gave continual emphasis to the need for Pathans to unite. For example, he would ask his listeners whether they had ever seen an English officer, a *Firangi* (foreigner):

> He is a man just like you. Like you he possesses only two hands and two feet. What is the thing which the *Firangi* possesses in addition to you? The reason why they, being men like us, rule over the Pakhtuns? They have got a spirit of unity which we people lack badly. Now you should get up and put your house in order and become brothers. (Ramu 1992: 93)

Noor Akbar recalled that: 'Again and again Badshah Khan told us that the British could be removed without any violence if the Pathans could only unite' (I.14).

To break the vicious circle of dubious verdicts and further feuds, Badshah Khan urged Pathans not to take their disputes to the official *jirgas* or to indulge in the feuding violence that would result in they themselves being dragged before the *jirga*. He urged them instead to talk disagreements over peacefully, through informal discussion in their own men's house or with the *mullah* in the mosque, or if necessary through small-scale *jirgas* convened at the local level, involving neutral representatives from one or two neighbouring villages: 'The message of Badshah Khan was "Don't go to courts. Resolve things among yourselves in *hujras* and mosques. Don't go to British courts for their justice, because they cannot give us any justice"' (I.5). The thrust of such speeches is indicated by the reports filed on them by British surveillance: 'Abdul Gaffar Khan still busy touring villages in the Peshawar district. His propaganda have hitherto been carefully adjusted to the understanding of village audience and he has confined himself to lectures advocating the formation of village *jirgas* for the promotion of unity and settlement of cases.'[30] 'Report of Badshah Khan touring the villages of Swabi tehsil urging villagers to form "panchayats" for the settlement of disputes.'[31] By stressing that the bastardised *jirgas* run by the big *khans* could not dispense 'justice', Badshah Khan was also seeking to convey not only ideas about unity, but also about the illegitimacy of colonial administrative mechanisms more generally, and the need for Pathans to withdraw from interaction with them through non-cooperation.

I asked each of my informants about the circumstances of their joining the KKs and all had vivid images of when they had first heard Badshah Khan's message. It is noteworthy that so many stressed that both they and those around them had been largely unaware of British rule before hearing him speak.

[30] Chief Secretary's Report, April 1930, emphasis added, L/P&J/12/9 IOLR.
[31] Report, February 1930, L/P&J/12/9 IOLR.

I myself did not know that the British were ruling India until Badshah Khan made us aware of the fact. (I.10)

We did not know about the British presence till Badshah Khan told us about it. (I.14)

I heard Badshah Khan speak for the first time in Marguz. Subsequently he spoke in many villages and I heard him on several of those occasions. He explained to us about the British and said how they had come from 80,000 miles away and were occupying our land that was not theirs. They were here to colonise us. He said that we must demand our independence and fight for it. This was the first time that Pathans had heard anything about independence or colonisation. (I.18)

This low level of awareness reflected the lack of democratic structures in the Frontier, the strict censorship, the suppression of civil activities, the poor educational levels and in particular the system of indirect rule channelled through the 'big *khans*' which served to occlude the realities of the colonial regime.

We did not know before that the British were ruling us. The *mullahs* and *khans* were in the pay of the British so they never told people the truth. No one in the whole Frontier had the spirit or the guts to speak against the British other than Badshah Khan. (I.47)

Badshah Khan's message was the first which spoke out against the British. The *mullahs* of the Province were in the pay of the British. We called them 'toadies' [the KK used the English word] and they spied and told on people and their activities. (I.12)

For many Pathans, therefore, the British had seemed remote from everyday problems of life, and their grievances and discontent were more often directed towards other lineages in feud, or Hindu moneylenders, or the landlords and their tax collectors. Badshah Khan was thus faced with the task of trying to get his fellow Pathans to grasp the bigger picture of colonial domination by explaining that it was the British who oppressed them and kept them impoverished. Several informants remembered being struck by the discovery that they were being ruled by a foreign people:

Badshah Khan told us that we must realise that the British have come from thousands of miles away and are ruling a land that is not theirs. Now, this was the first time that any of us had heard of all this. We did not even realise till Badshah Khan told us that we were being ruled by the British. We had always hated the imposition of the *chowkirdari* [tax collector] system on us, but it was only then that we realised that it was the British against whom our hate was really directed. (I.30)

The experience of suddenly understanding something new and important was a powerful one and for this reason Badshah Khan's words are often remembered as having the impact of a great revelation:

After I joined the movement my life changed. Life was too simple before Badshah Khan came on the scene. People were ignorant. They did not know that the British were ruling us and our country. But Badshah Khan changed all that. At first we heard that there was a man around from Hashtnagar who wanted to serve the Pathan people. He told us to stop all expensive customs and to stop feuding ... . When Badshah Khan spoke we ran through the village spreading his words and message. People listened to him and agreed with us ... . (I.5)

Mir Rahman Jarnail of Doaba recalled how his own involvement began:

It was some time before 1930. I heard Badshah Khan talk about reform in our mosque. He said that in order to get rid of those [the British] who were in land that was not theirs, we first had to reform our ways. He said that he needed volunteers to help him in this task. He said that he had nothing to offer, no salary or money. What he wanted was not very many people; but at least one man who would be honest and willing to serve the people. Therefore I joined the movement by vowing my allegiance to Badshah Khan. (I.11)

The often-quoted request for 'at least one man willing to serve' seems in its pragmatism and concreteness to have persuaded many listeners to volunteer.

The British initially viewed the motivation of the new membership as a combination of economic frustration and generalised trouble making. The Chief Commissioner warned that 'the movement in fact is in danger of assuming the character of a mass organisation of the poorer and needier classes with a large and potentially dangerous admixture of the riff-raff and hooligan element'.[32] This is precisely the kind of dismissive colonial description of mass movements so well critiqued by the Subaltern Studies school, with the peasant activists dismissed as basically rowdies who constituted merely a law and order problem rather than a political one. On the basis of all the written records and oral sources it is undeniable that the Pathan peasantry's standard of living was far from buoyant:

Everybody was very poor, even the *khans* were poor, we were poor ... the taxes were very harsh ... [T]he irrigation system in those days was very bad as well ... . [W]e sold wheat, corn, oats and *ghee* at low prices, and if we ran out we had to buy them at high prices ... the middlemen took everything. The unemployed and the poor were fed up ... the time was right for the movement ... .(I.13)

Although Badshah Khan was personally contemptuous of the big *khans* for being British lackeys, however, he was not seeking to stage a class-based peasant rebellion. He was well aware that many of the small *khans* were potentially progressive and supportive of the nationalist cause, and it was thus important to the long-term strength and durability of the KK movement not to alienate them and their support (as I discuss in Chapter Five). Rather, Badshah Khan sought to harness economic exploitation as a key motivating factor in a larger *nationalist* protest.Thus in his speeches and consciousness-raising work he strove to channel feelings of resentment away from the *khans* and tax collectors and towards the British who maintained the framework in which they flourished. It was in comparison to the British, rather than the *khans*, that he repeatedly stressed the ordinary Pathans' own relative deprivation, as Gurfaraz Khan and others recalled:

Badshah Khan had come to our village ... I was married then ... . He told us that this country was ours, and talked to us about love and about unity ... and that we should wear red clothes ... . He told us that it was wrong that this land was ours but rule was in British hands ... he pointed out the injustice of our children running barefoot and they being in their suits ... they could even afford to kick bread and we did not have enough to eat. (I.69)

Badshah Khan used to say 'what kind of justice is this? The buffaloes are ours ... they get the butter and we the whey!' (I.61)

---

[32] Chief Secretary's Report, 1931, L/P&J/12/32 IOLR.

Haji Abdul Wadood, who always wears a red kerchief to remind him of his involvement in the movement, told me: 'It was an afternoon like this ... Badshah Khan had come to our village for the first time ... . He told us about the British and explained that they were looting our country' (I.16). In such ways Badshah Khan tried to encourage Pathans of all social strata to join the struggle against the British. 'The biggest lesson that I learnt from the KK movement was that this is our land and that we should do everything to remove the British from here. There was no difference between rich and poor in this' (I.49).

While Badshah Khan's rhetoric in respect of class inequality was thus always temperate, it was undoubtedly the case that for many in the Frontier the KK's actions were a channel for expressing discontent with the existing system of taxes and the resulting economic hardship. The KK's civil disobedience, for example, through its refusal to pay dues, struck effectively at the authority, income and prestige of the tax collectors and their big *khan* masters. Others, meanwhile, specifically recalled Badshah Khan's initiatives on increasing business opportunities for Pathans, notably the cooperative sugar depots, and his efforts to wean people away from extravagance and the reliance on moneylenders it produced. Thus, while the KKs offered neither a Bolshevik nor millenarian elimination of want, they did offer the possibility of improving the difficult material circumstances through hard work, cooperation, non-payment of taxes and ultimately the removal of British colonial rule as the arbiter of the unjust status quo.

Many other KKs, however, emphasised quite different and non-economic issues when discussing why they had joined the movement. Some stressed Badshah Khan's call for unity: 'We were all tired of the British ... they were constantly trying to create divisions in our society. They just wanted us to accept our lack of independence. They used to have their own kidnappers and raiders to create trouble among people ... . They made us feud' (I.61). Others seemed to respond more to Badshah Khan's initiatives for social reform – like Sadar Musa Khan, who joined the movement in 1930:

> Badshah Khan made two or three points in all his speeches. He said people should stop all their bad habits ... he said that when people joined they must swear by the Quran that they will not tell lies, that they will boycott foreign cloth. My life changed ... I started to wear *khadi* [homespun cloth] ... . Badshah Khan stopped people from going to moneylenders and borrowing money from them and becoming dependent on them. He had roads built. (I.23)

> Badshah Khan came around to our villages telling us about his ideas. He said that we must start with some kinds of reform. He told us that we could do this by serving the people, cleaning *hujras* and the village. It was by cleaning villages, touring them and telling people to send their children to school that Badshah Khan managed to make people join the movement. The *mullahs* used to educate their own children in British schools but stopped the people from doing the same. (I.48)

Other informants said their main motivation for joining the movement had been concern about the place of Islam in Pathan society. Though never sectarian, Badshah Khan did appeal to the rural Pathans as pious Muslims, highlighting the various British offences against Islam. For instance, the British carried out inspections of land and property to make tax assessments and this often resulted in male officials entering *purdah* areas. As Badshah Khan stated: 'the *be-iman* [dishonest] government dishonoured women on the pretext of collecting land revenue ... if I do not die in the attempt I will prevent the English from ruling my country, and with the help of God I will succeed.'[33] Police and officials, always suspicious of disorder and foul play among the Pathans, were zealous in ordering post-mortems and these delayed burial beyond the two days prescribed by Islam. As Wazir Mohammed remembered it, 'People were attracted by the talk of reform and anti-British sentiment, and talk about an anti-post-mortem law and so on' (I.63). Akram Khan told me: 'The cause for our joining the movement was because of the Tranquillity Act. People opposed this Act. It called for a medical examination that we had to go through before marriage. This was against our principles' (I.35). Provisions under the Act allowed officials to order medical inspections of young couples before their wedding (presumably to check for venereal disease) and this broke all rules of modesty. Thus some became revolutionaries to challenge British flaunting of Islamic sensibility and to bring such indignities to an end through the nationalist struggle.

Buildings and businesses offensive to the Islamic sensibility were deliberately targeted for picketing activity. Brothels were one such:

> There used to be a lot of prostitution in this area as in others ... the British also used to visit these places ... . (I.55)

> We listened to Badshah Khan because he first opposed prostitution, ... earlier there had been some remnant of Islam in our society but then even that had been taken over by the British. (I.67)

> Badshah Khan tried his best to remove prostitution from this area ... and at least it was not done openly any more ... . (I.55)

Liquor stores were another target:

> I don't remember the year but I used to shave by then ... at the first picketing I was very young ... .The picketing of the liquor shops took place around 1930. I don't know about the exact dates but 1930 was very important because of the liquor movement ... . I was young ... and fully convinced that this land was ours and so when the Khudai Khidmatgars said that they were opposed to the British I decided to join them. We believed that, after the British, the law of *shari'a* would prevail. (I.67)

Some of my informants said they were spurred to join the KK by a particular incident, often of repression. Haji Lal Mohammed joined in 1942 as a young man:

> Ali Khan, Badshah Khan's youngest son, had organised a strike in the Charsadda school ... the police heard about it and were on the scene ... the Additional Police Commissioner threw him down on the ground and beat him badly. I did not know what the strike was about, but this incident made up my mind to join the movement. I went up to a General and asked for a uniform. I wore it and joined the movement. After the meeting it was decided that the next day there would be picketing outside the school to stop students from coming. (I.50)

Most people in one way or another emphasised the importance of Badshah Khan's personality and his powers of persuasion in inducting people into the movement. Shah Jahan Khan said simply: 'I joined the movement only because of Badshah Khan' (I.34). Others described his appeal:

---

[33] Chief Secretary's Report, 1931, L/P&J/12/32 IOLR.

He was a big man ... tall, handsome, good-looking ... he looked very distinguished on the stage. (I.67)

It was Badshah Khan's spiritual power that convinced us. We feel that he is still alive and among us today. (I.25)

We recognised Badshah Khan! People always recognise practical people with a drive to do things. (I.14)

Badshah Khan himself conveyed a sense of total self-sacrifice – that was the secret of his growing following. (I.7)

Ghulam Gilani recalled seeing Badshah Khan for the first time:

My father was a Khudai Khidmatgar. So I asked him at a meeting who this big man on the stage was and he told me that it was Badshah Khan. I remember a man asked Badshah Khan at that meeting why he was anti-British. He replied that he actually respected the British and that his disagreement was not personal but a political one. That statement of his struck me and influenced me a lot. (I.64)

Here, Ghulam Gilani was struck by the fact that Badshah Khan's grievances, unlike those in a feud, were not personal, centred around himself as an individual with honour, but rather concerned the larger shared interests of all Pathans, and in this way Ghulam began to understand the new political sensibility Badshah Khan was trying to promote. Equally, the idea of a respectful disagreement, rather than a visceral thirst for revenge, implied the abandoning of violent methods of challenge and confrontation.

Interestingly, however, despite the powerful influence of Badshah Khan's undoubted charisma, many of my informants' stories make clear that a lot of recruitment proceeded through 'horizontal channels', that is among peers. Derai Khan of Manikhela recalled the situation in his village: 'There used to be an annual meeting in Umanzai. It was started in 1930. Two people, Jarnail Sultan Shah and Umar Khan, went to this meeting and came back to the village and told us about it in the mosque. We heard them out and we immediately registered our names with them to be Khudai Khidmatgars' (I.46). Thus the movement spread village by village, family by family: 'When Badshah Khan came around to our villages telling us that the British were ruling us, I decided to become a Khudai Khidmatgar. My father's brother was already a president in the organisation. His son was a member too ... therefore I decided to join as well' (I.51). The 78-year-old Ghazi Khan from Pabbi described how practices of non-cooperation were spread in similar ways: 'In 1930 my brother Osman Khan got involved in the movement. Badshah Khan had held a meeting in Tangi. My brother had attended the meeting. He came back and told my father about it. My father used to take contracts from the British to deliver post. But my brother persuaded my father to return the contracts' (I.9).

Here, then, we see how people took the initiative in recruiting their peers, and how Badshah Khan's message apparently remained effective even when delivered 'second hand'. For all Badshah Khan's boundless energy in agitation, it is only through such horizontal recruitment that the exponential growth of the movement is explicable, as he could not possibly have spoken to so many tens of thousands himself in such a short time. We also need to recognise, however, that much recruiting reflected not so much the handing on of a clear and concrete message, but rather a robust peer pressure from a network of relatives and friends. In this sense we may think of the similar situation in Britain in the Great War, when many young men volunteered in response to peer pressure or else as part of a wider fraternal group enlisting *en masse*. Given the Pathans' acute sense of honour and pride, such pressure was particularly effective, as Wazir Mohammed's story illustrates:

> I joined the movement when I was 22 years old. I had gone to Charsadda to visit my relatives ... but they refused to shake hands with me because I had not become a KK and they taunted me and said that the men in Mardan were useless. When I returned to my village I told my people about what my relatives had said. Immediately 10 to 12 people volunteered to join. Then more joined, including prominent people like General Koti, Amir Mohammed, Sher Mohammed Salar. (I.63)

Thus, just as people would take part in feuds or factional struggles because their brothers or cousins did, or because neighbours or neighbouring villages taunted them and impugned their honour, so in the 1930s the values of family solidarity and even inter-village rivalry encouraged new members to join.[34] After the Kissa Khani massacre in particular, it increasingly became a question of honour for a family to have at least one member in the KKs. Bonner, describing the anti-Soviet resistance in Afghanistan fifty years later, noted that 'the *jihad* became an obligation that no one could shirk without losing honour ' (Bonner 1987: 45). A similar situation, I would suggest, developed in respect of the KK, in so far as there was a general awareness that membership entailed the likelihood of hardship, injury and imprisonment, and there was also an awareness that failure to enrol might be construed as a cowardly avoidance of these challenges.

Thus, whereas some men could describe in detail the particular issues and concerns which had led them into KK membership, for others the initial act of enrolment did not really stem from a careful consideration of the movement's aims, politics and ideology. Mohammed Roshan, for instance, joined 'because everybody else I knew was joining the movement. It was only when I joined the movement that I realised what we were doing and what it entailed' (I.41). Once a man had volunteered, however, he was required to attend training camps where he would be more thoroughly inducted through educational sessions into the true aims and means of the movement (see Chapter 3 below).

Shah suggests that each section of Pathan society interpreted the aims of the KK movement in its own way: the intelligentsia seeing it as a movement for the revival of Pashto culture and distinct ethnic identity; the smaller *khans* as a movement for demanding political reforms for the Province that would give them a greater role in governance; and the *ulema* as a crusade against the curse of the British infidel. The peasant rank and file, he suggests, were campaigning against their economic oppressors, the big *khans*, who happened to be agents of the British. The general thrust of Shah's description is not unreasonable but, as I have tried to show, it seems more accurate to say that even among the peasant rank and file there was a great variety of reasons for joining, and concerns about their own economic exploitation

---

[34] See Gilsenan 1996, for a particularly sensitive and phenomenological account of this sort of pressure from peers.

by *khans* was just one motivation among many. Certainly some marched in support of lower rents and taxes, but others were marching in the defence of Islam or stressed the promised benefits of social improvement and unity. Thus, while the government was happy to report that 'the average villager is ignorant and follows blindly', in fact, as we have seen, many people recalled rather precisely the specific reasons that had made them join the movement.[35] As Mukarram Khan wisely noted: 'It was different things that drew people together as part of the same movement' (I.70).

The motivation for joining the KK movement, therefore, was not a single, articulated, nationalist zeal but rather reflected a mixture of views and responses to social pressures. This variety, however, was very much a strength, since it meant that there were a number of criteria by which the movement could benchmark its own progress and success. In this respect it differed significantly from the earlier violent movements in the Frontier, which were of a more millenarian character (Ahmed 1976: 106). Premised on a single grand aim of salvation from the British infidel and the establishment of a religious utopia, such uprisings could not fulfil these magical promises and their leaders found that support quickly dwindled away. The varied social, political and material aims of the KKs, on the other hand, if more modest, were also far more likely to bring tangible and positive results.

This was demonstrated by the great achievement of 1931. As discussed in Chapter 1, the Frontier Province had been deliberately retarded in its political development by being denied the constitutional reforms introduced in the rest of India. The local intelligentsia had complained long and fruitlessly that the Frontier deserved the same measure of representative government as other provinces, and that their exclusion was tantamount to declaring that the Frontier people were not part of India (Shah 1999: 39). From 1930, however, the Khudai Khidmatgars made this demand a key part of their protest activities and eventually, as a direct result of this pressure from the mass movement, the British revised the Province's governance in 1931: the Chief Commissioner was replaced by a Governor and the Viceroy inaugurated the new legislative assembly. Although the assembly's powers were limited and it was elected by a very narrow franchise (less than 10 per cent of the population), this change meant that henceforth the Province would share the benefits of all future constitutional reforms enjoyed by the rest of India. It was thus a great early victory for the KK and a demonstration of the potential efficacy of mass non-violent protest.

The Alliance with Congress

Assessing the chain of events which had led up to the Kissa Khani bazaar incident, E. B. Howell, the Province's Home Secretary, admitted that the administration had failed to grasp the 'insidious growth of the Congress', as manifested by its growing conspicuousness in the Frontier and alliance with Badshah Khan. He remarked on 'the kaleidoscope fashion' in which Congress, Khilafat, Nau Jawan (the left-of-centre All India Youth League) and now the Khudai Khidmatgar movement, each with its own committees and volunteers, had managed variously to 'blend and sever, differ

[35] Chief Secretary's Report, June 1938, L/P&J/5/211 IOLR.

and unite, dissolve and resuscitate'. In particular, he noted with alarm the degree to which such blending had brought Muslims, Hindus and Sikhs together within the Congress fold.[36] While Howell focused on the Congress, in reality it was Badshah Khan who bestrode these various movements. He had led, or been asked to lead, each of them in the Frontier and had been instrumental in sustaining dialogue and achieving a closer cooperation and sharing of aims.

This process reached a climax in the formal alliance between the Khudai Khidmatgars and the Congress in August 1931, which was of mutual advantage. Hitherto the Congress presence in the Frontier had been very weak. Until 1928 it was a neglected sub-unit of the Punjab apparatus and was regarded by Congress's national headquarters with a degree of suspicion, as representing what was, to Delhi and Calcutta, a little understood and enigmatic part of India. Largely inactive, it had almost no popular following and its members and office-bearers were drawn from the mainly Hindu business and professional classes. The alliance thus promised to bring them a significant mass Muslim following and, in Badshah Khan, a leader of prestige and charisma.

The KK, for its part, was faced with a ban under statutes concerning seditious activities and so sought an affiliation with an established national political party: 'The British were very hard on us. Soon after the movement started, and all of us were in jail, there was a rumour that our main leaders will be hanged and that we will be beaten .... That is when we wanted to be affiliated to a political party in India' (I.53). As Secretary Wahidullah said: 'We had to form an alliance because charges of sedition were being constantly levelled against us' (I.26). Badshah Khan was in prison at the time but advised an initial approach to the Muslim League on the grounds of religious solidarity. The League at that time, however, was very lukewarm on the national question. 'The Muslim League wanted benefits, they did not want independence. That is why we then approached the Congress' (I.53). 'The Muslim League had been approached first but they rejected our offer because we were known to be revolutionary and anti-British' (I.26).

The KKs then turned to Congress, which, whilst seeing the obvious advantages, had some reservations about the credibility of a non-violent Pukhtun movement. Sarfaraz Nazim remembered that: 'Badruddin Tyabji, the Secretary of the Congress at the time, wondered how non-violence and the Frontier were ever going to be compatible. But our leaders then convinced him that NWFP had more non-violence than the rest of India' (I.1). 'Mahatma Gandhi asked us "What do you want and how?" Our representatives said that we wanted the British out of our country and with non-violence. Mahatma Gandhi sent Patel to the Frontier later to check out what we said. Only then did Gandhi agree to the affiliation' (I.53).

The alliance with the Congress had direct implications for the organisation of the KKs and the structure and nomenclature of each side were modified to suit the coalition better, the changes being announced in a widely issued official Congress statement. The district and provincial committees of the Congress and the district and provincial *jirgas* (councils) of the Khudai Khidmatgars were merged. They would

---

[36] 'A Secret Note on the Situation in the NWFP', E. B. Howell, 24 May 1930, F.No. 206/130, Home/Pol., NAI.

represent the Congress but 'in the language of the Province may be described as *jirgas*'. Thus the high-level Frontier Province Congress Committee became the Frontier Province *Jirga*, and the district committees became local *jirgas*, 'the fact that they are Congress Committees being also clearly stated'. Similarly, it was agreed that 'the KKs should become a Congress Volunteer organisation in accordance with the Congress Working Committee's recent resolution'. Again, however, the name 'Khudai Khidmatgars' was to be retained. In addition, 'The whole organisation should be conducted in accordance with the constitution, rules and programme of the Congress. The flag to be used henceforth will of course be the national flag', though the KK were to retain their red shirts and right to wave red flags. Lastly, it was stated that 'at the request of the Working Committee the Frontier leader, Khan Abdul Gaffar Khan, has undertaken to shoulder the burden of leading the Congress movement in the Province'.[37]

The tie-up was an unprecedentedly close alliance of a Muslim majority movement with the Congress, and as such it threatened to undermine the ongoing British efforts throughout the subcontinent to subvert the nationalist movement by encouraging tensions between Hindu and Muslim communities. It was thus of great political significance and severely worried the British, who, as we shall see in subsequent chapters, went to extraordinary lengths to try to disrupt it.

In December 1931, while Gandhi was in London holding talks with the government, the Frontier authorities launched a crackdown on the KK and its protest activities under special ordinances (Shah 1999: 35–8).[38] The KK and the Frontier Congress were both banned and Badshah Khan and other leaders were arrested and imprisoned. There was then an intensification of repression against the rank and file, with the police and army seemingly given an entirely free rein. Many KKs were beaten, incarcerated, their houses burnt and property and crops destroyed. Entire villages were blockaded and there were frequent march pasts of heavily armed troop columns. Demonstrating volunteers were often fired upon and killed, the worst incident being in the Kohat valley, where some fifty died.

Gandhi, having returned from London, tried to discuss the arrest of Badshah Khan and the repression of the KK volunteers with the Viceroy, but was refused. Subsequently, in a high-profile public speech in Bombay, Gandhi declared: 'Last year we faced *lathis*. But this time we must be prepared to face bullets. I do not wish that the Pathans in the Frontier alone should court bullets. If bullets are to be faced, then Bombay and Gujrat also must take their share' (quoted in *ibid.*: 36).

For over two years the Frontier authorities waged an attritional battle of wills against the KKs. Sympathetic English visitors from the India League said that the severity of repression had produced virtually a state of war in the Frontier. Yet while the vicious counter-measures did slowly begin to diminish the effectiveness of its civil disobedience actions, the KK's activity and agitation were continued throughout.

[37] Resolution passed by the Congress Working Committee at Bombay on 4–14 August 1931, Annual Report of Congress Working Committee, December 1931, F.No. 85 (1931) AICC Papers NMML.
[38] The Government of India issued three ordinances applicable to the NWFP – the Emergency Powers Ordinance, the Unlawful Association Ordinance and the Unlawful Instigation Ordinance. Taken together, these gave the Frontier authorities wide and almost limitless powers to arrest, detain or otherwise control any political workers suspected of opposing the government.

Moreover, as the English visitors observed, despite the extreme provocation and the ready availability of arms and ammunition in the region, the creed of non-violence had been steadfastly sustained. Congress, too, praised the role of Badshah Khan and the KK in pursuing protest in the Province in a non-violent way, and praised the Pathans' restraint, without which we 'would by now [have] witnessed a wholesale massacre of the European population' (quoted in *ibid.*: 38).

The nationwide civil disobedience campaign was eventually called off by Gandhi in April 1934. The Congress activists throughout India who had been imprisoned during the previous three years were released. Again, however, the Frontier was an exception: the KK leaders and Congressmen remained imprisoned and the movement remained under ban. The KK leaders were released finally in 1935, but Badshah Khan and his brother Dr Khan Sahib were not permitted to return to the Frontier. Almost immediately Badshah Khan was rearrested for making 'anti-government and seditious speeches' in the Punjab and he was sentenced to a further two years of 'rigorous imprisonment'. Badshah Khan returned to his home province only in November 1937, after some six years of imprisonment. By this time the political atmosphere in India as a whole had moderated. Under further constitutional reform, the legislative assemblies in each province had been granted more extensive powers, and political parties were permitted to contest elections. The highly dramatic civil disobedience campaigns of the early 1930s thus gave way to a more subtle struggle of parliamentary politics – a shift which, as we shall see in Chapter 7, brought new challenges to the Khudai Khidmatgars and their leader.

Conclusion

By 1930 Badshah Khan had completed the first stage of a long journey which had involved many of what Gandhi called 'experiments in truth'. Drawing on his varied experiences of social and educational projects and political mobilisation, he eventually designed and inspired a political movement which, in its scope and numerical strength, was unprecedented in the history of the Frontier. Recruitment into it was achieved through a remarkable combination of vertical and horizontal mobilisation – responses both to the message of a leader and to the pressures of peer groups and kin networks. The civil disobedience campaign carried out by these Khudai Khidmatgar recruits between 1930 and 1934 was arguably the most heroic and extraordinary of all such episodes in the Indian nationalist movement. In the following chapters I explore the organisational and ideological features of the KK that helped sustain its own coherence and dynamism in the face of the unprecedentedly severe repressive response of the colonial authorities.

3
Training, Service & Protest

Induction and Training

The Khudai Khidmatgars grew substantially through the 1930s. By 1938 British intelligence reported 386 Congress local committees across the Province (compared to 81 in 1932) spread across 220 towns and villages.[1] The wider Red Shirt membership was far larger, however, and the Governor reported that over 50,000 'would call themselves Red Shirts': 'The organisation is therefore widespread, and for the moment seems to have reached saturation point ... . Without wishing to minimise the danger of an organisation of this nature – for no large crowd of organised Pathans can be anything but a potential danger – it can be said that the majority of the Red shirts now are very different from the Red shirts of 1930 and 1931.'[3] The British thus acknowledged that the KK had matured as an organisation since its early days. What was referred to in 1930 as the 'dangerous admixture of riff-raff and hooligan elements' was by 1938 described almost admiringly as a 'formidable organisation' which had covered the Province in committees and could put thousands into the field of protest.[4]

The British authorities were well aware of the importance of this transformation of the tribally and economically segmented and 'unruly' Pathan masses into a unified and orderly movement. The Pathans seem to have been almost as surprised themselves. As Waris Khan recalled: 'I know it is difficult to believe. It was so incredible that we were like this, that Iqbal [a nationalist poet] wrote in one of his poems that Badshah Khan tackled Pathans like he was feeding grass to lions!' (I.2).

What were the particular activities, features and structure of the KK which helped it sustain an agitation over nearly two decades until its successful conclusion? Each new KK recruit was inducted into the organisation through the solemn swearing of an oath while the right hand rested on the Quran. The oath, along with the person's name and date of birth, was recorded on an enrolment 'Form Aliph' ('Form A'). Like all rites of initiation, this was a memorable moment which my informants recalled

[1] The fully paid-up Congress membership was assessed as 20,000. Chief Secretary's Report, March 1938, L/P&J/5/211 IOLR.
[2] Governor's Report, January 1939, L/P&J/5/214 IOLR; another report recorded that a recent census of the fee-paying members of the Congress Party in the six major districts showed Peshawar 7,000, Mardan 7,562; Kohat 1,353; Bannu 595; DIK 730; Hazara 1,243; Total 18,483.
[3] Governor's Report, June 1938, L/P&J/5/211 IOLR.
[4] Chief Secretary's Report, March 1938, L/P&J/5/211 IOLR.

vividly. Sayyid Mohammed Fasi Badshah told me: 'I joined the movement in 1930. I had only 27 teeth then, I remember ... . I was in Class VII. I became the President of the school boys' group' (I.39). Haji Awal Khan from Matta recalled: 'I was born into the movement! My father had told me that Badshah Khan and his four companions, dressed in their red shirts, had come to Matta to talk to the people and to enlist members. My father decided that his would be the first membership from his village and he took the oath there and then' (I.13). Enrolment also entailed small membership fees: 'We had to donate two annas for the Form Aliph which was our enrolment form for the movement. This was an annual membership' (I.22). These fees contributed towards the running costs of the movement.

The oath is recorded in several versions in written sources (see, e.g., Shah 1999: 44). Most of my informants, even the most elderly, could still repeat it in some form or other. That there was no single, standardised version appropriately reflects, I think, the nature of the movement, which never fetishised orthodoxy – everyone had the essential gist and that was considered the most important thing. Here I record the version that was recited to me by Sarfaraz Nazim:

> In the name of God who is Present and Evident, I am a Khudai Khidmatgar.
> I will serve the nation without any self-interest.
> I will not take revenge (badla) and my actions will not be a burden for anyone.
> My actions will be non-violent.
> I will make every sacrifice required of me to stay on this path.
> I will serve people without regard to their religion or faith.
> I shall use nation-made goods.
> I shall not be tempted by any office. (I.1)

The solemnising of the oath on the Quran and the reference to God point to a concern always to emphasise the Islamic legitimacy of the movement (a theme which I discuss in detail in Chapter 6). But the oath also contains a clear non-sectarian statement, which was important, given the KK links to the Hindu-dominated Congress and also its own sprinkling of Sikh and Hindu members. The pledge on the refusal of office concerns both the ethic of personal humility and the campaign of non-cooperation with the state. The position on nation-made goods clearly aligns with Gandhi's belief in the importance of national economic self-sufficiency and was concretised through the distribution of spinning wheels (charkhas) among the Pathans. While the oath commits the volunteer to serving the nation, there is no explicit statement concerning the end of British rule in India. To that extent the oath is more of a philosophical framework and moral undertaking than a narrowly political one, and at its heart is a commitment to principles of service, self-sacrifice and non-violence.

Badshah Khan's call for Pathan unity in the struggle against the British was important and novel. In earlier centuries rebellions against Mughal and Sikh rulers had been confined mainly to particular tribes: the Khattaks under the leadership of Khushal Khan Khattak, or the Yusufzais under the leadership of Ahmad Shah Abdali. Badshah Khan fervently believed that liberty could be achieved only by a concerted effort of all the Pathans together. But it was equally clear to him that achieving such unity would not be easy, given the high levels of disputes and the segmented nature of the social structure. Moreover, in addition to asking Pathans to put aside their traditional differences, he was also asking them to adopt a method of non-violent protest which was quite contrary to their martial traditions and ferocious responses to insult. Hence he was asking Pathans to put aside violence and aggression in both their internal and external relations.

As the son of a wealthy landowner, he well knew that the issue of violence was closely attached to that of honour, which in turn was deeply embedded within *Pukhtunwali*, and hence that violence was bound up in a cultural complex linking financial self-sufficiency, family pride and individual autonomy. The acute sensitivity to insult and sense of egalitarianism of the traditional man of honour made Pathans unpromising candidates for a disciplined and hierarchically organised army of activists. Equally, the Pathans' prickly individualism made it difficult for them to cooperate with one another and either to proffer or accept assistance; this presented a further problem for Badshah Khan, who envisaged thousands peacefully working together both in demonstrations and in the other activities which he linked with self-reform, such as the construction of educational and hygiene facilities. Lastly, Badshah Khan felt that the Pathans had become fatalistic and dispirited, doing little to help themselves in improving local life. Any progress in either the material or political sphere required that ordinary people begin to think that they could really improve matters, that contrary to the advice of many of their *mullahs* they need not simply forbear but could change their conditions of life themselves in the here and now.

The nationalist project as envisaged by Badshah Khan thus required significant changes in traditional patterns of Pathan thought, behaviour and social interaction, and in order to bring these about Badshah Khan designed and utilised a thorough regime of training and instruction. In 1941, an English Congress sympathiser, Mary Barr, visited a KK camp and described what she saw in a short article published in *The Modern Review* (January 1942: 54–6. The full article is reproduced in Shah 1999). The camp lasted about a week, and was marked by the flying of a Congress national flag. A large *pandal* (marquee) was used for meetings, school and spinning, while two compounds full of tents housed camp participants. The Red Shirts themselves were billeted under the strict discipline of their officers in a separate area where they did regular pack drill. The other tents were filled by people from the surrounding villages who had come for more general training and instruction. Separate marquees housed a medical dispensary, a small mosque and quartermaster's provisions. Barr noted that all the tents were clean and warm, with straw and carpets.

The standard day's activities began with drill. The Red Shirts would be trained and put through their paces by their drill masters. Running and other physical fitness training were also undertaken to provide the stamina necessary for long marches and all-day demonstrations, and Barr noted that despite the variety of ages there was 'not one corpulent man among them, all were slim around the waist, a tribute to their regular physical discipline'. After taking tea and a light breakfast there would be 'village cleaning': detachments would march off to surrounding villages to undertake cleaning and repair work for the inhabitants. Other participants would remain in camp to be instructed in proper cleaning and sanitation techniques, and would practise by cleaning the camp itself. Then 'school' was held. This consisted mainly of political education about the nationalist struggle, with particular regard to the history and duties of the KK. There was then a break for bathing, eating and rest. In the early afternoon, during the worst of the sun, the main activity was spinning raw cotton into thread on the *charkha*. Others, meanwhile, were grinding wheat to make the flour for the bread that fed the camp.

In the late afternoon the public meeting was held. All the camp would attend but they were also joined by anyone who was interested from the surrounding villages. Such meetings were of an agitational character, with performances of political verse, poetry and drama, and with speeches from senior members, including visiting leaders, not least Badshah Khan himself. These would discuss the key themes such as the importance of unity and the need for adherence to non-violence, but would also give lessons of a quite direct and practical nature. Jarnail Hazrat Gul recalled attending a camp near Khazana village, where he heard Badshah Khan 'teach us what jail was like and how to behave there. He also taught us to make speeches' (I.24). After another rest there were activity periods, with further physical exercises and drilling for the Red Shirts but also opportunity for music and dancing. The day would end with a further meeting for discussion and instruction.

The day just described was one of the more inward-looking ones, focused on training and practical tasks. During protest campaigns, however, the camps were used as bases where protesters would congregate together and be addressed by their leaders before marching off to the scene of the day's picket or demonstration. All the camp activities were coordinated by the camp commandant, usually a senior KK rank holder. Haji Mohammed Hussain Khan was a Camp Commander in 1942–3:

> The district general chose me because I had a good track record. He asked me not to get arrested any more and asked me to be Camp Commander instead. I was in charge of the *langar* (communal kitchen) for 800 people. I had to see that discipline was maintained. Volunteers used to collect the money to run the camp from willing donors. The Red Shirts were sent out for picketing and for courting arrest at different venues. (I.15)

At this point Haji Sahib produced his old camp register and read out a page which listed the names and addresses of the various people attending the camp at a given time and the various activities that they had been entrusted with. 'Later I gave up my camp commandership so that I could court arrest and someone else became the commander. Many men became commanders in this way' (I.15).

At the end of the week the commandant presided over the dismantling of the tents and the whole camp moved elsewhere. Concluding her account, Barr noted the 'atmosphere of unity and happiness which seemed to pervade the camp. There was much laughter and no strained looks, except occasionally in the early morning cold. The whole atmosphere was one which is only attained where people work together with a common purpose, a purpose which demands some self-sacrifice and entire sincerity.'[5] Barr's account comes from 1941–2, by which time the camp regime and infrastructure was well established. The first training camps held more than a decade earlier would have been smaller and less elaborate; none the less, the mix of activities and prevailing spirit would have been much as Barr describes.

[5] F. Mary Barr 'A Red Shirt Camp' *The Modern Review* (January 1942): pp. 54–6, reprinted in Shah 1999: 268–71.

The immediate initiative for setting up the early camps was usually Badshah Khan's visit to a village, when he would recruit the first KK volunteers, preferably from among the senior men. They would then form a *jirga* committee and elect individuals to particular positions and responsibilities:

> Our village was situated near a cremation ground. Badshah Khan had come to address a meeting there. I remember that he spoke a lot about Pathan unity. After the meeting the group got organised in our village. Committees were formed. A unit of the movement was slowly formed in our village on Badshah Kan's request. We elected a secretary, a president and so on. There was no difficulty in deciding these. After all, we were doing this to serve our country! (I.5)

> When he was setting up the organisation in our village the posts were decided by a *jirga*. First the *salar* (president) was decided, then the others. (I.24)

Badshah Khan would explain and demonstrate the main reform activities in person. Jarnail Abdul Rahim recalled: 'When a camp was set up, Badshah Khan would be there personally, cleaning the houses, sweeping the *hujras*, teaching people to spin their own cloth' (I.3). Jarnail Hazrat Gul told me: 'Badshah Khan had started a programme of reform. He said that we needed to start by cleaning our villages ... . Badshah Khan had personally swept all the 150 villages of Daudzai. I had accompanied him on these trips. He used to collect the rubbish in his own shoulder bag' (I.24). The fact that Badshah Khan, a respected *khan*, was willing to do dirty work himself made a great impact and contributed towards generating an improved civic sense. Whilst he might not in reality have swept all the 150 villages in Daudzai, it is significant that people remember the magnitude of his efforts in these terms. On the other hand, even the literal truth of the statement is not implausible, since Badshah Khan spent more than twenty years tirelessly trekking around the villages of the Settled Districts: 'I used to roam around this whole area with Badshah Khan ... there were meetings held in Bahadur, Sarband, Sayur ... I remember that at night Badshah Khan's legs and feet used to be swollen because he had walked so much' (I.67). Others recalled their surprise when the great leader turned up at their camp on a bicycle.

The senior KK generals of the district would travel with Badshah Khan from village to village, establishing camps, while the rest of the volunteers stayed in their villages to carry on with the reform work (I.3). 'Once the organisation was formed and Badshah Khan had left the village we used to hold parades and runs, do patrolling, educate people and prepare them for the struggle' (I.24). The committee was entrusted with the induction of further members from the surrounding areas and the implementation of the main reform activities. The work centred on establishing schools for basic literacy and political instruction, and on cleanliness drives in villages, with people helping to sweep the *hujras* and village lanes and acting upon the instructions they had been given on the principles and structures of good sanitation: 'Badshah Khan himself wore a red shirt when he came to us. The oath of the Khudai Khidmatgaran was printed and used to be read out. Then the *Islahi* (reform) programme was implemented. A school was opened and it spread Badshah Khan's message and his teachings' (I.5).

Unlike the ultimate aim of the ejection of the British, the camp activities could reward people's energy with immediate results, and the initiatives seem to have won the genuine enthusiasm of the Pathans. Noor Akbar of Matta told me: 'I liked to go to meetings. I liked the idea of serving my fellow Pathans' (I.14). During our interview, Grana suddenly stood up and began to give me demonstrations of how they used to sweep the villages and spin cloth on a *charkha* (I.17). Thus were they energised.

Like Congress in the rest of India, the KK distributed spinning wheels and instructed villagers in the techniques of spinning thread to supply and support India's handloom weavers against imported British cloth:

> There was also a lot of propaganda saying that it was a woman's job to spin thread. The British used to say that weavers are a low caste, but this was not the traditional belief. It was the British introduced the idea of hierarchy in Pathan society. Anyway, we could see that all the big leaders used to spin. Even *khans* had *charkhas* at home. *Charkhas* were placed on the stage during political meetings. The weavers used to have their own workshops and all sections of people used to go to these weavers with their own yarn and have it spun into cloth. Women did not even keep *purdah* in front of the weavers. This was the extent of our easy mixing with them. So *charkhas* were very popular in the Frontier. (I.24)

> We didn't worry that weaving and spinning were women's activities ... . All our leaders used to carry *charkhas* on their shoulders on a demonstration. We learnt to spin from our women, mothers, aunts and grandmothers. (I.66)

The *charkha* had the advantage of being an activity which could be done by the individual alone outside of the excitement of camp, and as such it could serve as a constant reminder of the lessons of the camp and the wider aim of national self-sufficiency and independence. 'The intervening periods between camps were sometimes dull and quiet, so people used to spin cloth at home regularly'. (I.3)

In addition to spinning, another important activity in the camps was grinding wheat for flour and rape-seed for cooking oil. These were arduous tasks and needed to be done in prodigious quantities since camps were attended by up to a thousand people. While Badshah Khan had a long-standing and genuine commitment to such practical activities, however, he saw them as much a means as an end. The self-sacrifice, humility and cooperation involved in such tasks were designed to help de-emphasise what he saw as the the traditional independence and aloofness of the Pathan psychology. When I asked why they cleaned other people's houses, Jarnail Hazrat Gul said: 'We did it to render *khidmat* (service) to them' (I.24). Noor Akbar recalled cleaning being used as a gesture to end traditional animosities, in particular by appeasing and wooing the *khans*, ever suspicious of peasant activism: 'The *khans* of Matta were in the pay of the British. So we used to sweep the *hujras* of the *khans'* houses so that they would soften their stance towards the KK. We did this to render *khidmat* (service) to them' (I.14). Serving them in this selfless way was also an attempt to inspire and shame the *khans* into abandoning their British ties and making common cause with their fellow Pathans.

From the modern perspective such tasks as digging a latrine trench also look like classic team-building exercises which could help reduce fractiousness and improve unity. By working with and for each other, the Pathans were rehearsing the kind of mutual support and endeavour that the mass demonstrations against the British would require. More fundamentally, the activities of cleaning and spinning were part of the psychological preparation for non-violence. Since non-violent civil disobedience was a new idea, the KK were given specific instruction and practice in how to behave in the heat of confrontation. Such instruction was both practical and philosophical. Haji Lal Mohammed gave me an illustration of how the idea was disseminated among the ranks of KK soldiers: 'The General gave us instructions about how to go about our picketing. He also warned us that we might be fired on or caned. We were told that if this happened, then we should grasp the cane and say, "We are ashamed to hit back" and not to say "Shame on you" because that would amount to an insult' (I.50) – an act of aggression which dealt in hate. But to react in this way was far from easy, of course, and required great forbearance. Hence the prolonged and unglamorous nature of the social tasks carried out in the camps – such as cleaning, digging and spinning – was also designed to inculcate a sense of patience, stoicism and forbearance in the Pathan at the expense of his more usually explosive reaction to such provocation. Such a psychological adjustment was vital if they were to adhere to non-violent responses when confronting the British. As an old KK explained to me: 'such tasks were simply preparation for a battle of patience' (I.19). Such a rigorous, labouring induction was also necessary in order to guarantee the continued discipline and steadfastness of the KK over an extended period of time, when hardships and disappointments would be inevitable.

Sarfaraz Nazim gave me a cogent explanation of why the notion of service, *khidmat*, was so crucial:

> To induct people into the philosophy of the movement the first step was to instil a sense of service. Then came a sense of non-expectation and humility and from there on came a feeling of non-violence. The KK had to first understand the importance of humble, selfless service (*khidmat*) to the people. The term Khudai Khidmatgar literally means 'the one who serves God'. Badshah Khan said that the best way to serve God was to serve one's fellow beings. Revolutionary political activity, the picketing of liquor shops and courts of justice and so on, could come only later. (I.1)

Badshah Khan explained to the KK that the notion of service he had in mind was one of 'serving others without self-interest'. As such, it was different from the grudging and contractual relationship implicit in the colloquial use in the Raj of the term *khidmatgar* to refer to an orderly or servant. The synthesis of this more elevated sense of service with ideas of humility and restraint is well reflected in Jon Anderson's elegant translation of *khidmat* as 'grace' (Anderson 1980). In preparing for non-violent protest the KK were being trained to display such grace under pressure. Hurmat Khan recalled: 'Badshah Khan came to our village and made a speech in the mosque. He said that we will serve God till we die. We must realise that the only way in which we could do that is by serving human beings. Because God himself needs no service' (I.30). Waris Khan said:

> Let me tell you about an incident which exemplifies Badshah Khan's attitude and humility. One night he sat up all night beating a piece of tin, fashioning it into scales. In the morning he asked the president and secretary of our movement to pick spinach from the Centre's vegetable garden and sell it in the nearby villages, using the scales he had made for them. At the end of the day they had made only 12 annas but Badshah Khan had managed to imbibe in them a sense of humility and respect for labour. (I.2)

In this way the activities of self-reform – village-centered, low-key and self-effacing – helped to pave the way psychologically for the restraint and sacrifice required in activities of public, visible and dramatic protest.

Such physical training in restraint and non-violence was supported by explicit religious and ethical teachings during the 'school sessions' and public meetings held in the camps in the afternoon. I shall discuss in Chapter 6 the themes which were prominent in this instruction; here I merely note that Badshah Khan constantly drew on examples from the Prophet's life in discussing patience and restraint. My informants remembered Badshah Khan as having constantly stressed those ideas in every possible context, emphasising that patience and faith had been the weapon of the Prophet. Gul Rahman of Pdang remembers: 'Badshah Khan taught us patience. He told us that we were at war against the British, for our independence; but we have no weapons. Our only weapon is patience. He used to tell people: "If you can fight this war then wear a red uniform and come and join us"' (I.40).

There were many occasions when resisters were wounded and even killed but the message was always that the best course of conduct was restraint: 'On the many occasions when Badshah Khan was arrested, he used to ask people to remain calm and to pray. And he said that if they did not want to do that, then they should offer themselves up for arrest as well, two at a time, as a mark of their protest. He said, "If you are struck on one cheek then turn the other to your enemy"' (I.14). It was hoped that such action would make the enemy realise his mistake, showing him the error of his ways, but the basis of this action had to be an emotion of genuine love for the enemy, not hate. Lieutenant Mohammed Wali asserted in his testimony: 'We learnt that non-violence, unlike violence, did not breed a bad feeling and hatred. Badshah Khan used to tell us to turn the other cheek if struck on one' (I.19). The deeply religious and moral nature of this restraint is seen in Haji Abdul Wadood's comment: 'He [Badshah Khan] used to ask us to be patient and said that if we retaliated with violence we would no longer be innocent. He used to ask us to turn another cheek if we were hit on one' (I.16). As he said this Haji Abdul turned his wizened old cheek for me to see what he meant. Gul Rahman said, 'He taught us to practise non-violence at every level. He told us not even to tear paper or break a pen because he saw them as acts of violence' (I.40). Through such exhortations Badshah Khan hoped to encourage people to internalise the principles of non-violence, forbearance and forgiveness, incorporating them into their everyday behaviour and manners.

The KK's practical and ideological entwining of political protest in the public sphere with extensive social work in the private always puzzled the British administration: 'It has been difficult to find a policy which fits all the various aspects of the agitation, and to decide how far ... [these activities] constituted a serious challenge to the government.'[6] This wrong-footing of a regime geared to the use of force was of course part of the cunning of non-violent modes of protest. If the British were puzzled, however, the KK themselves increasingly grasped the linkage between the ethic of service and self-reform and the nature of the colonial struggle. A wonderful example of the ways in which KK soldiers combined their identities as servants and soldiers is provided by the following anecdote:

[6] L/P&J/12/9 IOLR.

A letter came to me one day from Salar Amin Jan saying, 'Come to the KK office with one *charkha* (spinning wheel) and a broom.' So I wore my red clothes, picked up my grand-mother's *charkha* and left for the office. On the way to the office a man called me a *kafir* [infidel] for carrying a *charkha*. I said that it was not a *charkha* I was carrying but a cannon – a cannon that would finish London. (I.24)

The man's grasp of the potency of peaceful service is here vividly expressed. The transposition of the *charkha* as cannon – a metaphor that cropped up several times in my interviews – neatly brings together ideas about self-reliance, labour, non-violence and political struggle.

Feud Resolution

All the training in service and non-violence would come to nought if it was not accompanied in practice by the cessation of internal violence among the Pathans. Only when their own feuds and divisions had been put aside could they be said to have properly mastered the principles of non-violence and only then would they be ready to go forward on the basis of a political unity that bridged traditional cleavages of tribe and kin. Of all Badshah Khan's speeches and persuasive rhetorical devices, it is his teachings on the need for Pathan unity that are remembered most clearly by my informants.

The need for unity was explained by Badshah Khan to ordinary people with fables such as this one, which Hurmat Khan related to me:

Badshah Khan told us a story about three boys, the sons of a *khan*, a *mullah* and a police officer. They went out and stole melons from a field. The owner of the field could deal with them because he knew that they would not have any solidarity among themselves in a crisis. And so he punished them in turns. Badshah Khan said that it was a similar case with Afridis, Waziris and all the tribes of the Frontier. It was because all the other tribes kept quiet and did not raise their voice in protest when one tribe was punished that the British could get away with it. Therefore, Badshah Khan explained that without a feeling of being one people, without a single Pathan front, we could not stand up to the British. (I.30)

The centrality of the theme of Pathan unity was corroborated by others: 'Our drilling parade was always followed by an hour-long meeting. Every day a different person stood up to address the meeting. We did it by turns. Badshah Khan talked about how *Pukhtunwali* would not do us any good against the British and that people would have to settle their feuds before they were allowed to join the movement' (I.3).

As the induction oath suggests, and as Haji Lal Mohammed's testimony confirmed, an individual was only allowed to join the KK if he had withdrawn from any feuding:

When we wanted to join the movement, Badshah Khan used to ask us if we were involved in any feuds. If we were, he did not let us join. He used to insist that we settled them first. He wanted us to give an undertaking stating that: If we are slapped we will not slap back, but turn the other cheek. If our crops are burnt then we will not burn the crops of others. We will not take revenge on anybody. (I.50)

Sarfaraz Khan made the same point: 'No feuding families were allowed to join the movement. They had to settle their disputes first' (I.45).

I heard many stories and anecdotes about the widespread process of feud resolution that swept the Pathans during the early 1930s as they strove to meet the
conditions for membership of the KK. I asked Sarfaraz Khan how people actually
settled their feuds and he told me about a conflict between his own clan and another:

> Let me tell you a story about a feud that was settled and how it was done. We are
> Muhammadzai. We had a tenant who was killed by Musahib Khan of Mian Kaka *khel* (clan).
> In retaliation my father had killed three of theirs. Nearly ten years had passed since this
> incident, but the feud had remained alive. But now we went to their side to talk about it. My
> father and his two sons, that is my brother Ghulam Ali and me, went to our enemy's house.
> We went due to Badshah Khan's pleading that we settle our disputes. This was 1930 and
> Badshah Khan was on the scene and persuading us ... . He told us that one way to settle
> disputes was to put a knife and rifle in the hands of our enemy and ask him to kill you. If he
> spares you, then you can become a KK. When my father made this appeal, Musahib Khan
> fell to his knees and kissed my father's feet. He also decided to join the movement and more
> people from his clan joined with him. (I.45)

The resolution of the feud thus removed the barrier on membership from both the
clans involved, and in this way a single resolution could add significant numbers to
the KK. In addition, the resolution of the long simmering feud meant that the two
parties could now come together in normal social intercourse and cooperation
within the movement.

I asked Sarfaraz Khan whether Badshah Khan had taken on the role of mediator in
settling cases: 'Badshah Khan would think of strategies that would effect settlement,
but he did not mediate personally. That is, he was not physically present. He felt that
it was our problem and that we must sort it out ourselves before we joined the
freedom movement' (I.45). In Weber's description, the prophetic leader typically has
a specifically charismatic way of settling disputes – he conducts arbitration
according to his personal evaluation and through its effectiveness establishes the
absolute truth of his revelation. Such practice is seen with other 'segmentary saints'
such as those among the Nuer or the Sanusi in Cyrenaica.[7] But Badshah Khan did
not arbitrate personally in disputes in this way. Partly this reflected his general determination to play down the prophetic authority his supporters sometimes attributed
to him (see Chapter 5). More specifically, it reflected his conviction that feud resolution would be more genuine and robust where the methods were selected by the
participants themselves.

Like all social systems which regulate social conflict through the exchange of
violence, Pathan tradition itself provided several appropriate methods for peaceful
resolution of disagreements. One such was the *jirga* and Badshah Khan urged
villagers to talk over disagreements calmly among themselves, or if necessary to
convene small-scale *jirgas* taking in elders from other villages for neutrality, in order
to resolve disputes. 'The elders helped in effecting these settlements, but the opinion
of the young men was also heard. If someone still had a disagreement, or another
point of view, in that case we would call a *jirga* and try to explain our repective
points of view. If he was defeated ... he had to obey or else he was cut off from the
movement' (I.59). Thus the KK's emphasis on calm, impartiality and consensus

---

[7] See Johnson 1994; Evans-Pritchard 1949.

helped reinvigorate the traditional function and spirit of the *jirgas* which had been eroded by their cooption by the colonial authorities.

Another, more symbolic, method of peacemaking was described to me: 'In Pashto, settlement of dispute is called *kaunda*, which literally means a stone ... . A stone is placed on the ground between the two feuding groups and the settlement is made. It is a term with very serious implications ... . Badshah Khan told us to do a *kaunda* and settle our disputes' (I.59). Latterly, participation in KK activities seems itself to have become such a symbolic marker of resolution, as in the case that Jarnail Abdul Rahim remembered: 'Two *khans* in the Daudzai area, had been feuding for 29 or 30 years. But they agreed on a settlement and were soon seen joining in the same KK procession. They never fought again ...' (I.3). It was repeatedly emphasised to me that 'old enemies sat in each other's *hujras*, walked in the same processions' (I.56). I asked whether these settlements lasted, or did people revert back to their old enmities over time: 'There were lots and lots of cases of settlement. And these were lasting ties ... we became brothers' (I.45).

Whereas traditionally Pathan social interaction and exchange of women were confined largely to one's own *biraderi*, the network formed by relatives and close friends grounded in lineage and locality, the resolution of feuds and the shared participation in training, reform and protest activities together helped spread new ideas about loyalty and identity, in which status as a Khudai Khidmatgar and commitment to the movement superseded older local and family loyalties. Lieutenant Muhammad Wali confirmed the success of this idea: 'Whenever we were asked our names we said simply "Khudai Khidmatgar". And when we were asked where we came from we said Sardaryab (where our main provincial centre was situated)' (I.19). In adopting this naming practice the Pathans signalled that they had raised the scope of their sentiment and vision beyond that of village or lineage toward a wider provincial or even pan-Pathan domain: 'Badshah Khan never drew on clan loyalties, he said that we were all Pathans' (I.66). Haji Meherban reiterated this idea: 'Earlier people used to stay and interact within the confines of their tribes. But Badshah Khan changed all that' (I.36). As a result, many of my informants said that for the first time in their lives they made friends and acquaintances in other villages and that the range and frequency of their visits generally greatly increased.

Intermarriage across lineages and localities also greatly increased and seems even to have become rather fashionable. This was a particularly significant development because traditionally it was held that marriages which marked the end of enmity or the opening of a social relationship where none existed before were the most difficult to negotiate (Anderson 1982). Equality of the negotiating partners is an important notion in all Pathan marriages and is usually established through the exchange of huge bride prices or the giving of close female kin. With the intra-KK marriages, however, equality came to be demonstrated not through extravagant bride price, which Badshah Khan had long criticised, but rather through shared participation in the KK and the exchange of political camaraderie. Informants like Mohammed Pir Sher Shah told me:

> Earlier marriages took place only within the *biraderi*. But Badshah Khan changed things. Friendship grew among men across different *biraderis* and these were cemented by women. Now we praised intermarrying. Badshah Khan's personal example made a big difference. He

gave his own daughter in marriage to a Peshawari, a city person from a quite different people … . (I.59)

The Khudai Khidmatgari created links across all our tribes. Ali Khan (Badshah Khan's youngest son) was married to Qazi Attaulah's daughter. They were Mohmands. Yahya Jan was a Peshawari but Badshah Khan still gave his daughter in marriage to him. (I.34)

Thus the numerous marriages arranged between the families within the movement gave rise to a quite new network of alliances and solidarity.

The identities and loyalties associated with village and kinship were thus de-emphasised and subsumed within membership of the KK as a whole. Anticipating the authorities' anxiety about this new solidarity, Badshah Khan delivered a poignant speech, shortly before one of his extended prison sentences:

Oh the brethren of Pakhli, listen attentively, perhaps I may not be able to see you again. Listen to a word of mine. If a servant of the *Firangi* [foreigners – i.e. the British] comes and threatens you, you should say 'Is forming a brotherhood a crime? If it is a crime, then why have the *Firangis* formed a brotherhood of their own? If all the other nations have got a brotherhood of their own, why should the Pathans not have one?' … What for have you worn Red clothes? What do these clothes signify? The Red Shirts that you see are a new 'brotherhood', a new 'Pashto' we have formed. (Ramu 1992: 44, 100)

In this way Badshah Khan celebrated the Pathans' new solidarity and awareness of the nature of their own pan-Pathan community. Sher Khan recalled this message:

Badshah Khan's message created a sense of solidarity among us. Earlier in the village we all used to know each other. But later we began to love each other. Even strained relationships became friendly thanks to Badshah Khan's message of brotherhood and love. He told us to get over our tribal loyalties … . It took time … but it happened. We made an effort to befriend the other tribes and so on. (I.29)

The bringing together of the Pathans was an essential preliminary to the main battle – the non-violent confrontation with the British.

Building a Non-violent Military Structure

Badshah Khan went to a great deal of trouble to instil non-violence as a moral and psychological reflex in the KK membership, and he did this, as we have seen, by culti-vating ethics of service and teamwork, by moral and religious teachings and by encouraging the settlement of feuds. What was particularly distinctive about the KK, however, was the fact that Badshah Khan sought to bolster personal belief in non-violence with the unthinking discipline and obedience of mechanical military drilling, which was very different from the more individualistic Gandhian approach to teaching and acquiring non-violence. The KK was organised around a strict hier-archy of military ranks and titles, each of which commanded a certain number of sub-units and men. In Chapter 5 I consider this hierarchy in detail and in particular its novel relationship to Pathan social structure. For the purposes of the present discussion, however, the salient fact is that Badshah Khan established an explicit chain of command and instilled a strict discipline.

The question of discipline had more than the merely practical importance of helping conduct effective demonstrations and the like. Because the Pathans were perceived and portrayed as a wild and ungovernable race by the British, Badshah Khan felt that it was vital for the KK to demonstrate that the Pathans were in fact capable of self-discipline and organisation, and hence were worthy candidates for self-government. Jarnail Hazrat Gul recalled his early career and contribution to this discipline:

> As a lieutenant I used to conduct parades in Shabkadar, the central meeting place for several villages. Parade was held from 2 p.m. to 3 p.m. every day. We were taught to do parade by retired army officers who had served in Malaysia and elsewhere. The soldiers enjoyed the parade and did it gladly. Before leaving the camp for a demonstration or picketing, speeches used to be made on non-violence and it was clearly stated that whoever wanted violence should leave immediately. Badshah Khan told the people that the British had promised to leave after 180 years when they had first arrived. That is after India became self-sufficient. But they still had not left. So the parade and the reform movement were to prove to the British that we were in fact self-sufficient. The camp was a preparation for a battle of patience. We believed that if we practised non-violence consistently then one morning we would awake to find the British gone! (I.24)

In a colourful conversation, Colonel Mohammed Sayid gave me a demonstration by marching around the *hujra* in which we were sitting, explaining that this was how they used to march in and manoeuvre on parades when the bugle sounded – and he could still remember the tune (I.44). The 75-year-old Turab recalled that 'the bugle used to sound like a British army bugle' (I.52). The memories of belonging to this army are evidently still vivid and the pomp of the parades and uniforms appears to have caught the imagination of the Pathans. The authorities reported that excitement and enthusiasm was kept at high pitch through these meetings and drills.[8] 'We were similar to soldiers. We had a Captain, Drill Master, Major and General. We had to do drill and parade for one hour every evening' (I.3). 'There were 8,070 uniforms in the Daudzai area. Our Captain was Aslam Khan and the General was Akram Khan of Taktabad, who was the general for the entire Daudzai area. We liked doing parade for discipline' (I.46).

Kudrat Shah said: 'Obedience was total in our army-like organisation' (I.6) and 83-year-old Fazle Karim of Pabbi told me an anecdote to illustrate this: 'On our arrival in Meerut, Section 144 [of the Frontier Crimes Regulations, limiting public gatherings] was enforced. I had gone ahead on business leaving behind four other KKs. The police asked them to move on, but they refused saying that I had asked them to wait and that they would not take orders from anyone else but their own KK commander!' (I.10). Hama Gul provided another instance: 'Our army training was done in order that we could learn discipline which was needed for picketing activities and so on ... . Our obedience to the organisation was so strong that once when we were doing parade, our Commander said 'March!' but forgot to say 'Halt!' and the whole company marched into the river that lay ahead!' (I.51). Gul Rahman said that 'The secret of all this discipline was that it came from the several camps that were held ... there used to be at least one camp held once in 3/4 months' (I.40).

[8] L/P&J/12/32.

Such discipline paid dividends in the heat of confrontation with the British. Kudrat Shah told me: 'We used to parade just like the army. With bugles, drums and a band. A man called Colonel Sayyid used to play the bugle in our village ... . In a procession in Charsadda bazaar we were once ordered to fall before the horses of the British troops. We did so without any hesitation' (I.6). Similar instances are confirmed by the reports of the colonial administration: 'There occurred an illuminating fiasco ... there was a false alarm about a noise which caused a panic ... the only processionists who stood firm were the contingent of "Red Shirts" who had accompanied Abdul Gaffar Khan.'[9] Practically, such steadfastness and calm helped avoid the kind of mass panic which had contributed in the past to such tragedies as the Kissa Khani bazaar massacre. Symbolically it demonstrated a fearlessness and strength of will to the colonial adversary.

I asked whether their drills, like those in more conventional armies, were intended as practice for battle and attacks. The answers, however, were always similar to that of Jarnail Mohammed Umar, who stressed that 'The only function of the drills was discipline, never for fighting purposes' (I.21). Mukarram Khan recalled that 'Badshah Khan said that we were unable to defeat the British on the battlefield ... we were doing politics and that we had to defeat them politically ... there was nothing to say but agree to that' (I.70).

In its emphasis upon the combination of self-reform, grace and discipline, the KK had more in common with the Salvation Army than it did with the British Army. Like the Salvation Army, the KK was based on voluntary work and service, yet also prized virtues such as discipline and efficient organisational machinery. The Salvation Army was already very active in India in the 1920s and 1930s, and one of its programmes was the establishment of settlements for the reform of members of the 'criminal castes'. In his description of these settlements, Tolen argues that the reformatory practices of the Salvation Army were enforced primarily through the disciplining of the body, with methods closely resembling those chosen by Badshah Khan, namely drills, labour and uniforms (Tolen 1991). Such bodily discipline was intended to help transform souls by inculcating obedience and honesty, an aim comparable to Badshah Khan's desire to help Pathans pass through a transformation to non-violence and self-sacrifice. Although the official category of criminal castes did not exist in the Frontier, given that the Pathans were viewed by the British as incurably violent and anarchic, Badshah Khan was in a fairly literal sense seeking to rehabilitate the Pathans through the same principles of army-like discipline, obedience, cleanliness and service favoured by the Salvation Army. Despite the differing pedigrees and ultimate aims of the two organisations, the similarity of approach and methods is striking. As Tolen concludes: 'Industry, cleanliness, honesty, and obedience' were taught to members of the Army settlements in India and their children were 'trained to become worthy citizens of India'.[10] Badshah Khan had much the same ultimate aim for the Pathans.

Comparison can also be made, thanks to Robert Alter's research, with the network of *akharas*, or wrestlers' gymnasia, in North India. In modern India the wrestlers have

---

[9] Chief Secretary's Report, April 1931, L/P&J/12/32 IOLR.
[10] Salvation Army, 1923: 60, in Tolen 1991.

had an uneasy relationship with the state and have developed an ideology that is deeply fearful of the physical and moral weakness which the corruption and sloth of modern Indian society has brought. They have thus evolved a cult of intensive disciplining of the body in order to achieve a 'structured escape from docility and degeneracy' (Alter 1993: 51). By examining the gymnasia's discourses on their utopian visions of the ideal society, Alter shows that what the wrestlers are doing 'is confronting the power of the state at its most basic level by making physical fitness a form of political protest and civic reform' (*ibid.*: 65). The wrestlers' physical training imposed on them 'such values as hard work, humility, honesty, and public service', and also an egalitarianism, with brahmins and untouchables working out together. In this way, Alter demonstrates the way in which the wrestlers refuse to make a Cartesian distinction between body and mind, and treat moral and physical health as synonymous, with the whole body taken as a 'comprehensive agent of reform' (*ibid.*: 65). The wrestlers' political logic is that 'to be a strong, healthy, and moral wrestler is to be a strong, healthy, and moral citizen of the modern Indian state' (*ibid.*: 51). While the KKs did not explicitly articulate this kind of holism, their combining of physical fitness (through the discipline imposed by drills and parades) with moral fitness (the cessation of feuding and forgiveness of past enemies) can be seen as an analogous preparation of healthy citizens to challenge the decay of colonial rule.

Besides its military structure and discipline, another key feature of the KK was, of course, its Red Shirt uniform (complete with Sam Browne belt), which bore clear similarities to various units of the Indian army. British intelligence reports constantly remarked upon the KK's 'red shirts' and military paraphernalia: '... Red Shirt activity has increased, particularly in Peshawar and Mardan districts ... numerous Congress Committees have been formed and there have been many meetings and flag hoisting ceremonies; it is now a common thing for parties of Red Shirts with flags and bands to march in formation'.[11] Haji Sarfaraz Nazim, an ideologue of the movement, told me: 'Uniforms were worn for discipline. The young are happy to have physical activity, it keeps them out of mischief. Sam Browne belts looked good and made the uniform smart and tight and practical. Generals and presidents wore Peshawari turbans and trousers (not shorts) and the rest wore simple caps. Every youth looked like a flower!' (I.1).

The technique of non-violent confrontation was the very opposite of guerrilla campaigns and in place of the Pathans' traditional use of stealth and camouflage the KK was a determinedly extrovert and highly visible presence. Badshah Khan made this clear in his speeches: 'Just as the policemen wear uniform for identification so the Khudai Khidmatgar wear Red Clothes for the same purpose.'[12] 'The Red dress is meant to be a distinguishing mark to enable the people to know them as those who felt ashamed for the country of their fathers and have girded up their loins [to resist]'.[13]

Deran Shah recalled: 'I bought some white *khadi* and dyed it red. It was a matter of great pride for us. We used to fight over who was to be the one in uniform all the time

---

[11] Chief Secretary's Report, September 1937, L/P&J/5/211 IOLR.
[12] 14 December 1931, in a mosque in the village Khalabat, Police Station. Swabi, Ramu 1992.
[13] 15 December 1931, Torlandi, Police Station. Kalu Khan, Ramu 1992: 228.

.... My brother became one of the prime targets of the police attacks. They took away his uniform and burnt it. But that didn't stop him. He just made another one!' (I.5). It cost between five and eight rupees – a significant sum – for eight yards of material, but cloth was generally available because there were as many as twenty weavers in every village, who were of course being supplied with much of their thread by the KK's own spinning (I.25). Where uniforms had been burned repeatedly and no further replacements could be afforded, red badges were sometimes used instead. Secretary Wahidullah said that in 1931 more than 1,200 Khudai Khidmatgar uniforms were burnt by the authorities (I.26).

The uniforms acquired an immense popularity. My informants said that they always wanted to be seen in uniform, and this is confirmed by reports which record that KKs were even seen wearing their uniforms to the mosque, at the festival of Id, when it was traditional to dress in new clothes. I was also shown photographs of my informants getting married in their red shirts, with a wedding procession consisting of a long line of Khudai Khidmatgaran comrades, also in their uniforms.

This pride in the uniform largely reflected pride in the wider organisation and their own participation in it; we can recall the peer pressure exerted on young men to join (see Chapter 2 above). It also seems, however, that in a society which traditionally attached great value to egalitarianism, but had been experiencing growing inequality and class divides, the uniforms restored some measure of equality between rich and poor. On her visit to the Red Shirt camp, Barr noted that the ranks contained 'a great variety of status and wealth', yet all looked alike in their uniforms. As Derai Khan said: 'We had uniforms like schoolchildren have uniforms' (I.46). Though military ranks were marked on the shoulders of the uniform – for example, a colonel had shoulder pips, a *hawaldar* wore his on his arm (I.27) – this gave no clue to social status, since in the KK army – unlike the British – rank was deliberately disassociated from social position and traditional status, with Badshah Khan encouraging several methods of 'positive discrimination' to ensure the poor were well represented among the officers (see Chapter 5 below).

The KKs themselves generally offered fairly simple and straightforward explanations for the choice of red, such as its brightness and visibility, or the ready availability of the dye. For the colonial authorities, however, red had far greater historical and political resonance. Red cloth was a peculiarly military colour in India. In the eighteenth century, as European military advisers and armaments became more common, princely Indian rulers sought to enhance the prowess of their armies by dressing them in scarlet English broadcloth. As Chris Bayly writes:

> Thick dyed cloth and red harness were peculiarly appropriate to the traditional colour-coding of the Indian warrior classes and the use of red serge spread from the Nawab of Awadh's 60,000-man army to those of his competitors and by degrees to a whole range of irregulars, guards and doormen. The potency of the image of the 'red coat' is evident throughout the nineteenth century in India and persists even today. (Bayly 1986: 304)

These red uniforms gained further significance in the 1857 mutiny. Eric Stokes, discussing the reasons for the failure of the mutiny, describes how the rebel military units often began with well-defined unit identity, with all regimental forms and usages carefully preserved, but then gradually degenerated to the point where the sepoys became ragged and confused bands under warlords, finally melting into the countryside to join the general civil rebellion and bringing the mutiny to an abortive end. 'While military defeat was the main agency of regimental disintegration, the inability to refurbish their increasingly tatterdemalion appearance was also of significance. During the revolt, a number of the soldiers abandoned their shakos and jackets for ease of fighting, but this also increasingly obliterated the distinction of company and regiment, adversely affecting *esprit de corps* and turning them increasingly from regular soldiers into civil insurgents' (Stokes 1986: 66). Uniforms, therefore, could play a significant role in maintaining *esprit de corps*, and Badshah Khan had seen at first hand how the spirit of resistance of the Akali activists he had shared gaol with appeared to be bolstered by the togetherness that came from their wearing of black turbans.

In 1922, eight years before the first sightings of Red Shirts in the North West Frontier Province, red again emerged as a potent image in the Chauri Chaura incident in North India. Red turbans were the official symbols of *chaukidars* (police) in North India; in fact, it was the only symbol which gave these lowly officials credibility, the rest of their dress being cheap indigo-dyed blue jackets and *dhotis*.[14] During the violence at Chauri Chaura they were identified by their distinctive red turbans and Amin reports that 'it was this four-yard strip of red cloth that peasants attacked even after its owner was dead' (Amin 1995: 150).

By virtue of the military and police associations, therefore, red was clearly the colour of the establishment in India. Its adoption by the KK for their own uniform could thus be read as a clear statement of intent to challenge that establishment and deny its monopoly of authority. If one compares pictures of the Frontier Constabulary from the 1880s and the Red Shirts in uniform fifty years later, the similarities are striking. Indeed, my informants told me that often it was deserters from the Army who provided the accessories of belt and buckle for their own red uniforms. The 1857 mutiny was the first instance of a serious revolt within the colony, and the KK with their red uniform and quasi-military manner disturbed the authorities' collective memory, which goes some way to explaining the apprehension felt by the officials in the Frontier towards the Red Shirts. For the British, uniforms and ranks were necessarily military, thus entailing force and violence. For the KKs, however, they were a method precisely of disciplining the Pathans and *preventing* violence.

The pride that the KK took in their uniforms was matched by the British irritation with them. While my informants insisted that the uniforms made them look like 'flowers', the colonial officials frequently mocked and deplored the rough *khadi* cloth. Badshah Khan put an inspired spin on being perceived as 'slipshod'. He said that if the government servants and army needed uniforms, then how much more entitled were the KKs to wear them, as the servants and army of God. He also argued that the KK uniforms were in fact far superior to those of the British and their lackeys, because the KK themselves were 'really much superior to [the English] servants, their military, their slaves and to the Englishmen themselves':

> Do you see the English? Their servants and their employees are selling their country and their religion in these days for a few pennies. I say these Khudai Khidmatgaran are noble

---

[14] 'Proper' policemen, on the other hand, wore khakhi uniforms, leggings and boots.

because they eat what is their own. They wear is their own and it is bought with their own money. They prepare a uniform with which they serve God's created beings and His religion. Superiority does not depend on keeping an automobile, possessing large lands, riches and big property. This is the *Fauj* [army] of God. Just as God is supreme, similiarly the *Fauj* of God is superior to the servants of the English'.[15]

In short, however imperfect the uniforms, they were produced by the efforts and honest labour of God-fearing patriots. The red uniforms of 1930, unlike those of 1857, were not made from the famous broadcloth of the Lancashire mills, but rather of homespun *khadi*. Gandhi intended the use of *khadi* by Indians to make a statement of self-reliance, indigenous technology and *swadeshi* (nation-made) ideology. Its use for the home-made uniforms of a self-declared anti-colonial army made this statement an even more striking one. The KK were certain that the British hated their red shirts because it was the uniform of anti-British feeling (I.63).

The red shirts could thus be read as triply threatening. They gave the appearance of an army to a band of peasants; they used the colour of the military and the establishment in India and hence appeared subversive; and they were made from handspun cloth, which was itself a noble symbol of personal and national self-reliance. In this respect, the KK shirts are further evidence of the fact that codes of dress in the Raj were of great political significance, particularly in the contrasts between ruler and ruled and in the way in which twentieth-century rebellion was clothed (see Cohn 1987 and Tarlo 1996).

For most of the KK themselves, however, the significance and emotiveness of red shirts came not from older allusions or similarities but from its association with the KK themselves. One of my informants went beyond the more usual functional explanations of the colour: 'It was the colour of challenge ... it was the colour of blood ... as if our uniforms were steeped in our own blood!' (I.1).[16] In verses written at the time, the colour is similarly celebrated by a Khudai Khidmatgar:

Youths always win the field at the cost of their lives.
Autumn winds always blow at red flowers.
Oh tyrant! You have sharpened the sword of tyranny.
Youths have already given red colour to their clothes.[17]

Last, we should note that the colour was not confined to clothing and took on a symbolic and defiant life of its own. Today my elderly informants still wear and carry red handkerchiefs, red walking sticks and red notebooks. One recalled that 'People were really enthusiastic about the movement. They even painted their bulls red!' (I.23). In 1933 G. A. Cole, Assistant Commissioner of Sardar, filed an angry report on what he described as 'a minor recrudescence of Red Shirt cum Congress movement' in his area. On 9–10 August 1933 a Red Shirt meeting was held on the canal bank between Sardar Garhi and Chamkani. The following day a second meeting was held at the Pushti Sag police station, Daudzai. During the night of 12 August the milestones between Tarnab and Sardar Garhi were all painted red. On the following night all the milestones from Sardar Garhi to the Sardar police station were painted red.

---

[15] 12 November 1931 at Qila Maidan in the village of Nawanshehr, Ramu 1992: 100.
[16] In the Salvation Army flag red stands for the colour of blood and sacrifice.
[17] The poet is Khan Ghulam Haider Khan, *jirga* president, Hangu. NAI.

Cole's furious response to this impertinence was to arrest several dozen activists from the nearest villages.

Communications and Agitation

The extensive network of KK camps and committees across the Settled Districts required a sophisticated communications framework to bind it together and ensure coordinated activity. There were two main kinds of communication – one inward-looking and administrative, which I discuss in Chapter 5, the other public and agitational.

The journal *Pakhtun* was the main public forum. Launched in 1928, it was produced in runs of several thousand copies, and came out three or four times a month – although it was frequently banned and suppressed, as it was for most of the time between 1932 and 1937 (Shah 1999: 43). The actual printing presses were in Peshawar but it was distributed from Utmanzai, Badshah Khan's home village (I.7).

> There was a system for distributing *Pakhtun*. Copies were mailed to every president and secretary which they circulated. After people had had a look they usually wanted it too and subscriptions increased. (I.65)

> The journal *Pakhtun* was read by many people. It was distributed at the local sugar factories and other such centres of activity and people would read it out aloud for those who couldn't read. It was very inexpensively priced so people could afford it ... it was only 2 annas. (I.53)

> All of us were made to read the journal *Pakhtun* – we used to collect money in order to buy a copy; articles in these helped us understand non-violence and convert to it. Badshah Khan used to write that if we did not leave violence we would not ever be able to solve our problems. He taught us patience and told us to end our feuds. Badshah Khan used to say that people will learn what you teach them. (I.62)

> Everybody read *Pakhtun*. (I.11)

In addition to the main journal, a wide range of bulletins and information sheets were reproduced and distributed, and the authorities went to great lengths to unearth them, sometimes literally. A Congressman reported in 1932 that since the start of the movement two years earlier some half a dozen cyclostyle machines had been seized, but that to the frustration of the police this had not curtailed the flow of bulletins. When four KKs who had been arrested on charges of sedition refused to reveal the location of their machine, a ground area to the extent of one square mile round (perhaps a slight exaggeration, the report admits) was dug up to unearth the machine – but without success.[18]

Protest Activities

Having undertaken their own personal training in patience and service, resolved their feuds, put on their uniforms, practised their drill and advertised times and

---

[18] 'A Note on the NWFP by Kripalani', File No. P-16/1932 NMML.

places to meet in their bulletins, the KKs were ready to march against the British, with various kinds of manoeuvre in their repertoire.

The simplest was to march in procession through a settlement. An old colonial tradition which survives in modern India and elsewhere in the post-colonial world is the 'flag march'. In situations of tension or curfew the army is ordered to march in formation through the city centre and along important roads, bearing the flag of the government, as a statement of state power. By marching through villages in formation, the KKs appear to have made a similar show of force to the administration, as a statement of anti-state power.

Often, the KK column would stop halfway to hold a public meeting in the centre of the area it was marching through. 'A band used to head our procession ... I remember always running the first lap of any march in my enthusiasm!' (I.40). 'We used to walk to meetings in processions; at these meetings we used to organise our various activities and try to talk to people to convince them to join our organisation and movement '(I.6). The centrepiece of these meetings were political and agitational speeches, exhorting the local people to support the nationalist cause through their time, effort and finances and to join the KK. They would also discuss particular Congress initiatives and current events. Extensive use was also made of other agitational genres: 'Inspiring poetry used to be recited at the meetings' (I.11). 'I began to write poetry at the age of 10. I used to recite poetry at the Khudai Khidmatgar meetings. Badshah Khan's speech used to follow. The poetry was the result of nationalist ideology. It was not romantic poetry like the poetry in Persian' (I.7). 'A lot of poetry like this circulated among the people. Poetry used to create enthusiasm among the people and the Khudai Khidmatgaran' (I.52). Such poetry evidently made a great impression and several of my informants spontaneously recited political poems that had been popular during the life of the movement (e.g., I.7, I.11). Turab recited a couplet for me which described the feeling of bondage and oppression that the people felt, but then urged that the only way to shed these feelings was by selflessly serving the nation (I.52).

Plays were performed, too – and evidently stirred the emotions, judging by Sayyid Mohammed Fasi Badshah's recollection of a moment worthy of Pirandello:

> In 1931, Amir Nawaz of Utmanzai wrote a play called *Dard* ('Pain'). I myself played the part of an Englishman and my line was 'We will treat you the way we have treated Bahadur Shah Zaffar' [the last Mughal emperor, overthrown by the British]. The story's intention was to highlight British atrocities in the Province. But when I was saying my lines one night, people hated the Englishman so much that one man got up to shoot me. C. Barnes [presumably a police chief] heard about this incident and arrested several people during the night. (I.39)

Demonstrations and pickets were directed at specific targets. Often these were shops selling foreign cloth and goods, particularly liquor. Government reports and KK testimonies give equally colourful descriptions of the demonstrations and methods of picketing:

> The number of Red Shirt picketters no less than 900; as many as 30 on duty at a time. Picket reliefs marched through the city (Peshawar) in formations of some 50 at a time ... the method adopted for picketing is to send parties up to 100 strong and marching in formation

to the village selected. Pickets are then posted in the bazaar and outside the village, the number is then gradually reduced.[19]

In Bannu city marked revival of Congress activity ... picketing of foreign cloth shops ... as one batch removed [i.e. arrested], another took its place ... finally there were 140 prisoners ... . Next day an unusually large number entered the city at an early hour ... . Gates of the city closed and officer removed the villagers who offered no resistance and obeyed with good humour, but at the close of day ... 200 prisoners on his hands ... . Next day gates closed again but foreign liquor shops being picketed by women, including 5 or 6 Bannuchi women.[20]

Haji Lal Mohammed told me: 'Picketing used to start at six a.m. We were six men ... . There were additional police at each of the gates of the building we were picketing and they were playing with the bolts on their guns in order to pressurise us. Nothing happened for three hours, then the next shift of police took over ... . People used to stand and cheer successful picketings and arrests' (I.50). Maulavi Inayatullah said he remembered that 'during the picketing when one batch of picketers were beaten up by the police they were carried away and a fresh one took its place. The police used to give up and leave in resignation sometimes' (I.65). It is interesting to note that Haji Inayatullah's description was of picketing in Mardan, while the government report describes a picket in Bannu, 400 miles away. The method had obviously been tried, tested and standardised across the Province (and in the rest of India), and this gave the nationalist movement's operations a new consistency and rigour.

A very important aspect of the civil disobedience movement was its boycott of institutions of the colonial state, notably the courts, police, army, tax offices and officers, and schools. Such non-cooperation was practised in a variety of ways. A member of the All India Congress Committee reported: 'The Red Shirts have preached the non-payment of revenue and have simultaneously with this refused to avail themselves of the canal water offered by the Government. They have success-fully dissuaded the agriculturalists from using canal water and where their advice has been unheeded, [they] picketed the openings [outlets] of the canals.'[21] The Swat and Kabul river canals were high-priority projects, undertaken at great expense by the colonial administration (see Chapter 1) and the villagers' boycott of these canals thus hurt efforts to show the benevolence and dynamism of the Provincial colonial administration. The tone of the reports suggests that the bureaucrats took it almost as a personal affront, lamenting the natives' ingratitude. But the boycott was clearly not unanimous and seems to have caused tensions among the Pathans, since it nega-tively affected peasants' productivity and to that extent was somewhat contrary to the ideals of self-improvement and modernisation shared by Badshah Khan himself. Rejection of the administration's initiatives ultimately took precedence over self-improvement, however, and the boycott was vigorously upheld by the KK.

The institutions of law and order, the heart of the colonial administration, were also boycotted. In their place, villages with a strong KK presence set up their own *jirgas* for the settlement of both civil and criminal cases and urged that people report incidents to them rather than the police or the official *jirgas*. Thus, while Badshah

---

[19] Chief Secretary's Report, September 1931, L/P&J/12/32 IOLR.
[20] Chief Secretary's Report, June 1930, L/P&J/12/9 IOLR.
[21] G. Kripalani, 13 February 1932, L/P&J/12/43 IOLR.

Khan demanded that feuds be settled in order to promote non-violence, he did not want this to be done with the help of British functionaries. Self-reform had to be achieved through indigenous institutions. Gul Samand Khan recalled a particularly successful example:

> When Badshah Khan came to my village he talked to us and said 'Why do you work for the British? This is your own land. Don't report to the British for any help. You have your own laws!' After the meeting, his words had a good effect. People were enthused. After Badshah Khan left I called a meeting and we decided to form our own courts and enforce the *shari'a* law. We had our own *munshi* [scribe] and judge and other officials. We informed the people about our institution and told them what Badshah Khan had said. People came not only from within our village but from other villages as well. There were not even enough guest houses for them to stay while their cases were heard, but somehow we organised 50 *maun* of wheat to feed them. The *ulema* had a meeting and they declared in their *fatwa* that if anyone went to the English courts then they would have to divorce their wife! For one year and three months this plan worked. The British could do nothing. Then one day the Assistant Commissioner came to investigate one of our court meetings in the mosque. The A.C. asked on what basis was the law in our courts to be considered valid. Maulana Sahib said that it was based on the Quran and the A.C. looked shocked and said: 'But that is in Arabic!' (I.55)

In addition to boycotting British courts, however, the KK also took more direct action against them to demonstrate the Pathans' desire for self-rule and ownership of the legal system. 'We were given two [Congress] flags ... one to plant inside the court and one outside to prove that the country was ours and that the courts were also ours' (I.16). 'We raided a court. The magistrate ran away and we occupied his chair!' (I.27). Kudrat Shah remembered an occasion when they had picketed a court in Mardan so successfully and intensively that the District Commissioner of the place ran away into hiding (I.6).

Gul Rahman remembered picketing a court of justice in 1943: 'We had gone to picket the courts. We managed to take over the courts and got hold of the book in the court in which the judgements passed used to be recorded. We managed to pass four judgements ourselves ... (1) This Magistrate has not followed the rules of the nationalist government and therefore will be arrested and locked up and kept in a "hanging chamber". (2) In this court, all the decisions made so far are annulled because these judgements were passed according to the wrong law. I cannot remember exactly what the others were ...' (I.40). When I asked him whether these decisions were ever implemented, he said quite firmly: 'All the decisions except the first one.'

The administration constantly reported that Badshah Khan had been 'exhorting people to civil disobedience'. He indeed stressed to the Pathans that the police and tax collectors were *civil* servants, that is, the servants of citizens, and that people therefore should not hesitate to question their authority and actions: 'As long as we see the police and the tax collectors in our district we know that the Government is going on as it used to.'[22] The Chief Secretary reported some of the results of such exhortations in November 1937: 'Villagers assaulted a police patrol because being illiterate Muslims they misunderstood Abdul Gaffar Khan's reference to the Police

[22] Governor's Report, November 1937, L/P&J/5/211 IOLR.

being their servants and took his suggestions that they should no longer be feared literally.'[23] The reference to 'illiterate Muslims' is a nice example of the bureaucrats' continued underestimation of the strength of the political forces at work: the villagers, I would suggest, enjoyed full awareness of the significance of their defiance and cheek, not least due to tireless KK agitation on the topic of non-cooperation. Another of the Governor's reports noted: 'Undoubted effort on the part of the Red Shirts to interfere with their work ... when police go for investigations and other duties, they are sometimes openly told by Red Shirt sympathisers that they are of no account and one or two villages in Peshawar have actually organised village police.'[24]

The parallels in this respect between the KK's subversion of the police and similar tactics by other volunteer forces in the rest of India are striking. In Chauri Chaura, the mark of the *otiyar* (volunteers)[25] described by Amin was wearing a Gandhi cap, patrolling the village at night and 'behaving like a policeman' at a fair or gatherings. As Nandini Gooptu notes in her study of the politics of the urban poor in Uttar Pradesh, usurping the functions of the state by 'behaving like a policeman' was an established practice of volunteer forces in the 1930s, since it was precisely during this inter-war period that the police became increasingly involved in suppressing disorders: 'Defying or attacking the police, thus emerged as a recurrent motif in the political action of the poor, not simply to contend with direct police repression or petty tyrannies, but also as forms of resistance against the state or elites ... . Participation of the poor was also prominent in the Congress sponsored volunteer corps, which were organised as a means to usurp or undermine the authority of the police' (Gooptu 1991: 88). The volunteer groups Gooptu describes modelled themselves on the police by regularly organising drill, parades and marches, and some of them armed themselves with simple weapons such as *lathis*, swords, spears or mock rifles and attempted to maintain order at processions or public meeting and demonstrations.

The KKs differed from these volunteer forces in eschewing weapons and violence, but the remaining features are clearly similar. The 80-year-old KK Hama Gul remembered helping a Hindu candidate in the elections in neighbouring Punjab. The man had asked Badshah Khan for some KK 'soldiers' to help him. They were duly supplied and were given the job of keeping order at polling booths, collecting the ballot papers and putting them in the right boxes 'in an honest fashion'. Hama Gul recalled that the police used to try and stop the KKs usurping their function in this way, but the KKs would protest their righteousness by throwing their canes away and surrendering themselves for arrest (I.51).

As a result of Badshah Khan's exhortations, the Pathans found the confidence not merely to oppose the authorities, but to meet the challenges of local governance by setting up their own alternative institutions. The boycott of state institutions and provision of alternatives had a direct bearing on the government's credibility and the fact that the KK was striving to provide parallel functions to the state was a constant preoccupation of the colonial officials. On one famous occasion the KK audaciously

---

[23] Chief Secretary's Report, November 1937, L/P&J/5/211 IOLR.
[24] Governor's Report, December 1937, L/P&J/5/211 IOLR.
[25] The north Indian creolised term for volunteers.

set up a rival quarter guard right outside the regimental quarters of the famous Guides Cavalry in Mardan. Such symbolic actions, each relatively modest in itself, had a cumulative effect, gradually but irresistibly eroding the colonial authorities' prestige, legitimacy and morale in the Frontier.

Last, I should note that not all demonstrations were of quite such a politically profound nature, with some being positively mischievous, although no less effective for that, as Haroon Kaka recalled:

> I remember a particular incident when the Governor of the Province was visiting our village. We organised to surround the house where he had been put up for the night. We worked out an elaborate system by which a number of bugle players and drummers kept up a constant noise through the night. They tried to catch us but were totally unsuccessful because we had worked out a relay system by which every time they closed in on an area where they thought the noise originated, another group would start playing from another distant place. We managed to hold out all night and heard the next morning that the police thought we were mysterious *jinns* (spirits)! (I.27)

In all the activities described above the KK were on the offensive. They were often forced onto the defensive by police actions, however, particularly when the state launched raids on villages to root out activitists:

> Ours was the biggest village in the area with a KK army about 400 strong. This army of God used to surround entire villages to protect them. When the police came to attack the houses we protested and held our line in front of them and got arrested for this as well. A hundred and twenty people were arrested from here on that occasion. Some were imprisoned for three years. (I.27)

In the same way the camps were also used as defensive sites: 'When a warrant was out to arrest one of us, we always went to the camps so we could get arrested in large numbers' (I.5.).

Social Support for Injured and Imprisoned

The overwhelming majority of participants in the KK movement were ordinary peasants already burdened by exploitation and poverty. As I was told time and again: 'It *was* a movement of the poor after all.' When men courted arrest and were away in jail for long stretches of time, how did their families cope? When I asked Mukarram Khan this I was told that uncles and cousins and friends and relatives looked after the families of these men. His own butcher's business was taken on by his extended family until he returned (I.70). When a family did not have such resources of kin, then either the breadwinner was not expected to court arrest or, if he was arrested, donations would be collected for his dependants among other KKs (I.66). KK members would also help out on each other's land if someone was in prison during the crucial sowing or harvesting periods. Thus to deal with the new problems created by the revolutionary struggle existing networks of kin and community were utilised as support structures and mechanisms of mutual aid. 'When people went to jail, the others used to look after their fields. Badshah Khan taught us brotherhood' (I.34). Haji Zamir Gul also recalled the solidarity that the movement had engendered: 'The families used to help each other out while we went to jail. There was a lot of love among people ... Once on Id day, all the elders of our village were taken away and their Id clothes were stripped off and left in a heap in the middle of the village. They [the British] stood back to see what would happen. But everybody went and collected what was theirs and did not steal what was not theirs ...' (I.49).

Despite such mutual assistance, however, it was also recognised that some people simply could not afford to be away in prison. Haji Sarfaraz Nazim Sahib told me that this was one of the main reasons for the demographic distribution of KK membership, which he said was strongest in districts which had a high proportion of peasant culti-vators and reasonable average size of landholding, such that families had relatively more economic independence and resources with which to sustain periods of impris-onment. But economic vulnerability was a major disincentive to KK activity and the leaders accepted this as unavoidable. As Mohammed Pir Sher Shah explained, 'We did not take landless labourers into the movement ... they were affiliated to us ... and if by their involvement they did lose money then the wealthier people in the movement would help them out' (I.59).

Even where families were slightly more prosperous they were not expected to risk losing all their male workers to the British prisons: 'From every family one or two sons were given up to the movement ... the others remained passive supporters' (I.67). Badshah Khan was always aware that the bulk of the KK were people who had little idle time to devote to politics. As Mohammed Pir Sher Shah emphasised, 'We did party work only one or two days of the week. The rest of the time we had to work on our lands' (I.59). People recalled with gratitude the fact that when Badshah Khan went around villages and wanted to talk to farmers working in the fields, he used to make his escorts plough the land so that the farmers could sit and talk to him without losing valuable time (I.54).

The physical return of men from jail did not mean that they would necessarily be able to slip easily back into their former roles. As we shall see in Chapter 4, while in jail they were often subject to torture, bad food, illness and hard labour; many returned broken in body, if not spirit. Rehabilitating them required a great deal of care on the part of the support groups. One man was sent home from jail, having been severely beaten and stripped of his clothes (he still carries the scars on his head and legs). Seeing his parlous condition, the authorities had sent him home to die. When he reached home, however, the women of his family looked after him and helped him recover. When the authorities got wind of his survival, police were posted outside his house to keep him under surveillance, and the villagers had to feed them too while they did their duty! Eight days later he was taken back to Haripur jail (I.63).

The Role of Women

I had opportunity to speak to only one surviving female KK activist, the 90-year-old Grana. I asked her if she was an exception, or whether there were other women in the area who were involved in the movement in the same overt way. Grana could recall only one other woman who was from Babda, but unfortunately she was already dead. Many of the men I spoke to recalled women who had participated in the KK, however, and such activism was a major breakthrough for Pathan women, since it brought a relaxation of *purdah* and unprecedented access to public activity.

A Chief Secretary's Report from 1931 stated that:

> In and around Lund Khwar ... increase in the active participation of women. On 30 April ... 15 women volunteers paraded ... in Lund Khwar it was announced that meetings would be held ... about two or three thousand at meetings ... Speech prepared by Abdul Gaffar Khan read out by a boy and resolutions passed that, if permanent peace was not concluded, the women should join the men in future struggle, that *khaddar* [*khadi* cloth] only should be worn by the women and that the full rights of women under the *shari'a* should be conceded to them by men.[26]

Amazingly, Grana had said to me: 'You will see in the British records that you are reading in England mention of a little boy who once stood up and addressed a meeting. That was my son, Qasim Khan' (I.17). Deputing a little boy to read out the resolutions at a meeting was a standard solution to the problem of women otherwise having to keep *purdah* in front of Badshah Khan or another adult male speaker. Badshah Khan's speech-by-proxy urged women to show solidarity with the nationalist struggle by wearing *khadi* and by assisting their men in the non-violent civil disobedience. His emphasis on *shari'a* law was specifically related to his long-time support for proper women's inheritance rights, which the Quran prescribes but which Pathan tradition neglected. Badshah Khan had also long argued the importance of educating women as part of ensuring a healthy society.

Many of my informants confirmed the substantial presence of women at these meetings. 'Before Badshah Khan came on the scene, there was the custom of *purdah* in our society. But he talked about educating Pathans, even women. When Badshah Khan went to any village to hold a meeting and discuss his ideas, women flocked to meet him and lined the streets to greet him. And the men didn't mind' (I.29). Mohammed Badshah of Mardan recalled that at Badshah Khan's first meeting in Jamalgarhi more women than men attended (I.62). Haji Saifur Khan felt that women were attracted to the movement because they were typically more religious than men and responded to the religious element in Badshah Khan's message. 'Badshah Khan wanted women to join the movement ... . He addressed them as "mothers and sisters" ... women used to stand on rooftops ... *purdah* did not allow them to come out but at least they could hear the speeches ...' (I.31).

The British reports document several protest actions by women:

> A four day tour in this area by a squadron of the Guides Cavalry ... reception sullen ... one village demonstration against the Squadron ... a party of some 50 Red Shirts marched out in fours just as the squadron was leaving and raised revolutionary cries, while women of the village placed heaps of tamarisk branches, *bhusa* [straw for fodder] and cowdung in the road in front of the Squadron and set fire to them.[27]

More traditional techniques were also used. In April 1932 local elections were declared, but Badshah Khan was in prison and the KK decided to oppose the elections

---

[26] Chief Secretary's Report, 1931, L/P&J/12/32 IOLR.
[27] *Ibid.*

in protest: 'Biggest demonstration in Pabbi ... 200 to 300 women appeared on the scene with Qurans on their heads to persuade voters not to record their votes. In Charsadda ... only one vote was recorded.'[28] Traditionally all arbitrators and peace-makers in Pukhtun feud resolutions carried Qurans on their heads (see Edwards 1986) and this symbol of reconciliation and persuasion would have been well understood by the people of Charsadda.

In 1931 officials reported the preparations they were making to police a large KK demonstration that was being held in Peshawar on 23 April to mark the first anniversary of the Kissa Khani massacre. Women were intending to participate but wished to have their own marching routes: 'difficulty in getting all parties to agree ... the women's party insisted on marching in a separate procession to join men's procession [only] in the City ...'.[29] This wish to march separately presumably reflected the wish to retain at least a modicum of *purdah*. Although women's activism undoubtedly increased, it remained somewhat problematic in many districts for women to be seen participating too brazenly in public activities. Wazir Mohammed from Mardan related an incident when Badshah Khan had come to his village to address a meeting. Prior to the speech, the wife of the local *chowkirdar* [rent collector] made a speech and read a poem on stage. He remembered that 'people heckled initially on seeing a woman on a public platform, though the woman remained undaunted and carried on ... and at the end people applauded her' (I.63). Generally, women seemed more than willing to conduct protest activities, but generally wished to continue to maintain some symbolic and spatial separation from the male mass of KKs: 'Lots of women were involved and joined in processions. They came to the processions and stayed in the front where they were guarded by a cordon of linked sticks. Badshah Khan had explained that the women must also be involved and break *purdah*' (I.16).

As always, women also exerted a powerful influence within the home: 'Women certainly played a role in the movement – they egged the men on. They used to procure the red colour to dye the uniforms with and demanded that it be sold cheaply for two *paise*' (I.11). One young bride on her wedding night sent her bridegroom away to picketing and possible arrest, saying she preferred him to carry out his political duties than rest warmly with her in the nuptial bed! (I.30). And when the President of the KK in Bannu, Yakoub Khan, defected from the KK to join the Muslim League, his daughter and sister cried so much at the news that the whole village came to their door to find out the cause of their grief! (I.53).

Badshah Khan recognised these more private influences and felt that, at the very least, women had to be included in the enlarged political consciousness in order to ensure the success of the movement. He felt that some KKs had submitted apologies to the authorities to gain early release from jail because they had been pressured to do so by their wives. Success thus demanded that women be aware of the political climate and the issues involved, since without support and backing from home it would be much harder for men to undertake civil disobedience and cope with its accompanying trauma. But Pathan women had always been key players and instigators in traditional

---

[28] Chief Secretary's Report, 1932, L/P&J/12/43 IOLR.
[29] Chief Commissioner's Report, 1931, L/P&J/12/32 IOLR.

games of honour and they had a reputation for dealing with moments of crisis and responding to them with extraordinary fortitude.[30] In that sense, then, Badshah Khan's call on them to support the struggle being waged by their menfolk was not such a departure.

Badshah Khan became increasingly convinced of the need for women's involvement as the movement progressed, and in the end took the decision to invite them to become fully paid-up Khudai Khidmatgars. Partly this seems to have stemmed from his attending Congress meetings in Delhi, where he noted that women were being consulted in decision making about the nationalist struggle. This led him in 1945 to make the following observation in an article for the journal *Pakhtun*: 'Men and women are two companions necessary for the development of life and they are like the two wheels of the human cart. If one of these wheels is strong and the other weak then the cart cannot move forward smoothly. The cart can move successfully only if the two wheels are similar, identical.' Previously, Badshah Khan had remained conscious of the social taboo against involving women in any public activities – the *mullahs* had already labelled KK *kafirs* because of their non-violence and to have recruited large numbers of women into the actual KK ranks would have provided them with further fuel for propaganda. In his 1945 article, however, he put caution aside and made an unequivocal statement in favour of women's participation: 'We cannot stop people from spreading propaganda against us and that will continue for the next twenty years. There is no point waiting that long, for whenever we allow women to participate in our movement people will always talk.'[31] The vivid imagery of the *Pakhtun* article seems to have stuck in the minds of many men, Haji Abdul Wadood recalling that 'Badshah Khan had explained that no vehicle can move without two wheels. Therefore the women also must be involved and break *purdah*' (I.16). As ever, Badshah Khan led by example with the support of his own family. One of my informants recalled an incident when a demonstration suddenly came under fire from police and people started to panic and run away. Badshah Khan's sister's daughter had marched to the front to face down the bullets, setting an example that stopped the retreat (I.40).

Grana was one of the women who was willing to break *purdah* in order to become a KK. She was 25 years old when Badshah Khan visited Matta for the first time. By then, her brother, Khaista Gul, had died from his injuries in Haripur jail after being shot by a soldier and she said this personal tragedy had motivated her to become a KK: 'I used to lead processions with a flag in my hand; 3,000 to 4,000 people used to follow me. These were very large processions ... . I led several men's demonstrations as well' (I.17). Grana's jobs as a member of the movement did not sound very different from those described by other KKs. She used to campaign for the Congress during elections, sweep villages and spin cloth on a *charkha*. She did not know how to spin at first and was taught by Badshah Khan and Khurshid Behn.

I asked her if she had to face a lot of opposition from menfolk because of her involvement: 'The men did not object – after all, I could do what they could not. I persuaded other women to come along to the meetings.' Grana was able to participate

[30] See Edwards 1986 and 1996.
[31] *Pakhtun*, 17 November 1945.

because she had the support of her family and, above all, Badshah Khan's encouragement. She remembered him saying: 'If there are not enough young people in the movement, then include the women.' Grana did not seem to think that her experience of participation in the nationalist struggle was any different from the experience of the male KKs. The only exception was the fact that she had not been arrested: 'I remember feeling cheated when I used to offer myself for arrest because the jail authorities used to refuse to take me in because I was a woman' (I.17). Nor did she think women were naturally better suited to non-violence, saying that when Badshah Khan had taught non-violence men and women had understood him equally. I persisted and pointed out that Pathan men are known to be hot-headed and prone to passion for *badla* (revenge) to defend their honour: 'Never mind what Pukhtun men are known for.' she said, cutting me short, 'they all listened to Badshah Khan'(I.17).

The number of women like Grana who were fully involved in KK activity was probably rather small and they were mostly older women, their *purdah* being less strict (I.70). But Jarnail Abdul Rahim said that in every village there were at least one or two women who were involved in the movement and named Alif Jaana from Ahmadi Banda, who was also a poetess (I.3). Many other women activists are more dimly remembered, often anonymous but always picturesque. Mukkaram Khan remembered 'a woman Wazira, who always wore red clothes ... had a flag and led processions ...'(I.70).

Non-Violence versus Guerrilla War

The protest activities of the KK may be contrasted with the guerrilla warfare which was the model of resistance prevalent in the Frontier before 1930. The Afghans had won great victories in the three Anglo-Afghan wars on the basis of such tactics, and the fear of guerrilla attacks constantly plagued the British government. In this respect non-violent demonstration had the virtue of a surprise tactic, as the British did not expect it from what they saw as an archetypal warrior race.

Guerrilla warfare is predicated on surprise, ambush and quick retreat, and such tactics demand secrecy, camouflage and nimbleness, with bands melting back into the hinterland. Civil disobedience, in contrast, faces the enemy out in the open in a public confrontation, with deliberate visibility. For civil disobedience, retreat is undesirable since it marks moral defeat – the only honourable way to leave the field is to be carried away. While a guerrilla fighter has to wait patiently for the enemy to approach, the non-violent protest movement moves to the target of its choice and thereby constantly seizes the tactical initiative, an important consideration given the need to sustain the morale of its members over many years.

We can say with some confidence that if the KK movement had employed guerrilla tactics it would not have lasted 17 years. Assessing the fate of insurgencies in the colonial world Michael Adas observes: 'Although small-scale guerrilla warfare was more effective than pitched battles in the short run, its exclusive adoption foreclosed any chance for ultimate victory by the rebels ... [unless they] have faced incumbent regimes unable or unwilling to employ fully all the resources available to suppress dissident groups' (Adas 1979: 169). In the North West Frontier the British were more than willing to deploy effective force and substantial resources to suppress an armed uprising. Rather than attack this formidable force head on, therefore, the Khudai Khidmatgars used their numerical advantage to organise numerous protest actions concurrently throughout the Province, and thereby stretched the resources of the colonial government to the full. In this respect the KK made an attritional contribution to the nationalist struggle which was more like 'the patient ... struggles stubbornly carried on by rural communities ... which accomplish more than insurrectionists who are doomed to defeat and eventual massacre and are mere flashes in the pan' (Marc Bloch, quoted in Scott 1985: 28).

Guerrilla warfare historically arises between unequal parties and by 1930 there had been many instances of such confrontation between traditional societies and colonial powers. As Barnes argues, however, the inequality lay not merely in arms but in status and powers of definition: 'if both sides of a conflict perceive themselves as fighting a war, each grants to its enemy a formal equality of status which legitimises its opposition. In general, colonial powers under attack have strenuously denied this legitimacy to their subject populations' (Barnes 1990: 105). Instead, violent acts by such groups were categorised by colonial states as revolt, rebellion, insurrection, sedition, terrorism, banditry, brigandage, mutiny, piracy, faction fighting or murder – as anything other than legitimate wars of independence. Classified as domestic troubles requiring police action, the acts of violence by the indigenes were thereby denied any political status. Thus, when the Waziris launched a guerrilla campaign against the British in the 1930s they were simultaneously denied the dignity of war's status, being condemned by the authorities as mere insurrectionists and bandits, but given full 'benefit' of modern air raids and bombardment.

In contrast, by adopting non-violence, the KKs avoided becoming hapless victims in this kind of 'one-sided war' and made it that much harder for the British to deny political content to their protest actions. In appealing to the civilised and humane face of their enemy, rather than to its brutal one, the Khudai Khidmatgars made a statement about their own value and that of their cause, and about their right to equality. In this way, the Pathans had managed to set new and unexpected rules for the Great Game.

Conclusion

Though the Pathans are famous for their bravery and powers of endurance, their fortitude during the long years of protest, beatings and jail had to be grounded in something more than purely personal courage. As I have tried to demonstrate in this chapter, individual KKs were braced and strengthened by an elaborate system of training and infrastructure. In some respects the movement's organisation drew on tradition, such as the way in which extended kin groups were used as sources of moral and financial help for those who had been incapacitated during the struggle. More often, however, the organisation brought about significant alterations to traditional Pathan social life – the way in which co-participation in the KKs helped to resolve feuds and to extend social relations beyond the usual limits of lineage and village was perhaps the most notable example. The involvement of women in public political activity was another.

4

The British Riposte

Political Counter-propaganda

In this chapter I wish to consider the nature of the British response to the rise of the Khudai Khidmatgar movement, which embraced both sophisticated counter-propaganda and a surprising and disturbing range of violent and oppressive techniques. These measures often forced the KKs to refine and adapt their own approach, particularly in the ideological sphere, but they also reveal the depth of anxiety within the colonial regime's image of the Pathans.

After the serious disturbances and political events which followed the Kissa Khani bazaar massacre in 1930, the colonial government paused to take stock. Previously the Deputy Commissioner had dismissed the political speeches being made by Badshah Khan and others, saying that 'the general public are unaffected by this flood of oratory' and he was now reproached for not having sensed the trouble brewing.[1] The local administration, too, was accused of a 'considerable degree of supineness' for its failure to take timely counter-measures. In what was described as the spirit of 'better to be wise too late than never to be wise at all', however, new policies and initiatives were now put forward. These were outlined in an official memo as follows:

1. for Govt. to show its strength
2. for Govt. to give a lead and provide a rallying point for the well disposed
3. for vigorous counter-propaganda
4. for timely generosity e.g. over real hardship due to crop failures and such matters as the Kohat loan
5. for getting on with reforms and the experiment of introducing the electoral principle in Municipalities and District Boards.[2]

These recommendations duly received full support from the Chief Commissioner. Proposals 2 and 4 reflected the reports from the Deputy Commissioner's offices around the Province which warned of growing unrest and the likelihood of future instability in the absence of improved provisions for drinking-water, irrigation, sanitation and educational facilities. The Commissioner agreed that welfare in the NWFP had lagged behind other provinces of India and extra budgetary resources began to be disbursed to Education, Medical Relief, Scientific Agriculture, Veterinary

---

[1] September 1929, L/P&J/12/9 IOLR.
[2] E. B. Howell, 'A Secret Note on the Situation in the NWFP', 24 May 1930, F.No. 206/130, Home/Pol, NAI.

Dispensaries and the like. He justified the expenditure by stating that politically 'the investment would prove to be an excellent one'.[3] Such increased expenditure in these areas could be counted as an early success for the KK's protest activities.

Proposal 5, concerning the introduction of local democracy, gained additional weight from the fact that local élites were themselves concerned that uncontrollable agrarian unrest might soon break out. In a collective letter to the Viceroy in June 1930, Muslim *zamindars* (landlords) in the Punjab wrote:

> we consider that one of the main causes underlying the unrest which has been prevalent in the NWFP during recent years is the keen disappointment felt by the people of that province over the manner in which their legitimate political aspirations have been consistently ignored by the Government during the past twenty years and we are of the opinion that no stable and peaceful administration would be possible in that province unless these just and natural aspirations are fully satisfied and the province is accorded its due place in the constitution of the country on an equal footing with the other provinces. We would, therefore, strongly urge that your Excellency may be pleased to press upon the British Government the justice of the claim of the people of that province to be placed upon an equal footing with their fellow citizens of the British Empire.[4]

Again, in another important success for the KK, the authorities met this demand and in 1932 the Province was changed from a Chief Commissioner's province to a Governor's province, which put it on a par with the other provinces of British India. Municipal and district elections were then gradually rolled out.[5]

These were significant successes for the KK campaigns. The government, however, was concentrating most of its effort on Proposals 1 and 3 – 'showing strength' and 'conducting vigorous counter-propaganda'. Counter-propaganda against the KK began immediately after the Kissa Khani bazaar incident. Partly this was simple derision on the part of military and administrative officers. The KKs were repeatedly referred to in terms such as 'the unthinking masses' and as 'criminally degenerate and undisciplined', as reports sought to explain away the growing anti-government feeling in the province.[6] The officials even went to the extent of depicting the Pathans of the districts where the movement was especially active as being 'addicted to sodomy'.[7] Of more interest, however, are the concerns expressed by the government concerning the military symbolism of the KK, in particular their red shirts. Such symbolism reinforced British preconceptions about the 'warlike nature of the Pathans' and the authorities became preoccupied with the question of whether the KK had 'para-military tendencies' and constituted a 'parallel force'. The reports make repeated nervous references to the 'aggressive and militant spirit of the Red Shirt organisation' and 'the large camps in which parades and manoeuvres in military formations' were held, and stressed the need for an 'appreciation of the special features of the Red Shirt organisation'. These concerns extended right to the top of the Raj – discussing the Congress alliance with the KK, the Viceroy warned

[3] *Ibid.*
[4] 4 June 1930, NAI No. 13.
[5] Home./Pol., 141/34 NAI.
[6] Letter from the Honourable Chief Commissioner and Agent to the Governor-General, NWFP, No. 602-P.C. 13 February 1931. File no. 453-F30 NAI.
[7] *Ibid.*

Gandhi's representative Charlie Andrews of the 'dangers of the war mentality of the Pathans'. The Red Shirt movement, he warned, unlike Congress, was unconstitutional and 'inclined to violence right from the start'.[8]

In a meeting with Badshah Khan, the Governor said that he failed to see any connection between drilling exercises and social reform, and that it seemed the KKs were making preparations for a fight. Badshah Khan denied this and pointed out that if the nationalist demands were met there would be no need for his movement or for further agitation. The Governor continued his initial line, however, saying that if the Pathans wanted a fight then they could certainly have one and he warned that the KKs should disabuse themselves of the notion that inaction on the part of the government was due to fear. As this aggressive position suggests, the administration remained constantly sceptical of the movement's non-violent credentials and contrasted it with the genuine peaceableness of Congress. There was no little irony in this, given that only a few years earlier Congress had changed the name of its own mass activist wing from 'Seva Dal' (where *Seva* means service and hence is equivalent to the Pukhtun *khidmat*) to the more militant-sounding 'Sena Dal' (with *Sena* meaning 'army'). This shift of emphasis from service to militancy seems not to have affected the regime's view of Congress, however, and the British remained obsessed with the intentions of the Pathans. As I explore in Chapter 7, despite all the evidence to the contrary, the British constantly tried to infect the Congress leaders with similar doubts about the extent of the KK's non-violence, and not without success.

I discussed in Chapter 3 the emotive imagery of red in the military and political history of British India. In the 1930s, however, these images had been overlaid in the British mind by icons and associations emanating from contemporary Europe, particularly those of Fascism and Bolshevism. The Frontier government argued (incorrectly) that the KKs were the *only* force of volunteers in India who served without payment, and this feature, combined with the fact that arms were 'readily available' in the Frontier, made them an especially dangerous *'quasi-fascist* movement'.[9] By the mid-1930s a number of political organisations in India had come to be associated with uniforms. In an article in the *Civil and Military Gazette* of 1936, Professor Gulshan Rai noted this emerging 'cult of the Shirt' and asked 'Do we want Fascism in India?' Rai drew attention to the sudden emergence of a number of new organisations in India, all of which were voluntary forces, wore uniforms and espoused military-style discipline.[10] The organisations he mentions are the Mahabir Dals or Lal Pagris (Red Turbans) and the Arya Bir Dals among the Hindus, the Akali Jathas among the Sikhs, the Khudai Khidmatgars in the Frontier Province and the Black Shirts and Blue Shirts among the Muslims in the Punjab. Organisations of this type were not confined to any one region or religion, and most (but not the KK) were initiated during the nation-wide campaign of non-cooperation in 1921–2. In the professor's opinion, it was the 'hooligans and young men' in these volunteer forces who had caused tragedies such as the Chauri Chaura violence. The author noted that each movement had displayed highly organised

[8] Serial No. 19 Telegram from Norwef, Peshawar File No. 116-S, 11 April 1934, NAI.
[9] Serial No. 19. Telegram R. from Norwef, Peshawar File No. 116-S dated (and received) 11 April 1934, NAI.
[10] *Civil and Military Gazette*, Sunday 5 July 1936, in Home/Pol. 24/11/36 NAI.

behaviour in securing its objectives: demonstrating, capturing Gurdwaras or main-taining order at public meetings. Such precision he claimed to find chillingly similar to the methods of the Nazi storm troopers or the Fascist forces of Mussolini. He concluded his article with a call for all such organisations to be suppressed and denied participation in elections so as to prevent them interfering with 'ignorant illiterate voters ... exercising their discretion freely'. In similar vein, in 1937 the Governor told Dr Khan Sahib, the Congress Chief Minister of the Province and older brother of Badshah Khan, that 'the wearing of uniforms is one of the most dangerous aspects of modern society and urged him to get the KK to give up the practice'.[11] The marginal note scribbled by the reader in Whitehall asks worriedly: 'Is this a parallel force?'

Along with these accusations of a fascistic tendency in the KK, there were even more frequent claims that the KK represented a kind of Bolshevism. In 1930 the Viceroy wrote to the Secretary of State for India: 'Although it may be true that the Red Shirt movement was not inspired by the Bolsheviks, there was a good deal of Communistic doctrine ... connected with it.'[12] Such comments were guaranteed, and probably intended, to set alarm bells ringing in the Russophobic Whitehall estab-lishment. As with the issue of non-violence, the question of social philosophy was used to try to split the KK–Congress alliance by portraying the KK as radical leftists to the broadly liberal Congress leaders. The Viceroy continued: 'A further point to be noted in support of drawing a distinction between the Congress and the Red Shirts is the fact that the latter have conducted the campaign not merely anti-British or anti-Government, but also anti-capitalist and have endeavoured to annihilate the *khan* and landlord interests.'[13]

Attributing to the KKs the aim of annihilating the landlord classes was a gross exaggeration, to say the least. First, Badshah Khan had spent a good deal of time and effort seeking to elevate and redirect the peasantry's grievances, away from their landlords and towards the British. As Haji Abdul Wadood stated when recalling KK demonstrations: 'The slogans used to be Allah-o-Akbar, We never condemned any *khan* in our slogans. It was against the principles of non-violence. We were not against anyone but the British' (I.16). Second, Dr Khan Sahib imprisoned his own son Obeidullah for participating in a peasant uprising against their landlord, blaming it on mental disturbance caused by an earlier hunger strike. Third, Badshah Khan had intervened personally to win over as many small *khans* as possible into the movement (see Chapter 5 below). In fact, it was precisely this small *khan* involvement that was one of the main targets of the 'Bolshevik' accusation, since the British were desperately keen to discourage their participation in the nationalist movement. Overall, therefore, while there were some tensions within the KK over the degree to which they should support peasant interests (see Chapter 7 below), they could not in any meaningful sense be deemed a leftist movement, and were certainly not Bolsheviks. If anything, the KKs had more in common with the peasant Tolstoyans

---

[11] Chief Secretary's Report, September 1937, L/P&J/5/211 IOLR.
[12] Extract from a private letter, 16 August 1930, from H.E. the Viceroy to the Secretary of State for India. Halifax Collection, Mss. EUR., C.152, IOLR. We know that the Naujawan Bharat Sabha, with which the young Gaffar Khan had been involved, had a socialist agenda.
[13] *Ibid.*

who had clashed with the Bolsheviks in the Soviet Union after the revolution. Gandhi had been influenced profoundly by Tolstoy, and the peasant Tolstoyans had stood for ideas of non-violence, non-cooperation and the dignity of manual labour (see Edgerton 1993). And, as KK leaders often pointed out, it was curious to accuse a movement called the 'Servants of God' of following an atheistic doctrine such as Bolshevism.

Dr Khan Sahib strenuously objected to the British refusal to use the movement's proper name of Khudai Khidmatgar, their constant harping on the label 'Red Shirt', which they themselves had coined, and their insinuations about the movement's so-called Bolshevik aims. Cambridge-educated, he knew enough of European politics to understand the implications of such propaganda and he repeatedly tried to remove the misapprehension that the KK organisation had anything to do with 'red' politics in its European sense. To this end he stressed that the KK wore coats of dark red merely because the ingredients of the dye were cheap and easily available, and he attributed the accusations of Bolshevism to the delirium of British propaganda.[14] In a speech delivered to an audience of Indian Muslims at Lyall Library, Aligarh, Badshah Khan himself argued:

> The name given to us by the English newspapers is meant for the purposes of propaganda. They want to frighten you Indians with the idea that we are Bolsheviks. You also know that they want to frighten the British because the English race is very much afraid of red. ... You might have actually seen red signals on the crossings. Red signifies danger to Englishmen. The railway train stops immediately when it notices a red flag. ... So this is all propaganda. It is with the help of propaganda that a handful of Englishmen are ruling over us. ... Another thing which I want to tell you is that our Red Shirt movement is not like that of Hitler or Mussolini.[15]

And nor was it like the Bolsheviks: 'The uniform of the Bolsheviks is not red. It is [only] the colour of their flag which is red.'[16]

But the KK's explanations and disavowals of class war were ignored by the authorities and it seems clear from the records that this was done deliberately. In calling the KK 'Bolsheviks' the British were not innocent dupes of political semiotics but were intentionally spreading counter-propaganda. In a letter to the Secretary of State for India, the Viceroy admitted that the name 'Red Shirts' was introduced purposely by the NWFP administration as a popular substitute for the name 'Khudai-Khidmatgaran', which 'would have implied some kind of admission that we are dealing with an association of the pious and godly'.[17] The Viceroy concluded that the 'red shirt' label and its associations with Fascism and Bolshevism had 'supported its practical purpose pretty successfully' by helping discredit the ethical basis of the movement and forcing its leaders on to the defensive.

Ironically, however, the Secretary for State was not altogether pleased with this stroke of cunning. He had queried the term 'red shirts' as inaccurate as 'the shirts are

[14] Dr Khan Sahib on Red Shirts in *Tribune*, 5 August 1935, Home/Pol. 22/19 1936 NAI.
[15] 27 November 1934, from Ramu 1992: 228.
[16] 15 December 1931, Torlandi P.S. Kalu Khan, from Ramu 1992: 145.
[17] Extract from a private letter, 16 August 1930, from H.E. the Viceroy to the Secretary of State for India. Halifax Collection, Mss. EUR., C.152, IOLR.

actually a chocolate colour and a young Pathan informed me that they were that colour because the local dye-works happened to produce it'.[18] In his letter – significantly entitled 'Courtesy and civil disobedience' – he objected that 'The term has provoked a great deal of suspicion among our critics that Bolshevik agencies are at work. So far as I can judge from the latest telegrams the organisation of the red shirts has little or nothing to do with the Bolsheviks and we should have saved ourselves some trouble if we had never employed the word.' Clearly the two officials had different audiences in mind. The Viceroy needed 'Red Shirts' as a pejorative shorthand with which to denounce the movement. The Secretary of State, in contrast, was wary of raising a 'red scare' among anti-Bolshevik hawks in Whitehall; hence he recommended the exercise of 'extreme restraint' in dealing with civil disobedience so as not to cause a stir. Such restraint was not forthcoming, however.

These tensions emerged again in July 1940 when under the Defence of India Rules a ban on uniforms and prohibition on drilling was announced.[19] The Governor of the Punjab reported from Lahore that the Congress volunteer organisation there had promptly and openly defied this ban.[20] The Governor of the Frontier reported that there had as yet been 'no violent reaction to ban on drilling and wearing of uniforms' but he feared it might only be a matter of time.[21] It was 'not safe to say that Red Shirts will not attempt to challenge the ban ... but I impressed on Dr Khan Sahib the unwisdom of doing so'.[22] After this build-up of tension, it came as something of an anti-climax when the Viceroy's office in Delhi wired through that the Red Shirts were not in fact affected by the ban. Whitehall registered its surprise in the margin of the news report: 'It seems surprising that the Red Shirts do not come under the ban on uniforms.' The Frontier Administration then gave a rather peevish response justifying the Viceroy's decision: 'The Red Shirt uniform is generally regarded as not being affected by the ban on uniforms, and I must admit I should be sorry if any Government formation were thought to present anything like the appearance of a body of Red Shirts with their deplorable garments and generally slip shod air.'[23] Again, these more relaxed kinds of comments in high-level private correspondence suggest that there was in reality rather less real concern about either the paramilitary or Bolshevik nature of the KK than the statements of public counter-propaganda made out.

By its use of pejorative counter-labels for organisations like the KK, the administration sought to dismiss their political agenda and to treat their activities as simply criminal, thereby avoiding having to 'dignify their riot' by calling it anything as grand 'as waging war against the King' (Piggott 1930: 296 in Amin 1995: 111). By the 1930s this was a familiar ploy on the part of judges and administrators, who, in Amin's words, used 'extraneous criteria of the political/criminal buttressed by the rule of colonial difference' to obscure the true nature and aims of such protest movements (Amin 1995: 111–12). In the case of the Frontier such counter-labels also

---

[18] Extract from letter from Secretary of State, S/S Q -25/7/30 NAI.
[19] Volunteer movement in India, copy of despatch by Reuters, Simla, 5 August 1940, L/PJ/8/678.
[20] Sir Dawson's letter to Mr Walton, 22 August 1940, NAI.
[21] Governor's Report, July 1940, L/P&J/5/216 IOLR.
[22] Governor's Report, August 1940, L/P&J/5/216 IOLR.
[23] Governor's Report, September 1940, L/P&J/5/216 IOLR.

served to reinforce the stereotype of the Pathans as violent and martial. As we saw in Chapter 3, the KK attempted to revise traditional beliefs about honour and feud in favour of unity and non-violent civil disobedience. By evoking images of paramilitaries the administration thus attempted to occlude the new impression the Pathans were striving to make on the world. More crudely, the more aggressive the native population was depicted to be, the more armed resources the province could attract and the more repressive the punishments that could be justified. It is therefore not a surprise that so many reports blatantly ignored the actual ideology of the KKs.

Ultimately the emphasis put on the shirts by the government was probably somewhat self-defeating. On the launch of the KK movement at the end of 1929 the shirts had been of little significance, tending to be merely ordinary clothes dipped in the brown or chocolate colour which was most readily available. After the insistent official emphasis on the red shirts, however, the KK began to take increasing care with their shirts, making them more consistently red. As we saw in the previous chapter, the shirts, and the colour more generally, became a great source of pride to the KKs and made a valuable contribution to the movement's ongoing morale and *esprit de corps*.

Religious Counter-propaganda

From the regime's perspective, one of the most worrying features of the KK's emergence was its convergence with the Hindu-dominated Congress, and the government thus continually strove to disrupt the alliance. As we have seen, one way it did this was by constantly alleging that the KKs were violent and paramilitary, and hence not compatible with the Congress philosophy. Another method, however, was to cultivate religious tensions between the two sides. In this respect the British were fishing in promising waters, since from the very beginning Badshah Khan and the KK had been in conflict with some Islamic leaders in the Frontier. Some were traditionalists who disliked his social and educational radicalism, and in this respect they acted as Gramsci's 'traditional intellectuals', furthering colonial hegemony through creating a false consensus by preaching the virtues of ignorance, passivity and obedience: 'The *mullahs* used to tell us that there was no point in hitting our heads against the mountain. That is, there is no use in opposing the British' (I.34).

In contrast, Badshah Khan and other 'organic intellectuals' questioned the status quo by emphasising the possibility of self-improvement and giving liberationist interpretations of Islam, thereby seriously threatening the authority of the clergy. Moreover, it was common knowledge that some *mullahs*, particularly in the tribal areas, received a stipend from the government and in return delivered anti-nationalist propaganda (see Chapter 7 below).[24] A retired civil servant who served in the Frontier records in his memoirs that the Governor 'had sources of information not directly available to us through his underground network of pro-British *mullahs* scattered throughout remote parts of the whole Frontier' (Noble 1997: 195).

[24] See Shah 1999: 161, Mss. EUR., D.670/16 IOLR.

On the other hand, however, there were many *ulema* and *mullahs* who did vigorously oppose British rule. Their favoured mode of opposition, however, was the classical violent *jihad* against the infidel, and they thus criticised the KK for the timidity of their non-violent approach. Though Badshah Khan's ideas about non-violence had developed largely independently of Gandhi, for the militant *mullahs* non-violence was incompatible with their reading of Islam and with *jihad*: it represented the softer, weaker philosophy of Hinduism. This view was shared by the British as well, since the Governor, reporting on Badshah Khan's return to the Frontier after a visit to Delhi in August 1937, noted that the tone of his speeches was 'comparatively moderate' and wondered whether this was the result of the 'influence of down-country Hindu contacts'.[25]

So, while there were prominent religious leaders who supported the KK and became active in it,[26] there were many others who subjected the movement to fierce criticism on religious grounds, and throughout the life of the movement the KKs were labelled *kafirs* – that is, infidels and unbelievers.[27] As Mukarram Khan remembered, 'people used to say that Badshah Khan was a friend of Gandhi and was therefore Hindu' (I.70). My informants recalled that Badshah Khan's personal faith was frequently challenged in this way: 'Badshah Khan was once asked by a man why he did not slaughter cows (because you know that Hindus don't) and he replied, "I am not a butcher, that's why." However, the man persisted in asking him the same question and after the third time Badshah Khan said: "Why don't you bring me one of the bulls from the pair that pull *your* plough and I will certainly slaughter him!" That silenced the man!' (I.24).

Haji Meherban Shah felt that people were encouraged to come up with these sorts of questions because of the propaganda against Badshah Khan: 'He had changed Pathan people, you see. Earlier people used to stay and interact within the confines of their tribes but Badshah Khan changed all that. The British and the *mullahs* opposed this and started a lot of propaganda against him. They used to say that he was a Hindu, a Sikh and that *halal* [meat] from his hands was not valid. He finally decided one day to take off his turban to prove that he was not a Sikh [by revealing his short hair] and never covered his head again' (I.36). That he was compelled to deny that he was a Sikh partially reflected his close association with prominent Sikh leaders like Baba Kharak Singh during the Akali struggle in the 1920s (see Chapter 2 above). Since even the poorest Pathans wore a head covering, for a *khan* like Badshah Khan to have an uncovered head also inadvertently contributed to his enduring image as a *faqir*, an ascetic world renouncer.

My informants all remembered being harassed themselves in the street, not least by children, who called them Hindus and *kafirs*. It will be recalled from the story in Chapter 3 how merely carrying a *charkha* spinning wheel left activists open to ridicule as 'Hindus'. The authorities actively contributed to this climate of opinion by

---

[25] Governor's Report, August 1937, L/P&J/5/211 IOLR.
[26] Maulana Hamdullah Jan mentioned Maulana Aziz ul Haq in Tangi, Hazrat Maulana Fazle Mahmud Maqwi and Abdul Aziz of Utmanzai, and he told me that they had supported Badshah Khan by discussing and spreading his ideas at graveyards, mosques, public meetings, and wherever people would gather (I.12).
[27] Thus in November 1940 it was reported that a *mullah* had addressed a congregation in a mosque in Badshah Khan's village in which he stated that Abdul Gaffar Khan himself and all others who preached non-violence were *kafirs*.

parading arrested KKs in special saffron prison clothes in order to publicise their 'Hindu' identity (I.66). Badshah Khan urged his supporters not to be drawn into such discussions: 'Badshah Khan used to say, "Don't argue, it only leads to violence ... argue only with an *alim*"' (I.24) – a learned man of Islam, that is, and by implication not with *mullahs* who were usually less well versed in scripture. He also constantly re-emphasised the importance of maintaining good relations with Hindus: 'Badshah Khan used to explain by saying that after independence we will have to live with them [Hindus] and they are three times the population of Muslims so we should make friends with them' (I.70).

This was precisely the spirit of cross-faith unity and reconciliation which so concerned the British. They asked numerous senior Muslim leaders from the rest of the country to talk to Badshah Khan to prevail upon him to exit the alliance.[28] The editor of the journal *Zamindar* in Lahore referred to 'the blunder that has been committed by the worshipper of Hindus, Abdul Gaffar Khan, by subjecting the Khudai Khidmatgars to the control of the Congress and by this blunder he has destroyed the future of the Muslims and the Afghans'.[29] From the mid-1930s onwards the British would expend increasing time and money supporting the emergence of the Muslim League in order to weaken the KK–Congress axis and the ferocity and bitterness of such religious criticisms were to increase still further (see Chapter 7 below). As with the case of the 'Red Shirts' label, however, the KK often appropriated or ironically subverted such criticisms. Fazle Karim recalled with amusement that, after its conspicuous success in getting its people arrested in the campaigns of 1930–1, his home village of Pabbi was nicknamed 'Wardha' by the KK, in honour of Gandhi's *ashram* (I.10).

Torture and Repression

It will be recalled that Proposal 1 in the post-Kissa Khani memorandum was 'for government to show its strength' and this was done with a vengeance. Initially the authorities sought to arrest all those participating in demonstrations and picketing activities and by December 1932 British reports estimated that over 12,000 people had been imprisoned since April 1930. Haripur jail was specially constructed to hold participants in the civil disobedience movement and at times it alone held as many as 7,000 Red Shirts in severely cramped conditions. The severity of sentencing for innocuous crimes can be judged from the following case: On 3 December 1932 when the Governor of the Province came to Mouza Gardai to take tea, Abdul Ali and three KKs handed over a copy of their grievances and oppressions. For that they were arrested and they were sentenced to three years imprisonment and a Rs 250 fine.

The English Congress activitist Verrier Elwin collected many eye-witness accounts[30] of batches of Red Shirt volunteers, stripped of turban, shirt and shoes, clad only in pyjamas, being marched through Peshawar by the military, the 'noble

[28] Home/Pol. 33/8/31 1931 Part I NAI.
[29] Governor's Report, L/P&J/12/32 IOLR.
[30] 'What is happening in the North West Frontier'? Report by Father Verrier Elwin, 1932. F. No. 11 AICC Papers NMML.

Pathans bearing it in the true spirit of non-violence'. In one typical incident, Red Shirts from the Peshawar area who were arrested for picketing foreign cloth shops and sentenced to six months complained it was too little! Another of my informants recalled that 'Filling jails was our joy!'

Dr Waris recalled the living conditions of the jails:

The jails were overcrowded ... there was not enough space ... so the British had to pitch tents to keep us. I was once arrested in May, it was summer, and we were in tents out in the heat. Nobody could lie down, there was no space ... it was terrible. They used to link our fetters so that if one person wanted to turn over then the entire lot of us had to ... a stick was placed between our knees ... . We had to grind 40 *seer* of corn and oilseeds ... we were made to wear saffron clothes because we were labelled 'Hindus' ... some men were even castrated. All this was done so that we would ask for mercy and pardon ... there were so many lice and all kinds of bugs ... men were stripped of their trousers so they could not go back home after being released ... . Some people went on hunger strike ... I also did for 14 days ... that created quite a stir and the amount of oilseed was reduced and we were given some bread to eat. You see, ordinary Khudai Khidmatgaran were ordinary 'C' class prisoners [i.e. not counted as political prisoners] and we were treated worse than animals. (I.66)

Mir Rahman Jarnail said: 'I spent a year in the Haripur jail in 1930. My friend, Abdul Kalus Khan, was also there with me. The police were very tough. They searched us five times during the night. We had to sleep on the floor with only two torn blankets in the bitter cold' (I.11).

Extended time in prison became a mark of distinction and achievement for the KK activists. 'We learnt so much in jail. We used to go in illiterate but came out of them educated' (I.50). Most honoured of all were those who continued their protest activities within the prison:

We used to be weighed on being arrested and were given grain equal to our weight to grind. There was an incident when all of us in the jail decided that the grinding we were expected to do was far too much and that we had to find a way out of it if we wanted to survive our sentence. We all decided that we would simply refuse to grind more than two *seer* of grain in a day. We told the jailer that we gladly accept wearing shackles on our feet and the rest of it but we would not grind any more than we had decided to ... . We defied all his threats. Finally, Smutt, the jailer realised after ten days that it was futile to threaten us with anything and left us alone. (I.29)

To disrupt KK solidarity and morale and subvert their glorification of being arrested and imprisoned, the prison authorities would constantly tempt inmates to give in by offering them the opportunity of paying a fine, apologising for their behaviour and recanting their KK membership in return for immediate release. Given the appalling conditions, in which deaths from illness and brutality were common, it required great strength of character to decline such opportunities.

The British used to goad us to give bail. When they asked my father to do the same, he said, 'Why should I give bail in my own country? You are the ones who should give bail. After all, you are the ones who have robbed our country and are now about to run away.' The police and the army used to beat us and torture us in order to get us to curse Badshah Khan but we wouldn't. We used to feel that we might die, anything might happen to us ... but it did not matter as long as our country became free. (I.45)

Fazle Karim said: 'I was arrested again on 25 December 1931 and this time I contracted TB in jail. The jailer summoned my mother's brother and asked him to produce Rs300 as bail to have me released. But he refused, as that was my wish also, and I was released only in the following April' (I.10).

Inevitably, however, not everyone was able to endure: 'One or two per cent of the people asked for pardon. But these were people who did not know the implications of asking for pardon and how it was used by the British to weaken us and our organisation' (I.20). One man sadly recalled his own failure:

> People chose me to be their Captain … . I had to go to jail for six months myself … this was in Bannu jail. I left the movement when I was in jail … because I was disheartened. I felt that the *shari'a* law could never be enforced … that the British will never give us what we want. When I returned to the village, people scorned me and treated me badly … I was very ashamed of myself. But then, only I lost the game … the movement did not. (I.57)

As may be seen from this testimony, men who did break down received a harsh reception upon their return home. Even sixty years later Secretary Wahidullah remained unforgiving, saying that 'people who asked for pardon were stooges of British loyalists' (I.26). Haji Sarfaraz Nazim Sahib denied that social boycott was a Khudai Khidmatgar method, stating that 'When people asked for pardon it was attributed to their weakness, moral or economic. All fingers of the same hand are not the same, some people are weak' (I.1). While this may have been the leadership's approved response, however, in reality the shame associated with early release from prison led to numerous individual tragedies. 'Shah Nawaz from Utmanzai asked for pardon and was terribly ostracised socially and he was driven to suicide. There was another case from Badragi who had a similar fate' (I.10). 'If anyone asked for pardon, the others taunted him so much … . I know of three men who were driven to suicide …' (I.66). 'It was very difficult for any one to do that [ask for pardon] and then hope to return and live normally in his own village. Khan Mohammed, one man who did ask for pardon, had to kill himself in shame' (I.8). 'One *khan* from Charsadda who asked for pardon committed suicide in the end because of shame' (I.26). As far as I am aware, such events as these did not occur within the nationalist movement in the rest of India, and such stories emphasise again the power exerted on the Pathans by the notion of personal honour.

The vast majority of men came through their prison experience with their honour enhanced, however, and their experiences were passed on to other KK members, so that the movement as a whole became increasingly 'battle hardened'. Discussing a training camp for KK leaders held outside in Peshawar in 1940, a district officer's report wryly noted that: 'In addition to physical training and instruction in every kind of self-help, members were taught how to behave in jail. They ought to find a good staff of fully qualified teachers for this!'[31]

As the authorities recognised, the demonstrable sacrifices made by the KK through imprisonment gave the movement immense prestige and popular political legitimacy. A memorandum from 1940 noted the difficulty this posed for the authorities' efforts to undermine the KK:

[31] L/P&J/5/216/10LR.

The leaders [of KK 'disturbances'] must of course be dealt with, even though their imprisonment may in the end raise the political stock; jail is looked upon by many as a sure step to attaining office. It is, I am afraid, useless to hope that the Muslim League would make any advance once civil disobedience is launched. They could provide nothing to counter-act the propaganda eulogising the self-sacrifice shown by the Red Shirts leaders who had gone to jail for the sake of independence.[32]

Imprisonment was only one part of the government response to the rise of the movement and numerous other techniques were developed to deter and intimidate. When the prisons became full the police tried to disperse the demonstrators rather than arresting them. Elwin described what happened:

The authorities soon found it impossible to accommodate all those who offered themselves for arrest. They decided therefore to take a hint from the London Metropolitan police and to order picketeers to 'move on', beating them if they refused ... but this 'moving on' is nothing like the genial and almost friendly orders of a London policeman. The beating is very severe. The *lathi* blows fall like a heavy shower of rain. A policeman told me: 'Not even a donkey could bear it' ... . It is common practice for the police, after knocking a man down, to throw him into the icy water of a pond or river.[33]

Elwin made a distinction between the regular police, on one hand, and the police irregulars and military, on the other:

Regular police hate to use *lathis* and as friends of the people resent the policy of repression ... . But it is a very different story when we come to the additional police and military. The Additional Police are not Police at all, they are not even soldiers. They use military reservists, undisciplined, untrained, accustomed to loot and plunder. The bulk of the 'excesses' are due to them. The rest of the excesses are due to the military who urge the police on to more violent measures and themselves use the butt-ends of their rifles with deadly effect.[34]

In some cases, whether through malice, panic or indiscipline, the authorities opened fire with rifles, the worst incident subsequent to the Kissa Khani Bazaar being at Kohat in 1932, when, following the arrest of Badshah Khan, detachments opened fire, killing some three hundred Red Shirts and injuring a thousand more.

Another measure adopted when the prisons were full was forced labour, with those arrested made to work on public roads, military establishments, delapidated mosques and the like. Meagrely fed and sleeping out on-site, they were sent away at the end without any payment. Refusal to work led to further beatings with *lathis*, and, in the case of the mosques, to additional abuse as 'servants of Satan' for refusing to repair the abode of God. In 1940 a memorandum suggested that 'It might be wise in the event of an emergency to consider putting political prisoners into concentration camps instead of jails to avoid the privileges of the classification scheme and to enable labour to be undertaken by the detainees.'[35] Political prisoners were exempt from forced labour. This so irritated these officials that, a year into the war with Nazi Germany, they sought to establish concentration camps of their own to get round this restriction.

[32] L/P&J/5/216 IOLR.
[33] 'What is happening in the North West Frontier?'
[34] *Ibid.*
[35] L/P&J/5/216 IOLR.

The measures taken by the authorities were far from being confined to the actual scenes of demonstrations. Direct and covert measures were taken against the KK training camps. There were several incidents where the supplies to the camps of tea, milk and other goods were deliberately poisoned or adulterated. 'Our opponents were constantly on the lookout to poison food at camps so as to debilitate our force' (I.5). Haji Abdul Wadood recalled a particularly notorious incident. 'Someone was paid by the British to poison a camp that was set up in Peshawar to enforce picketing of liquor shops by poisoning the milk that the *gujjars* used to supply' (I.16). The result was mass vomiting and diarrhoea, with some older Red Shirts even dying.

> Dr Khan Sahib used to have a clinic in Kissa Khani bazaar those days and when he heard about the poisoning he sent his compounder with medicines and joked that perhaps the people from Doaba had overeaten. When the medicines did not work, however, he went to have a look himself and then discovered the source of the poison. He exclaimed 'Scoundrels, they have killed these people!' He returned again with a third set of medicines and prescribed a red coloured tablet for the diarrhoea and a white one for the vomiting. The people experienced a sense of great relief and went to sleep. (I.16)

Haji Mohammed Hussain Khan also recalled 'the terrible incident of the food being poisoned. Dr Khan Sahib, Dr Ghosh, Behari Lal and several others came personally to treat the sick. It was terrible that it should have happened' (I.15). On another occasion the army simply physically removed all the people from a camp in lorries, drove them out into the middle of nowhere and dropped them off, leaving the tired villagers to trek the many miles back home (I.27). Another technique was to stop the supply of water to camps by closing the relevant irrigation outlets (I.24).

The villages of the Settled Districts which provided the Red Shirts with activists and supplies were also targeted for punishment. A report from 1932 stated that some 92 villages had been fined nearly 20,000 rupees.[36] Such fines weighed very heavily on people who were far from prosperous. In addition the collection of fines was accompanied by a good deal of aggression and intimidation. 'The soldiers collected money as if they were Moghuls .... They took Rs180 from each villager and said, "If you have not got it, send your wives to earn it."' This was an obviously provocative insult to Pathan men, demeaning their jealously guarded women as prostitutes. A similar linkage of money and female sexuality is visible in the threats made by military officers to carry out the wholesale rape of the womenfolk of a village for failure to pay the Punitive Police Tax.[37]

Still more grievous, however, were the measures of systematic intimidation and violence that were carried out: 'Attempts were made to strike at the movement by dealing with village centres which had made themselves conspicuous for organising meetings and processsions; such villages were rounded up by troops after which the police entered the village, effected the arrest of the agitators, and in some cases collected firearms and burnt homes.'[38] Under special ordinances the officials had the widest powers to search wherever and whenever they wished and to arrest and

---

[36] *The Tribune*, 8 February 1932, NAI.
[37] Girdhari Kripalani's report, File No. P-16/1932, AICC Papers NMML.
[38] Chief Secretary's Report, L/P&J/12/9 IOLR.

detain people on suspicion. The penalty for disobeying any official instruction was two years' imprisonment, or a fine, or both.

> In the case of a raid upon one village the majority of the male members being absent, the women are severely beaten and their upper garments torn off their bodies. The person giving this report would say no more. It was evident that he did not wish to mention the worst that happened to these women left entirely at the mercy of the tommies. Two women had their legs broken by a *lathi* charge ... report from doctor. It appears that the Government are bent upon harassing the people in every way. When they do not find anything worth looting in any particular house they break the earthen pots, the only property of the poorest and mix together the flour, rice, dal, salt, chillies etc. with dust to make it unfit for their use. ... The old mother of a Captain, Burham Khan, was beaten until unconscious by a posse of 30 constables because she pleaded ignorance about her son's whereabouts. Then they ransacked the house.[39]

Elwin reported that these measures of repression had temporarily driven the activists underground. Owing to the police confiscation and burning of uniforms and red shirts, smaller and more discrete red badges were used as well. He also described frequent night searches, which meant that 'sleep can never be secure'. Sleep deprivation is of course an always reliable method of weakening the will to resist. Girdhari Kripalani's report confirmed that the use of the special ordinances had caused a sharp fall in picketing. Sayid Karamat Shah recalled that: 'Troops used to surround our village and keep us captive and immobile ... once this went on for 22 days. But we used to make all kinds of excuses to get out of the village and hold meetings in spite of the ban' (I.42). Villagers started holding KK meetings at night to hoodwink the police.

The worst outrages, however, were reserved for the KK activists themselves, and these were reported in the Congress reports filed from the Province to the All India Congress in Delhi. A report from the Swabi *tehsil* (sub-district) said that, apart from being fined and having their cattle confiscated, KKs had been beaten severely and made to lie in the burning sun with a heavy stone on their chests. Such beatings left some men senseless for days. A weekly Congress report from Mardan on 28 June 1932 recorded: 'Eight volunteers made to sit on burning sand from 10 a.m. to 5 p.m. and thereafter given a cold bath ... . President beaten and given cold bath ... indiscriminate beatings at a wedding ... volunteers made to stand for hours holding their ears ... made to carry water and bricks from long distances in scorching heat ... sixty flogged for shouting "Inquilab Zindabad" (Long Live Revolution).'[40] Arrested KKs were often ordered to abuse their leaders and were beaten for refusing to do so.

In 1931 Devdas Gandhi reported further abuses:

> In Charsadda for instance the madness of Goverment methods was to be compared only to the heroism of the people. ... Fanciful punishments were awarded, one of them being that persons suspected of being connected with the KK movement were compelled to carry heavy loads of stone and run up and down a hill until they fell exhausted [a common punishment within the British Army]. This went on for days. A pile of stones thus erected still stands and a Military officer is reported to have sneeringly remarked that that was the tomb of 'Allaho Akbar' and Abdul Gaffar Khan. Elsewhere the police compelled the Red Shirts to beat one another and tried to make them the laughing stock of the village.[41]

[39] Congress weekly report from Mardan, 28 June 1932, AICC Papers, NMML.
[40] *Ibid.*
[41] Devdas Ghandi, 'Report on the NWFP 1931', File No. P. 16 (1932) AICC Papers, NMML.

Another particular focus of the regime's effort was to shame the KK in religious terms. As we saw in Chapter 3, upon their induction into the movement, the Red Shirt volunteers had to take an oath sworn on the Quran. When caught by the colonial officers, they were frequently told to swear a counter-oath on the Quran that they would now be loyal to His Majesty and dissociate themselves from Badshah Khan and the KKs. Sadar Musa Khan recalled such demands: 'In 1931 I went to jail for a year and a half, in Haripur jail. In the meanwhile the British burnt houses and *hujras* .... . When we returned the *khans* who were British loyalists suggested to the British officials that Khudai Khidmatgaran be asked to take an oath by the Quran that they will not revert to being Khudai Khidmatgaran. Those who did not take this oath were fined' (I.23).

In 1933 G. A. Cole, the Assistant Commissioner of Saddar district near Peshawar, filed a report describing the actions he took following signs of KK activism in his area (the painting red of milestones described in Chapter 3). He went to the nearby village, called all of its Red Shirt workers together, and asked them to undertake such oaths of loyalty to the crown. He reported that 'the final result of these proceedings has been that of 5,872 known Red Shirts of Sadder subdivision, 4,704 have abjured the Red Shirt and Congress movement and sworn loyalty henceforth to H.M. the King. Some more will take this oath so I estimate that of what is left only 200 are Red Shirts at heart'.[42] What Cole neglects to describe, however, are the methods used to gain such results. There were frequent reports of torture and intimidation designed specifically to extract a counter-Quaranic oath and Elwin gathered evidence of these:

> There is a horrid story of how some hundred and twenty men are kept in an open place near Kohat for the whole of a freezing winter night. They were given no food, and most of their clothes were taken from them. In the morning they were asked to apologise, and on refusing they were beaten. Their bodies were numb with cold and the bitter morning wind was blowing down from the hills – it was too much and they apologised. But when you read in the papers of so many apologies from among the Red Shirts, remember that they have sworn on the Kuran not to do so, and only something that is very like torture can extract an apology from them .... . Sometimes the thumb of a man who has been knocked senseless by a *lathi* blow will be moistened and pressed as a signature on to an apology paper.[43]

The counter-Quranic oath caused much anxiety to those who made it under this duress. Sadar Musa Khan said that on returning home, however, 'the Khudai Khidmatgaran checked with their local *qazis* [officiating priests] whether a previous oath on the Quran can be broken and contradicted and the *qazi* said no. This made the Khudai Khidmatgars happier about their actions' (I.23).

Most pernicious of all were the techniques of sexual humiliation used against the Pathan men. The memories and reports of these practices are simply too numerous and diverse to be dismissed. On some occasions KKs deemed to have participated in picketing or other actions were stripped naked and smeared on their faces and buttocks with black coal tar. They were then paraded on roof tops and in front of lines of women who had been assembled for the purpose and compelled to watch the shaming exhibitions. Kripalani reported for Congress that:

---

[42] Home/Pol., 166/33 1933 NAI.
[43] 'What is happening in the North West Frontier?'

Picketing of any sort has been discontinued of late partly because of Ramzan and partly due to the shameless methods of the agents of the Government to humiliate the Pathan. The Pathan was prepared for the prison, the *lathi* and the bullet; but his imagination did not count upon the various methods of humiliation employed by the Government. There is thus a temporary suspension, perhaps to devise means to out manoeuvre the Government inspite of its inhuman method ... . One response to the coerced nudity was the discarding of their clothes even before they started from their homes for picketting ... . Not general, but shows the callousness that the degrading methods of the oppressed have engendered.[44]

Haji Lal Mohammed said: 'In Pathan society, taking off a man's trousers is a very, very serious insult. But the British used to strip us ... we were proud of our suffering, but it was very hard' (I.50). Even more serious were the incidents of sexual abuse and mutilation. There were numerous reports of KK prisoners having had wooden tent poles hammered into their anuses, causing great pain and often infection. There were also incidents of castration (I.10, I.66).

Taken together, the various modes of torture and repression deployed by the British constituted an uncannily accurate assault on the canons of honour and *Pukhtunwali*. The home and hearth and their safety, integrity and defence are the foundation of the Pathan man's sense of honour, so in their searches of villages and destruction of domestic goods the authorities deliberately disrupted this ordering. The soldiers also shattered the *purdah* of the women, verbally and physically assaulting them, and through innuendo and threat undermined the carefully guarded privacy of sexuality. This transgression seems often to have been done with deliberate relish, for, as Kelly notes, *purdah*, like *suttee* (the immolation of widows), symbolised for the British the 'bizarre and immoral' in South Asian culture and both practices were the focus of reform campaigns and colonial legislation. It also provided the British with one of their favourite metaphors for their own relationship to Indian culture, namely 'penetrating the veil' (Kelly 1991: 178). In traditional feuds the home was always off limits for attack (as in traditional mafia feuds in Sicily), but the British authorities flouted this convention, flaunting their ability to destroy the home. Such actions were therefore carefully calculated to shame and provoke the Pathan men to the maximum.

The Pathans, raised to abhor any insult or impugning of their dignity, were also subject to all manner of further humiliation. Novel punishments were used to infantilise them – activists were often made to stand for hours holding their ears, or to slap one another, in order to make them look childish and silly in front of others. The stripping and baring of buttocks forced them to reveal themselves sexually in a way that otherwise would be unthinkable, shaming them in the eyes of their womenfolk and also demeaning the women who were compelled to watch. The word for black in Pashto is *tor*, which is also the word for dishonour, and consequently black is traditionally associated with dishonour; the smearing with black coal tar was thus another obvious semiotic insult.

The incidents of castration and sexual abuse were cruel and literal efforts to undermine the activists' masculinity, and must be seen in the light of the British conviction of the Pathans' so-called 'addiction to sodomy' (compare Chapter 1). As

[44] Girdhari Kripalani's report, File No. P-16/1932, NMML.

Krishnaswamy notes of India as a whole, in a society that strictly segregated the sexes and encouraged strong same-sex relationships, friendships could easily leak into the erotic domain, in similar fashion to English public schools. However, the colonial rulers 'never recognised this, and the Indian males' proclivity for homosexuality was considered a racial failing' (Krishnaswamy 1998: 160). Given the homosocial dynamics in the Frontier, the use of the tent peg in this way seems to express the colonialists' mixed feelings of cultural contempt and physical desire, their homosexual instincts and homophobic rules. More symbolically, the tent peg was an old Persian punishment used particularly against men who had violated the sanctity of the ruler's harem.[45] Its use by the authorities against political activists thus seems to be a warning to them to remove themselves from the sacred realm of the political, whose enjoyment must be the sole pleasure of the ruler.

As we saw, the authorities tried to make arrested KKs swear counter-oaths on the Quran. This struck at their honour in two ways, first by forcing them to break the obligations of loyalty to a friend and leader, and second by undermining their sense of piety through forcing an oath in contradiction to an earlier one sworn on the Quran. In addition it should be noted that the corpses of activists who died in jail were not released for burial by the family but put in a plot near the Haripur jail itself, thereby shaming the family, who were unable to provide the proper burial prescribed by the Quran (I.20).

In all these ways, therefore, the punishments meted out by the authorities showed an assured grasp of humiliation in the context of *Pukhtunwali* and hence a disagreeable mastery of psychological warfare. Although there were undoubtedly massacres and instances of brutality throughout the Raj, there can be little doubt that the severity and methodical nature of the repressive activity in the Frontier exceeded anything in the rest of India. As Secretary Wahidullah and another informant stressed: 'Mass arrests never damaged the movement and its morale. They in fact improved it. But the atrocities *were* terrible. In 1931 when we were arrested for picketing we were first severely beaten and then thrown into a dirty ditch' (I.26). 'Times were so bad ... the constables were Gods in his area ... if you so much as pointed a finger at them they would cut it off ... once they burnt a man alive in lime ... . But his son later married an English girl as revenge and continued to be in the movement!' (I.66).[46]

The extra brutality deployed by the colonial regime in the Frontier partly reflected the acute sensitivities about the area as a strategic border, particularly given the Communist regime now in power in Russia. It may also have reflected the simple fact that it was far easier to get away with such things in the Frontier, since its relative physical and cultural isolation made such actions far less conspicuous than they would have been in, say, Bengal or Central Provinces. Entry into the interior was very difficult and the reports that were compiled involved no little peril. Elwin wrote that the villagers were very frightened and would only talk to him in hideaways in the dead of night; he himself had to wear disguises and hide his papers.

---

[45] Burton, final essay of his translation of the *Tales of a Thousand and One Nights*, 1886, quoted in Krishnaswamy 1998).
[46] In the Police only ranks above that of the Station Master were British officers (I.26).

I would argue, however, that the main thing which helped the British officials to justify their actions to themselves and to their superiors was the stereotypical image they had inherited about the 'dangerous' and 'warlike' nature of the Pathans. For instance, in 1932 the Provincial government asked for increased police strength as well as increased perks and salaries for them.[47] They argued that they had been severely stretched and overworked through having to carry out the wide variety of measures we have reviewed in this chapter. The Intelligence Bureau supported these proposals and was confident that the government of India would give their sanction, 'if only as a gesture of goodwill in return for the sterling work done during the last year by the subordinate ranks of the Police'.[48] But the government refused the request, citing 'financial constraints' and the fact that it might set a precedent for other states to make similar demands. The provincial government then responded with an argument that such comparisons with other states were inappropriate:

> Recent events have proved that the existing police force is inadequate to deal with disturbances occurring on a large scale among people, who, once aroused are accustomed to proceed to lengths unheard of in other parts of India. There is a general tendency of people to make a comparison between the establishment of the Punjab and the NWFP. In fact, I submit, the temperament of the people, the proximity of the Tribal territory, the physical characteristics of the territory and to some extent the lack of communication in this province render such a comparison less than fair for the NWFP.[49]

This sentiment that the Frontier was 'not comparable' ultimately fed, I would argue, into the suspension of normal restraint and rules of engagement in responding to the KKs. The Frontier authorities acknowledged the ongoing 'excesses' in internal memoranda but declined to conduct any enquiries or take disciplinary action. The Governor defended the actions, saying the police were 'faced with a supremely difficult task in dealing with the Red Shirt movement and it was vitally important to take no action which might undermine their morale' (quoted in Shah 1999: 36). Elwin noted with some surprise that there was little effort to deny or apologise for the repressive actions on the part of the British authorities in the Frontier. In a passage reminiscent of Conrad's *Heart of Darkness*, Elwin wrote: 'It may be said that most of the "excesses" are fully admitted even by local officials. But they are not ashamed of these things – "This is the Frontier" they said "and you down country people do not understand"'.[50]

Sustaining Non-violence

In the light of these vicious practices in the Frontier, it is clear that the Pathans would have had every justification for directing aggression and hatred against the colonial government. It is therefore even more miraculous that the Pathans abandoned their

[47] Home/Pol., 103/VIII/29 NAI.
[48] Letter of CC NWFP, No. 20217-G 0 9/31 d. 27.9.1930, Home/Pol., F103/XI/30 NAI.
[49] Letter of CC NWFP, Hon'ble S. E. Pears to Secy Home GOI Simla No. 5/56 d. Peshawar 5 September 1930 Home/Pol., F103/XI/30 NAI.
[50] From 'What is Happening in the North West Frontier ?'.

traditional martial instincts and compulsion for revenge. Before commencing fieldwork I had read British reports and come across references to 'Red Shirts' in processions armed with 'axes, spears and agricultural implements', and I thus challenged my informants about the true extent of their non-violence. Most initially remained adamant about their spotless record: 'We used to be totally empty-handed ... there was an incident when a man would not hit a dog that bit him because he said that he had sworn to Badshah Khan never to use violence' (I.67). Kalam Khan said: 'We carried small sticks for walking, but never used them to hit anyone. We were hit on several occasions but never hit back. I had sworn against violence. Badshah Khan had explained to us that we were waging a war againt the British with non-violence and patience'(I.48). Waris Khan insisted that their leaders used to carry only symbolic *charkhas* (spinning wheels) on their shoulders during demonstrations. Wazir Mohammed gave a vehement rebuttal: 'We never carried any sticks or arms. All we carried was some dry bread and maybe an onion'(I.63).

Others, however, admitted in the course of long conversations just how hard it had been to stick to the path of non-violence. Hama Gul recalled the following incident: 'Once I lost my patience with the Assistant Commissioner who asked for my name three times. I told him that I did not obey his government ... I was put in jail for one year for this offence. Several *khans* were also arrested because of me.' He also recalled another incident: 'Once during Ramzan, there was a raid by the British. There were 1,100 of us. Badshah Khan told us to hold our canes and sticks when the British came to hit. But one of us in his anger threw a Britisher to the ground. Thirty of us were injured as a consequence of that. We should have listened to Badshah Khan' (I.51).

Turab recalled an incident of extreme anger:

> Fakruddin and Sahuddin were two brothers who were wonderful teachers in a school Badshah Khan had set up at Tangi. One day they were arrested and people were so incensed that they picked up any weapon that they could lay their hands on and marched to the police station. Badshah Khan intervened, however, and explained to the people that the British were so powerful that they ruled half the world ... there was no way that we could match that kind of power; so the only way we could match them was by adopting the path of non-violence. The people understood Badshah Khan and agreed with him. Badshah Khan taught everybody the lesson of non-violence. (I.52)

Jarnail Mohammed Umar recalled another lapse and the useful lesson that followed:

> There was one incident of violence. This was at a *jehnaza* [a funeral]. There was a skirmish with the *mullahs*. The *mullahs*, you know, were against us. They used to call Khudai Khidmatgaran the children of Lenin. Three *mullahs* were beaten up by our men. Badshah Khan fasted for three days after this incident. The fast meant anger and remorse at the way people had behaved. If you don't eat people get upset and that makes them ashamed and makes them think about what they did wrong. (I.21)

Here, then, Badshah Khan fasted to reprove and instruct his followers, much as Gandhi did in response to similar incidents, notably during the communal rioting of 1946–7. Shah Jahan Khan agreed that lapses did occur: 'There were sometimes incidents of people resorting to violence within the movement. Yes, such incidents took place. Such people were removed from the movement. Once even Ghani Khan

(Badshah Khan's son) was removed. Such people used to eventually ask for pardon. They were readmitted only after demonstrating good behaviour for at least three years' (I.34).

It was difficult to ask the KKs about lapses from non-violence, as understandably they wished me to know only of their successes. These sensitivities were evident in my conversation with Colonel Mohammed Sayyid and Sarfaraz Khan of Pdang. I asked them if they ever carried any weapons or sticks when they went on a demonstration. Colonel Sayyid responded promptly: 'No, we did not have anything.' I pursued the matter, nevertheless, and asked him what they used to carry in their hands: 'Badshah Khan used to insist that we carried our own food with us, so we might have had some millet and sugar.' With my mind on the records, I asked him again: 'So no weapons ... ?' This was too much for his self-respect and he lost his temper and shouted: 'Haven't you just heard? We were non-violent. Why would we need weapons!' I apologised, shaken, and explained that the only reason I asked was that the colonial records in England reported that people in 'Red Shirt' processions used to carry sticks. I needed to ascertain if this was really the case. Colonel Sayyid then conceded that 'I used to carry only a small cane ... but that was only to keep order in a procession!' At that point in this rather tense dialogue, Sarfaraz Khan interjected: 'We did carry sticks and we hot-headed Pathans used to throw stones when we were pushed too hard, too far ... especially the bereaved women of murdered KKs. But we had tried to learn patience. After all, even the Quran says that "War should be one of Patience" ' (I.44, 45). Such comments perhaps explain something of the reports from Congressmen who sometimes drew a distinction between the Pathan's genuine non-violence, but lack of a wider 'peacefulness'. When my informants were willing to allow failings in the movement they typically attributed such actions to women or hot-blooded youths.

While this conversation revealed occasional lapses in the practice of non-violence, such stories give a more realistic picture of the tremendous effort involved in not only acquiring a belief in non-violence but translating it into consistent practice, even in the face of extreme provocation. They thus place the many undoubtedly successful applications of non-violent protest in a more plausible context of effort, failings, ongoing lessons and gradual mastery. But successes there certainly were and stories about them abound even today. Kalam Khan from Nowshera said:

> We were hit on several occasions but never hit back. I had sworn against violence. Badshah Khan had explained to us that we are waging a war againt the British with non-violence and patience ... and we believed in him and followed him. Once a British police officer asked me why we followed Badshah Khan. He said: 'Are you paid to do this?' I said, 'No, we even have to take dry bread from our own houses to sustain us, and then go with Badshah Khan to oust you from our country!' The officer patted me on the back. (I.48)

I asked eighty-year-old Haroon Kaka if he had ever felt the urge to retaliate with violence against some of the atrocities that he had seen and endured:

> How could we!? We had sworn ourselves to non-violence. Once we had gone to Suddam, where there was a man Mahmud Khan who was in the pay of the British. He used to receive Rs30 every six months. As we went about our movement's business he came with a rifle and tried to stop us. We did not retaliate but continued with our business. This made Badshah Khan very happy. (I.27)

Dr Waris told me how he had protested about the poor conditions in prison: 'Some people went on hunger strike ... I also did for fourteen days ... that created quite a stir and the amount of oilseed [which the prisoners were made to grind] was reduced and we were given some bread to eat' (I.66). Here non-violent protest appears to have had its desired effect and successes such as these must have strengthened the KK's faith in its efficacy. Thus, increased confidence in the non-violent approach came about both from their own experience of its effectiveness and from the approval of Badshah Khan which they worked so hard to earn.

When confronting the British this growing conviction in the efficacy of non-violence bore fruit. Derai Khan remembered that 'Once at a parade, a British soldier caught hold of my cummerband from the back and hit me on my back but I did not say anything. I got arrested later for picketing outside the courts and the liquor shops ...' (I.46). Lieutenant Muhammad Wali remembered his ribs being broken by the police at a riot but 'even then I did not resort to violence. We removed the British by our patience. Non-violence gives a strength of mind' (I.19). Derai Khan and Mohammed Wali chose to court arrest and punishment through civil disobedience activities and there were innumerable such choices in the course of the mass civil disobedience movement. It was these myriad acts of small-scale heroism which helped ultimately to bring the movement to a successful conclusion.

Badshah Khan urged his troops on, exhorting them to forbear in the face of provocations and to stick to their non-violent principles. 'People were already very tired of the British ... Badshah Khan said that the British were only human like us ... and they will be tired of our resistance as well' (I.61). 'If we despaired of removing the British, Badshah Khan used to say to us: "One horn of the British is already broken, the other one is already breaking. Why are you scared of them?"' (I.42).

To encourage and inspire the KK he frequently likened their sufferings at the hands of the British to those of the Prophet and his followers:

Great troubles were given to the disciples [of the Prophet]. They were made to lie on the hot sand: a rope was put in their necks and they were dragged in the streets. Because of Patience, the Mussulmans succeeded and God gave them rule from East to West. You would say that these are old stories and relate a new one. I am going to relate a new story now. Last year when the *Firangi* saw the sympathy [for the KK] he began practising tyranny upon us. KK were thrown from the storeys of their houses, horses were run upon them, but they remained silent. Our KK were killed by machine guns but we observed patience. They entered into our houses but we observed patience, our youths were troubled and they were made to grind mills, but we observed patience. Jameson was a *Firangi* Superintendent of Police. In Charsadda, there was picketing on the liquor shops. Oh! Brethren, how should I relate further! The work he has done is such a work that I am feeling ashamed. The *Firangi* took off the clothes of the youth and that Jameson caught them by their secret parts. These are the civilised *Firangis!* They are civilised? Does someone touch that thing! This is *Firangi*. Such a *Firangi* who rules upon us, but we observed patience. Ay brethren, the result of that patience was that the Pakhtun became famous in the whole world. (In Ramu 1992: 29)

By adhering to the principles of non-violent protest the Khudai Khidmatgar movement seized the moral high ground and fundamentally challenged the existing British stereotypes of the Pathans. The transformation was a self-conscious one, and, when Badshah Khan said in his speeches 'Abstain from violence and do not defame your nation, because the world will say how could such a barbarous nation observe patience' (in Ramu 1992: 142), it was with an international audience in mind. The violent repressions carried out against the anti-colonial protest in the Frontier allowed Badshah Khan plausibly to deride British claims of greater civilisation and quality of governance:

> The greater their oppressions the more pleased I feel because a mad dog has a very brief life. They are on the point of becoming *rook* [rabid] because you have weakened the foundation of their government. I prefer the mad and enraged *Firangis* because their bites shall cause awakening among us [infection]. Had the *Firangi* been gentle this spirit and this love would never have sprung up among us. As God does not bestow kingship upon mad men, so He must take it upon other men. I say why should the 'Red Shirts' complain of it because they themselves have driven the English to madness and the fault is entirely theirs. The English became mad at seeing you! (Ramu 1992; 84)

Thus a neat and satisfying reversal was achieved. The Pathans, long condemned by their British overlords as being uncontrollable, violent and without restraint, had now, through the disciplined and steadfast efforts of the KK movement, driven the regime to such a pitch of anxiety and distraction that it could with every justification be accused of acting like a 'mad dog' that was unworthy of continuing to govern the Frontier and India. As Mir Mohammed of Tahkal proudly concluded: 'No other movement was as successful as ours ... from Bombay to Calcutta' (I.68).

Conclusion

Given the nostalgic and cosy image of the Raj which prevails in Britain's middle-brow literature and media, I have felt it important to discuss the colonial response to the KK movement in some detail, for it makes it clear just how bitter and often vicious the nationalist struggle was. Until the very last days of 1945–7, the colonialists were not initiating a graceful process of withdrawal but defending their position in a fierce political confrontation. They used techniques of crude physical violence, such as beatings and shootings. They also, however, used acts of coercion which were not necessarily accompanied by overt physical violence, but were designed to shame and humiliate, what Bourdieu has discussed as 'symbolic violence'. Shattering the sancitity of *purdah* was one kind of symbolic violence, labelling the KK Bolsheviks and paramilitaries another while the use of coal tarring, castration and the Persian tent peg constitute, a subtle synthesis of physical and symbolic violence, linking 'Maussian techniques of the body with the intersubjective world of signs and communications' (Barnard and Spencer 1996: 560). We thus see again how the human body is often a long-suffering site for the inscription of signs of power (Feldman 1991, Das 1995).

5

Leadership of the Movement

Badshah Khan as Charismatic Leader

As we have seen, the British authorities took severe repressive measures against the Khudai Khidmatgars. Yet the movement survived and flourished for some 17 years. In this chapter I wish to consider the nature of the leadership of the KK, both for its contribution to the movement's longevity and in the context of anthropological discussions of authority and charisma.

My elderly informants rarely talked for long without returning to the central figure of Badshah Khan, whose words and actions seem to have lodged indelibly in their hearts and minds, and whom they undoubtedly regard as an extraordinary man.[1] This view of Badshah Khan is not mere nostalgia. At the very inception of the KK movement, we find British reports that testify to his popularity and influence: 'Pieces of gold, silver and flowers showered upon Abdul Gaffar Khan's car by the excited and jubilant crowd, and all along the route the usual and familiar revolutionary cries were raised by the processionists ... '.[2]

Thereafter both British and KK accounts assumed a clear causal link between the activities of Badshah Khan and the fortunes of the movement. During one of the movement's leaner phases (reflecting the disruption in the nationalist movement created by the outbreak of the Second World War – see Chapter 7 below), a government report recorded that: 'In recent months Abdul Gaffar Khan, in particular, has faded into the background and no longer attempts to take the active part which he used to. *As a result*, the term Red Shirt is now uncommon and the garment itself is far less prominent than it used to be at political meetings' (my emphasis).[3] Some months later the Governor commented: 'The only danger I foresee is with regard to Abdul Gaffar Khan himself. He can still, for all his loss of following, work on Pathan sentiment of the lower kind. It is just possible that his arrest would lead to public meetings, and that these meetings might lead to further arrests.'[4] A month later, the Governor's report yet again returned to the issue of Badshah Khan's leadership: 'Everything depends on the way in which Abdul Gaffar Khan himself chooses to direct the movement for he can still work on Pathan sentiment to arouse

---

[1] Since many of his speeches in the 1930s were recorded by government agents and remain in the archives I have been able to see just how remarkably accurate their memories are.
[2] Governor's Report, 1929, L/P&J/12/9 IOLR.
[3] Governor's Report, September 1939, L/P&J/5/214 IOLR.
[4] Governor's Report, November 1940, L/P&J/5/216 IOLR.

the feelings of the more unruly elements of the population – not a difficult matter at the best of times.'[5]

What were the sources of this remarkable influence? An initial thought might be that Badshah Khan's family origins as a wealthy *khan* were significant. Certainly *khans* were powerful figures in the rural areas of the Settled Districts and any public meeting called by them tended to elicit attendance out of a well-advised wish to show respect. It is not clear, however, that this consideration is really applicable to Badshah Khan. He toured villages and called meetings in areas far away from his family's lands, so those who attended would not have done so out of a tenant's fear. Similarly, the numbers involved in the KK movement, being in the tens of thousands, were orders of magnitude greater than the factions mobilised by *khans* in the Barthian *parajamba* model, and so it was surely a different motivating principle that was at work. None of my informants referred to the traditional kind of *khani* authority as being an influence on their response to Badshah Khan. On the contrary, they repeatedly emphasised that Badshah Khan was actually very different from other *khans*.

The most obvious difference was that whereas the big *khans* were very close to the British, being in their employ and accepting land grants and subsidies, Badshah Khan had rejected any contact with British institutions, including its army (see p. 47 in Chapter 2 above). Moreover, the big *khans'* opulent lifestyle contrasted with his own life of austerity and service, and this encouraged people to trust in him because they were confident that he was not in politics for personal gain. As Haji Inayatullah put it: 'Pathans joined Badshah Khan because he was a good man, a good Muslim. People knew that Badshah Khan wanted to serve the poor ... he wanted nothing for himself ... and people liked this' (I.38). His penury also demonstrated beyond doubt his incorruptibility and complete non-cooperation with the British. Gul Samand Khan explained: 'Badshah Khan was not in the pay of the British like the other big *khans*; we knew that he was a big *khan* but he lived like a *faqir*. He did not even have a cap to cover his head ...' (I.55). As a member of a class which was not merely privileged but often collaborative with the colonial establishment, Badshah Khan's demand for non-cooperation with the regime was doubly radical.

In recruiting for the KK Badshah Khan always stressed that membership was a matter of giving and not receiving. Badshah Khan stated in his speeches that 'it is unselfish public service, and not a red shirt, that makes a Khudai Khidmatgar'.[6] As he often remarks in his autobiography, however, the only way of convincing Pathans of anything is by example, and so he travelled and lived among the rural population of the Frontier as one of them. Mohammed Yakub Khan told me:

> Badshah Khan came to this area again and again to convince people of non-violence. He lived by example ... when he used to visit he was never a burden on anyone. He was like a *faqir*, he carried his own food with him and he ate only dry bread ... people who went with him had to carry their own food too ... usually just a little *gur* and *channa* [chickpeas and unrefined sugar]. He ate once a day. If anyone offered him more than one course he declined it. (I.61)

---

[5] Governor's Report, December 1940, L/P&J/5/216 IOLR.
[6] Chief Secretary's Report, August 1937, L/P&J/5/211 IOLR.

This austerity and stress on 'living like the poor' helped break down social barriers, aiding his communication with the peasantry and letting him win their trust: 'Badshah Khan was as big a landlord as any ... but his behaviour was like that of the poor ... he used to sit with us on the floor' (I.67). Maulavi Inayatullah said: 'people listened to Badshah Khan not because he was a big *khan* – there were *khans* much bigger than him – but because there was something special in the way he spoke ... it was with love ... ' (I.65). Badshah Khan seems to have understood instinctively that, given the wide range of people he was dealing with, his personal manner and practice could often communicate what words and abstract ideas could not. Some of my informants could not remember many of his words, but all without exception remembered his behaviour, his simplicity and austerity, and total identification with the rural poor: 'Our leader Badshah Khan used to travel from village to village in torn *khadi* clothes. ... It did not matter whether Badshah Khan was rich or poor ... it was his character that people followed' (I.2).

My informants frequently referred to Badshah Khan as a *faqir*. While in the rest of India the term usually had connotations of a world-renouncing man, in the Frontier the more usual day-to-day meaning was of a Pathan peasant who did not own any land, had no voice in the affairs of the tribe and was generally at the bottom of the social ladder (see Chapter 1). My informants, however, used *faqir* in a wholly positive sense, and to my mind this is evidence of the impression Badshah Khan made on them and the way in which he was able to invest humility and austerity with virtue. His chosen position in Pathan society was so anomalous that they needed a new vocabulary to describe it and so appropriated the Urdu sense of the word to emphasise his spiritual status and his voluntary removal from the pleasures of the world. In summary, then, it was not Badshah Khan's position as a *khan* which fired the imagination of the rank and file, but rather the fact that he was a *khan* who had turned his back on the trappings of his social position to become a *faqir*.

In reviewing the testimonies I gathered in the field I was struck by the frequency with which my informants used words drawn from the Islamic tradition to describe Badshah Khan and his activities. One informant, for instance, recalled his seemingly inexhaustible energy and appetite for the struggle, which remained undimmed despite the difficult physical conditions he often faced: 'Badshah Khan had a spiritual quality ... he did not care about food ... he was like a *dervish* ... '(I.12). 'Dervish' is a term from the Sufi tradition describing holy men who dance with a tremendous energy while in a trance-like state.

More frequently, people attributed to him prophetic or visionary qualities: 'Badshah Khan could foretell things. What he said would always come true. He was prophetic' (I.17). Haji Sarfaraz Nazim Sahib said: 'Badshah Khan's entire manner had a distinctive quality ... . His every action was a lesson for everybody around him ... . He was a man of action, of practice, not only of words ... . Badshah Khan could prophesy things. Whatever he foresaw always happened. Therefore people never doubted his word' (I.1).

In trying to explain these qualities my informants used various Islamic terms such as *paighambar* (prophet), *nabi* and *wali* (seers or visionaries). Such terms were sometimes applied in the context of discussing events that we would be inclined to call 'miraculous'. Secretary Amir Nawaz Khan recounted to me the following story:

> Once Badshah Khan visited me in my house along with several companions. We wanted to offer him water but our well had run dry that summer. He suddenly pointed to one patch in my back garden and asked me to dig for water there. I was sceptical as it was August and there was not likely to be ground water. But he persuaded me. When I dug for a while sure enough there was water! He was prophetic. Everything that he said came true! (I. 22)

For Secretary Amir, Badshah Khan's divining of water demonstrated that he was prophetic, and that in turn seems to have helped convince him that everything else Badshah Khan uttered – whether about the independence struggle or the need for unity – was equally true. Sadar Musa Khan of Chamkani, Peshawar district told me a story in a still more dramatic vein:

> It is true that Badshah Khan had very long arms ... and that is the sign of a *nabi*, a *wali*. It was said that when he slept his body lay in seven parts. In jail, food and water used to appear for him from nowhere. It came from *jannat*, from heaven. Once, Shamsul Haq, the Muslim League minister, was abusing Badshah Khan at a public meeting. People did not think it was advisable but he carried on. You may not believe this but suddenly he had a stroke and had to be carried off. His mouth went crooked and was paralysed. No one who abused Badshah Khan could get away with it. (I.23)

Given his commitment to non-violence, doubtless Badshah Khan would have been disconcerted to have such devastating powers attributed to him. None the less, the fact that his adversary's misfortune is spoken of in this way shows again the high regard the KK rank and file had for their leader's powers. Striking his enemies dumb and being fed by angels while in prison, Badshah Khan confirmed Sadar Musa Khan's conviction that he was on a divinely sanctioned mission.

What was it about Badshah Khan that made some people at least believe he had miraculous abilities? To some extent we can rationalise such claims. Badshah Khan was undoubtedly a wise and intelligent man, a far-seeing politician and a shrewd psychologist. He was also able to draw on a wide range of intelligence sources from the All India Congress, and so could make warnings and predictions of future political events and likely British responses which impressed the rank and file with their accuracy. Even his water divining may have reflected the two decades and more in which he had been helping Pathan villagers to improve water-borne sanitation. Yet I think the real key to the question is that in the minds of the KK he had already brought about a far greater miracle, namely the transformation of the once-violent and divided Pathans into the non-violent unity of the KK movement: 'Pathans are so hot-headed that you have to tie back their hands to stop them from fighting. Badshah Khan *must* have had spiritual powers to have converted us' (I.65). Others cited the fact that people had begun intermarrying across traditional lines and that friend-ships had grown between men of different tribes as evidence of Badshah Khan's prophet-like stature (I.32). Noor Akbar said:

> We were ready to believe that Badshah Khan was a spiritual leader ... and he was considered such because he had managed to introduce political awareness among the people. He had managed to convince people of non-violence in such a way that they cannot ever be convinced by another different ideology again. They can never take on the colour of any other ideology, even if we were to live for another 100 years. He was the *buzurg* [holy man] of our times ... . (I.14)

Thus what the British reported as Badshah Khan's manipulative working of 'sentiment of the lower kind' is, for my informants, the achievement of a miracle which brought them together in unity and political awareness.

There seems, therefore, to have been something of a virtuous circle at work. The personal qualities of austerity, sincerity, love and service which Badshah Khan demonstrated in his own life and dealings helped him gain people's initial trust and persuaded them of the rightness of his message. In turn, the growing number of people accepting his ideological principles helped bring about the wholesale transformation of Pathan society in the Settled Districts, through both improved social relations and a marked reduction in crime. This amazing success in turn convinced people that he must have extraordinary spiritual qualities and that Allah was on his side. As Shah Jahan Khan of Swabi said: 'Even the hot-headed youth who earlier always quickly resorted to violence were willing to listen to and believe in Badshah Khan. This happened only because of Badshah Khan's *karamat* [blessedness]. It was him. If other *pirs* [holy men] had spread this message it would not have had any effect on us' (I.34). Thus miracles such as divining water seemed trivial in comparison.

When I asked people whether it was strictly permissible in Islam to call someone other than Mohammed a prophet, they would generally explain that they did not mean Badshah Khan was a prophet in that sense, but that he had some qualities which were *like* those of the Prophet Mohammed. Thus they were aware that they were bending somewhat the usual meaning of *paighamber* to express Badshah Khan's distinctive qualities. The English term 'prophet', with its emphasis on future-oriented vision, is also not entirely appropriate to what they were trying to convey. It may be more accurate, therefore, to think of the older English term 'mantic', which Douglas Johnson has usefully revived in his discussion of Nuer prophets. Johnson distinguishes 'prophetic' and 'mantic' activity, where the latter 'refers to the acquisition, cultivation, and declaration of knowledge; knowledge of the commonly unknown present and past, as well as of the future' (Johnson 1994: 35).[7] In such mantic activity, the powers involved are not so much those of peering into the distant future, but rather of being perceptive and prescient about the present in a way that demonstrates powerful and 'uncommon' sense. In the light of this, it is perhaps more accurate to view my informants' comments as attributing 'mantic powers' to Badshah Khan. When my informants told me tales of miracles he had performed, they were always accompanied by expressions of equal wonderment at his more 'conventional' powers to persuade, reconcile, reassure and convince, and his ability to encourage people to reinvent themselves and their behaviour through self-examination, such that they developed sufficient patience, self-sacrifice and fortitude to take on the seemingly hopeless battle against the mighty colonial regime. In this way, Badshah Khan's mantic powers, like those of the Nuer prophets which Johnson describes, can best be seen as revealed through the contribution they made to 'defining and sustaining a moral community' (*ibid.*: 34).

---

[7] His distinction is based on Nora Chadwick's *Poetry and Prophecy*. Chadwick uses the word mantic (a cognate of the word prophetic) to delink the idea of prediction implied in the word 'prophecy' and to draw our attention to the other creative powers of prophets in uncovering the truth, healing rituals and other related activities of healing and affliction.

As the use of these various terms – *paighamber, wali, nabi, buzurg, pir* – suggest, therefore, not only was Badshah Khan the most prominent political leader of the Pathans, but he is also remembered as a profoundly spiritual leader. His political mission was perceived by many as part of a larger prophetic mission and this perception was a key element of his charisma and authority. Badshah Khan never made such claims for himself, however, and in fact was intensely distrustful of charismatic leaders who did claim religious authority (see Chapter 2 above). Weber states that the charismatic leader can gain and maintain his authority only by repeatedly demonstrating and proving his powers (Weber 1948: 249). Thus a prophet must perform miracles, a warlord martial deeds. Gilsenan observes of saint-like figures that part of their mystique lies in their silence, which leaves it to their followers to praise their miracles, thereby magnifying their reputation as enigmatic religious figures. Badshah Khan's dismissal of his own charismatic status went far further than this kind of coyness, however. He made no attempt to 'perform' miracles in this way to earn the status of a *paighambar*, and rebuked those who attributed miracles to him. When telling me stories of his *karamat* (blessedness), my informants were careful to qualify that he did not acknowlege any such qualities and disapproved of such talk: 'When people wanted to call him *buzurg* he stopped them. He always stopped them. He used to tell them "I am your *khidmatgar* [servant]" '(I.22).

Maulavi Inayatullah's anecdote illustrates this: 'Once in Mia Beda, a locality near our village, Badshah Khan suddenly arrived for a visit. The *gujjars* who supplied our milk brought some before Badshah Khan for him to blow on, in order to bless it. Badshah Khan did not believe in superstition and refused. But they insisted and so he had to reluctantly oblige because he said he did not want to disappoint people' (I.65). In this incident the *gujjars* extended 'recognition' (Weber's term) to Badshah Khan's spiritual power – milk blessed by him was 'good to drink' and promised prosperity to its consumers. Weber argues that this 'recognition' of the powers of the charismatic leader springs from 'faithful devotion; it is devotion to the extraordinary and the unheard-of, to what is strange to all rule and tradition and which therefore is viewed as divine. It is devotion born of distress and enthusiasm' (Weber 1948: 249). Weber's description gives an uncannily accurate portrayal of the circumstances in the North West Frontier. There was certainly existing distress (recall Chapter 1) and the project of transformation which Badshah Khan launched and led was certainly unheard of and in particular 'strange to all tradition'. On Weber's analysis, therefore, it should not be surprising that Badshah Khan won not only the devotion of the KK but also their recognition of some divine nature in his project and person.

Much of Badshah Khan's appeal was thus due to various qualities and circumstances that Weber would define as 'charismatic'. Like Weber's 'natural' leader, Badshah Khan emerged at a time of 'psychic, physical, economic, ethical, religious, [and] political distress' to set his people free and held specific gifts of body and spirit which were believed to be supernatural and not accessible to everyone (*ibid.*: 245). Also, like Weber's ideal type of a charismatic leader, he seemed to his followers to be in but not of this world, since he shunned the possession of money and gave up the lifestyle of a *khan* (*ibid.*: 247). He was widowed and did not remarry, and therefore stood outside domestic ties and routine obligations. Weber's important condition that the 'charismatic claim breaks down if his mission is not recognised by those to whom he feels he has been sent' was also met, since Badshah Khan's powers and mission were explicitly recognised by his followers (*ibid.*: 247).

In his charisma, moral authority and mass following, Badshah Khan was often compared with Gandhi and he was even dubbed the 'Frontier Gandhi' by Congress publicists. The comparison remains an interesting one, but perhaps in unexpected ways. In an iconoclastic article, Shahid Amin discusses the way in which subaltern and vernacular representations of Gandhi emerged in the months following his brief visit to a small town in North India. By reviewing incidents and reports in the local newspapers, Amin traces the growth of a 'trail of stories' about the Mahatma. The most interesting point for my purposes is Amin's argument that the stories show just how remote and unfamiliar Gandhi's presence was. Thousands would gather at stations at night to glimpse his train roll through, yet only a handful ever gained even a meaningful glimpse of him. Despite this limitation, Gandhi's charisma 'registered in the peasant consciousness' (Amin 1984: 22). It did so in quite specific ways, however, which often bore little relation to the actuality of Gandhi's person or message. The 'trail of stories' told of various ways in which the Mahatma's powers had been tested, of the dire fates that befell his opponents, the serious consequences of violating the taboos (also fictive) which he had supposedly set out, and his ability to enact miracles. Such stories were generated, however, in a context where few among the local population knew even what he looked like – Amin recounts incidents where crowds excitedly clamoured to see complete strangers in the mistaken belief that they were Gandhi – let alone what he stood for. Thus Amin shows that the ideas which most people had about Gandhi, his powers and his instructions, were at considerable variance with those which the Congress leadership took for granted.

At first glance there appear to be some similarities with the position of Badshah Khan, who, as I have shown, appears in a similar 'trail of stories', which takes in his miracles and stricken foes. I would argue, however, that in contrast to Gandhi Badshah Khan was never such a remote or mysterious figure in the Pathans' imagination. As I showed in Chapter 2, the vast majority of people who joined the movement could vividly recall when and where they heard the key messages from Badshah Khan himself. On innumerable occasions I was told that there was not a single village, or even household, in the whole of the Frontier, which Badshah Khan had not visited. Moreover, such statements were backed up with very concrete details – in several households, they pointed me to a room at the end of their courtyard where Badshah Khan had slept when he was in their village. Others remembered noticing his long legs, or his 'big feet, like those of the *powindah* [pastoral nomads]'. They tell stories about his big nose or of how little he ate, and the ways in which he spoke, all of which indicate an intimacy and familiarity of a kind which did not arise in India with Gandhi the Mahatma:

'We used to know Badshah Khan from before ... . We used to see him at the weekly fair' (I.47). 'All kinds of people were members of the organisation. There was Inzar Gul from Charsadda who was a kebab maker. But Badshah Khan knew everyone personally' (I.1). 'He was a very sensitive man. Our meetings very often would go on through the night until 4 o'clock in the morning. Once when the meeting took place in my house I remember Badshah Khan asked people to leave and go home and not expect the host to serve tea for so many of them. He was very considerate to the poor' (I.22).

Haroon Kaka confidently stated that: 'There is no village, no home in the whole of the Frontier that Badshah Khan has not been to personally. In jail, I remember Badshah Khan recounting a story by which we realised that he had even been as far as Chitral and Dir' (I.27). We cannot know whether the claim that he slept in every house is true or not – given his untiring agitation and the relatively small area of the Settled Districts he must certainly have visited many in the twenty years of the movement. What is significant, however, is that the KKs believed that he had made this effort to communicate with each of them, that he had touched each of their lives, and persuaded them that their individual contributions could help achieve the improvement and independence of Pathan society. Thus a particular feature of Badshah Khan's charisma was his ability to make every KK feel they had received the message directly and personally from him.

The various aspects of Badshah Khan's leadership, his personal qualities as a man, and his status as *khan*, saint, *faqir*, holy man, prophet and miracle worker all contributed to creating a larger-than-life presence which encouraged thousands to vow allegiance to his movement and follow his leadership. Without him there would have been no movement. Many of the anti-colonial and political movements discussed in the anthropological literature have been led by such talented and charismatic figures. Very few, however, have been able to survive over extended periods of time or been sufficiently robust to pass through periods of doubt and disappointment. That the KKs were able to sustain their struggle for some 17 years in the face of fierce British resistance is thus of some significance and I now want to consider the ways in which structures were specifically established for the KK in order to reduce its reliance on Badshah Khan.

Bureaucratic Structures

Most of my informants were always referred to by a title, their names preceded by a rank. I met, for instance, 'Jarnail' (General) Abdul Rahim, 'Secretary' Amir Nawaz, 'Sadar' (President) Musa Khan and so on. As I learnt in the following months, these titles referred to the jobs the men had held in the movement over fifty years before. The suppression and marginalisation they had suffered in the intervening years had not weakened their pride in these titles, and they continued to cherish them just as they still sported their red handkerchiefs, turbans, buttonholes and painted walking sticks.

Jarnail Abdul Rahim of Daudzai began by explaining to me that 'there were two parts to the organisation of the movement. There was the Khudai Khidmatgar wing, which was basically a social reform movement, and there was the Congress *jirga*, which was the political or civil wing' (I.3). Each had a hierarchy of ranks and positions. The two parts had broadly different personnel and functions. Those in the civil wing tended to be older and of higher social status, and its role was to make political decisions and run the movement efficiently. The military structure, the Red Shirts, tended in contrast to consist of younger and lower-status people. Its role, as we saw in Chapter 3, was to carry out social reform activities and political protest. Lieutenant Muhammad Wali explained that: 'The young men in the movement were sent to the military wing and the older men to the civil. The elders formed the *jirgas* and they did not wear the red uniforms' (I.19). Maulana Hamdullah Jan elaborated further: 'the civil wing had educated people in it like the *maulavi* (seminary-trained Islamic theologians) and so on. The military wing was comprised of soldiers. But there was no hierarchy between the two. And that was true even with respect to the British. For them both categories of people were as bad an enemy!' (I.12).

A revolutionary movement requires both strategy and planning, on one hand, and execution, on the other: the dual organisational structure allowed the movement both to meet this need and to draw on traditional Pathan divisions of status between old and young men. The age of the senior members could be given due recognition in the civil wing and their experience was called upon to formulate the policies which the younger members could then energetically execute. The activities of the two wings, however, were not necessarily mutually exclusive. Mohammed Badshah made me aware of this fact: 'The young ones were expected to go to the military ... but that did not mean that the old ones wanted to be left out of the army! They also wanted to be a part of the *jihad*. They used to join in the picketing and so on .... Also, the people in the civil wing used to come and treat the wounded, fish them out of rivers, and carry them home' (I.62). Equally, Red Shirts could sit in on the *jirga* discussions to observe, but they remained volunteers who were meant to simply enact the *jirga's* decisions (I.22).

Each of the wings had its own clear hierarchy of posts and corresponding duties. Haji Sarfaraz Nazim Sahib, who was Badshah Khan's secretary until his death, described for me the structure of the civil wing:

> The elders were called members and they formed a committee in every village. These were called branch committees. Every ten to twelve branch committees formed one *tappa* [area] committee; and twelve *tappa* committees formed one *tehsil* [sub-district] committee. Two or three *tehsil* Committees formed a *zilla* or district committee. There were several such district committees in the Province. The committees at every level each had a president, secretary, deputy secretary, treasurer and so on. One man would have the rank of 'branch president', a more senior man 'sub-district president' and so on. (I.1)

In this way the organisation of the civil wing extended right down from the Provincial *jirga* at the top to the grassroots activists in every participating village. As we described in Chapter 2, after the 1931 alliance, this hierarchy of committees within the KK movement was co-extensive with the hierarchy of committees of the Frontier's Congress Party – at each level the KK *jirga* was also a Congress committee.

This information about the civil wing's structure has been largely neglected by earlier accounts of the movement, but for my informants it was a key feature which they were keen to describe. Several of them drew a hierarchical diagram in the dust to show me how the division of labour and delegation of duty was achieved. Haji Abdul Wadood, a 'district *naib sadar*' (vice-president) elaborated further: 'The civil wing stayed in the villages and mobilised more people to join the processions. The military wing used to organise the procession. But the civil wing leaders would lead the processions' (I.16).

Secretary Amir Nawaz Khan, himself a member of the civil wing, told me: 'The men who joined the *jirga* did so because they were educated. My duty, for instance, was to take minutes' (I.22). For this reason he still has the title 'secretary'. The more junior office-bearers of the civil wing were required to take care of a great deal of administrative work in order to track membership, control funds, gather intelligence and information and distribute communications. Mohammed Badshah gave me some idea of the scale of work involved: 'There were about 80 villages under the district president and this produced a tremendous amount of correspondence which had to be taken care of. I had to tour through all these villages, keep reports, record any differences of opinion that people might have. Sometimes I spent every night in a new village' (I.62).

The senior office holders in the civil wing were responsible for discussing and making decisions upon strategic, political and ideological matters. Many of the most prominent individuals, such as Khan Amir Mohammed Khan and Mohammed Abbas Khan, belonged to the same category of small *khans* as Badshah Khan himself and they often joined the movement due to his personal persuasion. He went to great lengths to persuade and shame the small *khans* into joining, as in the following speech:

> Our *khans* are so foolish ... . The Englishman wants to make us fight among ourselves. The whole government of the English is based on this. He makes one fight against the other and he enjoys himself. I ask the *khans* to open their eyes and not to have faith blindly in the Englishmen. The Englishman is a friend [only] of his [own] object [i.e. aims]. He shakes hands with a *khan* if his object can be achieved from him. He shakes hands with another if the object can be achieved from him. He is a friend of nobody. He is a friend of [his own] object and gain. (Ramu 1992: 72)

When *khans* did join the movement it was an important event. Wazir Mohammed remembered one such occasion:

> I was trying to set up a public meeting. There were big *khans* in our village, Fateh Mohammed Khan, a big *khan* of Mardan, Sarfaraz Khan (Fateh Mohammed's son) and Abdul Rahman, and all three were in the pay of the British. Fateh Mohammed wanted to join the movement but when the Governor heard of this he took him away to Peshawar to stop him. So then we did not get any backing from the *khans* of our area. Then Amir Mohammed Khan came forward and said 'I am a *khan* and I will join you.' With his support we then organised the meeting. (I.63)

It was very important to have a local *khan* participate in this way. First, they could provide the wherewithal to organise meetings by allowing the use of their *hujra* (men's guest house) for the purpose and by supplying food for the crowds or for visiting activists.[8] This was important because only *khans* had their own *hujra* – ordinary men were not allowed them (I.23). Second, their support helped to encourage other people to join who might otherwise have hesitated for fear of annoying the *khans*. This was particularly true in respect of their own tenants: the involvement of a *khan* typically brought the involvement of his tenants as well, echoing the estate-based mobilisation discussed in Chapter 1 above. Deran Shah recalled that: 'When we saw that the *khans* of our village had joined we joined in as

---

[8] See Anderson 1983 for a superb discussion on the role of *khans* in Pakhtun society. He writes, 'A Khan can bind together the members of a khel by standing, like a *mashar* [head of household], at crucial organisational intersections where their residual unity can be put into action' (*ibid.*: 133).

well. I was about 12/13 years old at the time. My father was dead by then but my older brother also joined' (I.5).

The British realised the importance of the *khans* and, as in the above story, tried to prevent them from giving support to the KK. Deran Shah remembered that the Deputy Commissioner once came to a camp that they had organised and threatened the *khans* of the village with dire consequences if they did not leave the movement. On that occasion the *khans* did withdraw and this was followed by a period of severe persecution of the villagers by the police, in which Deran Shah's brother, an active member, was a prime target (I.5). Other *khans* were not put off, however. Once when the police had surrounded a village and required the villagers to pay a fine of Rs 800, one of the *khans* offered to pay the whole amount if the military left the rest of the population in peace. He was severely beaten for this expression of sympathy, however, and the village was looted, the people assaulted.[9] Sadar Musa Khan, himself a *khan*, described the sense of responsibility he felt: 'I became a *sadar* (president) in the KK *jirga* partly because I was a *khan*. There was a large number of very poor people in my area, in fact the majority were poor. There were no other *khans* from my area who joined the movement' (I.23). Sadar Musa felt obliged to join the movement in order to provide some leadership to the poor, and, since he was the only *khan* in his area to join, his support must have been vital in establishing the credibility of the movement there. He added that his own prestige had also benefited: 'To tell you the truth I too had several bad habits before I joined the movement. But I was totally reformed by Badshah Khan, and only because of him ... . My *khani* prestige doubled because of my involvement with the movement' (I.23).

If *khans* could be valuable friends of the movement they could also be powerful enemies, encouraged by the authorities to join in the activities of repression and intimidation against what was officially portrayed as peasant rebellion. Sadar Musa Khan said that 'most of the people who did not join the movement were bound to *khans* who were loyal to the British' (I.23). Haji Abdul Wadood broke down in tears as he recalled the actions of his local *khans'* servants and henchmen: 'They used to mix kerosene with the wheat, they insulted our women...' (I.16). Gul Samand Khan recalled another uncomfortable encounter with such hostile *khans*:

> One day the Assistant Commissioner came to visit our mosque. One Khudai Khidmatgar stood up on a string cot and shouted to the gathering 'Who among the people present here wants independence?' Forty-eight people came forward. The *khans* were angry and stood stock-still. The British asked them if *they* thought that the British were likely to go away? They replied that they did not think that at all ... . Then the *khans* pointed to us and said, 'We cannot do anything about them – why don't you drown the lot of them in the river Sind!' Then records were made and kept of these 48 people. (I.55)

Here the *khans* displayed a clear loyalty to the British government and a cavalier contempt for their fellow Pathans; for my informants such instances of betrayal and enmity remained vivid even fifty years later. Nabad Khan reiterated that 'people knew that *khans* persecute' but he felt that, overall, incidents of this kind ultimately increased the popular support for the KK movement (I.18).

[9] 'A Note on the NWFP' by Kripalani, File No. P-16/1932 AICC Papers NMML.

The military side of the KK organisation had a far more elaborate hierarchy of ranks and posts than the civil side, and Jarnail Abdul Rahim explained them to me. There would be one Captain, two Lieutenants, two *naik sahibs* ('sergeants') and two *lance sahibs* ('corporals') for every twenty or thirty Khudai Khidmatgaran soldiers. Two or three captains would report to a major, who would thus have about fifty to eighty men. A large village would have two or three majors. Two or three villages would report to a colonel, who would thus have three or four hundred men. Above colonel, there were higher ranks of *hawaldar*, *jamadar* and *subedar* before finally reaching the half-dozen generals, who each ran a district with several thousand KK soldiers (I.3). They reported to the *salar-e-azam* or commander-in-chief of the Province, who alone was entitled to ride a horse (I.40).

The accounts I received of this hierarchy varied somewhat, as with any good social structure, in the details and numbers. None the less, it was clear that the military wing had an organisational logic of considerable power and flexibility, which was demonstrated in practice by their ability to place several thousand Red Shirt demonstrators in the field at short notice. The parallels with the colonial army (and bureaucracy) are obvious. Badshah Khan had seen these structures in operation and they doubtless guided the design of the KK military structure, which proved its flexibility and effectiveness in the way it absorbed the fast-growing numbers of volunteers and channelled them into some semblance of order. The KK also received advice on organisational structures and techniques from the Congress party.

The military and civil wings had quite different criteria for selecting personnel. The *jirga*, as a political body, had its posts filled by election, and in practice they tended to be filled by *khans* and other senior men. Things were quite otherwise, however, in the military wing. Gul Rahman explained: 'Because the KK organisation was a military one, there were no elections. Elections were held only in the *jirga*' (I.40). The military rank holders were thus simply appointed by their superiors. Badshah Khan himself was involved in appointing the top echelons and I was told that the commander-in-chief of the entire KK army was invariably a person of his choice and took orders directly from him (I.40, I.28). For a period it was Rab Nawaz, who was his nephew. Clearly Badshah Khan wanted key lieutenants he could trust implicitly and felt confident appointing his own kin to the highest posts, but he would always consider the personal qualities of the candidates carefully. According to Mir Rahman Jarnail: 'During the time spent in jail, Badshah Khan decided who would be given the tasks of leadership and who would hold posts. Our behaviour and conduct in jail determined this' (I.11). Jail thus served as the KK staff college, and qualities such as honesty, fortitude and steadfastness were rewarded with senior rank, encouraging people to adhere to these principles. Did the appointment of leaders cause rivalry in the ranks? Jarnail Aziz insisted that it did not, since the post holder did not want the post: 'In fact, the man who shied away from taking on an important post was given the responsibility for it. This was Badshah Khan's lesson. "Don't give it to the man who wants it," he used to say' (I.25).

With less senior appointments other considerations applied. Majors and colonels were chosen from among the men who were good speakers, good-looking and smart (I.3). For the captains, lieutenants and NCOs, however, appointments were often made in novel and quasi-random ways. I was told of men being appointed on the strength of winning a short-distance sprint, or even for being the most tongue-tied man in the section! Such methods were used to emphasise, first, that posts were simply to facilitate the delegation of duties, rather than being sources of personal power, and, second, that all khidmatgars would get a chance sooner or later to be at least an NCO or lieutenant.

The selection procedures of the military wing deliberately ignored social status and imposed a social egalitarianism. This was obvious in the quasi-random methods of picking the lower ranks; in appointing the higher ranks too, however, the emphasis was put on personal qualities, not status or wealth. My informants recalled several instances in which very poor people were appointed as generals: 'In Parmooli there was a general, a very, very poor man. He was the general of the entire *tappa* Razad area. Another general was a very weak man physically, but he was appointed because he had the quality of *khidmatgari*, the ability to serve with love. Very often lower castes with such qualities were appointed into high posts to prove this very point' (I.25). By pointing out to me several similar examples, my informants were keen to convey that the poor, low-born and weak were encouraged and given a chance and often became leaders, with inner quality the determining factor. Haji Meherban Shah commented: 'Our biggest commander in Swabi was a butcher. The lower classes were made leaders. There was no question of big or small. A man had to have the right calibre ... we did not believe in high and low' (I.36).

I asked if people found it difficult to obey these leaders, who in ordinary circumstances would not have been respected or listened to. Mohammed Roshan replied: 'We used to follow the command of anyone who became a commander and some very ordinary people became commanders, they were not necessarily *khans*'(I.41). Jarnail Aziz thought that obedience was a fundamental value. 'Never was a general disobeyed ... . People realised that, if they did, then the very principles of our movement and our ideology would be damaged' (I.25). To disobey such a general would have subverted not merely the military principle of discipline, but also the deeper ethic of humility, respect and pan-Pathan solidarity upon which the movement rested.

The participation of a wide range of people in leadership roles was popular since it gave volunteers a sense of importance and focus. Badshah Khan's message was that 'Every man should think himself a leader.'[10] But it was also a practical necessity, since a single demonstration or police *lathi* charge could eliminate dozens of rank holders through arrest, imprisonment or injury. They needed to be replaced by equally responsible and reliable men: 'There was a lot of fluidity in the filling of posts. There was always a second line of defence. If a lot of office bearers got arrested then a new *jirga* would be formed to appoint the new post holders' (I.36). This 'second line of defence' was vital if the struggle was to be kept going. In some cases a capable man could change roles completely: 'I joined the movement as a colonel and then had to move to the *jirga*. This was because there were gaps in the posts of the *jirga* created by arrests and there was an urgent need for leadership in the civil wing' (I.27).

The different criteria of selection of leaders in the civil and military wings are crucial in explaining the way in which traditional structures were both continued

[10] Speech at Shah Nazir Khel Mosque at Swabi, 14 February 1931 (Ramu 1992).

and modified in the Frontier's nationalist movement. Seniority and age were recognised in the civil wing and this largely maintained the existing distinctions of status. This was important for the smooth functioning of the organisation, since people were used to having *khans* and elders as leaders, and they in turn were comfortable being leaders. Friction between elders was largely avoided through having regular elections within the *jirgas*, such that the presidency of committees was rotated around the various candidates.

In the military organisation, however, a great social innovation took place. As Derai Khan said: 'Earlier, the leaders in a village were always the wealthy or the *khans*. But, after the movement started, even a *shah khel* [a wedding musician] became a general' (I.46). Thus, hierarchies based on economic power, caste and occupation were displaced by a new idea of organisation based on a meritocracy of commitment to the movement and its principles. None of the titles in the civil or military structures were extant in Pathan society at the time and they were adopted from the colonial army in order to draw a veil over earlier sources of identity and hierarchy and create a new solidarity.[11] The title and the rank given by the post often replaced the ascribed status of the member, and the KK office holders, irrespective of birth, are still today respectfully addressed as General or Secretary or Lieutenant.

I would suggest that the egalitarianism and dignity which was thus achieved through membership in the KK answered a deep-seated need among Pathan men. I showed in Chapter 1 that the economic and social changes wrought by the colonial presence between 1850 and 1920 had generated a growing rift between the new economic base and the traditional cultural superstructure of *Pukhtunwali*. Having suffered the abolition of the tribal system in the Settled Districts, increasing numbers of Pathans suffered the anomie consequent upon their having become too impoverished, indebted or socially subservient to live up to the image of the 'man of honour' which *Pukhtunwali* prescribed. In contrast, the KK movement, particularly on its military side, provided a surrogate tribe to which to belong, and set new criteria for honour which were ideological and behavioural rather than material, thereby allowing each and every man to be, and feel himself to be, a member of full and equal worth.

Thus the dual civil–military structure allowed a brilliant combination of conservatism and innovation, ascribed status and meritocracy, hierarchy and egalitarianism. In this way it resolved and avoided many of the problems of leadership which typically afflict subaltern protests and enabled the KK to attract the widest possible range of Pathans into activism, irrespective of their social rank. This achievement of 'vertical' social unity mirrored that of the 'horizontal unity' which was achieved by the KK's transcendence of feuding and clan identity, and was similarly important and creative.

---

[11] Quasi-military structures were not unknown, of course, in the history of protest in the subcontinent. Guha discusses the presence of a *fauj*, a formally constituted army and its commanders, as law-enforcing personnel in peasant rebellions in India. The adoption of these structures is interpreted by him as an 'anticipation of power' by the rebels, who simulated the function of a state apparatus. Guha points out, however, that in this way the imagined free state merely replicates the present status quo and hence appears as a limitation of the particular politics of the rebellion. The rebels in Guha's account chose the titles of *daroga, subahdar, dewan or naib*, which were extant in society.

Communications and Administration

The administrative structure of the KK demonstrated great efficiency in conveying the communications crucial for coordinating individual efforts into a mass movement. News and messages somehow spread across the Frontier from one village to another despite the lack of motorised transport or access to wireless. I asked Jarnail Hazrat Gul and others how meetings were planned and summoned on the military side: 'Every time there was a meeting planned Salar Amin Jan used to send a letter to the district general informing him about it. These letters always began with a greeting of good tidings ... . We used to gather up people from the surrounding five or six villages and go out in a procession with a drum and bugles spreading the news. People used to come forward and help to spread the news. All this, mind you, was done on foot' (I.24). 'There were close links between about four or five villages and there was a colonel for a group of villages that size. Every Friday, after the prayers, a meeting was held for passing on any information and orders. Orders came from the Centre in Utmanzai ... . I was in charge of the post on Friday' (I.34). 'We used to transport our mail ourselves ... . I remember doing it myself when there were no men to do the job ... . I did these jobs even after I was made a Colonel. Right down the hierarchy everybody followed orders' (I.46). 'I took up the job of a messenger, of distributing mail. I used to take orders from my general ... . I was very happy to do this job' (I.42).

There was a similar hierarchy of reporting in the civil wing: 'We Khudai Khidmatgars used to meet once a week by turns in one village every time. Each *tappa* [sub-district] branch used to meet once a week and the president gave orders and the latest news. At the district level meetings were held once every month. ... 'A monthly report from the *tappa* committee went to the *tehsil* committee and from there to the *naib sadar* of the District. He then reported to the *salar-e-azam* [provincial president]. In this way news was quickly spread, and by means of a very efficient foot postage system' (I.25).

The police special branch used to try to unearth and interdict these communications. One month they excitedly reported the 'important arrest of Fazal Rahman of Hoti Mardan, Peshawar, agent of Jupiter Insurance Co. ... who has been for some time in close touch with the Congress Party in Lahore, Delhi and Bombay and one of its most active liaisons in the Province. His arrest led to information about a number of other Congress agents ... under the guise of employees of various insurance companies'.[12]

As a result of such surveillance, the KK had to invent ways of covertly conveying sensitive notes. Haji Mohammed Sher, who worked in the postal system of the organisation, used to hide letters under his *chaddar* (shawl), in his shoes or turban, or sometimes even sewed letters into the hem of his trousers. He recalled that 'there was a cobbler in Mardan city who used to deliver letters through the night. He was never suspected by the police because every morning he used to be back in the same place mending shoes!' (I.33). Jarnail Hazrat Gul, a particularly delightful old man, narrated the following story:

[12] Chief Secretary's Report, May 1932, L/P&J/12/43 IOLR.

Let me illustrate it with a particular incident. I had an important message and was asked to come to Peshawar Gate. There were three more gates after the one to which I was assigned. They were the Dogbari, Kohat and Yakatoot gates. I had to pass my message on at the first gate. We had a code word that was first exchanged. On that occasion it was *badmash* [scoundrel]. We each had a [coded] stick with one, two and three leaves on it respectively. In spite of there being very strict night patrol by the police we were not detected ... that was the level of secrecy. (I.24)

Charisma and Bureaucracy

Akbar Ahmed has famously discussed the rise in the Tribal Areas of the North West Frontier at the end of the nineteenth century of the millenarian movements which ultimately established the princely state of Swat (Ahmed 1976).[13] These movements shared characteristics with other millennial movements in that they were led by 'messianic leaders, nationalist heroes and prophets, often claiming mystical talents, promising some sort of utopia in the future or reversal to a happier order in the past, and supported by the dipossessed and the rural' (*ibid.*: 105). Unlike cargo cults, however, their agenda was 'cultural and religious rather than economic and material' (*ibid.*: 106). The Ada Mullah, the most famous of the Swat leaders, saw the process of opposition to the British government as *jihad*, a fight for salvation and a return to true Islam. This *jihad* was predicated on disrupting the existing social order and was thus viewed by the British and the big *khans* of the area as 'anarchic'. These messianic leaders, unlike the more prosaic local *mullahs*, 'were men of charisma claiming supernatural powers or having such powers attributed to them'(*ibid.*: 108). The eruption of these movements is explained by Ahmed as the result of British penetration of the Malakand Pass, which lifted the '*purdah* of Swat', and as a response to a call to save Islam from the infidels.

Michael Adas discusses five other 'prophets of rebellion' who led 'millenarian movements against the European colonial order' in Burma, India, East Africa, New Zealand and the Dutch East Indies (Adas 1979).[14] Adas notes that the leaders of these movements came from élite groups in their societies, yet all were marginal figures in some way – due to exile, disruptive childhoods or the early recognition of their preco-cious powers. Each emerged in a society where there had been a tradition of millenarian thought and a history of resistance to the colonial regime: 'Though the overall millenarian visions were characteristically vague, they conveyed a sense of supernatural concern for the sufferings and anxieties of the groups and often dealt with the resolution of specific grievances' (*ibid.*: 112). Their ideologies were often eclectic, drawing on various traditions, and as leaders they typically occupied a pivotal role as cultural brokers between these traditions: '[The] emphasis placed on

[13] Ahmed's thesis is that the first set of millenarian movements set the scene for the rise of the longer-lasting leadership of the future Wali of Swat and his success in establishing the State of Swat. See also Edwards 1996.
[14] These were Prince Dipanagara in the Dutch East Indies (1825–30), Saya San in Burma (1930–2), Kinjiktile Ngwale who led the Maji Maji rebellion in German East Africa (1905–6), Birsa Munda in east-central India (1895–1900) and Te Ua Haumene, who led the Hau Hau movement of the Maoris in New Zealand (1825–30).

the revival or assertion of ancient rituals and behaviour in part represented attempts to build up cosmic support and magico-religious strength for the coming confrontations with the technologically superior overlords' (*ibid.*: 113).

These various anti-colonial millennial movements provide a useful counterpoint in our understanding of the KK movement. Although Badshah Khan's leadership had clear features of charismatic authority, unlike these millenarian leaders in Swat and elsewhere, he did not himself lay claim to charisma, mystical talents or religious authority, and it was precisely his knowledge of the Frontier's failed uprisings that made him wary of such an approach. Unlike the movements discussed by Ahmed and Adas, the appearance of the KK movement was not sudden and unforeseen but rather the culmination of twenty years of sustained activities to raise educational levels and political consciousness. Many of those young men who joined the KK in the 1930s had been educated in the various schools which Badshah Khan had established in the 1920s, where they had been exposed to discussions of politics and world affairs (e.g. I.25).

Instead of the 'anarchic content and threat to disrupt societal structures' which Ahmed discusses in the uprisings in Swat, the KK attempted to create a new social order which drew upon traditional loyalties, status and institutions but attempted to incorporate them into a more egalitarian and nationalist framework. Popular enthusiasm was regulated and supported within strict structures of discipline and organisation. The KK protest was not based on violent conflicts but on civil disobedience. This approach undoubtedly required steady personal resources of bravery and resilience from its participants. While the chances of injury and death were ever present, however, they were not as inevitable as in the heroic charges of the millennial movements into the withering fire of British machine guns; hence there was less chance of the KK running out of that nervous and moral energy so vital to sustain a long-term attritional struggle.

The goals of the KK movement were not religiously or materially utopian, and demonstrated an ongoing and prosaic concern for the practical resolution of problems of food, transport, education and economic prosperity. This steered the KK away from what might otherwise have been yet another case of an unworldly 'Islamic' movement. On the other hand, while having material concerns, it did not, unlike the cargo cults, promise instant wealth descending from heaven or the redistribution of earthly riches and land, instead offering only hard work, cooperation and the gradual improvement of community life. The success of the movement, therefore, was not directly dependent on the fruition of larger promises, as was the case with millenarian movements. The community reforms of sanitation and feud resolution and the political successes of constitutional reform in the Province were tangible individual victories which encouraged people to feel they were winning and that their continuing efforts to overcome their own anger and fear remained worthwhile. Much of this improvement came from the Pathans' own changes in attitude and behaviour as they laid aside their mutual feuding.

In this respect a more appropriate comparison can perhaps be made with the case of Ngundeng, another segmentary saint, who was the greatest modern prophet in Nuer society and led his people's resistance against the British administration in southern Sudan in the early part of this century. The Nuer had gained a stereotype in the colonial mind as archetypal 'savages': naked, stubborn and warlike men (Johnson 1981: 515). The Pathans wore more clothes but otherwise endured similar stereotyping. The Nuer also had a segmentary social structure and were similarly prone to feuding and internal strife. Ngundeng had great success in managing to persuade the Nuer to live peacefully both with one another and with their neighbours, the Dinka. As one British official noted, he was the first to unite the Nuer 'in common and peaceful cause that promised no rewards in plunder' (*ibid.*: 521). Badshah Khan and Ngundeng each adopted positions outside the system of clan and tribal segmentation in order to exhort their peoples to lay violence and feuding to one side. Both delivered this message with a power and authority that was more than simple political skill and which persuaded listeners that they promised real deliverance.

The Nuer and Pathans had received very little material or social benefit from imperial rule, and both Ngundeng and Badshah Khan were instrumental in seeking to improve the material conditions of life around them. Ngundeng encouraged the Nuer to gather grain surpluses together in central stores for subsequent distribution, thereby ensuring that the poor and weak did not go hungry, and that in bad years a grain reserve was available for all.

A further significant similarity is the challenges both men launched against the authority of 'chiefs', who were largely British puppets. After the colonial authorities' difficult experiences with the Mahdiyya and other millenarian Muslim movements in northern Sudan before the First World War, 'the administration saw its main task as "recreating" the position of "chief" among the Nuer in such a way that would diminish the political power of the prophets' (*ibid.*: 515). Ngundeng struggled against such 'government chiefs', just as Badshah Khan struck at the collaboration of the big *khans*.

In common with the movements discussed by Ahmed and Adas, however, Ngundeng's ideas largely lived and died with him. When his energy or health declined, so did that of his movement: this meant that ultimately the authorities were able to destroy it through the simple expedient of killing Ngundeng himself. In Swat, too, the nature of the uprising changed dramatically when its leader moved from resisting the British to becoming one of their hired princes as the Wali of Swat. In contrast, although people attributed prophetic status to Badshah Khan, the KK movement, with its immense structures of post holders and delegation of duty, was not critically dependent on Badshah Khan's presence. It continued to function, if at lower intensity, even during his prolonged periods of jail and exile, notably through much of the 1930s. The organisational structures of the KK transformed the Pathans into a formidable opponent for the British administration, channelling their individual dissatisfaction with the status quo into concerted dissent expressed through well-rehearsed and coordinated manoeuvres of protest. Methods of recruitment, delegation of duties and communication of commands were all regularised in a way which allowed them to be sustained through difficult periods. The importance of the movement's structure for morale and confidence is suggested by the persistence and enthusiasm with which my informants (often spontaneously) insisted on explicating it.

In this sense, after the KK's initial creation, it was not dependent on the presence of a central charismatic figure. This is why it must be viewed very much as a political movement, rather than a rebellion or protest. Badshah Khan's repeated denial of his supernatural powers gains in significance when we note that the colonisers never doubted that prophetic visions would prove illusory, that magical charms would not prevent European guns from firing, and that the groups in rebellion would suffer or die fighting for a hopeless cause (Adas 1979). Thus in his creation and leadership of an extensive political organisation, Badshah Khan combined revolutionary appeal with a capacity for state building, using his charisma to establish a bureaucracy, thereby proving an exception to Weber's celebrated claim that charismatic domination is the very opposite of bureaucratic domination. Its combination of spiritual vision and sound administration gave the KKs the characteristics of both millenarian and more routine political movements.

If Badshah Khan brilliantly reconciled charisma and bureaucracy, on one hand, I would suggest he also reconciled religious and secular authority. Barth's discussion of the Swat Pathans presents the figures of chief (*khan*) and saint as complementary figures who share the political limelight and responsibilities (Barth 1959). There is a clear division of labour in Barth's model, whereby chiefs initiate violence and saints act as mediators to resolve it – both are necessary components of a political bloc opposing other such blocs. In the politics of the KK movement, however, Badshah Khan commanded the combined authority of both saint and chief. He undoubtedly drove the political agenda and initiated the struggle against the British, as would a chief, but his principled personal example also raised him to the stature of a saint as he brought the feuding Pathans together in resolution and unity.

Last, by not allowing the KK to be either an exclusively Pathan organisation or an exclusively Muslim one, he provided an extra-parochial vision which drew the KK volunteers into membership of the larger nationalist movement and into interaction with politics at the level of the modern state. This brought added strength and credibility to the movement and had serious implications for the British response to it, since the KK could not now be suppressed as some minor local difficulty or rebellion without taking on the suppression of the nationalist movement in the subcontinent as a whole.

In the light of this discussion, it becomes clearer why the KKs survived for 17 years (in the colonial period alone) and broadly achieved their goal, whereas none of the other millenarian movements discussed above achieved their goals or lasted more than five years.

Conclusion

I noted, in the context of discussing the prophetic powers attributed to Badshah Khan, that he always disavowed such attributions. But he was equally suspicious of secular power. He wrote in his autobiography that quite early in the life of the movement, when people had started to call him 'Badshah' (emperor), he tried to explain it away by saying that it was because they 'were uneducated and poor people and therefore they did not know the difference between "president" and "Badshah"' (Khan 1983: 127). 'Badshah' was a term of elevated secular power with which he was uncomfortable. As we saw in Chapter 2, he had seen at first hand the malign effects of excessive trust in leaders who all too often proved to be erratic and lacking in judgement, and he constantly warned the KKs about it: 'Be careful, do not make me king. If I die some other man may become king by deceiving you. There is one [only] object in making me king, because if I die you will stop wearing red clothes, for you will say that as our king has died, we should stop wearing red clothes ... brothers, do not forget your real object. This part of the country belongs to the Pathans ... the Pathans will utilise the produce of it, not the king' (in Ramu 1992: 122). Thus we see him trying to convey to his followers the modern political idea of a set of policies and beliefs which can live on independent of any particular leader. Despite the veneration offered to Badshah Khan, he never became complacent or arrogant. Rather, like Gandhi, his ethical aspirations constantly developed and his life remained an unremitting struggle to achieve them. Thus he was never a prophet who lost his following 'as a result of his incapacity to live up to his magical exploits and inflated promises' (Ahmed 1976: 116). Rather, he was a man whose steadfast example until his death led him to be called 'Badshah' Khan, an emperor in this world and a martyr in the next.

6

The Ideology of Islam, *Pukhtunwali* & Non-violence

Badshah Khan and Gandhi

The Pathans have been portrayed by travel, colonial and anthropological writings as a fierce and volatile people living by a strict code of honour and feud in a wild and hazardous environment, who have risen up numerous times in violent *jihad*. The North West Frontier thus seems an unlikely setting for a movement with an ideology of non-violence. In this chapter, I try to demonstrate the ways in which Badshah Khan was able to ground his ideas of non-violence in both Islam and the traditional Pathan code of *Pukhtunwali*.

Of all the nationalist leaders it was certainly Badshah Khan who was most like Gandhi in character and practice. The two men were very similar in their asceticism, strength of principle and abhorrence of public office; and while they shared great spiritual authority, as respectively *mahatma* and *paighambar*, both were intensely practical men who elaborated concrete social programmes in which they were themselves untiring participants. Like Gandhi, Badshah Khan was conscious that his followers would have to purge themselves of anger, pride and impatience in order to undertake civil disobedience successfully. As the British reported: 'Abdul Gaffar Khan has been touring Southern districts ... main tenor of his speeches that the country is not yet fit to undertake civil disobedience, and that *satyagrahis* must undergo a course of self-discipline before they can become worthy. He calls for picked men only, and says that he wants quality rather than quantity.'[1] Both men demanded high standards from their followers and did not hesitate to rebuke failure, as Badshah Khan did during the war when Pathans enlisted in the army. As one informant put it, 'Badshah Khan and Gandhi were reformers born to this world which needed them. They were men who were unshakeable in their beliefs. Mountains would move but their beliefs would not' (I.1). Badshah Khan was in agreement with Gandhi's teachings and principled practice, and admired the older man. Often during crises and difficult decisions in the nationalist struggle, Badshah Khan would side with Gandhi when most other leaders disagreed. The Governor remarked during one of Gandhi's visits to the Frontier that '[Badshah Khan] continues to sit at Mr Gandhi's feet as a veritable *chela* [devoted disciple]'.[2] Congress commentators gave him the nickname 'Frontier Gandhi', although Badshah Khan

---

[1] Chief Secretary's Report, April 1940, L/P&J/5/216 IOLR.
[2] Governor's Report, July 1939, L/P&J/5/215 IOLR.

deplored it, feeling it created a sense of competition in what was a relationship of teacher and disciple.[3]

In the light of these similarities it is understandable that previous commentators have attributed the KK's non-violent ideology to the influence of Gandhi's thinking. This simple process of diffusion was similarly assumed by both the KK movement's Congress allies and its Muslim League critics. In reality, however, the constituents of the KK ideology are quite otherwise. Although the KK undoubtedly drew on Congress's experience of the precise techniques of civil disobedience, the basic underlying principle that violence must be eschewed had been grasped by Badshah Khan long before he met Gandhi, through his own reflections on the needs and shortcomings of Pathan society (as we saw in Chapter 2). More fundamentally, Gandhi's philosophical inspiration for non-violence was the Gita, a text sacred to the Hindus, whereas Badshah Khan was a devout Muslim, who had gone on *haj* (pilgrimage) to Mecca and who was well versed in the Quran and Hadith. He would have been well aware of the impossibility of popularising a Gandhian non-violence that was so steeped in Hinduism. So, while it would be implausible to say Gandhi's thought and presence had no influence on Badshah Khan himself, in respect of the wider KK the main elements of the non-violent philosophy were conveyed in very different terms.

Islam and Non-violence

The relationship between violence and political protest remains highly relevant in the contemporary Islamic world and has been discussed carefully by Quranic scholars.[4] Asghar Ali Engineer, with his eye on the stereotype of the crusading Muslim, seeks to show that violence is not intrinsic to Islam (Engineer 1995). The primary meaning of *jihad*, he argues, is not war to spread Islam, but rather the rescue of the weak from persecution. The Quran says:

> And what reason have you not to fight in the way of Allah
> and of the weak among men and the women and children, who say –
> Our Lord, take us out of this town, whose people are oppressors,
> and grant us from Thee a friend,
> and grant us from Thee a helper
>
> 4:75 (Engineer 1995: 122).

In this context the primary virtue recommended by the Quran is the intolerance of injustice, and so the essence of *jihad* is the struggle against the enemies of justice. Engineer suggests that in the conditions prevailing at the time of the Prophet, violent *jihad* was unavoidable, and so violence was central to the early political and social development of Islam: 'The Quran sanctions violence to counter violence ... the philosophy of passive resistance would not have worked in that environment' (*ibid*.:

---

[3] Some young Pathan friends tell me that the title of 'Frontier Gandhi' also had derogatory connotations for chauvinists in modern-day Pakistan.
[4] For example, Ahmed 1990. 'Islam' is derived from the root 'silm', 'to be at perfect peace'. The word for peace in Arabic is 'salam'. A Muslim is one who surrenders to the will of Allah and by definition it is the religious duty of every Muslim to aid the establishment of peace in society.

124). But Engineer's purpose in placing the early *jihads* in their historical context is precisely to remind us that they were a response to certain imperatives and conditions. The Quran, he argues, views violence as a last resort which should only be employed, rationally and dispassionately, with the intention of serving divinely sanctioned ends, rather than to express hate or enmity: 'Fight in the way of Allah those who fight you, but be not aggressive. Surely Allah loves not aggressors' (2: 190).

In this vein, Syeda Hameed notes that, when after battle the victorious Quraish avenged earlier wrongs against them by mutilating their defeated enemies' corpses, the Prophet exhorted them to restrain themselves: 'Bear wrong patiently; verily, best it will be for the patiently enduring' (quoted in Hameed 1995). Thus, while the Quran commends struggle against injustice in the form of *jihad*, it also commends patience as a virtue, both in triumph and in suffering, since it is patience which prevents hatred and aggression:

> But indeed if any
> Show patience and forgive,
> That would truly be
> An exercise of courageous will
> And resolution in the conduct
> Of affairs.

(**Al Shura** 42: 43)

Here, then, patience and forgiveness – the hallmarks of non-violence – are celebrated as qualities of the brave and resolute.

The concept of forgiveness is not always given prominence in popular representations of Islam, with the following famous *sura* often quoted to demonstrate Islam's sanction of violent revenge:

> We ordained therein for the
> Life for life, eye for eye,
> Nose for nose, ear for ear,
> Tooth for tooth, and wounds
> Equal for equal.

However, the inclusion of the verse's following four lines provides a more complete picture:

> But if anyone
> Remits the retaliation
> By way of charity, it is
> An act of atonement for himself.

(**Al Maidah** 5: 45)

So, while the Quran recognises the duty to seek justice through revenge, in these lines it also values the renunciation of retaliation as an act of benefit to the individual's soul. Revenge is honourable, but forgiveness is still more worthy in the eyes of Allah. The Quran appreciates, however, that such forbearance and forgiveness require great self-restraint:

> While the Unbelievers
> Got up in their hearts

Heat and cant, the heat
And cant of Ignorance,
Allah sent down his tranquillity
To his Messenger and to
The Believers, and made them
Stick close to the command
Of self-restraint.

(**Al Fath** 48: 26)

The true believer is thus able to show self-restraint because he has knowledge of Allah and shares in His tranquillity; demonstration of such self-restraint is therefore pleasing in the eyes of Allah (Hameed 1993: 108).

In her study of the Islamic revivalist movements which arose in India during the nationalist struggle, Barbara Metcalf discusses two key concepts that constantly recurred in the central discourse of these movements (Metcalf 1982). The first is *tajdid*, a commitment to the way of the Prophet; the second is *jihad*. She argues that these movements used the concept of *jihad* to refer to the great effort or action required to conform to the way of God. Such *jihad* encompasses struggle at two levels. The 'lesser *jihad*' (*jihad-i-asghar*) relates to legitimate military struggle and 'holy war' against injustice. But the 'greater *jihad*' (*jihad-i-akbar*) denotes the inner struggle of an individual to develop a true commitment to Islam and cultivate the spiritual qualities which the Quran cherishes.

I was at first puzzled by my informants' frequent use of the word *jihad* to describe their experiences in the KK, since they seemed to use it to refer to a great variety of actions and contexts. In the light of Metcalf's discussion, however, it becomes clear that they were referring interchangeably to the physical activities of demonstration, on the one hand, and their inner spiritual struggle and development, on the other, since the KK movement demanded of them both types of *jihad*. They undertook the external 'lesser *jihad*' against the injustices of the colonial rulers, but they had first to undergo their internal 'greater *jihad*' to develop the necessary qualities of service, self-restraint and patience. In this light, Badshah Khan's continual emphasis on self-reform before self-determination takes on added significance. Rebutting calls from religious leaders to attack the British with violence, he stated that: 'The Quran teaches *jihad*, which in its real sense means to struggle for the welfare and advancement of its followers.'[5] The KK thus used the greater *jihad* to prepare for and achieve the lesser *jihad*. As al Hakim al Tirmidhi, a ninth-century Sufi saint, put it: 'Now the person who is patient despite his character traits, his manners and defects, is the person whose heart God fills with knowledge of Himself, and God expands his breast with His light and thereby bestows life on his heart. Patience consists of persevering at something and remaining firm in it. But can anyone achieve that except the person who is filled with what we have described above?' (in Radtke and O'Kane 1996: 205).

In short, as with any of the great religious texts, one can find passages within the Quran which justify very different actions and ethics. The militant religious leaders

---

[5] Speech delivered in the Juma Masjid on 15 June 1931, in Ramu 1992.

in the Frontier who led the tribesmen in *jihad* against the British repression were acting in a thoroughly legitimate Islamic way, taking up arms in righteous rebellion where they saw no alternative way to alleviate the forces of oppression. Equally, however, Badshah Khan was perfectly justified in Quranic terms in urging his followers to abandon the aggression that comes of hate and to identify an alternative means for combating colonial injustice: a non-violent practice which built upon virtues of patience and self-restraint.

My informants were certainly convinced that the inspiration for their non-violent struggle came from Islam. 'Badshah Khan told us that Allah does not answer the prayers of a people in a *ghulam* [bonded, enslaved] land and that we must therefore free ourselves' (I.31). In seeking to draw support to the KK Badshah Khan constantly drew on Islamic idioms and images. Mira Khan recalled: 'Badshah Khan saw a vision when he was in Mecca .... It told him that his country was in bondage, and asked him what he was doing so far from it. Badshah Khan told me about his vision when we were in jail together. It was after this vision that he decided to start the independence movement. Badshah Khan said that we must be able to get rid of the yoke of dependence and slavery' (I.56).

Haji Sarfaraz Nazim said that: 'When Badshah Khan was at a loss for a suitable strategy, inspiration came to him from the example of the Prophet's exile in Medina, and he decided upon a complete lack of violence' (I.1). Badshah Khan himself stated in his public meetings that: 'It is wrong to assume that Gandhi was the first to set foot on a non-violent campaign in order to attain *swaraj* [self-rule]. About 1,300 years ago, the Prophet of Arabia had recourse to non-violence.'[6] I asked Deran Shah whether he had heard of Gandhi and whether he knew that Gandhi had advocated the path of non-violence for the Indian people in their fight against British rule: 'Non-violence was started only after our meeting with Gandhi. But we did not follow it because Gandhi told us to and because he was a leader. We followed it because in Islam our Prophet also said that violence does not solve anything' (I.5). Mohammed Yakub Khan remembered that: 'Badshah Khan always talked of peace ... in our movement, fighting was considered bad. He used to quote to us from a [Quranic] *hayat* which said that war is a bad thing ... whether with one's own or with the British' (I.61).

In his speeches at the KK training camps Badshah Khan continually emphasised the Quranic virtues of patience as a basis for non-violence:

> When the Musalmans in Mecca were oppressed and helpless and poor like us, the infidels of Mecca were resorting to various sorts of tyrannies over them. The Musalmans came to the Holy Prophet and asked him how would they be able to combat with infidels. The Holy Prophet told them that he would show them such a thing that no power on earth would be able to stand against it. The thing is patience and righteousness! (Ramu 1992: 102)

> Do not be anxious brothers. Only a couple of days ago, they shut eighty men in a cell in the village of Ganbad. In seeing such sights I get pleased and displeased at the same time. This may appear strange to you. The reason for this strange feeling is that the English cannot be turned out until they become oppressive and inflict pains on you, flog you and send you to prisons. Those of you who are acquainted with the Quran should know that God destroyed

---

[6] *Ibid.*

all those nations which began to exercise tyrannies upon other nations. I warn the English that we also have a God who watches over us and who must send retributions upon them! Why should we be anxious when God is there? I admit that they have got machine guns, army, guns and police but we have got God. We have also got patience! (*Ibid.*: 151)

The 95-year-old Haji Abdul Wadood still vividly remembered this message: 'Badshah Khan's message spread everywhere. We did what he told us to do ... it was a war of patience ... we shouted slogans against the British, picketed the courts ... . But we did not use violence ... it was a war of patience' (I.16).

Closely linked to *jihad* is the notion of *shahadat*, martyrdom. The tradition of martyrdom is particularly strong in the Shia branch of Islam, with the voluntary deaths of Hassan and Hussayn being the archetypal acts of *shahadat* which remain celebrated today. While their deaths can be explained in political terms – their opposition to the authority of the Caliphs in the struggle for power after the death of the Prophet – their *shahadat* is remembered primarily as an act of religious witness. In discussing this story and the tradition it inspired, Ali Shariati notes that a *shahid* bears witness to the injustices of the status quo, and that the essence of martyrdom 'is bearing witness to what is taking place in this silent and secret time ... it is the only means of attack and defence and the only manner of resistance to truth, right and justice that can remain alive at a time and under a regime in which uselessness, falsity and oppression rule' (Shariati 1986: 79). Thus when the balance of power is such that *jihad* is not a feasible option, the righteous course of action is to court martyrdom.

Though my informants are Sunni Muslims, they drew heavily from such images of martyrdom, which they seemed to find apposite in encapsulating their own political and spiritual experience: 'Such a tradition provides a rich repertoire of symbols and interpretations within which the idea of a suffering community of believers can be formulated and dramatically expressed' (Gilsenan 1982: 55). In particular, they remember Badshah Khan as a martyr precisely because at a time of 'silence and secrecy' in the Frontier he stood up to bear witness to untruth and injustice. Standing by his principles in the face of constant danger, he gave up much of his life to the jails of his opponents.

But the martyr's witness must also bring his death. As Shariati puts it, through his martyrdom, 'the dying of a human being guarantees the life of a nation. His *shahadat* is a means whereby faith can remain. It proves that truth is being denied. It reveals the existence of values which are destroyed and forgotten. It is not a death imposed on him' (Shariati 1986: 79). The martyr is not a victim and his passing is not a tragedy, since he courts it willingly in order to help win redemption for others.[7] Badshah Khan's death was undramatic at the age of 98, but by that time he had spent much of his life in British and Pakistani jails. His contribution to the freedom struggle was never given due recognition by Pakistan and the struggle of the Pathans for greater freedom continued throughout his lifetime. He had long abandoned his status as a *khan* and was reborn as a *faqir* who identified completely with

---

[7] Uberoi also observes that 'In order to be martyrs human beings have to possess the qualities of truthfulness, fearlessness, poverty and chastity' (Uberoi 1994). Again, Badshah Khan met all these criteria, being amongst other things a widower.

the poor, and whose austerity and principled lifestyle was a perennial statement against corruption and exploitation. In all these ways he willingly embraced suffering and social death, and it is for this that his followers honour him with the name of martyr. As Shariati comments: '*Shahadat* is not an accident ... a death imposed upon a hero, a tragedy, [it] is a grade, a level, a rank' (*ibid*.: 80). Haji Abdul Wadood explained: 'It was Badshah Khan's spiritual power that convinced us. We feel that he is still alive and among us today. Anyone who is *shahid*, a holy martyr, is felt to be alive ... and only beyond *mortal* sight' (I.16).

On the basis of his study of martyrdom in the world's great religions, Uberoi argues that, sociologically, martyrs are born of the tension between power and status, state and clergy (Uberoi 1994). By rejecting both realms, the martyr occupies a third realm (what Weber terms 'other-worldliness'), from which he denounces both temporal power and established religion. The martyr rejects society's rules and chooses to die in order to secure its salvation. We can see something of this in the case of Badshah Khan. His programme of education and self-improvement questioned the fatalistic dogma of the established religion represented by the *mullahs*, while his non-cooperation with the colonial institutions overtly challenged the legitimacy of the state.

Most of the martyrs whom Uberoi discusses were highly individualistic, however, and restricted the domain of their 'third realms' to their own spiritual state and embodiment. It was the individual deaths of Hassan and Hussayn which redeemed the fate of their followers. Badshah Khan did not restrict the third realm in this way. As we saw in Chapter 5, he resisted efforts to attribute to him a monopoly of vision or wisdom, and instead tried to embody the third realm within a newly formed collective, the Khudai Khidmatgars, thereby sharing with them the opportunity to challenge church and state. Following Uberoi's logic, we can see how this necessarily made all the KKs eligible for martyrdom themselves. When he appealed for volunteers to join the KK, Badshah Khan made it quite clear that, given the brutal actions being taken by the authorities against the KK, death was a real possibility. He stressed, however, that it would be a noble death in a great cause:

'Whether you belong to the army of the Khudai Khidmatgars or the army of the English you shall die. Even if you are hidden in a cave you cannot avoid death. As death will come only once therefore it is much better to die for the sake of one's nation and country' (Ramu 1992: 130). 'Nobody is safe from death,' he reminded his audience a few days later in another speech. 'A man is sure to die whether he is brave or not. But there is a difference between every sort of death. Do not forget your object – your object is to liberate your country. "The best death is that when one dies the way of God and Holy Prophet."'[8]

It has become usual in modern Muslim states who have been at war, such as Iraq and Iran, to refer to those who have died in battle as martyrs. I would argue in the light of our discussion of the Shia tradition of martyrdom, however, that this usage is not strictly correct. It is not the intention in war to die, and it is preferable to survive as a glorious and righteous victor. The essence of martyrdom, however, is to commit oneself to death as an act of witness to untruth when there is no way to fight. As

[8] Speech at mosque in Toru on 16 December 1931, from Ramu 1992.

Shariati puts it: 'The martyr's death is not a means but is a goal itself. It is originality. It is completion ... it is the only reason for existence' (Shariati 1986: 79). Non-violent civil disobedience offered the chance of martyrdom in its purest form, since putting one's life conspicuously in one's enemy's hands was itself the key act, and death incurred in the process was not a defeat or a tragedy, as it would be in war, but rather an act of witness to the enemy's injustice. Thus, unlike in a military *jihad*, the choice was not between death and victory; rather, the act of witness and the choice of death were themselves the victory. In his recruiting speeches, therefore, Badshah Khan was offering to each and every Pathan not the mere possibility of death, but rather the opportunity of glorious sacrifice and martyrdom.

Accordingly, my informants used the discourse of martyrdom to refer not only to Badshah Khan but to their own roles as well. Gul Rahman, for example, used it to refer to those killed during a civil disobedience campaign: 'We heard that there had been firing in Utmanzai ... I ran all the way there to find out more ... the graves of the *shahid* had been freshly laid' (I.40). The terms *ghazi* and *mujahid* were also frequently used. I asked Maulana Hamdullah Jan, who had trained at a *madrasah* seminary, about who was considered a *mujahid* or a *ghazi* in Islam:

> Anyone who has made a sacrifice, who served the people and did *khidmat* (service). Every *khidmatgar* was a *ghazi*. In the Pashto sense of the term *ghazi* is used to describe any sacrifice. In the older Arabic sense it was used to describe a warrior who had died in a battle waged and fought by the Prophet. In contemporary times therefore it describes any warrior who fought against the British with Badshah Khan. (I.12)

This explanation is a fine example of the vernacular nature of Islam. Terms like *ghazi* and *jihad* were coined during the early life of Islam to describe particular kinds of sacrifices in specific struggles for the establishment of the new religion. Thirteen centuries later, the same terms were adapted to provide continuing Islamic legitimacy for new meanings and events.[9] By using the term *ghazi* for themselves as nationalist revolutionaries participating in a *jihad*, my informants implicitly elevated Badshah Khan to a prophetic level, placed themselves by his shoulder as his compatriots on the battlefield, and aligned their own sacrifices and deaths with those of the early Muslims in the defence of their new faith.

Islam and *Pukhtunwali*

Islam plays a very important role in Pathan life and is an ancient and important component of Pathan identity. Akbar Ahmed makes the observation that Islamic symbols are highly visible in Pathan society and that their social significance is obvious from their frequent reappearance, even if the precise religious meaning may not always be readily comprehensible (Ahmed 1980: 105). He argues that the unity of *Pukhtunwali* and Islam is symbolised and expressed in village social life by the

[9] See Andreyev 1998 for a discussion of how the founder and followers of the Rawshaniyya movement among the Pathans in the sixteenth and seventeenth centuries often compared the results of their activities with those of the Prophet and his followers, in their attempts at sowing the seeds of a 'true Islam' among the Pathans.

physical juxtaposition of the mosque and the *hujra* (men's guest house), and by the way in which the four 'pillars of Islam' – prayer, fasting, *haj* and *zakat* (tithing) – are embedded in local practices and social structure. Ahmed also notes the importance of *sunnat* (the actions of the Prophet) in people's own explanations of their personal habits and the frequent usage of tags such as *Inshallah* and *Mashallah* in conversation (*ibid.*: 109–15). Ahmed argues, therefore, that 'The Pukhtun accepts religion without doubts or questions, there is no conflict between his Code and Islam ... . The problem for the Pukhtun is not one of accepting colonial law or tribal law but one of bringing Pukhtun custom into focus with accepted Islamic law' (*ibid.*: 106). On this logic, Badshah Khan's demonstration of the Islamic basis of non-violence should have been enough to convince the Pathans to embrace it, with the practice of *Pukhtunwali* simply adjusted to conform to the (newly interpreted) Islamic law in the way Ahmed indicates.

I would suggest, however, that neither now nor in the 1930s were things quite so straightforward. By way of illustration I relate a conversation I had with a *khanzada* (son of a *khan*) in Charsadda during Ramzan, the holy month of prayer and fasting. It soon became apparent to me that not all the men were keeping a strict fast.[10] Very often they came home during the course of the day from the fields or office to snatch a cigarette, a cup of tea or something to eat. Nor was this done very surreptitiously, certainly not by the young *khanzada*, who was served by his wife and servants at home, all of whom were fasting themselves. I asked tactfully whether he perhaps did not believe in fasting. He replied that he said the first of the five prayers of the day every morning in the *hujra* with the village folk and overnight guests. But he drew the line at going without food or a smoke from dawn to dusk for thirty days of the year. I asked why he could not assert that in public – was it because of the strict Islamic laws of the Pakistan government? That was not the reason, he said – the government of Pakistan did not bother him. Rather, he could not, as a *khanzada*, be seen to violate the laws of Islam. Was this because Pathans were strict about their Islamic beliefs? It had nothing to with religion, he explained impatiently: 'Pathans do not eat during Ramzan and as a Pathan *khan* I cannot be seen to eat. As my father says, we Pathans are Pathans first, Muslim second and then Pakistani.' Here, then, while respecting Islam is seen as a very important part of being a Pathan, being a Pathan is certainly not seen as equivalent to, or synonymous with, being a Muslim.

It is well established that the workings of a Muslim society cannot be grasped merely through an understanding of Islam and the Quran (Gilsenan 1982; Gellner 1981). Subsequent interpretations of religious texts and laws and interconnections with pre-existing cultural and social structures or the practices of non-Muslim neighbours together combine to produce the great variety of Muslim communities and practice we see around the world.[11] Given that in this sense all Islam is vernacular, we can expect the fact that the core elements of *Pukhtunwali* are thought to date to the eighth century – as old as Islam – to have had a good deal of influence on the precise way in which the Pathans have adopted and used Islam. This, of course, is

[10] These were also men who scoffed at my attempts at keeping the fast and insisted that my resolve would break soon.
[11] James and Johnson 1988.

precisely what Ahmed shows in the close intertwining of the symbols of Islam and *Pukhtunwali*. What I am arguing, however, is that this is a coming together of equals, with *Pukhtunwali* being just as influential as Islam.

Equally, I would argue that, even if non-violence had been portrayed as authentically Islamic in the way I have explored, it would not have been an acceptable idea to the Pathans if it had been seen to be in complete contradiction to *Pukhtunwali*. The right to exchange violence through feuding was fundamental to the whole business of 'doing Pukhtu' and was intimately connected to the obligation to defend and assert honour. Violence was not some criminal aberration but had a central place in this wider ethical system. Therefore, it was equally important for Badshah Khan to show that being non-violent did not compromise the Pukhtunness of the KKs, and this was done by drawing rhetorically on the traditional elements and idioms of *Pukhtunwali* but applying them to novel contexts which subtly changed their meanings.

Pukhtunwali and Non-violence

In calling men to participation in the KK movement Badshah Khan challenged the Pathans' sense of bravery and honour. He chided a gathering at Jehangira in the following terms:

> Have some shame! You call yourselves Pakhtuns. Do not be so shameless ... . Your heads are full of slavery. It is for this reason that you free yourself from the servitude of one to fall into the servitude of the other ... . O you cowards! ... Have some sense of honour ... . Have some *gherat* [honour] in the cause of Islam ... . Feel a little *gherat* for your mothers, sisters and children who are dressed in rags ... get up and throw the yoke off your country (Ramu 1992: 114).

Here he challenged the Pathans' lofty boasting of their own honour by contrasting it with the realities of life in the Frontier. How could a man be truly honourable when he had allowed the British to insult Islam in various ways and reduce his women and children to wearing rags? How could men of honour have allowed themselves to be enslaved to the wills of both unscrupulous factional leaders and the British? The idea of freedom was an integral part of the wider framework of *Pukhtunwali*. In the traditional system associated with *wesh* and tribal lands (see Chapter 1 above) only the freeman was a true Pathan and member of the tribe – a man who lacked independence and served others was merely a worthless *faqir*. It was thus a grave charge to accuse the audience of servility. It was a still greater slur to accuse them of cowardice, and in a less unusual context and with a leader of less stature such insults would have been sufficient in themselves to provoke challenge and feud. Badshah Khan was thus explicitly impugning the Pathans' honour and laying down a challenge before them.

This speech also drew implicitly on notions of *nanawati*, the giving of refuge. Throughout the Middle East such refuge entails the defence of the guest from hostile third parties throughout the time of his stay: 'guests in another's house are "in the face of" the householder ... he is ... disgraced or insulted if someone else does them harm, or most of all, if he harms them himself ... the protégé is "on the honour" of his protector, or in his charge and must be defended by him' (Dresch 1989: 59). Badshah Khan's speech implied that the whole population of the Province, particularly its women and children, were appealing to men of honour to give them refuge and sanctuary from the British enemy, and hence that the truly honourable Pathan should join the KK in order to draw the weak under his protection. This approach was also made explicit in the course of promoting non-cooperation with government institutions. Gul Rahman recalled: '*Nanawati* was used to appeal to people personally. There were a lot of Pathans in government jobs ... for instance Yahya Jan (later Badshah Khan's son-in-law) resigned his Professorship in response to this appeal and others also resigned their posts and joined our *biraderi* [fraternal network]' (I.40).

Badshah Khan used a similar approach to persuade Pathans to lay aside their feuding with one another. As he berated them: 'You cut the flesh of your own brother yet you are afraid of him who has taken the country of your forefathers.' Here, Badshah Khan used emotive language by referring to the country not merely as 'their country' but as 'that of their forefathers', thereby appealing to the sense of honour and pride that Pathans had in their lineages and ancestry. He often said in his speeches that the KK movement was accessible to everyone but cowards. But, since people who were feuding could not join, there was a clear implication that to continue feuding in the presence of the British was a cowardly act which evaded the true enemy. This brilliantly put the onus on the people themselves to decide if they were in fact as brave and honourable as they considered themselves to be.

Despite his own personal ethics and exasperation with feuding, when appealing to Pathans to settle their feuds, he pragmatically urged them not to permanent saintly behaviour, but rather to make their peace at least until the British had been ejected. As Mohammed Pir Sher Shah recalled: 'Badshah Khan said: "After they leave you can do what you want, but before that we need and must have unity"'(I.59). My informants admitted that some feuds and tensions had in fact remained unresolved but they stressed that they had never let those ongoing enmities interfere with the 'national interest' as embodied by the KK movement. Such self-restraint was vital since Khidmatgar activists had constantly to visit one another and sit together to meet, work and plan, and march and demonstrate together irrespective of the relations between them. Unlike in the traditional meetings between men involved in blood feuds, these interactions would take place without any mediators or peace-keeping elders. By asking for at least a temporary and conditional cessation of feuding to allow such work to take place unhindered, Badshah Khan's request was again implicitly made within the tradition of *nanawati*, where sanctuary had to be extended even to an enemy who asked for it and restraint of one's own violent feelings was vital.[12]

Another aspect of *Pukhtunwali* which Badshah Khan sought to adapt was the principle of *melmastia* (hospitality). Traditionally, hospitality in the Frontier was often carried to excess and could be aggressive in its expression of status, oppressive in the indebtedness that it created for the guest, and burdensome for the demands it made on

---

[12] In addition, the call for a temporary cessation of feuding has to be viewed in the light of the fact that it was not unknown for feuds to fall into abeyance for many years at a time, only to splutter erratically to life in due course, often upon the coming of age of the following generation of sons.

the host. The ostentation, waste and underlying aggression were incompatible with the principles of frugality and humility advocated by Badshah Khan. As Haji Lal Mohammed recalled: 'When we used to celebrate the 23rd of April as the anniversary of our struggle, we were instructed to carry our own food. We might have had to spend a night in a village, but were not allowed to impose on them for hospitality, to ask for food or even water. We had to sleep in the mosque. Like soldiers, we carried our own rations' (I.50). This practice helped avoid the problem of peasants trying to outdo each other in welcoming the honoured guests, or of poorer peasants feeling embarrassed that they were unable to sustain the burden of feeding the activists. By carrying their own standardised rations, rich and poor could eat the same together, while the poor could now offer Badshah Khan and his associates as satisfactory a hospitality as the rich, namely simply a place to lie down. This was in line with the general downplaying of social status among the Red Shirts (see Chapter 5). Further, in the context of the repressive measures that were taken against villages who collaborated with the KK, those who were willing to receive activists into their homes put themselves at risk. Hence the warmth and adequacy of hospitality came to be judged not by its material lavishness, but by what it said of a man's bravery and commitment to the cause.

For the sake of completeness we should also note that the movement wrought similar adjustments in the other main elements of *Pukhtunwali*, namely *jirga* and *purdah*. As we saw in Chapter 3, women's extensive if often unorthodox involvement in the movement's activism brought a considerable relaxation of traditional practices of *purdah*. Meanwhile *jirgas* were reconstituted as problem-solving bodies at the local and village level in a way which was quite different from the grand tribal councils which had been traditional, and hence implied a new approach to 'the honourable ordering of public affairs'.

The key task Badshah Khan faced, however, was persuading the Pathans to put aside many centuries of war and martial success to combat the British with non-violent techniques, even in the face of the brutal and shaming punishments dispensed by the authorities. Various rhetorical approaches were used to argue this. As Gilsenan notes of societies with strong institutions of feud, although honour always demanded revenge for insult, revenge was not necessarily synonymous with violence or killing, and could be had in other ways, for instance through the economic domination or social humiliation of the other.[13] Badshah Khan often suggested that the best way for the Pathans to avenge themselves on the British would be to show them up as the unprincipled villains they were and eject them from India with their reputation in tatters. The chosen method of non-violence and the violent responses it provoked were thus intensely satisfying in so far as they undermined colonial claims about both the Pathans' inherent violence and anarchy and their own civility and civilisation. Badshah Khan noted the many cruel acts being perpetrated by the regime, and asked rhetorically: 'And these are the civilised *firangis*? They are civilised?' Thus the KKs were reminded that if they could adhere to non-violence in the face of such provocation they would win honour in the eyes of people all over the world, who would marvel to see what they thought was 'such a barbarous nation observing patience'.

---

[13] See Gilsenan 1996: 159–88 for a pertinent example.

Since violence was not necessarily integral to revenge and honour, it was also possible to argue that, in a struggle against the overwhelming military force of the British, the highest expression of bravery and honour was to confront the British weaponless, defying them to strike first (Gandhi made a similar point that carrying any weapon reduces the risk of injury and so diminishes the courage required). In this way the volatile bravado of violence had to be replaced by the willpower and steadfastness of approaching a soldier in the sure knowledge one would be clubbed. This idea was not without appeal to the Pathans. Bonner relates an encounter he had at a *mujahiddin* camp during the war against the Soviets, when he saw a young man who had been arguing with a friend about which of them was the braver place his hand in the fire and hold it there until seriously burned. We may also recall from Chapter 1 the story of the Pathan who sought to raise the stakes of a confrontation by helping the British riflemen improve their aim. As Lindholm suggests, among the Pathans: 'Great value is placed on courage, which is not in the act of killing so much as the willingness to take ruinous consequences for the sake of cleansing one's honour' (Lindholm 1996: 52). Civil disobedience provided constant opportunity for this.

Badshah Khan also appealed to notions of manliness and masculinity. He repeatedly accused the British of slyness and cowardice for the way in which they beat women and children, or adopted tactics of stealth and subterfuge – poisoning the KK camp's milk, or using agents and provocateurs to whip up enmity and disunity: 'The *Firangi* is a cunning and tricky fellow ... . He is unmanly. He is a coward. Because if somebody flatters and respects him, he becomes obstinate and when somebody frowns at him then he begins to show respect to him. Is it the work of a brave nation? He has enforced Section 144 everywhere. I tell you he is not brave!'[14] Such techniques he contrasted with the public and straightforward methods of the KK protesters, which truly showed *meran*, which literally means 'manhood' and implies a strong will and the ability to resist and overcome any difficulties (Lutz 1989: 65).

However, *meran* itself was also somewhat redefined, since traditionally it was closely associated with physical strength. Non-violent protest, however, unlike war, did not require physical strength – as Gandhi said, the strength required did not come from physical capacity but from indomitable will and truth, such that self-restraint and forgiveness of the enemy could come only from a genuine inner strength. The weapon of civil disobedience was thus equally available to men and women, to the young, the old and the infirm. It may be recalled from Chapter 5 how some men who were physically weak still became generals in the KK became they were recognised as possessing great strength of will. For the first time, women could take an active part in struggles led by men of honour. Even children could play important roles, not least as examples which encouraged and pressured more mature men into joining the struggle. Turab recalled: 'One summer, I remember I was a small boy and I was carrying sand bags [for barriers] ... . I collapsed under the strain. There was Zyarat Kaka, Noor Kaka and others who came to help me up. I think that, when a little boy like me also joined, it gave the movement fresh impetus'

---

[14] Section 144 forbade the assembly of more than four people in a public space.

(I.52). Badshah Khan thought so too, and with great pride told an audience in India of an instance in Kohat when a young boy came up to him, in the presence of a policeman, and asked to be enrolled. When asked what he wanted to enrol his name into, he replied, 'into revolution'.[15]

In considering their adoption of non-violence, it is important to remember that Pathan violence had elaborate rules of its own. Only particular modes and contexts of violence could constitute legitimate revenge and thereby satisfy honour – attacks against a house guest or against the home and children of an enemy were not eligible acts. The man of honour thus required a great deal of self-restraint in order to control the emotional urge to revenge himself immediately; he had to wait for an appropriate moment and context. Lindholm shows through his work among the Yusufzai Pathans in Swat that they greatly value the restraint of anger, since they are all too aware that anger, once revealed, starts on a slippery slope to blood feud which can implicate the entire lineage (Lindholm 1996: 187–205). The non-violence necessary in a KK demonstration could thus be viewed as requiring a similarly honourable exercise of restraint.

A critical factor which must have aided the adoption of non-violent ideology in the Frontier was the realisation that, deep down, the British were an enemy who would understand and respect the use of non-violence. The approach could not have been used in Stalin's Russia or Hitler's Germany. While the British engaged in a wide range of brutal actions, including torture, and massacres were not unknown, they did not for the most part launch the mass killings that were perfectly possible given the firepower at their disposal. Although they launched their heavy aircraft to bomb the Tribal Areas they did not flatten the dense villages of the Settled Districts as they might have done. This reflected the restraint put upon them by those elements of the public, media and political classes who did not support colonialism, or at least not a colonialism which revealed itself to be too conspicuously brutal. In that sense, in laying down the gauntlet of non-violence, the KK hoped that the British would be sufficiently honourable to understand the challenge properly and to respond to it in an appropriate way, through similarly non-violent means.

Honour was a concept which both sides valued. If the Pathans had *Pukhtunwali*, then on the British side, too, particularly in the regular army, there were indigenous values of honour, notably in the regimental systems and the concept of the gentleman. In the words of Carlyle, 'It is a calumny on men to say that they are roused to heroic action by ease, hope of pleasure, recompense ... in the meanest mortal there lies something nobler. The poor swearing soldier, hired to be shot, has his "honour of a soldier" different from drill regulations and the shilling a day' (Carlyle 1983 (1840): 86). Gilmore terms such models 'vertical honour', each being a culturally specific understanding of honour. Among participants within vertical honour games there is fierce competition, for instance between regiments or between clans, as they seek to match and outdo each other's actions, for, as Gilmore reminds us, 'honour is about action not merely words' (Gilmore 1987).

---

[15] Speech delivered at the first session of the Jamiat-ul-Ulema on 19 July 1931, Cinema Hall, Budhana Gate, Meerut; from Ramu 1992.

Such games of vertical honour have to be played between equals. In the British army, for instance, violence by a senior officer towards a lower rank guaranteed a court martial, while the Guards regiment would not deign to compete with an obscure provincial yeomanry. Pathans, too, only fight over honour with other men of honour. Discussing the Mediterranean region, John Davis notes that 'honour functions as the coin of egalitarianism' (Davis 1977). The traditional approach of guerrilla attacks had always allowed the British to make self-serving criticisms of the rebels as furtive, unmanly and dishonourable for avoiding a 'fair fight'. In contrast, by framing their challenge to the colonial power in terms of open non-violent protest, the KKs avoided such slurs. The KK's unexpected deployment of non-violence thus took the initiative in throwing out such a challenge and placed the two vertical models into a direct contest of 'horizontal honour'.[16] In doing this, the Pathans asserted their own dignity and right to be held equal with the British.

In addition to being a physical confrontation between protesters and troops, therefore, the campaigns of non-violent protest became a competition to see who could be most civilised and honourable; thus the vertical games of honour became elevated into a tumultuous international match within the Frontier, a rather different 'Great Game' that lasted seventeen years. As Haji Sarfaraz Nazim told me: 'Non-violence was used to create situations in which the British could not use force or violence. That was the ideal and goal' (I.1). Ultimately the KKs could only demonstrate their honour through restraint and non-violent forbearance because the enemy, too, were concerned about their own reputation and sense of honour. As Gul Rahman pointed out, the KKs were amazed that 'the British did not in fact fire upon us when we stood up to them and were ready to face their bullets ... that was certainly different from Abdul Qayyum's policy after 1947!' (I.40). If the KKs set the rules for this new Great Game of honour, the British did not totally flout them.

As is well known from the classic works of Evans-Pritchard and Emrys Peters, in traditional segmentary societies particular kinds of violence were associated with particular levels of segmentation, with the violence increasing in seriousness and scale at higher levels of segmentation (Evans-Pritchard 1940; Peters 1967). Thus wars between tribes were more serious than raids between clans, which were more serious than feuds between lineages, and so on. This was largely true of the Pathans as well. With the feud resolution brought about by the KK movement, however, intra-Pathan conflict between tribes, clans and lineages was suppressed in favour of the unified struggle of the whole collectivity against a common enemy, the British. By the logic of the traditional typology of violence we would expect the nature of such a confrontation at this supra-tribal level to surpass the wars between tribes in violence and intensity. Yet, instead of embracing a still more severe type of violence, the KK movement made the confrontation between the entire segmentary system and the colonial state into a non-violent one. This idea was most succinctly stated by Ajab Khan in Charsadda: 'Violence is an intra-Pathan affair. With the British it was different ... we adopted non-violence' (I.43).

---

[16] See Jamous 1981 for a discussion of the importance of challenge in honour games.

Learning Non-violence

As I have tried to show, one of the reasons for the KK's great success was the extent to which its ideology was grounded in both Islam and *Pukhtunwali* – it was made clear to potential members that values such as patience and self-restraint were valued by the Quran, but equally cherished by Pathan traditions. By absorbing Badshah Khan's message and passing through the KK training camps the successful activist thus emerged simultaneously as a good Pathan, a good Muslim and a good non-violent protester. We may wonder how long it took for the new ideology of the KK movement to be accepted by the people of the Frontier – did people undergo a dramatic transformation overnight?

Mohammed Yakub Khan told me that the process had taken considerable time and effort: 'Badshah Khan had to come to this area again and again to convince people of non-violence' (I.61). Sher Khan similarly admitted that there was no sudden conversion: 'It was not easy for people to convert to this idea. It did not happen easily. But we persisted. People went back to their own *jirgas* to think over these ideas – (I.29). Maulana Hamdullah Jan said that 'People gave up feuding gradually over a period of several years. But the message of Khudai Khidmatgari lives to this day' (I.12). Mohammed Gul said: 'Talk of non-violence was new and difficult to understand initially ... . Fighting back was a Pathan custom ... but Badshah Khan explained that would not get us independence. It wasn't possible to defeat them on the battlefield ... they could have killed us with the local administration alone ... and besides the non-violence brought unity among the people' (I.67). Sarfaraz Khan remembered the way in which Badshah Khan made clear what qualities were desirable and undesirable for the KK movement: 'There was a man Abdul Rahman, a murderer and criminal, who was also an exceptionally brave man; but Badshah Khan removed him from the movement, because he said that we did not want this kind of bravado ... we needed honesty and a feeling of solidarity' (I.45).

Some comments suggested that, for all Badshah Khan's rhetorical use of *Pukhtunwali*, some people did perceive a tension between the tenets of non-violence and *Pukhtunwali*. Sarfaraz Nazim stated that: 'Non-violence was accepted by people because, even though it was incompatible with being a Pathan, it was compatible with Islam. It was accepted by people as a non-violent *jihad*' (I.1). Similarly Maulana Hamdullah Jan felt that the crux of Badshah Khan's success was that he had creatively *used* the message of Islam. For others, however, the philosophical ramifications were unimportant. They believed and trusted in Badshah Khan and were willing to do his bidding: 'Even if we had had guns, we wouldn't have used them because it was the order of Badshah Khan. I followed him right from the start. Badshah Khan's word was law' (I.42). 'I followed non-violence because it was Badshah Khan's order' (I.51).

I stressed in Chapter 2 that the motivations and reasons people had for joining the KK movement varied considerably. The ideological framework I have outlined here had a similar flexibility. The father of the young *khanzada* who believed he was a Pathan first and Muslim second could ground his own personal reconciliation to non-violence in aspects of *Pukhtunwali*. Those who placed their primary emphasis on being good Muslims could reconcile themselves to non-violence through the lessons

Badshah Khan highlighted from the Quran. And those who did not wish to think about such details could base their non-violence on the commands of a leader who was so conspicuously a true and honourable Pathan and a devout and saintly Muslim.

Community and Ideology

To see just how unusual and successful the KK's ideology was, it may be useful to compare it with those of other movements that emerged during the colonial period. First, we may contrast its attitude to Islam with those of its contemporaries. As Barbara Metcalf notes in her study of the Islamic revivalist movements which grew up in India during the nationalist struggle, a key concept in their discourse was *tajdid*, a commitment to the way of the Prophet (Metcalf 1982). In 1927 a religious teacher, Mawlana Muhammad Ilyas, founded the Tablighi Jama'at movement, which, from modest beginnings in North India, eventually reached out to Muslims all over the world, including Nigeria and England. The tenets of the movement revolved around the idea of *tabligh* (invitation) and sought to persuade modern Muslims to practise their religion with the same pride and diligence as had the early followers of the Prophet. The movement's message was kept simple; it did not believe in theological disputations and avoided conflict with the Islamic establishment of the *ulema*. It was also self-consciously apolitical (Van der Veer 1994: 128–30).

Very different was the Jama'at-i-Islami, founded in 1941 by Maulana Maududi, which was a self-consciously political movement. It also wished to revive the purity and devoutness of the Muslim community, although it was far more prone to theological disputation than the Tablighi Jama'at. Despite being a political movement which took views on goverment and the state, it was anti-nationalist. Initially, it did not support the Muslim League's idea of Pakistan, rejecting nationalism as a 'Western conspiracy' and arguing that the project of Pakistan entailed a particularism which would undermine the establishment of the transnational Muslim community which was Maududi's aim (Van der Veer 1994: 63). The movement was established as a tightly and hierarchically organised revolutionary force, run on almost Leninist principles; Maududi's idea that the state should be taken over by Islamic workers and then used to establish a revived and purified Islam has had considerable influence on revolutionary movements elsewhere in the Muslim world, such as the Ikhwan and the Muslim brotherhoods of Egypt and Sudan. Although it had limited success in elections it built up considerable influence in Pakistani politics through its campaigns to establish an Islamic constitution and *shari'a* (Islamic law) which would prohibit un-Islamic practices, a programme which in its radicalism attracted large parts of the intelligentsia, particularly university students.

The KK differed from these movements in very significant ways. It was not an exclusively Islamist movement, since 'a large number of Hindus and Sikhs joined the movement like everybody else' (I.12). Nor did Badshah Khan appeal to people to join his movement in order to either prove or improve themselves as good Muslims. Although he often accused the British of offences against Islam, he also accused them of many other things, such as economic exploitation and establishing corrupt systems of justice – complaints which were of equal concern to non-Muslims in the Frontier. The basis of the KK invitation, therefore, was to join a non-sectarian movement. The crucial alliance with the Hindu-dominated Indian National Congress also made this clear.

The other Muslim movements of the time placed great emphasis on the reform and revival of Islamic practice and the reanimation of Islamic ideals, with the first decades of Islam providing the fundamental examples of admirable Islamic behaviour. Although Badshah Khan did refer to acts of the Prophet, notably in respect of His acts of patience, and although he did pursue reform activities in Pathan society, he made no effort to improve or re-create the local community on the basis of an early Islamic blueprint. In fact, Badshah Khan had a relaxed attitude to orthodoxy and was impatient with the dogmas of the *mullahs*, as Jarnail Mohammed Umar illustrated in the following story:

> It was sometime in 1930. A Khudai Khidmatgar had died in a protest and was to be buried and a crowd had gathered to mourn him. Unfortunately it was raining. Badshah Khan suggested that the *jehnaza* (funeral) be conducted inside the mosque instead of in the pouring rain outside. The *mullahs* refused to do so, saying that Islam did not allow it. Badshah Khan said that it was in fact possible and that he had himself seen it done in Mecca. This led to an argument. (I.21)

Certainly the targets selected for picketing and boycott included some, such as brothels and liquor stores, which could be viewed as offensive to the religious sensibility. None the less, the majority of the reform activities conducted within the villages were of a religiously neutral type, such as sanitation and road building, or, in the case of education, even in contradiction to the prevailing religious orthodoxy of the *mullahs*. In that sense Badshah Khan's reform programme was premised much more on a utilitarian and modernist manifesto than on a retro-Islamic one.

Last, neither the Jama'at-i-Islami nor the Tablighi Jama'at addressed their messages to a constituency defined by regional or ethnic borders, since both aimed to reform and unite the Islamic community to its widest extent. Accordingly, while their influence has been extensive and geographically far-flung, they were not effective in mobilising the kind of dense membership and locally focused profile required for an effective mass political movement. In contrast, Badshah Khan was always very conscious of the constituency he was addressing. His resolve that the KK movement should be run by the Pathans for the Pathans was influenced, among other things, by his unhappy experiences of protest activities masterminded by ideologues elsewhere in India, notably the Khilafat.

A more suitable comparison, therefore, is with the Indian anti-colonial movement in Fiji described by John Kelly (Kelly 1991). Fiji bore some structural similarities to the Frontier: both were 'cut off' from the rest of India and suffered peculiar colonial atrocities, the main problem in Fiji being the severe sexual exploitation of female indentured labourers. Both areas suffered extreme neglect in facilities for education and colonial interference in marriage laws and traditional custom.

In response to these conditions Fiji witnessed the rise of two revivalist movements from two different sects of Hinduism, the Sanantanis and the Arya Samaj. Both worked on educational programmes and community uplift, including organising village councils, and both had to face colonial accusations of following Bolshevist Communism. The Arya Samaj movement subsequently launched a civil disobedience campaign against the colonial regime, but the movement was not a success. The Arya Samajists, in their 'back to basics' revival of the Vedic values of Hinduism, attacked the Hinduism of the Sanantanis, criticising their elaborate portrayals of the gods and ridiculing as degenerate their particular strain of emotional devotionalism. This was in much the same vein as criticism levelled by Christian missionaries and colonial officials, and the Arya Samajists may thus be seen as seeking to introduce something of an austere, quasi-monotheistic 'Protestant'-style Hinduism to demonstrate their own civilisation and modernity. Kelly calls this a utilitarian and 'modern retooled alternative ... which made god morally impeccable, but less relevant' (*ibid.*: 245). Isolated far from India and having to combat a hostile interfering colonial power, however, many of Fiji's Hindus remained deeply attached to the 'degenerate' Hinduism of the Sanantanis, which gave them greater comfort and hope of redemption, and their response to the Samajists' movement was therefore hostile.

The Arya Samaj's doctrinaire approach on religious practice precluded the island's Hindus from coming together into a unified community which could struggle effectively against the colonial regime. In the light of this failure and the contrasting success of the KKs, one may see the wisdom of Badshah Khan's decision to keep the KK ideology free of too much religious content or debate over theology and practice. Badshah Khan always specifically insisted to his followers that they should not enter into debate about religion with either religious leaders or anyone else. The KK similarly remained aloof from issues pertaining to the precise practice of Islam, or those concerning the relationship of Muslims to non-Muslims which were raised by Islamist movements elsewhere in South Asia. Given both the traditional Pathan penchant for *parajamba*, literally 'taking sides', and the numerous religious figures who dwelt in the Frontier, such doctrinal debates would have had great potential for divisiveness once unleashed.

But it was equally clear, as the failure of the Arya Samaj also illustrated, that in a broadly traditional and pious society a modernising political movement could not afford to alienate religious feeling or neglect the energy and solidarity which such feeling could bring. Hence Badshah Khan took it for granted that Islam was a very important part of the KK volunteers' lives and made considerable efforts to show that the newly introduced notions of non-violence and civil disobedience did not conflict with Islam. But he was also careful to restrict this religious content to the kind of generally accepted, everyday Islam which his followers unselfconsciously practised, avoiding any more precise specifications – in short, he sought to run a 'broad church'. Thus, while the movement was grounded in Islam in the same way as Pathan society as a whole was, it was not doctrinally prescriptive or disputatious.

Overall, therefore, I would suggest that Badshah Khan skilfully succeeded in creating a movement which successfully balanced the competing demands of religious affinity and ethno-cultural community. Wiqar Shah, himself a Pathan and author of an excellent monograph on Frontier politics in the years 1937–47, makes a similar point in considering the nature of the KK movement. He argues that for the Pathans Islam was one of the principal constituents of their self-definition, with a Muslim way of life and Pathan tradition being taken as complementary attributes of their identity (Shah 1999: 34). Their awareness of themselves as Pathans, however, and their love for what they saw as their traditional society distinguished them from other Indian Muslims. Thus, in his appeals for their support, Badshah Khan combined Islamic values of hatred against oppression and slavery with Pashto values of freedom and independence (*ibid.*: 36). He similarly used Islamic symbols of fraternity and love and Pashto terms of brotherhood to forge unity (*ibid.*: 35). As Shah concludes, therefore, the KK movement combined concerns of religion and concerns of Pathan identity, and the mix gave rise to a regionally specific political movement against the British.

I would suggest that what Badshah Khan sought to do above all was create an improved political and social context in which the people of the Frontier could live prosperously and fully express themselves as Pathans and Muslims. He had grown up in the violent and divisive climate of the turn-of-the-century Frontier, and the ideas of his untypical father, Behram Khan, had made a great impact: 'He was not like other *khans* ... . He did not take revenge and did not allow other people to either ... . He would tolerate any offence against him with patience.'[17] This was the kind of spirit Badshah Khan wished to spread among all Pathans, and he was not concerned about the precise balance of religion and custom which helped achieve it.

This kind of community-focused, common-sense ethics is similarly seen in the comments of my informants: 'Badshah Khan wanted to humanise Pathans' (I.1): 'For eight years between 1930 and 1938 there were no crimes, no court appeals. This was the effect of the Khudai Khidmatgar movement' (I.2). 'We used to like Badshah Khan because he said that we must fight against the British. But he also said the solution was not violence. Instead he told us that we should go from *hujra* to *hujra* telling people that all Pathans are brothers and about tolerance and honesty' (I.42). 'We used to recite a line which said "Those on whom God had grace would become a Khudai Khidmatgar, the others would support the British"' (I.56). Haji Sarfaraz Nazim Sahib argued that it was not its position on Islamic law or theology which made the KK popular, but rather its own distinctive framework of symbolism and practice: 'In the entire movement there were only ten to twelve educated people. For the rest it was the religion of the Khudai Khidmatgari that was attractive' (I.1).

Deran Shah recalled: 'In 1930 Badshah Khan came to our village along with two friends, and went to Amanullah Baba's house. He gathered people there and said to them "Let us populate this land with Pathans." Everybody was very enthused and joined him. We joined because the message of Badshah Khan and the Khudai Khidmatgar movement was irresistible' (I.5). Mir Mohammed said, 'Badshah Khan believed in the emancipation of his nation ... he always stood against anything that went against the interests of Pathans ... . Even recently, when he was so very old, he came here and condemned the Kalabagh dam project' (I.68). 'Badshah Khan's words seemed sweet to us. Unlike those of the people in the Muslim League. And therefore we took to non-violence. Talk to a Pathan sweetly and he will do anything! Badshah Khan formed human links between us that could not be broken by anti-riot police' (I.36).

[17] Khan 1983: 12. Some of my informants remembered Behram Khan as an extremely humble *khan*, who served his guests food himself rather than leaving it to servants.

Taken individually and together, these comments suggest the unselfconscious way in which the KKs perceived the unity of Islam and Pathan identity and understood that the movement's ultimate vision was neither of a better nation state nor of a better religious practice, but of a better moral and social community. It was 90-year-old Mohammed Gul of Tahkal who best summed up this balanced ideology: 'Everyone here remembers Badshah Khan with so much love. How can you not love a man who talks about Pathan brotherhood, about Islamic principles, about freedom from foreign rule?' (I.67).

Non-violence as a Lifelong Philosophy

If we imagine Islam, *Pukhtunwali* and non-violence as different ingredients in a cultural experiment, the solution the KK synthesised may have lasted long enough to be used and admired – but surely it was destined to fade once success was achieved? Yet the prolonged conversations I enjoyed with the surviving KKs suggest to me that upon the departure of the British they did not simply abandon non-violence as a tool which had served its purpose. Rather, the movement's emphasis on non-violence has stayed with them as a guiding principle throughout their lives.

I always asked whether they might have taken a violent approach to fighting the British if they had owned better weapons. Haji Zamir Gul stressed the renunciation of all types of weaponry, good or bad: 'Before joining the movement we used to have guns, including some good ones ... but after Badshah Khan we let them rust ... there was no place for guns in our movement' (I.49). Mira Khan said: 'Even if we had had weapons, we would not have fought. Badshah Khan brought light into our lives. His message was one of independence' (I.56). By 'independence', Mira Khan here seems to mean not merely political freedom from the British, but a spiritual freedom from the enmity and hatred that had dogged his people before Badshah Khan's message of unity and non-violence was accepted.

When I asked Gul Samand Khan if he still believed that non-violence was the best method of political struggle, he said: 'We believed in non-violence, we asked for our freedom with folded hands ... with violence we could not have won. But we did not want violence because although we were ready to die we could not assume the responsibility of the sacrifice of the lives of others' (I.55). As this statement and others like it clearly suggest, for many KKs non-violence acquired a moral and religious significance which far exceeded its tactical utility and which remains valid irrespective of the precise outcome of the political struggle: 'Badshah Khan will never be born again. It is because of his struggle that we achieved anything. His wish was to have an independent Frontier. That didn't happen. But he has left us his principles, his light ...' (I.67).

Fazle Rahim Saqi told me that when Mahatma Gandhi was visiting the North West Frontier Province for the first time in 1938, he expressed the desire to meet some of the leaders of the non-violent army of KKs:

So the Generals were summoned and twelve of them were introduced to Gandhi in the KK office. Gandhi asked them, 'Do you follow Badshah Khan as your leader? Do you obey him totally?' And they all said a prompt and vehement 'Yes!' Then Gandhi asked them, 'What will your reaction be if Badshah Khan one day decides to change and starts to believe in violence?' The Generals tried to tell Gandhi that he was making a mistake and that there was no way in which Badshah Khan would ever change his ideology. But, when Gandhi persisted, a General called Anwar, my father's brother's son, replied: 'We can leave Badshah Khan but we cannot leave non-violence.' This impressed Gandhi very much. (I.53)[18]

Some fifty years after the British had left, it was this spiritual victory which remained most important for the old men I spoke to.

When I turned back from the outer battle,
I set my face toward the inner battle.
We have returned from the lesser Jihad,
we are with the Prophet in the greater Jihad.

(Jalal ud-din Rumi, *Mathnavi-e-Ma'anavi* I: 1386–7)

Conclusion

I have argued that the non-violent ideology of the KK was thoroughly grounded in *Pukhtunwali* and Islamic thought. From Badshah Khan's speeches we can see some of the ways in which he negotiated a conceptual and cultural space for the virtue of non-violence and implied to his audiences that it was not as great a departure from their previous practice as it at first seemed. In this way, the key terms of *Pukhtunwali* – such as shame, honour, refuge and hospitality – were subtly redefined. My KK informants often argued that people were able and willing to adapt because 'Badshah Khan had raised our political consciousness so we could understand what was happening' (I.3). Statements about the importance of non-violence represent the convictions not only of the leadership but also of the average 'subalterns' of this non-violent army. In their *jihad*, the Pathans declined to take an eye for an eye, and instead decided to turn the other cheek. Their existing 'values and ideals were interpreted in terms of their function in a particular form of discourse rather than as timeless truths which stand beyond a speaker or writer' (Meeker 1979: 30). Accordingly, rather than conceive of culture as a passively received and immutable charter, we can see from the example of the Khudai Khidmatgars' ideology that people make selective and innovative use of traditional cultural elements in order to frame responses and solutions to the particular historical predicaments in which they find themselves.

[18] Even Wali Khan, who has taken over the mantle of Pukhtun leadership from his father, had not heard this story until May 1992, when I had occassion to narrate it to an audience in Delhi in response to a question expressing scepticism about the non-violence of the Pathans.

7
Pathans & Nationalist Politics

The political events of 1937–47 in the Frontier are complex and involved a number of tensions and oppositions. First, there was the tension between the kind of mass agitational politics which had emerged in the Frontier in the form of the KK, and the more sedate world of parliamentary politics ushered in by the Government of India Act of 1935. Second, there was the fierce party political rivalry between the Congress Party and the Muslim League. Third, there was the tension between the metropolitan, Hindu-dominated All India Congress party and the peripheral, Pathan, Muslim KK movement. Fourth, there was the three-way opposition between competing visions of India, Pakistan and Pathan regional autonomy. Last, there was the separation between the Settled Districts of the Frontier, dominated politically by the KK with its steady purpose and its non-violence, and the Tribal Areas, where violence continued to reign and alignments and attitudes were altogether more volatile. Meanwhile, the grey hand of the colonial authorities was exceptionally active in exacerbating these various oppositions in an effort to keep the Pathans divided and the Frontier quiescent. I do not wish to cover the political events in great detail – the interested reader is referred to the accounts of Jansson, Rittenberg and particularly Shah. I do wish, however, to highlight some aspects which add perspective and significance to the analysis of the KK movement contained in the previous chapters.

Parliamentary Politics

Under the new arrangements for the government of India around 14 per cent of the population in the NWFP were granted the right to vote. In the first elections in 1937 Congress stood on a manifesto which stressed its general aim of an independent, unpartitioned India, but also addressed issues specific to the Frontier, promising reform of the system of land tenure, rent and tax, with the specific aim of reducing the burden on the poorer peasantry. It also proposed to repeal the repressive laws operating in the Frontier, together with the system of grants and honours bestowed on the big *khans*. Mass demonstrations were prohibited during the election campaign, but the KK volunteers were mobilised to undertake canvassing work and ensure a good turnout, and Congress duly became the became biggest single party. After a brief minority coalition government of smaller parties led by a big *khan*, Sir A. Qaiyum, Congress was invited by the Governor of the Province to form a ministry, with Badshah Khan's brother, Dr Khan Sahib, as its Chief Minister.

The election of a Congress government was a great achievement for the KK and well remembered by my informants: 'In the 1936 elections we won 19 seats out of the 38 seats available for Muslims. The total number of seats in the assembly was 50. In those days people believed in *khadi* and cast votes like gifts. And this was possible despite Badshah Khan being in exile! If he had been here we could have won all the seats!' (I.2) 'Nineteen out of 49 seats were won by Khudai Khidmatgaran. But as Badshah Khan was in exile at the time he could not become the Chief Minister ... but in any case he did not want to be' (I.62)

On his return to the Province Badshah Khan worked closely with Dr Khan Sahib to address the demands of their supporters. My informants still remembered some of these successful measures – many of which had an egalitarian thrust, as Mohammed Badshah recalled:

> According to the Frontier Crimes Regulation, the common man could not make *hujras*, only *khans* could. Earlier, if they did, then the police came and demolished them. But Dr Khan Sahib changed that. Low-castes were given opportunity to buy land. They also became eligible for government jobs. Female education was started, because earlier even the Azad schools were only for boys. Dr Khan Sahib reduced taxes by one-third. Moneylenders were done away with ... everybody was treated equally. (I.62)

Particularly significant were reforms made to the *lambardari* system (see Chapter 1), restricting these minor officials' powers and replacing the quasi-hereditary status they enjoyed with the need to be elected by the village community, in a manner more like the *panchayats* of the rest of India. 'The *nawabs* and *khans* had implemented the *lambardari* system. When Dr Khan Sahib's ministry effectively banned it we were impressed. We felt that we really *were* going to be able to remove the British' (I.14). 'With Dr Khan Sahib the *lambardari* system was abolished. Earlier every *lambardar* who collected taxes had to be given a fixed fee for his job by the villagers' (I.65). Also significant was the law passed on women's inheritance. As in much of Muslim India, Pathan custom did not grant women the inheritance rights prescribed by the Quran. In 1937, the national Shari'a conference of Muslim leaders and theologians passed a resolution by which a daughter should inherit a share equivalent to half that of her brother's, and Dr Khan Sahib's ministry passed legislation to this effect: 'Ours was the only Province where this resolution was passed into law. It was a big help to women. People did not resist the change because as many people stood to gain by it as to lose' (I.2).

Overall, therefore, 'The Congress ministries made a big difference to the lives of the people. People were happy with the reforms they introduced' (I.53). 'In the elections, we managed to defeat some big *khans* and gained a lot of say for the first time in government' (I.36). While the election of the Congress ministry was a great success for the KK, however, it tended to reduce the former clarity of their struggle against the British regime in the Frontier. Because the Congress provincial government was now directly responsible for keeping order in the Frontier, campaigns of civil disobedience by the KKs had the potential to cause embarrassment to the ministry. For the most part, therefore, when Congress was in office the KK focused mainly on its social and self-improvement activities rather than on major acts of civil disobedience, and this was the case for the periods 1937–40 and 1945–6.

Although the KK placed great stress on its internal discipline, however, it was not always able to make its members 'unlearn' the new techniques of protest they had acquired. This was clearly seen in the several spontaneous actions of civil disobedience that occurred. In 1938, for instance, the 2,000 villagers of Ghalla Dher in Mardan District launched a protest against their notoriously grasping landlord, who was seeking to levy new illegal rents and fines upon them (see Shah 1999: 66–8). The villagers, led by men with extensive KK experience, refused to pay the money and when the bailiffs came to evict them resisted with sit-ins and other non-violent techniques, in which they were joined by other KK activists from neighbouring villages. The ministry blamed radical socialist elements within the wider Congress movement for encouraging the agitation, and the KK high command asked the rank and file to avoid involvement, warning of the need to avoid stirring up class hatred between peasants and landlords, which could lead to blood feuds and division in the Province. When the villagers were finally evicted, however, KK members from other villages came to cultivate their lands, just as they had done during the civil disobedience campaign for those who had been imprisoned. This gave much encouragement to the dispossessed families, who continued their resistance. Eventually the authorities felt compelled to arrest the village ringleaders for the sake of wider order and they were sentenced to two years' imprisonment. In protest their wives, mothers and sisters sat in the roads, waving red flags and carrying Qurans on their heads, and many were eventually injured when the police lost patience and charged with *lathis*. Eventually Badshah Khan himself had to visit to broker a compromise and the Congress ministry agreed to forbid the landlord's illegal taxes and stop the evictions.

A very similar incident took place the following summer at Muftiabad after tenants had been evicted by their landlords. The KK leadership urged volunteers to remain aloof from an agitation which it claimed was sponsored by 'anti-Congress elements', but again to no avail. Embarrassingly, Dr Khan Sahib's very own son Obeidullah was instrumental in leading the non-violent protest activities. Dr Khan Sahib had him arrested, saying his mind had been weakened during the long periods in jail he had spent in the course of the KK's previous civil disobedience campaigns. Badshah Khan denounced Obeidullah for creating disunity among the KK. Such events embarrassed the Congress ministry, while the official KK position of non-involvement tended to damage its own reputation among those peasants who looked to it as the main defender of their interests.

As Shah points out, however, not the least remarkable feature of these events is the way in which, despite the complete absence of any senior KK leaders, the peasants involved adhered totally to the principle and techniques of non-violent protest. This is good evidence, I would suggest, of the extent to which the principles of non-violence were now grounded in the minds and actions of the KK membership, and exerted an influence on the peasantry more widely.

The KK's stock also tended to suffer from its association with weaknesses in the Congress ministry's performance more generally. Although the ministry achieved much, the Governor's repeated refusal to give his assent to proposed legislation, the footdragging of the British-manned civil service and the ministry's own unwillingness to alienate the smaller *khans* meant that the Acts they passed to attack *khan* privilege and reform land practices were mostly watered down and often failed to meet the high hopes raised among the peasantry by the populist manifesto; this in turn tended to weaken KK activism. Official reports noted in 1939: 'It has now been realised how few of the promises made by the Congress leaders during the general election have been implemented during their term of office. This is probably the reason for the present lethargic attitude of the Red Shirts.'[1] As Maulavi Inayatullah put it: 'Dr Khan Sahib was not free to do anything ... the Governor constantly created obstacles in his way' (I.65). 'Yes, the Congress government helped us,' another informant recalled. 'They got us drinking water, cloth and sugar ... one and a half yards of cloth each and one and a half kilos of sugar. But the bureaucrats were British and did not always deliver these in order to discredit the Government' (I.61).

KK popularity was similarly vulnerable to adverse developments in the economy and to opposition party criticism. Sarfaraz Nazim told me that Dr Khan Sahib's ministry had earned much disfavour among the Pathans because of the shortages that arose in the supply of cloth after 1939 amid accusations that they were selling the material on the black market. Sarfaraz Nazim told me this was the result of propaganda: 'Most of it was spread by the Muslim League, who accused us of theft, saying that we were misusing our full access to government machinery. They incited people saying that we were depriving people of cloth for *kafans* (funeral shrouds)' (I.1). In reality such shortages mainly reflected the British rationing and control over supplies. None the less, this kind of emotive and religious propaganda directly affected the local reputations of the KKs, although ironically the main fall-out was borne by the local KK activists in the countryside, most of whom did not have the vote and for whom the world of parliamentary politics in Peshawar remained somewhat remote.

Badshah Khan always tried, therefore, to limit such collateral damage to the KK movement; he did not want it to overshadow his programme of social self-reform, which he still considered to be the Red Shirts' main aim. As a British intelligence report stated in 1939: 'There is general agreement that the tenure of office by Congress has increased the disruption in the ranks of the Red Shirts organisation ... . This view has often been expressed by Abdul Gaffar Khan and it was the principal reason for his determination to keep the Red Shirt organisation separate from the Congress.'[2] Badshah Khan was also well aware that the popular response in the Frontier was to *him* personally and to his own non-Hindu articulation of non-violence, and he thus needed to maintain the clarity of his leadership and avoid confusing it with that of the predominantly Hindu Congress. For example, a report to the Governor stated that: 'Abdul Gaffar Khan wishes to keep his dictatorship over the Red shirts free from interference by the Provincial Congress Committee ... . There is hardly any mention of Gandhi among Red Shirts.'[3]

For these reasons Badshah Khan always worked hard to ensure that the mass, military side of the KKs remained organisationally discrete from Congress, and this was one of the main motivations for establishing and maintaining the two separate wings of the movement (discussed in Chapter 5). The military wing, more populist and explicitly Pathan, was kept largely autonomous, while the civil wing kept far

---

[1] Governor's Report, November 1939, L/P&J/5/215 IOLR.
[2] Governor's Report, November 1939, L/P&J/5/215 IOLR.
[3] Governor's Report, May 1938, L/P&J/5/211 IOLR.

closer coordinating ties with the provincial Congress committee and ministry. The Governor, George Cunningham, accurately reported Badshah Khan's policy:

> Abdul Gaffar Khan insists on absolute independence for the Red Shirts, and maintains that any support or allegiance accorded to the Congress party by Red Shirts will be given under his orders and that the Red Shirts will take orders from nobody else. To ensure that this procedure is followed in practice he has appointed his nephew, Rab Nawaz, as commander-in-chief of the Red Shirts – thereby providing a further insulator against Congress interference. In this connection a general tendency in Ministerial circles is noticeable to avoid interference by the Congress Executive in Provincial administrative affairs .... Abdul Gaffar Khan ... has not attended recent Congress meetings, and has of late become more parochial in his activities. These ... go to show that the Red Shirts are determined to maintain their own independence as an organisation .... A corollary to this view is that the Congress executive will go a long way to retain the allegiance of the Red Shirts.[4]

A further concern on Badshah Khan's part was his continual fear of disunity. A further British report noted that: 'the Red Shirts continue to function as an autonomous organisation, the objective being to provide an insulator to prevent the rifts of opinion in Congress circles from affecting the discipline of the Red shirts'.[5] 'Badshah Khan has condemned the local Provincial Committee for intrigue and disunity and to some extent withdrew himself from it, saying that he intended to devote his whole energies to the training and organisation of the Red Shirts.'[6] Sarfaraz Nazim explained to me Badshah Khan's concern: 'We had the example of the Punjab Congress before us, you see. They spent more than half their energies reprimanding their own members! Therefore we always kept the KK organisation and the Congress separate' (I.1). Sarfaraz Nazim claimed that: 'Unlike the Congress, the KK organisation was never plagued by strife. That was because of the complete discipline and military organisation. There was always a reserve force of volunteers in the organisation who obeyed Badshah Khan totally' (I.1).

Both the logic of the dual organisation and the underlying tension between the functioning of the parliamentary party and the grassroots organisation are exemplified in the relationship between Khan Abdul Gaffar Khan and his elder brother Dr Khan Sahib. The two brothers were very different. Dr Khan Sahib, the elder, had been educated in Cambridge, married an Englishwoman, spoke English fluently, returned to the Frontier to be a Captain in the Guides Cavalry and later set up a successful medical practice in Peshawar. Only in 1930 did he get involved in his brother's political activities when Badshah Khan had been arrested and there was a need for someone he could rely on to provide leadership during his absence. When the 1935 Government of India Act opened the way for elections, Badshah Khan remained in prison in the Punjab, and so Dr Khan Sahib became the senior figure in the parliamentary Congress Party, and then Chief Minister.

In many ways the split of responsibilities worked well, since Khan Sahib's involvement in the fudge and compromise of legislation left Badshah Khan free to maintain a more pure and principled line on issues. It also gave him the necessary

---

[4] Governor's Report, June 1938, L/P&J/5/211 IOLR.
[5] Governor's Report, May 1938, L/P&J/5/211 IOLR.
[6] Governor's Report, July 1940, L/P&J/5/216 IOLR.

time and space to forge alliances with other nationalist leaders in India, and to travel extensively through villages in the Frontier, continuing to mobilise and sustain the KK volunteers with his own particular brand of charisma. The British government were very aware of the difference between the activities and personalities of the two brothers, always characterising Badshah Khan's politics as more 'extremist', which they saw as the main reason behind his success in whipping up support among the masses. In contrast, the British looked upon Dr Khan Sahib as having a moderating influence on the supposed 'volatility' of the KK activists. As the Governor noted with regret, however, 'unfortunately his influence with them is only a fraction of the power wielded by his more exciting brother, Abdul Gaffar Khan'.[7] This difference in their respective roles lives on today in the elderly KKs' memories. My informants did not have much to say about Khan Sahib, recalling him as a distant *khan* who was an important minister, rather than as someone who had visited and inspired them, although he did occasionally come out in red uniform at the Martyr's Day celebrations of the Kissa Khani massacre each 23rd of April.[8] Badshah Khan, on the other hand, with his pure and austere Pathan lifestyle and manner, was able to retain a direct empathy with the local rank and file, in spite of his frequent high-level visits with such national figures as Gandhi and Nehru.

Despite having a brother as Chief Minister, Badshah Khan never lost his abiding suspicion of politicans. Ahead of the 1946 elections Badshah Khan initially said that he was not going to canvas for Congress, so unimpressed had he been with its previous periods in provincial office and the self-serving attitude of some of its parliamentarians. One of my informants said that, for Badshah Khan, re-entering government was like taking something back into your mouth which you had already spat out! (I.1). Only when he became increasingly alarmed by the Muslim League's emphasis on religious tensions did he throw himself into the campaign to counter such influence. He insisted, however, that he and the KK would canvas only if the Congress parliamentarians promised to serve selflessly the poor majority of the population and agreed to follow the guidelines of the KK organisation (Shah 1999: 167).

Non-cooperation with the British War Effort

At the start of the Second World War, the national leaders of the Congress Party took the view that Britain was vulnerable and hence would be open to political pressure and negotiation. They undertook to commit Congress to cooperation with the war effort in return for Indian independence upon the conclusion of the war. Badshah Khan, however, was furious at this decision and resigned from the Congress. He argued that the principle of non-violence could not be put aside in any context, whether local or international, and that he and the KK could not participate in any way in the war effort. In this respect he emerged as more determinedly non-violent than the rest of Congress. This reflected the fact that Badshah Khan knew better than anyone the effort it had taken to persuade the Pathans to lay aside

---

[7] Governor's Report, June 1938, L/P&J/5/211 IOLR.
[8] Home/Pol. 48/5/44 NAI.

violence, and feared that even a brief cooperation in the war effort would undo years of hard work.

The Pathans had long been officially designated by the British as a 'martial race' and were natural targets for recruitment into the Indian army. Thus a key aim of KK agitation had long been to dissuade young Pathans from enlisting in this way, so as to wean them off traditions of martial endeavour and demonstrate non-cooperation with the state. Upon the outbreak of war the British redoubled their efforts and recruiting officers travelled widely in the Province offering 20 rupees to volunteers, a considerable amount. Mukarram Khan remembered men being recruited in this way (I.70). Sadar Musa Khan said that people also remembered 'that the British loyalists from the 1857 revolt had been made *khans* ... and families of soldiers who fought for the British and died in [the First World] War were later given lands that had been confiscated from *khans* who supported the KK' (I.23). Also, the big *khans* were keen to prove their loyalty to the regime in its time of need; long accustomed to providing levies of men to the British, they now exerted their great powers of patronage and intimidation to persuade tenants and clients to enlist.[9] Muhammadi Shah remembered being beaten up by his landlord's retainers in this way (I.47). Others recalled being pressurised by *mullahs* to join the war against Nazi Germany, 'the enemy of Islam'.

Badshah Khan toured extensively in an effort to combat these pressures, warning in his speeches about the unwisdom of having any association with the war. He stressed to gatherings the shortages and scarcities that arose in wartime and the adverse impact this would have on the nationalist political struggle. He also argued that, since the British had not consulted with the Pathans or Indians more broadly before becoming embroiled in war, it would reflect a lack of political maturity and weak sense of independence to accede to that decision.

The question of enlistment was a sensitive topic for my informants. Most assured me that neither they nor their immediate circle had enlisted. Some went further, saying: 'No KK ever went for recruitment', or that 'KKs never stopped wearing their own uniforms' (I.1). Muhammadi Shah, however, acknowledged that 'People enlisted in spite of Badshah Khan. A prophet can never convince everyone' (I.47). This view is more realistic and is supported by other interesting anecdotes:

> There was a man called Fazal Din from Pdang, a KK who had run away from home. He was in another district where people did not know him and a contractor noticed him for his excellent drill (due to his training in the movement) and recruited him. But then later they suspected him to be a spy and he was therefore given a three-month pay packet and asked to retire! (I.23)

Overall, the view emerging from my informants' narratives was that, in the KK's stronghold areas in the central Settled Districts, the discipline, support and mutual shaming among the membership successfully impeded enlistment – it appears that Fazal Din had to leave his own village and go elsewhere as a stranger in order to sign up. In areas where there were more non-Pathans and the KK was less influential, however, it seems more men did enlist – mainly for the money, according to my informants.

---

[9] Another way was to contribute tens of thousand of rupees to things like the aircraft fund. Governor's Report, October 1940, L/P&J/5/216 IOLR.

Badshah Khan's reaction to enlistment was both angry and sorrowful:

Reports of a tour by Abdul Gaffar Khan in Kohat and Bannu ... . Interesting for their
negative nature. All meetings poorly attended, and although Abdul Gaffar Khan
condemned Pathans as ruining their nation by fighting for the British who had declared war
without consulting them, he said that so many of the 'Red Shirts' had recently proved themselves unfit for self-government ... that he was not ready to lead them in a fight against the
British.[10]

As the British report rightly implies, Badshah Khan regarded participation in the war
effort not only as contrary to the ideas of non-violence, but as a betrayal of the whole
effort to deny the legitimacy of British rule. By joining its army he felt the Pathans
had demonstrated their unsuitability for self-government and his statement that he
was no longer willing to lead them was a clear attempt to shame them into staying
faithful to the principles of non-violence and non-cooperation.

As Badshah Khan had warned, the Frontier soon began to experience war-related
shortages and economic disruption, and these in turn exerted a negative impact on
the political life of the Frontier. Food prices rose, bringing benefit to the landlords but
hardship to the peasantry, who found little time or energy for protest. As the
Governor reported: 'Political inertia in rural areas ...: attitude of the people
undergone remarkable change ... . Interest now centred on *zamindari* [landlords] ...
complaints confined to purely parochial matters such as the supply of irrigational
water ... attempts to keep political interest alive fails.'[11] In short, the increasing
material distress led many to vent their anger against the profiteering landlord class,
and hence the war undid some of the progress Badshah Khan had achieved in raising
the peasantry's political vision to focus on the British. This fall in political interest and
turn to 'parochial' concerns was obviously of critical advantage to the colonial
government in a time of war.

Responding to the limited nature of British promises on India's future, Congress
subsequently reversed its position on cooperation with the war effort. In August
1942 it passed its Quit India resolution, authorising Gandhi to lead a mass non-
violent campaign for independence on the widest scale. In the Frontier Badshah
Khan rejoined the Party and toured the Settled Districts to popularise the Congress
initiative, urging the population not to pay their rents and taxes, to leave their jobs if
government servants and to desert the army. Deran Shah and others recalled the
launch of the campaign vividly: 'In 1942 on the 4th of September we declared independence. We declared an ultimatum that either we would finish the British or we
would finish ourselves. But we were confident the ultimate victory would be ours ...
This would be our last battle' (I.5). 'In 1942 disobedience was resumed. For Badshah
Khan, *Purna swaraj* (complete self-rule) meant that every child should get a vote on
the quality of his life ... and he was therefore not willing to rest before he had achieved
that' (I.26).

After a period of preparation the KK launched a wide-ranging campaign, picketing
liquor shops and government schools and arranging student strikes. There were also
'raids' on government offices and law courts to stage sit-ins. In October 1942

---

[10] Chief Secretary's Report, December 1939, L/P&J/5/215 IOLR.
[11] Governor's Report, January 1940, L/P&J/5/216 IOLR.

Badshah Khan was mercilessly beaten during a police *lathi* charge on a demonstration, and he and other KK leaders were arrested and imprisoned. For two years
the KK maintained the protest campaign in the face of continual beatings, arrests
and other repressive measures. Their efforts compelled the national government to
divert significant resources to the Frontier – police numbers increased from 7,500 in
1941 to 21,000 plus 9,000 auxiliaries by the end of the war, all equipped with
modern guns, radios and vehicles (Shah 1999: 139). Since these repressive
resources would otherwise have been used against protesters elsewhere in India, the
KK had once more taken on a heroic share of the hardship and pain of the nationalist
protest. And, as before, despite the fierce counter-measures and constant provocations, they maintained an unbendingly disciplined adherence to non-violence.

The Emergence of the Muslim League

Through the 1930s and early 1940s the Muslim League was in a very weak
condition in the Frontier. The Congress, as we have seen, gained considerably in
strength after 1930, swept along by Badshah Khan and the KKs. In 1937 officials
reported that 'the Muslim League ... are fast receding into the background ... for want
of leadership and funds. The Congress [is the] only party backed by real organisation.'[12] This 'real organisation' was provided by the extensive village- and district-
level KK structure which I described in Chapter 5. In 1936 the Muslim League's
national leader, Jinnah, visited the Frontier but failed to elicit mass support, and the
party made a poor showing in the 1937 election.

Although the measures on land and privilege introduced by the Congress ministry
of 1937–9 had fallen short of popular hopes, they had been more than sufficient to
disturb the larger landlords. The Governor reported a meeting in April 1939 with a
deputation of 'very influential *khans*' who had come to complain about being
specially discriminated against by the Congress ministry; he reflected that the administration could not 'afford to neglect a class of people who still have a strong sentimental loyalty to the British Crown'.[13] The Governor thus conveyed his regrets but
assured them of his support and added that the remedy really lay in their own hands:
they needed to form a party strong enough to win the next election. Thus the
Governor actively encouraged the big *khans* to put aside their mutual differences in
order to support and properly finance the Muslim League. The British hoped that a
strong party with an avowedly 'Muslim' agenda would draw support away from the
KK–Congress alliance.

The official encouragement of the League was part of a constant strategy of 'divide
and rule'. The memoirs of an officer who served in the Frontier between 1941 and
1947 relate a typical incident from 1942 and praise the finesse of a fellow
bureaucrat:

[He] had very skilfully succeeded in injecting some communal divisiveness into the
Congress arrangements for picketing local schools. Muslim opinion was 'outraged' by

[12] Governor's Report, November 1937, L/P&J/5/211 IOLR.
[13] Governor's Report, April 1939, L/P&J/5/211 IOLR.

alleged threats by the pickets to the modesty of their daughters and one of the most dangerous agitators was beaten up by some Muslims. 'Divide and rule' can be a risky tactic ... but it worked for him and I took over a quiet district.' (Noble 1997: 133)

The regime's tactics were quite transparent even at the time. As Muhammadi Shah put it: 'The way that Badshah Khan started the KK movement, the British then started the Muslim League' (I.47). My informants said they had been well aware of the close links between the Muslim League, the big *khans* and the British, and that they regarded the League as the agents of the British. Several recalled nicknaming them 'the Motor League' to mock the wealth and affluence of their membership, which contrasted so sharply with the average KK's penury.

In March 1940 the All India Muslim League took its decisive Lahore resolution, which committed it to striving for a separate Muslim state of Pakistan upon independence from the British. The League began to publicise the idea of Pakistan in the Frontier. Initially, however, the idea attracted little interest or popular support. Shah notes that, when two noted League orators toured Charsadda, the immediate upshot was increased KK enrolment in the area! Such was the apathy that in the 1943 by-election campaigns the local League decided not to mention Pakistan in their campaign at all.

The dynamics of Muslim League support in the Frontier remains the key debate in the historiography, but Shah sets out a cogent and plausible analysis. The primary political interest and aim of the majority of the Pathan intelligentsia was in the improvement of the material and political status of the Pathans of the Frontier, specifically through enhanced self-rule and cultural autonomy. Such regional autonomy seemed likely to be better served within the large, messy, diverse, quasi-federal structure that India was likely to become on independence, rather than the smaller, more ideologically focused and centralised nation that was the blueprint for Pakistan. Moreover, the Pathans traditionally had seen themselves as part of the wider Muslim world – their fellow Pathans were across the border in Afghanistan, and their wider 'imagined community' had taken in the Muslims of Central Asia and the Caucasus. They had not felt any particular affinity with the Muslims in the rest of the India, therefore, or any imperative to join them in a separate nation state as the League proposed. Last, much of the Muslim League's popular appeal in India tended to come from its emphasis on the spectre of Hindu domination and oppression over Muslims. Such a scenario was not convincing in the Frontier, given that the Hindus were such an insignificant minority there (well under 3 per cent). Throughout India, the League was always stronger in provinces with smaller Muslim minorities, who felt more vulnerable, than in those with substantial Muslim populations, such as Punjab and Bengal. In so far as the Frontier was the only majority Muslim Province in India, its neglect of the Muslim League was just an extreme case of this general pattern.

None the less, if for most of the period under discussion the League's actual support in the Frontier was modest, its activists and politicians subjected the Congress and KK alliance to a constant barrage of criticism in an effort to portray Badshah Khan and the KK as stooges of the Hindus. Shah presents numerous examples (Shah 1999: 107). It was said that a good Pathan 'should receive orders from Medina not Wardha' (Medina being the birthplace of the Prophet Mohammed, Wardha the site of

Gandhi's *ashram*), and that Badshah Khan had replaced his turban with a Gandhi cap, the crescent and star with the *charkha*. League publications carried photos of him sitting with Hindu Congress workers and eating from their utensils. It was alleged that the wily Gandhi had captivated the hearts of the simple-minded Khan brothers, who had shamefully taken shelter within a Hindu organisation. The League also criticised the KK for embracing 'an effeminate cult of non-violence', and after Badshah Khan's resignation from the Congress over its policy on the war, the League, which was more supportive of the British war effort, accused him of going against the Islamic injunction of *jihad.*

To contend with this propaganda Badshah Khan was compelled to reiterate constantly that he himself was a believing Muslim and that affiliation to the Congress in no way endangered Islam. He made a comparison with the strategic alliances which the Prophet entered into with the Jews to further the interests of the still-fledgling Islamic community. He also likened the Muslim League to gramophone records which produced sound only when touched by the British needle.[14] His sensitivities on the subject were apparent, however, as the Governor reported: 'Abdul Gaffar Khan has been making an intensive tour of Mardan, two by-elections coming up ... . He has refrained from using the word "Congress" and has referred to his party by the Islamic title "Khudai Khidmatgar" ... to forestall any anti-Hindu propaganda.'[15] More subtly, as we saw in Chapter 6, he was always careful to show that the idea of non-violence was entirely compatible with Islam.

The repetition of such accusations and the efforts the League made to widen the social composition of its membership after 1943 started to win over some popular support, including some converts from the KK. Fazle Rahim Saqi remembered trying 'to convince a lot of people not to join the Muslim League'. When I asked about this trend my informants typically argued that this was a quite different phenomenon from the growth of the KK. They felt that as KK political supporters they were independent volunteers and 'fully felt a part of the Congress', whereas they thought the mass supporters of the League were only there because 'the big *khans* forced their tenants to join' (I.53). Fazle Rahim Saqi went on to say that: 'the reason these people gave was that they had to tolerate a lot of beatings and torture from the British for being Khudai Khidmatgaran'. In support of this contention he stated that often the prodigal revolutionaries would change their minds again once the bullying had stopped and a discreet period had elapsed, whereupon 'Badshah Khan had an amazing capacity to welcome back defectors!' (I.53).

Congress Perceptions of the Khudai Khidmatgars

Badshah Khan had always made it clear that he had joined the Congress and allied the KK to it in 1931 because it was the only well-organised body actively struggling for the same objective as himself – the ejection of the British from India.[16] In contrast, the

[14] Ramu 1992: 109 and 137.
[15] Governor's Report, January 1938, L/P&J/5/211 IOLR.
[16] Home/Pol. 4/2/33 NAI.

Muslim League at that time was neither well organised nor militant in opposing the British. From the Congress perspective the KK provided the mass Pathan following from which the Congress Provincial ministries of 1937 onwards derived their popular legitimacy. The NWFP was the *only* province in British India with an overwhelming Muslim majority, and so being popular in the Frontier was a vital vindication of the Congress claim to represent both Muslims and Hindus throughout India.

Given the disciplined and determined way in which the KK maintained non-violent protest through the great campaigns of 1930–4 and 1942–3, one might have thought that their reputation within Congress would be very high. In some ways it was – many warm words were spoken and written in public about the valour of the KKs, and Badshah Khan himself was regarded as one of the most formidable leaders in the entire nationalist movement. Yet I would argue that the doubts which the Congress had expressed in 1930 about the Pathans' ability to master non-violence never entirely disappeared. The fundamental problem was that the Frontier was the subject of ill-informed curiosity in the rest of India. Its 'strange' customs of blood feuds and tribal loyalty were quite different from the caste-based order of village India. Consequently, Congress shared many British stereotypes about the violent nature of the Pathans. Despite the alliance and shared aims, the geographical and cultural divide at the Indus and the deliberate British security measures restricting travel and communication together meant that for much of the period there was a lack of the day-to-day interaction and contacts which might have eroded such incomprehension. Aside from the very highest levels of leadership, there was little involvement between the activists of the two sides; as a result, the Pathans were never really assimilated into the Indian National Congress alongside rank-and-file Congress workers.[17]

These difficulties were compounded by the fact that the political climate in the NWFP was very different from elsewhere. We discussed at length the severity and ruthlessness of the physical intimidation which the British were willing to deploy in the Frontier, actions which shocked even experienced Congress activists such as Elwin. Similarly, Gandhi's son, Devdas, reported with some surprise in 1931 that there was continuing repression regarding access to salt in the Frontier, an issue on which the British had already granted concessions in the rest of India after Gandhi's dramatic and decisive march to Dandi on the salt *satyagraha*.[18]

Stereotypes of violence, communication difficulties and knowledge that the Pathans were being subjected to particularly fierce repression and provocation combined to make the Congress executive continually doubtful about KK adherence to non-violent methods of protest. They were constantly concerned that lapses by the Red Shirts would damage Congress prestige and the authority of the non-cooperation movement in the rest of the country.[19]

[17] Some KKs attended annual All India Congress Committee Meetings, but they tended to live separately and, although befriended, were left somewhat to themselves, not least because not all spoke anything other than Pashto. See list of delegates from NWFP to 48th Congress of the INC, Bombay.

[18] 'The story of the salt concession in this area is sad indeed. I could not resist the feeling that the local authorities were hostile to the concession and made no effort to work it in the spirit in which it was made. There is great poverty in this area and it seems a thousand pities that the settlement should have failed to give the much needed relief in this area which it was intended to bring to the poor.' Devdas Gandhi, 'Report on the NWFP 1931', File No. P-16 (1932), AICC Papers, NMML.

[19] As had the violence at Chauri Chaura in Uttar Pradesh.

Such doubts were present from the start. When in 1930 Congress appointed Badshah Khan to coordinate the civil disobedience programme in the Frontier, it was not without some apprehension. The local committee received a letter from Nehru asking for their detailed proposals for carrying out the programme of civil disobedience and laying repeated emphasis 'on the importance of observing non-violence *in view of the traditional reputation of the people of the Frontier for the opposite characteristic'* (my emphasis).[20] In due course, Gandhi offered assurances that anyone meeting Badshah Khan in person would be convinced of his complete lack of any violent intent, and described him as a 'truthful man and out and out believer in non-violence'.[21] None the less, Congress continually sought to check on the KK activities and in 1934 the Congress General Secretary sent a letter to the Provincial *jirga* enquiring whether there had been any incidents of violence in the Frontier in the course of the ongoing civil disobedience movement, and demanding 'accurate information on this point'.[22]

In December 1934, Gandhi sent his aide Charlie Andrews to talk to the Home Secretary in Delhi about the KK. Andrews had been writing in the London press to defend the name of the KKs, who (as we saw in Chapter 4) were being represented as 'a dangerously violent Frontier movement akin to Russian communism'. In his record of the conversation, Andrews said the Home Secretary defended this characterisation of the KK on the grounds that Badshah Khan's speeches were of an 'inflammatory nature'. In reply Andrews initially described Badshah Khan as one of the noblest Muslims he had ever met, 'as tender as a child and as brave as a lion', and he drew a distinction between fiery rhetoric and physical aggression. The Home Secretary persisted with the allegations, however, until finally Andrews confessed his own surprise that Gandhi had accepted the Frontier movement so quickly and with so little enquiry, and said that he feared Gandhi had failed to appreciate or understand 'the mentality of the Pathans' (Andrews 1939). Here, then, was the strange scene of a trusted envoy of Congress confirming to the British their own worst prejudices about the Pathans.

For several years the British prohibited Gandhi from travelling to the Province. When finally he was allowed to visit, his main objective seems once more to have been to ascertain how well civil disobedience and non-violence were working in the Frontier. Most of my informants certainly remembered it this way, and retain to this day a vivid memory of the event and a great sense of pride in the impression they made on their distinguished visitor. Shah Jahan Khan and Gul Rahman told me: 'When Gandhi visited the Frontier thousands of Khudai Khidmatgars lined the streets from Utmanzai to Charsadda. At the meeting that was held, Gandhi said: "I congratulate you that you have the privilege of being led by Badshah Khan. I have been to many public meetings all over the country but the level of organisation in today's meeting surpasses all of them. There is so much discipline everybody is so quiet that one can hear the birds!" ' (I.34, I.40). This statement is particularly significant given that at the same period in the mid-1930s Gandhi was imploring crowds elsewhere in India to be more disciplined.[23] The KKs came out of the comparison very

---

[20] Chief Secretary's Report 1930, L/P&J/12/9 IOLR.
[21] Letter from Gandhi to the Home Secretary, Mr. Emerson dated June 13th 1931. File No. 206/1930 (Home/Pol.) NAI.
[22] Chapra (B&O), 17–7–34 NAI.
[23] For example, Gandhi had been asking them repeatedly not to shout slogans or beg *darshan* – a visual glimpse, usually of divinity – of their leaders in the middle of the night when they arrived at railway stations. See Amin 1984.

well, and the trip was successful in so far as Gandhi returned from it greatly reassured of the discipline of the KK and their adherence to non-violence.

The KKs were well aware of the image outsiders had of them as unruly and violent, and my informants still remember vividly the Congress scepticism about the Pathans' adaptation to non-violence. They thus told me about Gandhi's statement as a way of reassuring me that all they had been telling me about the organisation and peaceful activities of the movement was true: it really had happened, and *even Gandhi had acknowledged it*. Muffariq Shah, a *khan* involved in the movement, reiterated this: 'Our organisation consisted of hundreds and hundreds of workers, totally disciplined and ready to carry out any orders given to them by their leaders. Gandhi and Nehru used to be amazed and scared of this army!' (I.20). These recollections were accompanied by pride and conviction that their early assurances to Gandhi of the KK's adherence to non-violence were thoroughly vindicated in the long years of activism and struggle that followed.

In truth, however, the struggle to prove themselves in the eyes of Congress was never won, and much later Nehru was still purveying exactly the same stereotypical image. He had visited the Frontier in the late 1930s, receiving a warm welcome and seeing the KK in action, yet when he came to write his *Discovery of India* in 1944, he did not hide his disbelief: 'When it is remembered that a Pathan loves his gun more than his brother, is easily excited, and has long had a reputation for killing at the slighest provocation, this self-discipline appears little short of miraculous' (Nehru 1985 [1946]: 381). The British were were well aware of these continuing reservations on the part of Congress and did their utmost to foster them.

Relations with the Tribal Areas

An issue which always complicated the discussion of non-violence was the significant differences between the Tribal Areas and Settled Districts in the Frontier. The British viewed the Tribal Areas as the front line of the Raj, and were desperate to avoid any nationalist agitation there. They thus prevented any attempts to initiate political gatherings and organisations in the Tribal Areas, and carried out intense surveillance and other measures, including bombing raids, to ensure the 'loyalty' of the tribals. In addition, the authorities strove to minimise communication between the two regions in order to prevent the emergence of a pan-Pathan solidarity. Badshah Khan asked the Governor on a number of occasions for access to the Tribal Areas but was repeatedly rebuffed.[24] With Badshah Khan unable to carry his powerful message into the Tribal Areas and with no KK organisation allowed there, the tribals never took on board the idea of non-violence. When the news spread of

[24] In 1937, for example, Badshah Khan met with Governor George Cunningham and raised the question of access to the Tribal Areas. According to Cunningham's account Badshah Khan 'started by saying that Pathans were all one, and that the Pathan problem has to be tackled as a whole, both in the Settled Districts and in tribal territory. He did not actually say that he wanted permission to go into tribal territory himself, though he hinted at this. I said that all this was a very large question, and I would have to think over it, and he did not pursue the subject further. I told him that I was always ready to have talk and discuss any ideas he might have for promoting the common good of the people. I fancy that he will come and have another talk later on.' Governor's Report, 1937, L/P&J/5/211 IOLR.

British troops firing on unarmed Pathans at the Kissa Khani massacre in 1930, large numbers of Afridi arrived in the Settled Districts in a show of solidarity, fully armed and ready to fight. According to my informants the KK leaders thanked the Afridi for their support but declined their offer of military help, and ever after the Afridis seem to have had a genuine but slightly bemused respect for the KK. The conceptual difference between the KK's approach as a political organisation and the Afridis' experience of charismatic rebellion is suggested by Elwin's report that the Afridis 'do not altogether understand the cry of "Inquilab Zindabad" [Long Live Revolution]. They think that there is a living man called Inquilab, a great leader who has arisen to lead the people to freedom.'[25] The Afridis continued to demonstrate their sympathy in the traditional manner by harassing the English, capturing two English military officers and saying they would release them only when the government ceased its hostilities against the Red Shirts. In response the British established permanent army posts in the Afridis' vital winter pasture land as a disincentive to further involvement with the KK (Noble 1997: 173)

Throughout the 1930s, while the non-violent struggle was being waged by the KK in the Settled Districts, a series of violent insurrections took place in the Tribal Areas, on the initiative of various religious–political leaders, most prominently the Faqir of Ipi in Waziristan, and the British administration used these to create difficulties for the relationship between the KK and Congress. They constantly publicised reports of raids which the tribals were alleged to have conducted against the small Hindu minority in the southern Settled Districts. When I presented these British claims to my informants, however, they categorically denied them. Janan Khalifa, who came down from Waziristan (where I was not permitted) to see me, said that one particularly well-publicised raid on Bannu was targeted solely on English strongholds and depots, and had in no way been directed against Hindus. Sarfaraz Nazim Sahib said to me impatiently:

> All these reports of raids by tribals on non-tribals in the British documents that you are reading to me, are spurious claims because these raids were actually directed against the British. To prove the point, there have been no such raids between 1947 and 1980 [i.e. before the start of the Afghan war]. Pathans from tribal territories came into the Settled Districts to do business and work. The question of raids simply does not arise (I.1).

'Nobody was killed or robbed in the raid of 1938,' Mohammed Yakub Khan stated, and there was 'definitely no looting ... these raids were directed not at Hindus but at the homes of the British and the British loyalists' (I.61).

The truth is hard to ascertain. Certainly, as we saw in Chapter 4, the British were more than happy to use fictional propaganda against the Pathans and to allege attacks on Hindus would be perfectly consistent with their earlier attempts to manipulate religious differences between the KK and Congress (making KK prisoners wear saffron-coloured clothes, for example). None the less, it seems undeniable that raids of some kind were launched from the Tribal Areas, and throughout 1938–9 there was a wave of kidnapping and looting in Bannu and Dera Ismail Khan districts,

---

[25] From 'What is Happening in the North West Frontier?' Report by Father Verrier Elwin, 1932, F.No. 11 AICC Papers NMML.

where most of the non-Pathan minorities were concentrated. An exasperated Dr Khan Sahib eventually proposed draconian legislation empowering police to intern any suspects without evidence or reason (though the motion was not passed).

Badshah Khan argued publicly that the raids were mainly attributable to the anger and frustration of the Waziris in response to the very aggressive British actions being taken against the Faqir of Ipi, and that more humane treatment of the tribes would be the most effective contribution to law and order (Shah 1999: 78). Mohammed Yakub Khan told me that the raids aimed to get money to buy arms to fight off the British attacks: 'There were large concentrations of Hindu businesses and raids meant a means of making money' (I.61). Badshah Khan also argued that government officials helped organise the raids themselves to discredit the KK and the Congress ministry among the non-Pathan minorities in those districts, many of whom had fled to the towns to escape the raids. He personally toured the area in an effort to restore confidence to the minority communities: 'The Faqir of Ipi told his people not to harm Hindus and that their battle was only against the British. There used to be regular crossings across the Durand Line ... . British law was disregarded. But there were British agents in their ranks and they always spoiled things ... ' (I.61).

As a further strand in the British approach of divide and rule, the authorities sought to counterbalance the KK–Congress dominance in the Settled Districts by actively promoting the Muslim League in the Tribal Areas. Although Badshah Khan was consistently denied access, Jinnah, the leader of the All India Muslim League, was allowed to visit in 1936. More generally, the Political Agents made great efforts to promote criticism of the KK and Congress. The authorities paid the tribes of the Tribal Areas substantial subsidies to remain loyal to the Crown and keep the peace; they thus had significant leverage over most of the *khans*. When uprisings did occur they were led not by *khans* but by religious figures such as the Haji of Turangzai. The British similarly subsidised the regular clergy and put much effort into persuading the *mullahs* in the Tribal Areas to carry out helpful propaganda. In the 1930s the authorities encouraged the *mullahs* to denounce Bolshevism as the enemy of Islam, not least because this also allowed them to denounce as anti-Islamic the supposedly Bolshevik Red Shirts (Shah 1999: 138). During the war Nazism, too, was portrayed as an enemy of Islam, and Congress's position of non-cooperation with the war effort was denounced as collaboration with the enemies of Islam.

As a result, Badshah Khan had little confidence in the political leadership of the Tribal Areas. In his view most of the *khans* there were stooges of the British. The 96-year-old Haji Abdul Wadood recalled this for me in the following terms:

Relations with the tribal agencies were not good, because they were in the pay of the British. When Badshah Khan announced a meeting in the Mohmand agency they did not want it, and this was at the provocation of the British. Badshah Khan used to question their 'tribal' status. He used to say that if they were not under the British government then why were they given the benefit of macadamised roads? The *khans* of the tribes never wanted to support Badshah Khan for this reason. (I.16)

None the less Badshah Khan made constant efforts to try to remain in touch with the Tribal Areas, particularly those leaders who did try to stand up against the British. This was not easy, however, as Haji Chairman Meherban Shah, of the

Yusufzai in the Settled Districts, noted: 'We always wanted to form links with the Yusufzais in Swat but never could because the Wali of Swat was a loyalist and would not allow it. We have resumed links with them only after the princely states were abolished' (I.36). In 1935–6 messengers were sent to Bajaur in the Tribal Areas 'to tell them about the Khudai Khidmatgar movement and about the fight of the Pukhtun people against the British government ... and the importance of Pathan unity' (I.8). Haji Sarfaraz Nazim Sahib recalled that: 'In 1942 we went into the Tribal Agencies to extend links of *biraderi* (brotherhood) with them. Mohammed Israr Khan and myself were also sent later. We lived in the agencies of Bajaur and Mohmand for three years. Our people also went to Waziristan and the Afridi territories' (I.1). Janan Khalifa said the Faqir of Ipi kept in regular contact with Badshah Khan: 'Badshah Khan used to encourage us to go to the Faqir and help him. We used to supply food and provisions to him in the hills. Once we were caught ... about 30 or 40 lorries were caught. But Dr Khan Sahib got us released' (I.58).

British intelligence reports in the archive hint at secret communications between the Afridis and Dr Khan Sahib, who was said by the British to have 'positioned himself as the champion of Afridi malcontents'.[26] Another report said that 'it would appear for the most part the Red Shirts have been almost entirely absorbed in cross-border affairs' and identified conspiracies between the Settled and Tribal Districts:

> The local authorities at Bannu are convinced that one Malik Ali Akbar Khan of Bannu, a Congress worker (the host this week of Dr Khan Sahib) was largely instrumental in inciting the Daurs to rise up this spring. However, no concrete evidence of this was available ... . The Political Agent has informed us that a party of about 8 Red Shirts visited the Faqir of Spankhare recently and endeavoured to enlist his sympathy with a promise to act as a channel with Bajaur, but without success. Will supply names shortly.[27]

Although much of the detail of these events remains obscure, it is clear that Badshah Khan and Khan Sahib felt an acute sense of solidarity with their fellow Pathans in the Tribal Areas and took very seriously the importance of attracting their goodwill and support for the nationalist cause. They repeatedly intervened in their own ways to keep relations amicable: 'Dr Khan Sahib never criticised the Faqir of Ipi, nor did he ever fine the Waziris. He used to support him' (I.61). 'Dr Khan Sahib would never issue any statement against the Faqir of Ipi, even after the Bannu raid' (I.58).

None the less, the British stranglehold on the Tribal Areas forced the KK into what was at best a partial and covert relationship with the tribals. The KK movement was never allowed to gain a firm foothold there and the majority of the tribals never took on board the idea of non-violence or came together in effective opposition to the British. On the basis of these stories and reports it seems that Badshah Khan felt that the larger cause of pan-Pathan solidarity meant that the KK should cooperate with the tribals wherever possible, including supplying the Faqir of Ipi, even where that meant having to turn a blind eye to his continuing violent engagement with the British forces. Whether justifiably or not, the modest links sustained with the tribals further fuelled Congress suspicions about the Khudai Khidmatgars.

[26] 'Red Shirts and Tribal Affairs during 1936', L/P&J/5/211 IOLR.
[27] *Ibid.*

The Approach to Partition

Even after the end of the war, the Muslim League and its proposal for the creation of Pakistan remained of limited appeal in the Settled Districts of the Frontier and the relationship between Hindus and Muslims remained calm. On a platform backing an unpartitioned India, Congress won strongly in the 1946 elections, gaining 30 out of the 50 seats. But the Muslim League continued to berate Badshah Khan for his statements in favour of a united India, saying he was inciting Muslims to forget their religion and identity (Shah 1999: 173). The regime even sponsored the creation of the Anjuman Asfiya, or Group of Religious Leaders, who with great ceremony passed a *fatwa* declaring Badshah Khan and the KKs *kafirs* (infidels). This was merely the latest and most elaborate of the repeated attempts during the previous decade to cite the KK's non-violent method and alliance with the Congress as evidence of their supposed Hinduism.[28] The KK were told by their leaders to ignore such false propaganda and not respond. Badshah Khan re-emphasised that their main objectives remained constructive activity against social evils and factionalism, and that the principles of peace and non-violence meant direct confrontation with the League had to be avoided at all costs. When communal riots broke out in northern India in late 1946, however, the League sent delegates to the affected towns who returned to the Frontier with eye-witness accounts of atrocities committed against Muslims, and their reports were given wide publicity in the Province. Despite the best efforts of Badshah Khan and the KKs to argue against communal ideology, the continual slogans of 'Islam in Danger' began gradually to become more influential among the Pathans. The Muslim League gained in strength.

It was in this atmosphere that Jawarhalal Nehru made his fateful visit to the Frontier in October 1946. Ostensibly his mission, in his role as Minister of External Affairs and Commonwealth Relations, was to review living conditions in the Tribal Areas, where untoward events included British air raids on a clan who had kidnapped a government political officer (Noble 1997: 91). The underlying agenda, however, was to assess the truth of the reports he had been fed, often by British intelligence, that the influence of Badshah Khan and the KK in the Frontier was waning. When Nehru had visited the Frontier in 1938 he had received a good reception even in areas which were not Congress strongholds, such as Dera Ismail Khan.[29] In 1946 at Peshawar he met with a very different reception, as thousands of Muslim League demonstrators waved black flags and yelled slogans against his 'plans for Hindu domination' of the subcontinent. Badshah Khan, true to his principles of avoiding confrontation, had ordered the KKs to keep away from the area.

Things got still worse as Nehru moved on to visit the Tribal Area of Waziristan. As a British bureaucrat recalls:

When it was realised in the summer of 1946 that the Hindu Nehru had assumed control of the advice given at the Centre to the Viceroy about Tribal Affairs, tribal concern over Indian politics began to stir. The notion that there might be a Hindu master of their affairs, so long

---

[28] I discuss this issue in detail in Chapter 4.
[29] L/P&J/5/211 IOLR. During those visits Nehru had insisted, somewhat brazenly, that credit for anything done should go to the Congress.

dismissed from their thoughts as ludicrous, now acquired a new significance, and the existence of a provincial Ministry controlled by the Khan brothers, who gave their children in marriage to infidels, quickened their interest' (Noble 1997: 289).[30]

A fascinating account of the details of Nehru's visit is available from a letter which the Political Agent of South Waziristan wrote to his wife:

Abdul Gaffar Khan opened the proceedings by telling the Waziris that the great Nehru had heard of how they had been oppressed by the Firangis [foreigners] and had decided to come and investigate their condition. They were poor and the new Indian government was determined to give them schools, to teach them their religion, to build hospitals and to civilise them. The Wazir spokesman replied more in grief than in anger that Abdul Gaffar had got it all wrong. The Utmanzai Wazirs were oppressed by no one, nor did they need instruction in the teaching of Islam from a man whose son had married a Parsee and whose niece (Dr. Khan Sahib's daughter Miriam) was married to a Christian. This remark infuriated Dr Khan Sahib who called them paid toadies of the Political Agent. This remark was too much for the *jirga* who leapt to their feet in protest. Smouldering with indignation the party then departed [to meet the Mahsuds]. A Mahsud *jirga* was assembled in the Residency garden. Nehru spoke in Urdu. The Mahsuds probably did not understand much. But when he said that those present were all debauched by British bribery it was too much for old Kaka, Mir Badshah's father, who in the coarse way that Mahsuds have, said, 'Hindu, if the British pay us money, there's a good reason. Our private parts are of extraordinary size as you will find out to your cost before long.' With that the old boy stumped out. The Political Agent tried to persuade Nehru to end his tour after this but Badshah Khan begged him to continue. Things only got worse however as their car was pelted with stones, injuring the two leaders with flying glass. (Hunt and Harrison 1980: 231)

Subjected to further demonstrations and harassment, they finally arrived back in the Settled Districts to a warm welcome at a KK camp by 3,000 Red Shirts. However, much damage had been done. Badshah Khan accused the political department of contriving these hostile receptions and said that the British provocations had ruined the Pathans' reputation for hospitality and that in their promotion of religious communalism and division the British had changed their chosen weapon in the Frontier from 'an iron rod to a green flag' (quoted in Shah 1999: 180). The Governor subsequently denied any provocations and blamed Nehru's own lofty manner and loss of temper when addressing the tribes. Noble recalls, however, that 'Experienced political officers who were present were appalled at the breakdown in the normal conventions of communication' and the Viceroy himself acknowledged short-comings in the arrangements for protecting the visitiors (Noble 1997: 291–2).

Whoever was to blame, after the visit the authorities noted a swing in sentiment in favour of the Muslim League, and the League taunted Congress that Nehru had achieved in a week what the League itself had not managed in four years, namely to turn Pathans towards Pakistan (Shah 1999: 182). In the eruption of these religious tensions the British finally reaped the rewards of their long-term efforts to keep the KKs out of the Tribal Areas. Subject to constant propaganda from their *mullahs*, and denied both the countervailing voice of moderation that Badshah Khan could have

---

[30] Dr Khan Sahib's daughter was married to a Christian, Jaswant Singh (whom most assumed to be Hindu), and Badshah Khan's eldest son had married a Parsi.

supplied and the discipline and encouragement that membership in the KK organisation fostered, the tribals were left vulnerable to the clarion call of communalism. Long accustomed to rising up behind charismatic leaders to defend both Islam and their own freedom from government, the tribals once again rallied together to oppose infidels who wanted to rule them – previously it had been the British, now it was the Hindus.

Through the winter of 1946–7 communal tensions rapidly intensified and in retaliation for the attacks on Muslims elsewhere in India the tribes began to launch raids against the Settled Districts, attacking Sikhs and Hindus, some of whom were kidnapped and forcibly converted to Islam. Simultaneously the League came out in open defiance of the Congress ministry and utilised classic civil disobedience techniques of boycotts and pickets. The movement for Pakistan had gained support among the Muslim intelligentsia and civil servants in the Frontier administration and they, along with religious leaders and students, together 'created an air of religious fervour which the Congress could not withstand' (Jansson 1988: 242).

By the spring of 1947 the Frontier was the only major Muslim province in India which did not have a Muslim League ministry – the Muslim Unionist Party in the Punjab had recently fallen after a sustained destabilisation campaign by League activists, who now turned their attention to the Frontier. While rioting swept the Punjab, Peshawar began to suffer sabotage, arson (sometimes directed against Sikh and Hindu religious buildings) and bombs, all of which badly affected the life and economy of the city, particularly its Hindu-dominated trade. Badshah Khan said that the League was preaching hatred and his response was to march some 20,000 Red Shirts from all over the Province into the city, who conducted processions and patrolled the streets and bazaars, restoring a large measure of calm and greatly reassuring the minorities (Shah 1999: 203). But throughout March and April the KKs themselves came under increasing harassment and attack by armed League supporters. The KK leaders continued to urge strict non-violence in the face of these provocations in order to prevent further exacerbation of tensions, but after numerous injuries and deaths Badshah Khan's eldest son lost patience and in defiance of his father set up a youth wing, Zilme Pukhtun (Young Pukhtuns), to carry arms to defend the mass of non-violent activists. My informants recalled this new development:

> The Zilme Pukhtun was formed in 1946 during the elections. Major Khurshid, who had been dismissed from the Punjab Army for moral turpitude, belonged to the Muslim League and was inciting people to violence against the Khudai Khidmatgaran. He said 'Let's kill Badshah Khan and all the Khudai Khidmatgaran and then that will be the end of their movement.' (I.62)

> Ghani Khan gave orders for violent action. Badshah Khan, his father, had him removed. But Ghani Khan said that it was not in his culture to present the other cheek. He broke away and formed Zilme Pukhtun. (I.19)

> It was formed for the protection of the Khudai Khidmatgaran and the rest of the Pukhtun population. Yahya Jan used to come to meetings with a big gun. I remember having gone to Bannu with Ghani Khan ... where at a public meeting he invited people to use violence. Some people then joined .... (I.53)

Ghani Khan used to use the network of the Khudai Khidmatgar movement to build his own organisation. The young people who were not yet convinced of non-violence joined him. (I.62)

I did not join the Zilme Pukhtun because I did not believe in violence. But the Zilme Pukhtun created a split in the movement. In some senses it was similar to the split in the Congress between Subhas Bose and the Indian National Army and Nehru. The Zilme Pukhtun never came for our protection as they claimed ... they were just anti-British and against the creation of Pakistan. (I.50)

I in fact joined Zilme Pukhtun for a while ... but Badshah Khan explained to us that the methodology in it was that of violence, so I left it – some people left, some stayed. (I.49)

The Young Pathan wing, wearing black stripes on their red collars and cuffs, soon attracted many young men and in response the League formed its own formal militant organisation. In this way the communalist mire began dragging the younger generation of Pathans away from the principles of the KK and back towards older traditions of violence. None the less, the main body of KKs continued to strive to keep the peace and to resist the worst excesses of communal violence in the Province. As Shah argues, for all the League's agitation, the KK still held considerable strength and its determined protection of the lives and property of the non-Muslim minorities was one of the main reasons why large-scale rioting and killing of non-Muslims did not take place in the Frontier (Shah 1999: xxiii).

In the spring of 1947 Viceroy Mountbatten visited the Frontier and, despite his request to Jinnah to avoid all demonstrations during his visit, the League organised a huge rally in Peshawar. Again, the KK adhered to Badshah Khan's principle of avoiding clashes and stayed away. In so far as this restraint ceded the field of protest to the League, however, it seems only to have convinced Mountbatten of the need to take into account the League's position and its protests against the Congress ministry, and he raised the possibility of holding fresh elections to judge more accurately the true weight of opinion in the Province on the question of Pakistan. Dr Khan Sahib argued that it was only a year since Congress had won a clear election victory in the Frontier on the platform of a united India. The National Congress subsequently accepted Mountbatten's 3rd June Plan for a partitioned subcontinent, however, and Nehru agreed to Mountbatten's suggestion that a referendum be held (on the usual narrow electoral franchise) on the single question of whether the Frontier should join India or Pakistan upon independence.

Nehru's agreement to both Partition and a referendum shocked the KKs. First, Congress had always assured them that it would never allow Partition. Second, in the rest of the subcontinent the choice of joining either India or Pakistan was left to the elected government of each province. Hence, apart from Sylhet Province in Bengal, the Frontier was unique in being singled out for a referendum. Badshah Khan argued that both the majority of the electorate and the wider mass of Pathans desired to stay with India, but Congress acceded to the Muslim League's objection that this was unfeasible because of the geographical separation of the Frontier and India by Pakistan's half of the Punjab. As many of my informants noted, however, such an arrangement was far less impractical than the positions of West and East Pakistan (Bangladesh), with the whole of India between them. Badshah Khan then tried to insist on the inclusion in the ballot paper of a third option: an independent Pathan homeland of 'Pakhtunistan'. This was rejected by the Congress Working Committee, however, who were concerned that such an option would set a precedent for other states and provinces, and lead to the complete break-up of India.

In my view, Nehru's mind had been made up after his ill-fated visit to the Tribal Areas. Nehru was both notoriously vain and in possession of a considerable temper, and he is unlikely ever to have forgiven the Pathans for the humiliation he suffered at the hands of the Tribes. His unfortunate experience there had merely served to confirm every stereotype that he had held about the feckless and volatile nature of the Pathans, and seems to have convinced him that there would never be peace in the Frontier until it entered Pakistan. He returned to Delhi having given up on the Frontier.

The Tribal Areas had never adopted the discipline of the civil disbedience movement, and had never claimed to do so, yet their leaders' words and actions seem to have been taken by Nehru as representative of the entire Pathan population, including the KKs. Despite nearly two decades of discipline and sacrifice and attendance at Congress camps, ultimately the KKs were still viewed merely as 'Pathans', and the long years of struggle by the Red Shirts were forgotten. When the details of the 3rd June plan and the Frontier referendum came to be known, Badshah Khan could only comment poignantly that:

> The sacrifices the Pathans have made in the course of their struggle for liberty have borne fruit and we are on the threshold of freedom today. Now is the time to enjoy the blessings of freedom. But when I look at the prevailing conditions I fear that we may not probably be able to derive the full benefit from this golden opportunity.[31]

In response, Badshah Khan stated that the KK would be boycotting the referendum, calling it a meaningless exercise which gave them a spurious choice between an India which had rejected them and a Pakistan which despised them, with the option of an autonomous Pakhtunistan denied them. The KKs began to use all their well-practised methods of non-violent protest and agitation to call for Pukhtun autonomy and to urge those eligible to vote to stay at home. Throughout the period of the boycott the KK received absolutely no support from the Congress leadership. Gandhi merely harked back to the old stereotypes, warning that 'Any fight among the Pathans themselves who [are] a martial people would be most regrettable' and he reproached the KK for 'endeavouring to find means to avoid the referendum and its consequences'.[32] Badshah Khan replied wearily that: 'We have been working under very difficult and trying circumstances but have adhered to non-violence in thought word and deed. How long a state of affairs like this can last it is not easy for me to say' (quoted in Shah 1999: 224).

The result of the KK's non-violent agitation was a very low turnout, which clearly undermined the popular legitimacy of the referendum. Eighty-year-old Mohammed Yakub Khan from Bannu stated unequivocally that 'No Badshah Khan supporters participated in the referendum for Pakistan, it was the Muslim Leaguers who did'

---

[31] *The Hindustan Times*, 9 June 1947.
[32] 'Conflict among Pathans', *The Hindustan Times*, 19 June 1947.

(I.61). There were 573,000 registered voters, less than 14 per cent of the total population. The turnout among these was just over half, nearly all of them voting for Pakistan, reflecting the League's strength among the urban intelligentsia and bureaucracy. In addition to the effects of the boycott, there was much dubious electoral practice, such as bogus votes cast for absentee and deceased voters (Jansson 1988: 243; Rittenberg 1977: 395).

There had been some criticism among the KK leaders of the decision to boycott the referendum, since they argued that with energetic agitation they would still have a good chance to win a majority in favour of the India proposition (Shah 1999: 227). Badshah Khan refused this line of action, however, and it seems this was his final great act of principle. He feared that given the tensions and violence already simmering in the Province, particularly among the would-be *jihadists* in the Tribal Areas, a fiercely fought referendum campaign and narrow majority in favour of India would be tragically divisive and risk unleashing unbridled violence among the Pathans.

On 21 August 1947, a week after gaining independence, Dr Khan Sahib's ministry was dismissed by the Governor on orders from Jinnah. Badshah Khan took the formal oath of allegiance to Pakistan and said he would not seek to damage the new state in any way, but he sought to lobby Jinnah to grant a significant level of autonomy to the Pathans. He was persistently rebuffed, however, and in June 1948 the KK organisation was banned by the new Muslim League provincial government and its leaders imprisoned, branded as 'friends of Gandhi and Nehru' and 'traitors to Pakistan'. Thus the KKs were forced to watch as the Muslim League, whom most of them regarded as the tools of the British, prospered in this way upon an independence which had been won largely through the blood and bruises of the KK activists. The KKs expressed their feeling by reciting a bitter *tappa* (couplet) to me: 'The stick that used to beat us now has a flag on it' (I.66). The KK also felt a great sense of betrayal by Congress and each of my informants whispered to me at least once the famous parting words of Badshah Khan to Gandhi: 'You have thrown us to the wolves.'

Five decades later my informants still felt an overwhelming sense of bitterness at the way Congress had treated them: Why had Nehru allowed Mountbatten to impose a referendum? Why had their aim of an autonomous Pakhtunistan within India not been honoured? How could it be that twenty years of political camaraderie were forgotten in a few weeks? As Raghibullah Khan stated, 'we had believed in and fought for an undivided India' (I.32). I have tried to put such questions in context by considering the KK's disagreement with Congress over cooperation with the war effort, the role that the Tribal Areas played in disrupting the alliance and, perhaps most significant, the persisting stereotypes that the Congress leaders held of the Pathans. Shah, Rittenberg and Janssen discuss in detail the murky deal making and compromises surrounding these decisions at the highest level.

Badshah Khan felt that Partition and the Frontier referendum betrayed everything that he had promised to the KK. Muffariq Shah remembered that in earlier years Badshah Khan had explained to them how 'in independent India there will be one army for the whole of the country. It will not be like it is now ... where the Muslim League beat the Hindus here and the Hindus beat the Muslims in India' (I.20). Colonel Mohammed Sayid recalled that Badshah Khan had told them that 'in an independent undivided India, in Hindu majority areas Hindu law would prevail and in Muslim-dominated areas Muslim law would be introduced' (I.44). Partition dashed these hopes.

These feelings of betrayal intensified as the KK began to see how they would be treated in the new state. After Jinnah's rejection of any autonomy for the Pathans, the KK resumed its methods of agitation and non-violent protest. The response of the new state was equally if not more vicious than that of the British, however, and my informants repeatedly drew parallels between the colonial regime and its Pakistani successor. Many of the more prominent KK activists ended up in prison and had their lands confiscated, and many families were reduced to poverty, their children denied an education because their fathers were in jail for much of the time after independence. Mohammed Gul concluded that 'it has only been a change of uniform after Pakistan was formed' (I.67).

Aside from their personal sufferings my informants also expressed a variety of complaints about political developments after 1947: women had stopped participating in politics, with the government encouraging strict enforcement of *purdah* (I.16); Pakistan's centralising ideology had standardised dress so much that the Yusufzais no longer wore their flamboyant traditional *khaliqs* (I.36); the name of the province was never changed from the British 'North West Frontier Province' to one that better reflected the Pathans who lived there (I.27); and in the 1990s the KK's successor party, the ANP, still had to strive for more rights for the Pathans (I.12).

Some of my informants drew solace from the knowledge that they had fought a fair fight against the British and achieved independence. Mukarram Khan emphasised that 'Badshah Khan accomplished his mission ... the liberation of his country' (I.70). Others, however, felt that Partition had cut short what might otherwise have been achieved. Sarfaraz Nazim stated that: 'Badshah Khan wanted to humanise Pathans. But later the influence of the Muslim League on the people ruined it all and ruined the tolerant values of the region. All the Hindus were driven out' (I.1). Hence 'Partition itself is a lasting problem' (I.70).

Such personal suffering and political grievances led to a great sense of frustration. Eighty-year-old Sher Khan said: 'There was an evening when I remember sitting with Badshah Khan by the Sindh river at dusk, talking ... I remember telling him that I did not and could not accept Pakistan. I said that I wanted to kill off the "brown sahibs"' (I.29). When Badshah Khan's son, Wali Khan, was put in jail by the Pakistan People's Party, an enraged Hama Gul challenged the by then elderly Badshah Khan: 'I know it says in the Quran that if anyone wrongs you forgive him, but is anyone ever going to forgive us or are we expected to do the forgiving all the time?' (I.51). To this and many other such questions, however, 'Badshah Khan's response remained always the same – that violence would get us nowhere' (I.51).

Conclusion

As we saw in the preceding chapters, the Khudai Khidmatgar movement was the vehicle by which the modes of thinking and behaviour associated with the traditional segmentary–feudal society of the Pathans were gradually put aside in favour of a wider political unity in the struggle against British colonial rule. Yet this was only one aspect of the realignment of loyalties and political priorities. A further key element was the linkage of the Pathan freedom fighters to the wider body of opposition in the rest of India as represented by the National Congress. This linkage itself stretched across traditional barriers of religious difference and the social and cultural divide that lies at the Indus. It also had to bridge the conceptual and practical gap between parliamentary politics and a populist mass movement. These differences were a constant source of tension surrounding the KK movement, and, while often successfully skirted, they resurfaced decisively during the events leading up to Partition, not without the active encouragement of a colonial regime which in its governance of the Frontier was at its most manipulative.

None the less, if the overall outcome was not entirely that which had been hoped for by the KK, in their determination to avoid clashes with their political rivals and their steadfast adherence to the principles of non-violence and service, they played a key role in ensuring that the course of events in the Frontier did not decline from an intense political drama into an out-and-out bloodbath. To that extent they may forever remain proud of a great and good moral victory.

8
The Work of Memory

Anthropologists often refer to 'informants' or 'interviews' as an economical shorthand for what is in fact the extended and typically messy process by which they learned something new during fieldwork. Although I dignified my interview technique as 'semi-structured', in reality my questions would provoke a wide range of responses, only a few of which were immediately recognisable as direct answers. Often an initial question would lead to an uninterrupted outpouring of recollection lasting several hours, and it was clear that the significance of my question was not its precise meaning but rather the fact that it signalled my interest in their past and willingness to listen. On other occasions, especially where there were several old men together, a question would provoke a gale of laughter, energetic debate and mutual interruptions. In this chapter I wish to step back somewhat from the details of the KK movement to consider the conversations I had with my informants from the perspective of recent anthropological thinking about the nature of memory.

Khudai Khidmatgar Narratives and Oral Tradition

Over the last two decades there has been substantial interest in narrative within historiography, social science and literary criticism.[1] As a result of such work, it is fairly uncontroversial to assert that the canons of narrative form and of genre are culturally constructed, and that an individual's account of events will be shaped by the narrative forms and general metaphysics of cause and effect among which he or she has been raised. Moreover, as cognitive psychology long ago demonstrated, the effects of such narrative forms typically become stronger over time, as people unconsciously fill in the details they are forgetting with elements that are culturally plausible. The fact that human beings forget and remember in principled ways and use narrative structures to tell their stories has made oral history an interdisciplinary territory in which the form and content of stories and sources are treated as equally important (Tonkin 1994). For oral historians who are trying to establish concrete facts about far-off dates and events in societies without documentary records such phenomena can be challenging. In the context of African historiography, for example, Jan Vansina has warned of the way in which the historical accounts

[1] Prominent inspirational figures in this area would include Bakhtin in literature, Hayden White in historiography, and Bartlett, the 1930s Oxford psychologist who investigated the idea of cognitive schemata.

contained within oral traditions become increasingly influenced by older archetypal narratives until, over time, the individuating details of an event are lost and the account gradually transforms from reportage to myth (Vansina 1966 and 1985).

The narratives I have collected refer to events and dates which are for the most part well recorded and still remain within living memory. None the less, we may still reasonably expect these narratives to be undergoing already something like the process which Vansina discusses. David Edwards confirms the importance of such cultural expectations about narrative in the light of his extensive study of Pathan oral traditions about the Soviet–Afghan war, which are obviously even more recent than those of the KK:

> The act of transforming events into narrative involves a process of selection based on the narrator's cultural awareness of what is and is not significant. In this way, the narrative makes an intelligible discourse out of the raw material of events and perceptions. Intelligibility here involves coherence on the level of the cultural system and on the level of narration, which includes giving events beginnings, middles and ends, associating actors with acts and acts with consequences. In the intersection of these two planes of coherence – the system of cultural meaning and the metacode of the narrative – events become 'real' and 'true' because ... they have been shown to possess the character of narrativity. (1986: 68)

In the light of this it is not unreasonable to expect that some KK testimonies will bear the influence of older Persian, Pathan and Arabic/Islamic myths and tales. After all, such traditions are often incorporated into everyday speech and Anderson has remarked upon the use of multiple forms of folk quatrains, proverbs and quotes from the Quran and Hadith to punctuate conversation in Pashto-speaking Afghan communities (1985: 270). To demonstrate in detail the effect of such older forms and stories on the narratives which I gathered from my KK informants would take another book. None the less, I would like to sketch very briefly some of the resonances these narratives might have with older genres by comparing some with the excellent work of Margaret Mills on oral tradition among Persian-speaking Afghans.

I have quoted brief statements from KKs throughout this book; these have all been excerpted, however, from far longer statements. Typical of what happened was the style of Mohammed Yakub Khan's reply when I asked the ostensibly innocuous question: how did you become involved?:

> In 1930, Badshah Khan had come to Kakki, and a small meeting had been held at Shamshi *khel* (Bannu). Soon after this Ajab Khan's father's brother's son, Tur Lali, organised a meeting at Spin Tangi. There was also a secret meeting held in Ayub Khan's village which was called for a specific purpose. Then my father also declared a meeting in his own village. The Shamshi *khel* organisation was led by Qazi Fazl Qadir, a senior leader. The British were after him and there was a warrant out for his arrest. The *khans* in our village tried to stop my father's meeting. They said they would meet his demands in order to stop the meeting from being held. My father said to them, 'Let us shake hands on that then! Our demand is the removal of the British.' Mirza Sikander was the magistrate at the time and he sentenced my father to six months of rigorous imprisonment for saying this.
>
> It was the 8th of August when my father was arrested. People protested about this and wanted to hold a meeting in Bandar Kali. The elders of the village were worried, however, saying it would bring more trouble. Then the meeting was held in Abbassi, in Wazir country. Then another meeting was held in Shanwa, Guddi *khel*, which is in between

Khattak and Wazir areas. The Nawab of Teri, on hearing about these meetings, came down by plane and told Ayub Khan and Qazi Fazl Qadir that he was willing to meet all their demands provided they did not hold any more meetings. The agreements were made by swearing with a hand on the Quran. The Nawab promised to help in ousting the British but begged them not to hold any more meetings. On 24 August 1930, however, a huge meeting was organised in Spin Tangi. A huge number of people turned up at the meeting and this was in spite of the fact that a large number had been stopped on their way there by the British. During the meeting, Qazi Fazl Qadir was fired at by the British and a battle broke out. My father, Ayub Khan and Qazi Fazl Qadir were all followers of Badshah Khan. Badshah Khan had taught us non-violence and everyone accepted it .... But unfortunately one or two others carried arms. At Spin Tangi, 300 were arrested, 80 were martyred and many wounded who had to be treated secretly. On the British side, the captain of the battalion was totally dismembered by swords and axes.

The Qazi was taken to Domel police station ... the Deputy Commissioner taunted him to repeat his anti-British call ... but the Qazi just turned his head and died. In spite of this the British passed a 14-year sentence on him and buried him in Bannu jail. They did not even hand over his body for the *jehnaza* to be performed. (I.61)

And so on – and even this far longer version is still a summary of the whole description which meandered purposefully through various asides and sub-plots and lasted several hours.

This story is obviously informative. We see the concern of the *khans* and even the Nawab grandee to avoid any troublesome meetings as they tried to fulfil their part of British indirect rule. The nervousness of the village elders is also made clear, torn as they were between assisting the nationalist cause and risking the punitive destruction of their village by the security forces. The categorical nature of the nationalist demands is clearly articulated – there can be no agreements or concessions until the British have left. The tensions of non-violence are also revealed, with nearly everyone accepting Badshah Khan's message, but one or two still carrying arms and a British officer ending up dead and disfigured. The extent of the disturbance and deaths among the KK is confirmed in the equivalent British report of this event. Lastly, we see another example of the authorities' use of symbolic violence as they sentence a corpse and deliberately violate the Islamic injunction to grant a dead man a proper and speedy burial.

The general accuracy and informative nature of the account, however, does not require us to deny that it bears some generic similarities to pre-existing genres. The length, the extensive cast of characters and the heroic nature of the events make it something of an epic story, that 'generic scope of ... story telling ... [which offers] a lengthy, framed, multi-episodic novella-type adventure tale ... which school and test the hero in patience, fortitude, and faith' (Mills 1991: 120). It was precisely the schooling he received through the imprisonment of his father and his own experience of the dramatic and tragic events at Spin Tangi that led Mohammed Yakub Khan to join the movement.

Discussing the Afghan oral traditions, Mills argues that it is basic to Islam's egalitarian ideology that 'private citizens are morally situated to observe and critique the excesses of unrighteous ruling powers' (*ibid.*: 145), and accordingly there are numerous Afghan tales which are critical of despotic rulers. In such tales, episodes are first presented to establish the individual honour of the rebels and to establish their credentials as critics of the powers that be. In this spirit, the KK narrative clearly contrasts the principled integrity and courage of Mohammed Yakub Khan's father with the behaviour of those he is defying, the *khans* who collaborate and the colonialists who kill. Most striking of all is the death scene of the Qazi, who contemptuously ignores the British taunts and turns his head and dies, a paragon of dignified defiance. The presentation of this episode also seems to owe something to older tales of martyrdom, perhaps the Afghan tales which tell of the 'eagerness for martyrdom' of their protagonists (*ibid.*: 153).

Thus, by beginning our interview with this story, Mohammed Yakub Khan was demonstrating his critical credentials in the way Mills describes, in order to add weight and significance to all the other things he was intending to tell me subsequently. Similarly, in Chapters 3 and 4, I presented numerous KK accounts of incidents involving repression and suffering. Typically these first set out the precise tribulation suffered, then reiterate the ideals of the movement. 'The British used to strip us – but we were proud of our suffering' (I.50). 'My ribs were broken by the British police at a riot. But even then I did not resort to violence. Non-violence gives a strength of mind' (I.19). Again, such stories resonate with the Afghans' tales of *jihad* which discuss the commitment of a hero, 'his willingness as an ordinary man, inexperienced in battle, to die in holy war, and the use of his outlandish experiences *to illustrate the place of suffering in ethical development*' (Mills 1991: 152; my emphasis).

It is striking that, after nearly five decades, KKs could still quote to me statements made by specific people during the movement. Since these quotations are boldly declaimed and clearly the product of many repetitions one might dub them slogans of resistance. For example, I asked whether there were any heroic tales of KK bravery, and received a prompt 'Oh yes!' in response: 'There was one prisoner who was being whipped to elicit information. After 30 lashes he simply asked for a cigarette! He used to say "I have silenced 30 whip lashes." He was nicknamed *khamosh* (silence) after that' (I.21). Psychologically such a memory seems almost hybrid, since it has something of the automated nature of a 'habit memory' yet is clearly felt to contain ideas of great significance and meaning, something usually taken to be indicative of higher 'cognitive memory' (Connerton 1989: 22–3). We should also note that such stories can easily take their place within the tradition of ancient stories of those who have successfully defied the pressures of infidels:

> 'Even if you tear me apart piece by piece, I absolutely refuse to accept your religion, Praise be to God, whether you kill me now, or whatever you do!' They took me to prison sir, they said accept this religion, I said I won't, like that, and there was this piece of iron lying in the prison that weighed a hundred *man* ... they hit me over the head with it and split my head open .... My head is all swollen up, but no matter what they did, I didn't accept their religion. (Mills 1991: 106)

Another recognisably distinct genre of KK memories, told with particular relish when two or three veterans got together, was that of subversive narratives, the telling of events which punctured the dignity of the colonial administration. We may recall the noisy nocturnal demonstrations that kept the visiting dignitary awake in Chapter 3. Haji Mohammed Sher told me another lively incident:

> Let me tell you about an incident in one of our camps in Gujjar Garhi. There was to be a picketing charge outside the Mardan District Commissioner's office. There was no camp

commander in the camp. A frail-looking, lower-caste man called Hasham offered to be the camp commander. He was told that he had to capture the DC's office. When he arrived there the next day, he planted himself inside the office and refused to move when he was ordered out. After several repeated threats by the office staff he still had not moved. The DC heard the commotion and came out to find out what had happened. He was so exasperated by Hasham's stubborness that he finally picked him up and deposited him outside. Hasham laughed at the DC and said 'So far the British have been sitting on our heads. But today a Pathan was sitting on their shoulders!' (I.33)

This story resonates with a wider Afghan use of traditional forms of folk farce to artic- ulate their scathing critique of the state. In a similar vein, we can recall the story in which the initially hostile soldier eventually pats the KK on the back, disarmed by his dignified assertion that the KK serve for love not money. This seems cognate with Afghan narratives portraying 'little men dealing cleverly and successfully with the potentially abusive power of a king and moving the king to act generously' (Mills 1991: 299). Fazle Rahim Saqi told me that he remembered 'an old Hindu man in jail who hung a portrait of George VI upside down as an act of defiance. When we had been arrested he had started a "vow of silence" ... he was released after six months but died at the threshold of the jail' (I.53). Here we have a vivid and amusing image of subversion, followed by a denouement of great pathos, in which the combination of silence, martyrdom and thresholds again seems to resonate with older mythemes.

Most conspicuously indebted to older stories are the KK tales of the miraculous, some of which I reviewed in Chapter 5. I naturally doubted the literal truth of these stories about Badshah Khan's supernatural powers, although in so far as I was forming an interested audience for such tales I was an active participant in these miracles (Gilsenan 1982: 75). My lingering scepticism was perhaps obvious, and Sarfaraz Nazim used the following anecdote to convince me of their truth. He had noticed that I had stopped taking notes during the course of our conversation and suddenly said:

You have run out of ink. That reminds me of a story. One day Badshah Khan said to me that I must sit down and take notes on some of the thoughts that he was going to share with me. I agreed. Badshah Khan then pointed out that I must check to see if I had sufficient ink in my pen to avoid an interruption later. I assured him that my pen was always full enough for a week's work and did not heed his request to check the amount of ink in my pen. Not so long after we started my pen ran dry, to my astonishment. Badshah Khan was prophetic! (I.1)

The accounts given to me of Badshah Khan's prophecies about pen and ink, his divination of water, the striking dumb of his hostile critic, all smack of older Pathan and Islamic tales about righteous men with special powers. Badshah Khan's attributed ability to find water might be a frugal and wealth-renouncing form of older tales of men who could smell out buried gold, or even of the Prophet Himself, who smelt the sanctity emanating from Yemen (Mills 1991: 205–6). Badshah Khan's magical blow to his critic is obviously quite at odds with his non-violence and is clearly assimilated to older talk of such dramatic powers. As Mills comments, 'the images are received wisdom, but their placement is highly creative, even innovative' as they are juxtaposed with 'a particular human action or attitude observed in the real world' (Mills 1991: 272). These, then, are in a sense confabulations, but clas- sical confabulations whose connection to older tales in itself tells us a good deal about

Badshah Khan's standing in their tellers' eyes. As Feierman notes when discussing oral sources on nineteenth-century Tanzania, 'historical information can be integrated into a pre-existing myth' – for example – 'there is a partly formed epochal tradition which mythologises [King] Kimweri's actions, even though they took place in the relatively recent past' (Feierman 1992: 69, 10).

I would suggest therefore that in the KK testimonies we can see something of the influence of older pre-KK narrative forms. Equally, some of the stories seem so well rehearsed and widely known that they may be said to constitute a nascent oral tradition specific to the Khudai Khidmatgar. Most of my interviews contained numerous different episodes and tales, all varying in their content and mood but shedding light on one another. As Mills writes for the Afghans, it is 'part of the aesthetic of ... traditional story telling ... that stories of differing genres, scales of complexity and construction, as well as other kinds of discourse (proverbs, conversational remarks) are juxtaposed and caused to reflect on one another in a full-blown oral performance of varying verbal texture' (Mills 1991: 21).

Of Objects and Emotions

Theorising about narrative has provided many insights for social scientists and historians. It does encourage a tendency to take a very logocentric view of memory, however, which reduces all talk and thought to 'texts'. It is important, therefore, to allow for the non-verbal factors which can influence memories and accounts.

When I posed my first question to Noor Akbar, he gave me no answer and instead told me to wait until he returned as he had just thought of something. I waited more in hope than expectation for a couple of hours, but he eventually reappeared dragging a battered black trunk. I watched with growing excitement as he slowly extracted his old uniform, his Sam Browne belt, an old poster of Badshah Khan and other items of memorabilia. I recognised what some of them were and linked my initial questions to them. Gradually the discussion moved to more general issues, but Noor Akbar repeatedly went back to the other obscure items whose significance resided only in his mind. He did not always explain to me what they were and I did not always ask, but they clearly served as mnemonic devices that helped him recall. While this was the most dramatic uncovering, on other occasions, too, an old uniform or a faded photograph taken on a visit to a Congress camp were produced from well-hidden nooks and crannies to become the centrepiece of the conversation. The 72-year-old Gul Rahman had an original flag up on the roof of his house and a picture of Badshah Khan in his room (and also a daughter named Siyasat, 'politics'!) (I.40). The tactile and sensual nature of these objects helped release memories. The red flower in the buttonhole or red walking stick became props for the unfolding of more 'Red Shirts' stories. Thus, as Hoskins notes, such 'biographical objects' play a key role in telling the stories of people's lives; in particular, containers like Noor Akbar's chest, or elsewhere a betel pouch, hollow drum, or funeral shroud, all serve as 'memory boxes' (Hoskins 1998: 5).

These biographical objects helped turn what could have been a general and abstract conversation about civil disobedience into a story which was grounded continuously in personal experience. When I was talking to Sarfaraz Khan about his civil disobedience activities he said: 'In 1942 we picketed the law courts. Thirty of us were arrested' (I.45). He then produced an old notebook in which he had made a note of the twelve officers who were arrested along with him and imprisoned for a period of three years in Dera Ismail Khan jail. He read out the names, which prompted him to further recollections of dead associates and long-forgotten incidents. Moreover, reading his own handwriting appeared to remind him of the time when he had written the account down, which was some years later during the suppression of the movement by the Pakistan authorities, when he had feared that such information might be irretrievably lost. The memory of the making of the record prompted him to ruminate on these later years, too. Several other informants also pulled out such notes on scraps of paper and I wondered how many other such evidences of popular written sources I might be missing. Given the widespread use of such notebooks in South Asia, I share Margaret Mills's sense of opportunity when she writes that 'Despite the availability and ready sales of chapbooks throughout the Persian-speaking world, there has been virtually no research either on this form of vernacular literacy in general, or on the specific contribution of chapbooks to oral performance and vice versa' (Mills 1991: 136). Sayyid Mohammed Fasi Badshah, for instance, told me he could tell me with great accuracy the story from 1919 to 1942 since he had previously dictated the story to a teacher who had written it down for him in a notebook, which he regularly reread to remind himself (I.39).

During our conversations, my informants often felt compelled to enact their activities as KKs, sweeping, spinning and marching while they talked. Their evocative gestures were the re-enactment of previous revolutionary activities as they tried to persuade me to visualise them not as they were but as they had been – young, strong, and fearless. They were indeed transformed as they enthusiastically supplemented the ever-increasing amount of information with their mimes, striving to make the picture clearer to me, and these wonderful charades were certainly examples of embodied memory (see Connerton 1989). When I asked Gul Rahman if he remembered what made him join the KK movement he said: 'As a child, I had a natural inclination for the movement, I think. It was Id day, and we heard that there had been firing in Utmanzai ... . I ran all the way there to find out more ... the graves of the *shahid* (martyrs) had been freshly laid' (I.40). It was particularly striking that an old man in a wheelchair remembered running in his enthusiasm, an action that clearly belonged to another time. The dramatic sight of the fresh graves of the martyrs symbolised for him the sacrifice of the KKs and led to his own involvement.

If objects and actions helped the memories then so too did emotions, as I unwittingly discovered. Having already done some archival research in London I would mention certain British statements about the KK movement. These were sometimes so divergent from the views of the KKs themselves that they found it difficult to credit my attributions and in defence I had physically to produce my file of notes and translate the relevant passages. This in itself was an interesting exercise and I began to do it regularly, for in responding to these 'allegations' of the British the old men's narratives often became more focused and directed as they stared fiercely at my sheaf of notes. The 'false' claims made about their organisation provoked them to state their points of view with the clarity resulting from anger and pride. I thus witnessed a vivid virtual dialogue between the revolutionaries and the voices of the colonial offi-cials. Michael Lambek, on the basis of his work on spirit possession in Madagascar, persuades us to think of memory not so much as an object which individuals 'possess' and whose veracity we can measure, but rather as a phenomenon which can be acti-vated between people and 'is intersubjective and dialogical' (Lambek 1996: 239). This was certainly the case for my encounters with the KKs, where the answers they gave me were often the result of provocations, arguments, revaluations and exchange involving myself, the colonial records, the Pakistan authorities and the Khudai Khidmtagars themselves.

The Politics of Memory

The act of remembering is itself a political act and the 'politics of memory' has become a fast-growing area of anthropological interest. The usual sense of this phrase is the contestation or coercion that occurs over the proper interpretation of historical expe-rience (Tilly 1994: 247). John Davis utilises the Marxian phraseology of the social relations of production to signal his claim that historical statements are a type of commodity, a commodity moreover which some people, due to their wealth or power, are far more able to produce and distribute than others. Accordingly, as with money and commodities, the pattern of distribution of particular historical asser-tions, including memories, is greatly influenced by the structure and inequalities of the society in which they are produced: 'history is a social and cultural product, consisting of events plus the structure of relations among those who construe events' (Davis 1989: 116). Davis contrasts three such structurating models. The lineages within the Zuwaya tribe produce lineage-oriented accounts in which the events of Libya's last hundred years are viewed on the basis of their significance for the tribe and its own particular role in the country's history and battles. Events are fitted into a historical and genealogical narrative of the Zuwaya past, which is far older and more extended than that of the Libyan nation, and history is seen mainly as a sequence of homicides, marriages, trading expeditions, battles and narratives of feud and peace, and of constant efforts to evade the reach of the state. The Libyan state, however, in contrast to the small-scale Zuwaya histories, purveys a state-oriented and teleological nationalist account of the fighting against the Italians which stresses a long-term trans-tribal unity of will and purpose, directed toward building a Libyan nation and state. Third, on the basis of Lison-Tolsana's work on the Spanish village of Belmonte, Davis notes the way in which views of events can change dramatically from one generation to another, so much so that their respective accounts are almost incommensurable. The middle-aged men who were the village elders in the 1970s had grown up in the turbulence of the Spanish Civil War, and had chosen to renounce the turbulent politics of their fathers, focusing instead on village stability and agricultural innovation. Their children, however, growing up amidst such calm, complained about this parochial and apolitical nature of village life, to the anger of their fathers.

As befits its location on the Indus (see Chapter 1 above), both the village-based and generational patterns of memory are in fact present in the NWFP. There is certainly a lineage-based set of memories of the KK and its activities, since the old men often frame their recollections in terms of their uncles and cousins and their own feud resolutions, celebrate particularly the defiant non-violent feats of the members of their clan, and suggest that their clan or lineage had always been especially active and effective in struggling against oppressors. The young are more tolerant and proud of their own KK relative than they are of his merely tiresome and senile comrades. But there is also a strong generational pattern in the recollections. The old men describe what it was like to be swept up in the revolutionary and anti-British fervour and to follow an utterly charismatic leader in a spirit of complete self-sacrifice. Their offspring, however, already themselves well into late middle age, talk more in terms of the hardship and deprivation of being the children of pariahs, of their long-absent fathers and uncles and of the smell of prison visits. As Antze notes, 'to remember is never solely to report on the past so much as to establish one's relationship to it' (Antze and Lambek 1996: 240).

As in Libya, the official historiography of the Pakistan state has stressed a unity of will and purpose in nation building which left no place for the KKs, reflecting what Amin has called the 'hegemonic power of judicial and nationalist discourse' (Amin 1995: 118). The KKs, as we have seen, had strong links with the Indian National Congress and supported an unpartitioned India. Thus, when the Pakistan movement was successful, the KKs were regarded with a great deal of suspicion by the new government and the result was brutal repression of the Pathans; KKs found their movement banned, their lands taken away, their leader Badshah Khan in jail and they themselves placed under arrest or otherwise harassed. This was followed by a far longer period of continued criticism and marginalisation, during which they were represented as an unpatriotic movement and denied the support of memorials, memoirs or approbation.

Understandably, these intervening events have often muted the KKs' thoughts and memories about their political actions: 'The individual's remembrance is the meeting point of a manifold network of solidarity of which he is part' (Halbwachs, noted in Thompson 1988: 214). The authorities had done their best to destroy this network of solidarity. One old man I spoke to was convinced he was the only loyal KK who remained alive in the Frontier, while the great difficulty I had in tracking down veterans similarly illustrates their isolation. My presence as an Oxford academic, however, and perhaps particularly as an Indian, seemed to galvanise them as they replayed memories and convictions and recalled or reconfirmed the rightness of their actions. The most dramatic instance of this was my meeting with Secretary Amir Nawaz.

When I went to see him it was quite late in the day, just before sunset. We had been to two other homes that day and had driven for miles; I was getting late for the curfew hour of dusk at Walibagh and I was exhausted. But Habibullah persuaded me to meet another Khudai Khidmatgar in the vicinity; we had come so far we might as well go, and he had heard that this particular man was very ill. His son greeted us warmly but apologised that we would have to see his father inside the house rather than in the guest room. He was very ill and in bed. We readily agreed and I chatted with him for a long time, sitting by the side of his bed while he lay there, a frail figure, his head covered with a yellow towel held together with a safety pin under his chin. He gave me some wonderfully detailed information about how the movement was run and its organisational structure, and told personal stories about Badshah Khan, getting more and more excited. At the end, I asked him, as I did everyone, whether I could have a picture of him for my book. He agreed, on the condition that I would include myself in the picture. As I handed my camera over to Habibullah, Secretary Amir Nawaz insisted he had to sit up as he couldn't possible be seen lying down next to a lady! As I touched his feet in farewell, he got out of bed and insisted on seeing us to the door. One of his sons walked in on hearing the bustle. As he entered the room his jaw dropped. He looked at me and exclaimed, 'What have you done? My father hasn't left that bed for six months.' The old man was laughing cheerfully: 'You have worked wonders for me! Talking to you and remembering all those years and sharing them with you ... you are so interested in our history! In all these years no one has come to ask us why we did what we did, what we felt about our fight for independence .... I feel better already .... see, I can sit up! I can walk .... She has given me a reason to live!' (I.22).

The sense of jubilation that Secretary Amir Nawaz felt reflected the long decades during which he and the other KKs had been marginalised and repressed by the government and excised from the accounts of the nationalist struggle and birth of Pakistan. As Allessandro Portelli argues from his work on veteran commmunists in Italy, 'rank and file' histories are unlike the 'affirmative discourse' of official history, which is ready-made, articulated and available. Instead, a vernacular version 'must piece itself together from scratch every time, and is burdened by the fear of disapproval and isolation ... it is distorted, buried, deviated, and allowed to emerge only in between the lines, as dream, metaphor, lapses, digression, error, denigration' (Portelli 1990: 155). As a consequence, my interviews were intensely emotional experiences as I watched the KK veterans gradually piece together their accounts and slowly unburden themselves of the feelings of isolation and fear which Portelli describes. Now in the twilight of his life, Secretary Nawaz had had the chance to tell a stranger about his revolutionary past, someone, moreover, who would go abroad and write a book containing some of his most precious memories, and the exhilaration of this was enough to produce a temporary revival of health and morale. This kind of transformation was foreshadowed by part of a poem which another KK recited to me:

If I could hold our own flag in my hands,
the withering flower will flower again.

Tilly notes that there is a second sense to the 'politics of memory'. It is not only the political contest over the proper description of the past, but also the way in which 'accumulated, shared historical experience contains today's political action' (Tilly 1994: 247). In her work on the past of a Greek village, Anna Collard gathered oral testimonies from villagers about life during the past two centuries (Collard 1989). She found that they spoke readily of the pre-twentieth-century Ottoman period, despite not having lived through it themselves, and also of the Civil War (1944–9), in which many had participated; they were unforthcoming, however, about the 1930s and the period of Nazi occupation (1941–4). Collard argues that, for various political and demographic reasons, the Civil War period severely interfered with the community's ability and inclination to recall the decade which preceded it. For example, in discussing contemporary events, the villagers used 'before' to refer to the 'recent' Civil War. When discussing the Civil War period, however, 'before' was used to refer to the Ottoman period. Thus the inter-war years stand as an invisible, unremarked pivot, separating before and after. Here, then, we get a sense of how intervening events – such as chaos, dislocation, institutional change, propaganda and repression – can influence and interfere with corporate recollections and evaluations of particular historical events, and how the course of time in memory may be divided up in the classical Maussian way by discrete symbolic breaks.

Analogous influences can be seen at work in my own ethnography, where we can point to two pivotal points in the pattern of memories about the KK. The first is explicitly identified by the KK themselves as their introduction to the work of Badshah Khan. Their testimonies repeatedly stress that, before him, the Pathans were unruly and divided, after him, disciplined and unified. Before, they were ignorant and knew nothing; after, they knew more about both the wrongs of the British and of what was morally good behaviour for themselves. The second pivot is Partition in 1947, which clearly influenced their testimonies to me. The KK viewed their pre-Partition activities in the light of their post-Partition disappointments and sufferings. Their heroic tales of the movement's heyday were usually followed by the wistful comment 'But that was another time' – a veiled expression of their critical attitude toward the post-Partition state. In discussing the movement's aims they emphasise not an unpartitioned India and autonomous Pukhtunistan, each of which would imply failure, but rather that of expelling the British, which was certainly successful. They also stress their moral education under Badshah Khan – their cultivation of an ethic of non-violence, humility and service – as a great achievement in its own right. To some extent, therefore, the original means have been slightly re-emphasised, the original ends somewhat de-emphasised. In this, we see that processes of self-justification and self-presentation are not antithetical to the historical 'reality', but are an intimate part of it; and, as in Collard's work, we see how large-scale political events can act as defining points in the course of people's most personal memories.

But this stress upon the moral improvement and spiritual development which the KKs achieved under Badshah Khan is not simply a reaction to the non-fulfilment of their more overtly political aims. After all, it was not only large-scale events which intervened in and influenced their lives. By the time of my interviews, these men had moved through fatherhood, grandfatherhood and great-grandfatherhood, and lived through decades of the daily grind of making a living. They had seen a half-century of life, with all its pettiness, problems and conflicts, and had had much opportunity for reflection upon it. Recollections of the past are certainly influenced by the changing responses to the world which arise as an individual passes through his own life cycle, and this is one reason why the elicitation of life histories can be so illuminating and intriguing. It is not so surprising, therefore, that these days it was not the long-ago politics they should choose to emphasise so much as the moral guidance which they had received from Badshah Khan, a guidance which seems to have influenced their approach to everyday life long after the British had left. I felt also that they were clearly addressing themselves to the contemporary life surrounding them, and the many elements of it which disturb them. An old man's impassioned defence of non-violence and unity becomes highly resonant and understandable when one leaves his hut and encounters grandchildren playing casually with the automatic weapons which are increasingly deployed in intensified feuding. Similarly, the emphasis on the KK's frugality seems to be directed both at venal and corrupt politicians and at a younger generation, who they fear are being seduced by foreign goods and a nascent consumerism.

Thus it would be misleading to worry only about the 'factual accuracy' of KK statements and narratives. Instead, we learn more, and can do better justice to the stories we have heard, if we take seriously Lambek's suggestion that 'such tacit assertions and claims, based as much on cumulative wisdom and moral vision as on individual interest, form a kind of moral practice' (Lambek 1996: 248). It certainly felt like this to me as the forced silence and private musings of five decades charged the KK veterans with the desire and need to convince me of the beauty of their discipline, the selflessness of their comrades and the firmness of their faith in non-violence.

Conclusion

In his book *History in Three Keys* on the Boxer rebellion in China, Paul Cohen distinguishes the past that is known by the person who experienced it, the past that is known by the historian who strives to reconstruct the events, and the past that is known by the person who is concerned to mythologise it. The historian cannot know the past in the same way as the experiencer, however keen to do so, while the mythologiser is largely uninterested in the original experience. While acknowledging that experiencers can subsequently write history and that historians are not immune from myth making, Cohen argues that 'event, experience and myth, as alternative evocations of the past, are analytically distinct and grounded in very different bodies of historical data' (Cohen 1997: xiv).

In this book, I have tried to orchestrate the story of the Khudai Khidmatgars in all three keys. I have tried to convey at least something of their experience of these far-off events. I have also sought to make a historian's contribution by exploring the membership's motivations and their views on the KK's activities, organisation and ideology, all of which I feel are vital to the proper reconstruction of the movement's life and times. But the mythologisers are also present, albeit somewhat in the shadows, for the official mythologisers of the Pakistan state have systematically removed the KK from the historical record. In response the KK veterans have remained stubbornly determined to preserve their own account of the years between 1930 and 1947, and have created a corpus of memory which is enriched by its confrontations with the official myths. The KK narratives are not merely accounts of experienced events, therefore, but rather the result of long years of introspection and reassessment, silencing and reiteration, disappointment and defiance.

To be a custodian of these narratives is a great privilege but brings its own moral burden and duty, which I have tried to discharge by recording these stories and sentiments for posterity in as convincing a way as I could. All anthropologists crave credibility in the eyes of their hosts, who look after them with so much patience, but this trust can often take many months and much effort to gain. One day Habibullah, my constant companion and guide on the roads of the Frontier, suddenly stopped the car in the middle of nowhere to ask me a question: 'What do these talks with these brave old men mean to you? Are you going to just take them away and put them in your book and forget about them? Do they really *touch* you anywhere?' I was at a loss for words. We had just spent three hours chatting with an old KK who was now so poor he did not own his house and we had had to chat in my car. But his enthusiasm had been overwhelming and he jumped out of the car, into the rain, to show me how they used to march and drill, shouting the old commands, beseeching me to imagine him not as the desperately poor and toothless man who stood before me but as a manly youth, splendid in his uniform, marching with hundreds of other soldiers. The tears I had held back then, as I watched, now flowed at Habibullah's challenge.

Conclusion

Social Creativity and Peasant Intellectuals

Recent discussions of peasant resistance have contrasted sporadic violent uprisings and rebellion with the ongoing low-key and informal modes of everyday resistance which James Scott has so influentially described. Chatterjee (1999) argues that the moments of open rebellion give the historian a glimpse of the 'undominated region in peasant consciousness' and hint at what political feelings lie beneath the surface the rest of the time. On this logic, an extraordinary event such as the Indian uprising of 1857 reveals the enmity and political opposition to the colonial regime which was simmering away before and after. The weapons of the weak were certainly widely used in India. As Krishnaswamy notes, in numerous stories Kipling mocks natives who adopt such tactics as non-cooperation, flattery, obsequiousness, evasion, shirking, irresponsibility, lying and avoidance. He makes abundantly clear his contempt for their inability and refusal to be a 'proper victim' and stand up boldly and fight in manly fashion, regardless of the consequences. Although the variety and cunning of such tactics of daily resistance have been well described, the fact remains that there are clear limits to their efficacy and political content.[1] They cannot in themselves substantially alter the status quo and balance of power, and, although Kipling's characterisations were certainly hostile, they were not altogether without truth. In India the weapons of the weak, at least among the middle class, frequently manifested themselves in frustration, 'untargeted rage, fatalism and desperation, and could become a fantasy rather than intervention in the material world, marked by empty bombast and bluster' (Krishnaswamy 1998: 132).

In the Frontier, too, there had certainly been informal non-cooperation through foot dragging, arson, sabotage and thieving, the latter particularly a constant cause of British complaint. The emergence of the Khudai Khidmatgar movement radically changed this state of affairs, however, by encouraging the Pathans to abandon such negative activities and adopt formal techniques of non-violent protest, which raised non-cooperation to a far higher intensity. The KK boycotted all state institutions from courts to irrigation channels, and did so in a self-consciously open and defiant way. In that sense it was the large-scale 'unveiling' (to use Scott's word) of everyday protest. Furthermore, in the quieter times between these dramatic campaigns the resisters did not merely fall back on the weapons of the weak, as peasants usually did after sudden, short-lived uprisings. The KK movement had generated support for a whole new set of constructive activities, such as spinning, cleanliness drives, school maintenance, drilling and calisthenics, all of which helped the Pathans maintain the momentum of nationalist protest through the ongoing self-reform of their communities. The weapons of the weak thus gave way to those of the empowered.

---

[1] See Gutman 1993 for a robust critique of Scott's epistemology as evidence of a conservative backlash in Western academia.

The Khudai Khidmatgars' organisational structure was fundamental to the movement's longevity and success, but it demanded significant alterations in traditional behaviour and social interaction, notably through the cessation of feuding, the widening of social ties and affiliations, the provision of an alternative mode of solidarity, the addition of meritocracy to ascribed status and the introduction of women into public affairs. This supports Chatterjee's argument that within anti-colonial movements it was the 'community' which was the main site of peasant struggle 'with respective rights and duties established and contested' (Chatterjee 1999: 167). The innovative impact the KK movement had on Pathan social structure was matched by its creative ideological statements. Eric Wolf has complained that writings on culture pay 'too little attention to how groups mobilise, shape and reshape cultural repertoires ... to elicit participation and commitment' (Wolf 1994: 6). I have tried to show how, in the course of the Khudai Khidmatgar movement, the Pathans indeed reshaped their cultural repertoire. In order to accommodate non-violence, the symbiosis of *Pukhtunwali* and Islam had to be adjusted: the notions of *jihad* changed; martyrdom was promoted in place of conquest, and self-restraint in place of revenge; and customary terms concerning honour and sanctuary were subtly redefined or given a different emphasis. Thus from our study of the Khudai Khidmatgar movement we can conclude that Pathan culture is not *only* or *essentially* composed of strict codes of revenge, blood-feud and aggressive hospitality, as anthropology has sometimes led us to believe.

I suggested at the start of this book that studying frontier regions could be especially illuminating in respect of cultural mutuality and exchange. From our discussion of the ideology of the Khudai Khidmatgar movement we can observe that the brew stirred up in the Frontier was not the simple sum of its ingredients: the non-violence was not simply Gandhian, the Islam not simply Sunni, and *Pukhtunwali*, temporarily at least, became something quite different from its counterparts in the Tribal Areas and in Afghanistan. In frontier zones new influences do not obliterate old ones but rather combine with them to throw up novel syntheses, which in turn are carried back to the surrounding civilisations. As Aimé Césaire put it, exchange is cultural oxygen. Studying frontiers thus helps remind us that cultural creativity and synthesis are really the norm rather than the exception.

Civilisations are often compared to giant wheels, with central governments at the hub radiating power outwards to control otherwise inert people on the rim. Anna Tsing found it worthwhile exploring Indonesian state authority precisely where it was most remote and unreliable, because such 'an out-of-the-way place is, by definition, a place where the instability of political meanings is easy to see' (Tsing 1993: 27). Similarly, the North West Frontier Province was the site of vigorous contestations between state and people over concepts of violence, masculinity, honour and freedom. The significance of non-violence is particularly profound when it is adopted by martial Pathans on the subcontinent's periphery, while the colonialists' self-serving claims of their own civility are exposed by the brutal acts they were willing to undertake behind the modesty curtain of the Province's remoteness.

Lenin once wrote that: 'Literacy is a condition without which one çannot even talk of politics. The illiterate person stands outside of politics ... . Without the ABC there are rumours, fairy tales and prejudices – but not politics.' Yet in a region with only 6 per cent adult male literacy the KK movement managed to achieve a specific political and ethical agenda, a novel and practicable language of protest and a thorough-going, self-sustaining organisational structure. Further, the Khidmatgars were party to three Congress provincial governments voted into power largely through their support and canvassing. The KK movement thus embodied a transition from the kind of factional, volatile political activity associated with a segmentary–feudal social structure to that of a mass, nationalist and modernising movement. This transition was intimately connected to the process of state formation and prepared the way for the later post-colonial demands for an autonomous Pathan state.

The KK volunteers thus occupied a cusp between older-style peasant mass move-ments – what Hobsbawm called 'primitive rebels' – and modern political parties. In this respect I like Steven Feierman's characterisation of rural people who participated in the anti-colonial movement in Tanzania as 'peasant intellectuals': 'Even in the periods of intense political activity, most spent some time farming. To call them peasant intellec-tuals defines their historical role at moments of leadership, moments of organization, and moments of direction' (Feierman 1992: 18). This epithet is precisely applicable to the KK. The movement lasted some seventeen years and so necessarily included, between more dramatic episodes, long periods of calm during which they got on with the business of agriculture and everyday life. At crucial points in history, however, they conspicuously participated in political activities, organization and leadership.

Their status as peasant intellectuals was also evident from my conversations with the elderly KK, whose narratives and responses always showed that they had thought deeply about the meaning of the movement. The colonial bureaucrats were convinced that the KKs were either random troublemakers or else pursuing a thirst for land, but my informants' testimonies show that the rank and file joined and participated from a variety of motivations, some of them 'prosaic', like the desire to avoid their friend's scorn or to alleviate their tax burden, others 'high-minded', such as a wish to express national consciousness, a desire to give a better life to their children, the wish to defend Islam from offence or simply an intense faith in the goodness of Badshah Khan. Such accounts provide access to the *meanings* that people attribute to their actions, and bring alive in a compelling way an otherwise dry notion such as 'the growth of the movement'.

Similarly, my informants' narratives have allowed us to see that the non-violence embraced by the KK was neither Gandhian in inspiration nor a merely tactical manoeuvre, but rather a creative ideological position that was grounded in Islam and Pathan custom and which was genuinely embraced by many rank-and-file KKs as a guiding principle which they have continued to cherish and follow in the rest of their lives. For the KK's ideological discourse, 'long term continuity and active creation were in fact compatible ... [E]ven when forms of discourse are inherited from the past, the peasant must make an active decision to say that they are meaningful at this moment, to select a particular form of discourse as opposed to other possible forms, and to shape the inherited language anew to explain current problems' (Feierman 1992: 3).

I have deliberately quoted extensively from my informants, since it was they who lived through the events of the past and who had been denied a voice in subsequent decades. While obviously I have edited and selected excerpts from their narratives, I have for the most part avoided converting their statements into reported speech because I think the form in which the information is conveyed can be as important and interesting as the content itself. As Taussig puts it, 'Surely it is in the coils of rumour, gossip, story and chitchat where ideology and ideas become emotionally powerful and enter into active social circulation and meaningful existence?' (Taussig 1995: 163). The same is true for the colonisers, whose prejudices, judgements, confusions and pronouncements I have quoted as they were originally written, to allow the reader a sense of the language and mood of this discourse. In doing this, I have hoped to avoid the unwarranted coherence and uniformity that can arise out of an over-dominant authorial voice. As Tilly puts it, 'the contest and the contestability of shared memory ... [contribute] to an enriched, coherent, and verifiable history of politics' (Tilly 1994: 253).

None the less, I am well aware that, as with any other statement gathered in the field, such narratives require a huge effort by the ethnographer to interpret and understand them fully. To evaluate the testimonies I gathered, I have had to consider them in the light of Pathan culture and history, the structures and practice of imperial power, Islamic scripture, Afghan story telling and rhetoric, the politics of the Pakistan state, five decades of post-Partition history, the nature of Pathan ethical and customary terms, the life courses of old men, the experience of subsequent generations, the psychology of self-presentation and so on. This is the kind of 'thick description' required in any ethnography, but in the sort of historical ethnography I have attempted there is a particular need to achieve a dialectical synthesis of past and present.

Non-violence, Androgyny and Real Masculinity

In *The Intimate Enemy*, his path-breaking book on the nature and psychology of colonialism, Ashis Nandy explores the way in which the choice of non-violence as a political weapon defied the psychological limits which colonialism had set for the colonised (Nandy 1983). As we saw in Chapter 1 (drawing on Nandy's own work and later work inspired by him), after 1830 the colonial images of the Oriental became increasingly negative, with Indians encoded as superstitious, chaotic, cowardly and above all effeminate, thereby justifying the colonialists' new dominion over them (Nandy 1983: 72). Nandy points out that the 'homology between sexual and political dominance was not an accidental by-product of colonialism' but reflected a cultural consensus created in Europe which valued the dominance of men and masculinity over women and femininity (*ibid.*: 4). Thus, (hyper-)masculinity was seen as an essential quality of the powerful coloniser, while femininity-in-masculinity, or effeminacy, was attributed to the subjugated Indian man and viewed as a 'final negation of man's political identity, a pathology more dangerous than femininity itself' (*ibid.*: 8).[2]

There emerged two kinds of responses to the colonialists' hyper-masculinity. The initial response came in the form of various nineteenth-century movements, often

---

[2] Nandy explores this process through the personalities and writings of British men such as George Orwell, Rudyard Kipling, Oscar Wilde and Charlie Andrews.

but not always linked to religious revivalism, which valorised the *kshatriya* (warrior) as the ideal of a martial and authentic Indianness (*ibid.*: 7). The religious leader Vivekananda attributed contemporary Hindu weakness and emasculation to the loss of textual Brahmanism and social Kshatriyahood, which had robbed Hindus of those original Aryan qualities they had shared with Westerners. He therefore tried to make Hinduism more monotheistic (recall the similar efforts of the Arya Samaj in Fiji), declared manliness to be his new gospel and preached that the androgynous motifs of Hindu mythology were dissolute, enervating and effeminate: 'No more weeping but stand on your feet and be men. It is a man making religion I want. I want the strength, manhood and virility of the *kshatriya*' (quoted in Krishnaswamy 1998: 44). Such movements contributed to a kind of muscular Hinduism which despised the ancient androgynous aspects of Hinduism. This strain of martial Indianness continued into the twentieth century among various violent terrorist movements in Bengal, Punjab and Maharashtra.

The second response came in the form of Gandhi's political praxis. Rather than trying to live up to, and compete with, British hyper-masculinity, he sought to subvert it through the renewal and revaluing of Hindu androgyny. He revolutionised the terms of the confrontation by placing it within a philosophical framework in which androgyny was most valued, followed by femininity. Masculinity ranked third, being superior only to cowardice. For Gandhi, the desired goal of a man's personal development was *ardhanarishwar* – the encapsulation of the feminine within the masculine. The adoption of non-violence gave men access to the powerful, caring maternal principle of the cosmos, which in turn gave them the spiritual strength to avoid cowardice. Hence, it was through tapping the female side of their being that they became braver men. The truly authentic man therefore was 'one who admits his drive to be both sexes'. The courage he gains from the feminine 'is not linked to violence', and hence is unlike the martial courage implicit in masculine Kshatriyahood (Nandy 1983: 54). Thus Gandhi delinked violence from courage and aggressiveness from protest. By doing this he not only challenged the ideas of neo-Kshatriyahood which were in currency, but also the whole *raison d'être* of colonial culture with its 'inbuilt fears about losing potency through the loss of activism and the ability to be violent' (*ibid.*: 55). On Nandy's reading, therefore, Gandhi strove to liberate not only India, but also the British from their own psychology of violence-through-colonialism (*ibid.*: 49).

Nandy's reading of Gandhian non-violence seems to be a convincing one. If true hegemony lies in getting the oppressed to believe the representations of them purveyed by their rulers, then Gandhi's move was profoundly counter-hegemonic: rather than accept British criticisms of Indian effeminacy, as did the muscular Hindus, he challenged and subverted them.

But what of the non-violence of the Khudai Khidmatgars? The Pathans were never branded effeminate. From Elphinstone in the early 1800s to Dalrymple in the late 1990s British travellers and writers have stressed that the Pathans are unlike the other peoples of the subcontinent because they meet the stranger's gaze and treat him as an equal. As Olaf Caroe, the last governor of the Frontier, wrote, 'here were men who looked you in the eye and you knew you had come home' (Caroe 1958: xv). The British enjoyed jousting with Pathans in the Frontier since they felt that here at last was a place where their own hyper-masculinity had met a worthwhile match. In addition, as Muslims, the Pathans did not have any tradition of religious androgyny on which to draw, and Badshah Khan never made reference to ideas of femininity.

Badshah Khan's philosophical project in advocating non-violence was thus quite different from that of Gandhi. I would argue, however, that there was an important structural congruence in so far as Badshah Khan's move was equally counter-hegemonic. Though they had not been portrayed as effeminate, the Pathans had been stereotyped in other important ways, as we saw in Chapter 1. To recapitulate, they were alleged to be riven by tribal prejudices; quarrelsome, intriguing, and distrustful of each other; vengeful of real or imaginary injuries; wanting perseverance; and unfit to govern either themselves or others. The Pathans were viewed and portrayed as fundamentally infantile, engaging in continual strife and argument without rhyme or reason. The regime could afford to praise the Pathans' fearlessness and virility because they did not pose any political threat to the status quo.

Badshah Khan recognised that the Pathans were acting in ways which entirely confirmed the British stereotypes, thereby undermining their own dignity and worth, and the precepts and activities of the Khudai Khidmatgars can be seen as a deliberate attempt to disprove each negative stereotype. In place of excessive pride and quarrelling came feud resolution and humility; in place of ungovernability a process of self-reform and establishment of indigenous institutions; in place of extravagance and fecklessness, an austerity and sense of service.

In respect of non-violence, where Gandhi drew on traditions of androgyny, Badshah Khan drew instead on traditions of self-restraint. While Islam condoned revenge, it valued forgiveness more highly. And within *Pukhtunwali*, while it was creditable to seek revenge, a man gained even more honour by showing restraint and responsibility, particularly in the context of an enemy who requested sanctuary. Thus I would argue that the strength of will which Gandhi attributes to the feminine principle in Indian cosmology is similarly present as a virtue of ideal Pathan manhood. It was thus possible for the KKs to establish a non-violent persona from within their own cultural resources without the need for Gandhian philosophy. Where Gandhi mocked and subverted British hyper-masculinity through androgyny, Badshah Khan and the KK subverted it by providing a countervailing image of *truly manful* restraint and self-control, as opposed to the cruelty and noisy bluster of the colonial 'mad dog'.

The Pathans' adoption of non-violence greatly surprised the British.[3] Furthermore, they appeared to resent it as almost a breach of trust. Having long enjoyed the homosocial bond of sparring and fighting with their manly adversaries, they now found them adopting practices associated with the effeminate down-country Hindus. In Nandy's terms, we may say that the Pathans' refusal to fight threatened the British with the collapse of their own carefully constructed ideals of masculinity, denying them the opportunity to be violent and thereby threatening an associated loss of potency and power. From this perspective, the range of homo-erotic and sexually shameful punishments unleashed on the Pathans appear as efforts *literally* to emas-

---

[3] Gandhi himself commented that the efficacy of his philosophy would be proved when it could be successfully practised by the Pukhtuns, whose ethic seemed most opposed to it.

culate the Pathans as penance for their turning away from hyper-masculine violence. But such cruelties could not hide the fact that, through the KK movement, the Pathans had matured from martial infants into political adults.

Politics and Ethics[4]

In 1918, in a war-torn Germany, Max Weber gave a lecture entitled 'Politics as a Vocation', which sought to consider the ethical implications of his famous definition of the state as 'the agency which in a given territory has the monopoly over the means of legitimate violence' (Weber 1946 (1919): 118–28). If the state is inextricably tied to violence in this way, is not politics similarly tied? If so, can we ever seriously talk of political ethics? Does 'everything that is striven for through political action endanger the salvation of the soul'?

Weber argues that there is an ethic in politics but that it is different from a religious ethic. The politician's ethic is the 'Ethic of Responsibility'. The politician is responsible for securing satisfactory utilitarian results or ends, and he can be justified therefore in using dubious means. The politician is obliged to recognise that good can come of evil and that ethically dangerous means can be used to achieve good ends. This is the reason why violence is often used as a decisive means in politics. Weber argues, therefore, that a true politician of passion and responsibility has to follow his *dharma*, his duty, and not worry about the moral consequences of his means. Weber cites the similarly pragmatic advice Krishna gives to Arjuna in the *Mahabharata* and Kautilya's writings in the *Arthashastra* in support.

Opposed to the politician's 'Ethic of Responsibility' is the 'Ethic of Ultimate Ends' of the religious saint. This adheres to absolute values and so would never embrace morally dubious means. Unlike the politician's ethic, it does not have to take account of the foreseeable results of its chosen actions. Thus, when faced with violence or war, the politician's obligation is to fight, control and punish, since otherwise further deaths would follow. The saint's position, however, is always to 'turn the other cheek', as most famously in the Sermon on the Mount, and the saint does not discriminate between just and unjust violence or recognise the notion of self-defence. Weber says that while such an extreme ethical position can appear justified and convincing in individual saints, such as Christ or Buddha, who are entirely good and truthful, when it is adopted by those who are ordinary and not so extraordinarily truthful, it becomes an 'ethic of indignity' and submission.

Weber argues, therefore, that the opposition between the two ethics cannot be reconciled. The proactive, pragmatic ethic of the politician embraces violence; the reactive, other-worldly ethic of the saint eschews violence. Exploring historical instances of the intrusion of the saintly ethic into politics, he concludes that they are invariably ineffectual, not least because the saints are let down by their followers, who lapse into motives which are 'ethically base', such as revenge, booty and spoils, or else take a millenarian turn and decide to carry out the 'one last violent deed' in

---

[4] I thank Keith Hart, Murray Last and Charles Stewart for their detailed comments on this section of the argument.

order to bring about the new world of ultimate good. Thus religious leaders who do not acknowledge the deficiencies of ordinary people, presuppose the goodness and perfection of the enemy, and believe that bad means can never justify good ends are dismissed by Weber as 'political infants'.

Weber died two years later in 1920 and so did not see the effective use of non-violence against British colonialism. In his terms, however, we may view the non-violent protest of the nationalist struggle as an experiment in reconciling the saintly ethic to the politician's ethic. Gandhi and Badshah Khan must undoubtedly be counted as political leaders. They led substantial movements in campaigns against the state and supported overtly political aims. Yet both attached great importance to religion and morality as a basis for political action. Both used the same religious image from the Sermon on the Mount, of turning the other cheek, to embody a *political* ethic. On several occasions Badshah Khan clearly rejected the politician's ends-focused *dharma*. He rejected the opportunity which world war offered to pressure the British and bargain with them, remaining firmly non-cooperative with the war effort. And he rejected the possibility of seeking to win a referendum he did not believe in and which he feared would cause division and bloodshed. In each case his distrust of the means led him to renounce an otherwise desirable end, and he thus displayed something of Weber's saintly ethic.

Yet the adoption of non-violence never became the ethic of submission which Weber thought inevitable. This largely reflected the fact that, like Weber, Gandhi and Badshah Khan realised the importance of ensuring that every activist had a high degree of 'truthfulness', or integrity and self-awareness. As I have shown, the Khudai Khidmatgars' struggle was directed not only outwards to the enemy, but also inwards, to free themselves from 'ethically base' motivations such as pride and envy. Far from being an 'ethic of indignity', non-violence thus gave its practitioners unprecedented pride in themselves and their actions, a pride which still remains fifty years after the event.

At the end of his lecture, Weber warned that religion should not despise politics for its violence. It is true that 'anyone who wants to engage in politics as a vocation lets himself in for the diabolic forces lurking in all violence'. But violence in the world, he argues, itself stems from the central place of violence in religion. Violence entered religion with the ancient sacrifice and retribution made for the original sin. In turn, the violence inherent in religion has allowed for the easy 'integration of violence into ethics as a disciplinary means against sin'. Thus Weber reaches the gloomy conclusion that politician and saint are in the end equally bound by the realities of life in a 'Paradise Lost'.

Rene Girard's *Violence and the Sacred,* on the other hand, shows that we can look at the relationship between religion, violence and politics in a different and more positive way (see Girard 1977, Das and Nandy 1985). Girard directly addresses the question of why violence is central to religion. Contrary to Weber, he argues that the significance of violence for religion lies not in its destructive or disciplinary function, but rather in its role in the regeneration of social order. Girard argues that sacrifice involves the ritual annihilation of a sacrificial victim who stands as an idealised other on to whom worshippers project their own most vicious and unholy desires. The killing of the sacrificial victim thus symbolically annihilates the 'feelings of violence and hostility which lie behind attempts to carry out violent activities'. Thus what is destroyed is destructiveness itself: 'The function of ritual is to purify violence, to "trick" violence into spending itself on victims whose deaths will provoke no reprisals' (Girard 1977: 36). Religious rituals thus safely expend violence and violent urges, and thereby regenerate the social order.

Girard's analysis affords us an interesting perspective not merely on Weber, but on the Khudai Khidmatgars' achievement. By renouncing the practice of violence and revenge, the Pathans of the KK movement themselves became people 'whose deaths provoke no reprisals'. In their ritualised, weaponless confrontations with the well-armed colonial forces many of the KK died, and by the criteria of Pathan tradition they remained forever unavenged. In Girard's terms, therefore, we can surely see them as sacrificial victims who literally and symbolically drew upon themselves the poison of the violence that was wracking the Frontier, and thereby dissolved it through their own self-restraint and that of their kin. But they were not marginal or helpless victims who had the role of scapegoat imposed upon them. Rather, they chose to take up this burden and were fully aware of the price that many of them would pay. Equally, they were not looking to sacrifice some proxy, the idealised other which Girard describes, but instead were offering themselves up for destruction. Thus, as one commentator on Girard argues, sacrifice can also take the 'symbolic form of noble self-destruction' and it is this 'internalisation of sacrifice' which we typically refer to as martyrdom (Juergensmeyer 1992: 104–5). On this view then, and contrary to Weber's claim, it is not violence against others which lies at the heart of sacrifice and hence religion, but rather a willingness to suffer violence upon oneself in the name of purification and renewal. In the long years of the nationalist struggle, the opportunity for such self-sacrifice in pursuit of the community's regeneration was presented not merely to Badshah Khan, an authentically saintly figure, but also to the tens of thousands of ordinary rank and file activists who joined him in resisting the British. Ultimately, then, Badshah Khan and the Khudai Khidmatgars were able to resolve the apparent incommensurability Weber described, and establish a truly *ethical politics*, through their constant determination to avoid violence against others and continual readiness to embrace martyrdom for themselves.

Afterword

In *Peasant Intellectuals* Feierman relates President Julius Nyerere's experiences of seeing old nationalist fighters while attending district meetings in the 1960s:

> It is always a government affair. I am met by the provincial commissioner and by the district commissioner both of whom are likely to be ... the very men who TANU fought but a few years ago. I am then introduced to the chiefs and to the officials of the native authority and again I am meeting men who either opposed TANU or who carefully stayed out of the political struggle. Then off to one side I notice a few chaps in torn green shirts wielding banners but looking somewhat forlorn. (Pratt 1978: 108, in Feierman 1992: 224)

When I had almost given up all Khudai Khidmatgars for dead, I happened to attend in Peshawar the fourth annual ceremony marking Badshah Khan's death.

There among the dignitaries and thronging crowds, my eyes alighted upon some red shirts. Standing far back from the stage, right on the fringes, dressed in the old uniforms they had lovingly preserved over the years, a handful of old Khudai Khidmatgars waited patiently for the proceedings to begin. One could imagine the same Shahi Bagh arena in the 1940s, full of thousands of red shirts, when they would have blended in noisy solidarity with the rest. Today, however, they stand on the periphery, proud but silenced, as they continue to mourn the death of their leader and their movement.

Bibliography

A Note on the Records

Communications were efficient between Delhi and Peshawar. In general replies came back within two weeks. Between Whitehall and Delhi and Peshawar: fortnightly reports travelled on time through the telegraph system.

Documents British reports were mostly typed; Congress reports were either typed or handwritten, and sometimes were illegible.

The unpublished sources fall into two categories.

1. The collections at the India Office Library and Records, in London; the National Archives in New Delhi; and the Manuscript section in the Nehru Memorial Museum and Library, New Delhi, were the archives consulted.
2. Interviews/conversations were conducted with surviving Khudai Khidmatgars in NWFP, Pakistan. A table with names of informants, date on which interview was conducted, the area to which the interviewee belongs and the age of the interviewee can be found in Appendix I. Interviews are cited in the text with reference numbers.

An entry which looks like this in the table:

5) 20.I.92 Deran Shah Khatkale, Nowshera *b*. 1900

is cited in the text as:

Deran Shah [I.5].

Unpublished Sources

India Office Library and Records, London (IOLR)

Records of the Political and Secret Department 1929–45
L/P&S/10; L/P&S/12; L/P&S/20
Records of the Public and Judicial Department 1929–45
L/P&J/5; L/P&J/6; L/P&J/7; L/P&J/8; L/P&J/9

National Archives, Delhi

Records of the Home Department (Political) 1929–45 (cited as Home/Pol. in the text)

Nehru Memorial Museum and Library, Delhi (NMML)

AICC Files 1929–47

Pakhtun *1945*

Published Sources

Aberle, D. (1970). 'A Note on Relative Deprivation Theory', in *Millenial Dreams in Action*, New York, New York University Press.

Adas, M. (1979). *Prophets of Rebellion: Millenarian Protest Movements against the European Colonial Order*, Cambridge, Cambridge University Press.

Ahmed, A. (1976). *Millenium and Charisma among Pathans: a Critical Essay in Social Anthropology*, London, Routledge & Kegan Paul.

—— (1980). *Pukhtun Economy and Society: Traditional Structure and Economic Development in a Tribal Society*, London, Boston & Henley, Routledge & Kegan Paul.

—— (1985). *Resistance and Control in Pakistan*, London, Routledge & Kegan Paul.

Ahmed, H. M. T. (1990). *Murder in the Name of Allah*, London, Guernsey Press.

Ali (1966). *And Then the Pathan Murders*, Peshawar, University Book Agency.

Almagor, U. (1986). 'Institutionalizing a Fringe Periphery: Dassanetch–Amhara Relations' in Donham, D. & W. James (1986).

Alter, J. S. (1993). 'The Body of One Colour: Indian Wrestling, the Indian State, and Utopian Somatics', *Cultural Anthropology* 8(1): 49–72.

Amin, S. (1984). 'Gandhi as Mahatma', in *Subaltern Studies, Volume 4*, Delhi, Oxford University Press.

—— (1995). *Event, Metaphor, Memory*, Berkeley, California, California University Press.

Anderson, B. (1991). *Imagined Communities*, London and New York, Verso, second edition.

Anderson, J. (1979). 'Doing Pakhtu: Social Organisation of the Ghilzai Pakhtun', PhD thesis, University of North Carolina, Chapel Hill.

—— (1980) 'There Are No Khans Anymore: Economic Development and Social Change in Tribal Afghanistan', *The Middle East Journal* 32(2)[1978]: 167–83.

—— (1982). 'Cousin Marriage in Context: Constructing Social Relations in Afghanistan', *Folk* 24/25: 7–28.

—— (1983) 'Khan and Khel: Dialectics of Pakhtun Tribalism', in *The Conflict of Tribe and State in Afghanistan*, Tapper, R. (ed.), London, Croom Helm.

—— (1985). 'Sentimental Ambivalence and the Exegesis of "Self"', *Anthropological Quarterly* 58(4): 203–11.

—— (1992). 'Poetics and Politics in Ethnographic Texts: a View from the Colonial Ethnography of Afghanistan', in *Writing the Social Text: Poetics and Politics in Social Science*, New York, Aldine de Gruyter.

Anderson J. & D. Eickelman (eds) (1985). *Self and Society in the Middle East, Anthropological Quarterly* (Special Issue) 58(4).

Andrews, C. (1939). *The True India: A Plea for Understanding*, London, George Allen & Unwin.

Andreyev, S (1998). 'The Rawshaniyya Movement', unpublished DPhil thesis, University of Oxford.

Antze, P. and M. Lambek (eds) (1996). *Tense Past: Cultural Essays in Trauma and Memory*, New York & London, Routledge.

Appadurai, A. (ed.) (1986). *The Social Life of Things: Commodities in Cultural Perspective*, Cambridge, Cambridge University Press.

—— (1988). 'Putting Hierarchy in Its Place', *Cultural Anthropology* 3(1): 36–49.

Asad, T. (1972). 'Market Model, Class Structure and Consent: a Reconsideration of Swat Political Organisation', *Man* 7(1): 74–94.

Aya, R. (1990). *Rethinking Revolutions and Collective Violence: Studies on Concept, Theory, and Method*, Amsterdam, Het Spinhuis.

Baha, L. (1978). *NWFP Administration under British Rule 1901–1919*, Islamabad, National Commission on Historical and Cultural Research.

Banerjee, M. (1990), 'A Study of Segmentary Political Systems from the Atlas to the Indus', unpublished MPhil thesis, Delhi School of Economics, University of Delhi.

Barnard, A. & J. Spencer (1996). *Encyclopaedia of Social and Cultural Anthropology*, London, Routledge.

Barnes, J. A. (1990). 'Indigenous Politics and Colonial Administration with Special Reference to Australia', in *Models and Interpretations: Selected Essays*, Cambridge, Cambridge University Press.

Barr, F. M. (1942). 'A "Red Shirt" Camp', *The Modern Review*, 71(1).

Barth, F. (1959). *Political Leadership among Swat Pathans*, London, The Athlone Press.

—— (1981). *Features of Person and Society: Collected Essays*, London, Routledge & Kegan Paul, two vols.

—— (1987). 'Cultural Wellsprings of Resistance', in Klauss, R. (ed) (1987).

Bayly, C. A. (1986). 'The Origins of Swadeshi (Home Industry): Cloth and Indian Society, 1700–1930', in Appadurai, A. (ed). (1986).

Bellew, H. W. (1862). *Journal of a Political Mission to Afghanistan in 1857 With an Account of the Country and the People*, London, Smith Elder & Co.

—— (1880). *The Races of Afghanistan Being a Brief Account of the Principal Nations Inhabiting that Country*, Calcutta, Thacker, Spink & Co.

Bondurant, J. (1958). *Conquest of Violence: the Gandhian Philosophy of Conflict*, London & Princeton, OUP & Princeton University Press.

Bonner, A. (1987). *Among the Afghans*, Durham & London, Duke University Press.

Bourdieu, P. (1977). *Outline of a Theory of Practice*, Cambridge, Cambridge University Press.

Boyarin, J. (ed.) (1994). *Remapping Memory: the Politics of Time Space*, Minneapolis and London, University of Minnesota Press.

Bright, C. (ed.). (1984). *Statemaking and Social Movements: Essays in History and Theory*, Ann Arbor, University of Michigan Press.

Burke, P. (ed.) (1973). *A New Kind of History from the Writings of Febvre*, London, Routledge & Kegan Paul.

Butalia, U. (1998). *The Other Side of Silence*, New Delhi, Penguin.

Carey, G. (ed.) (1990). *Frontiers*, London, BBC Books.

Carlyle, T. 1983 [1840]. *On Heroes, Hero Worship and the Heroic in History*, New York, Chelsea House.

Caroe, O. (1958). *The Pathans 550 BC–AD 1957*, Karachi, Oxford University Press.

Chadwick, N. (1952) [1942]. *Poetry and Prophecy*, Cambridge, Cambridge University Press.

Chatterjee, P. (1999). *The Partha Chatterjee Omnibus (comprising Nationalist Thought and the Colonial World, The Nation and its Fragments, A Possible India)*, Delhi, Oxford University Press.

Coen, T. C. (1971). *The Indian Political Service*, London, Chatto & Windus.

Cohen, P. A. (1997). *History in Three Keys: the Boxers as Event, Experience and Myth*, New York, Columbia University Press.

Cohn, B. (1987). 'Cloths, Clothes and Colonialism: India in the Nineteenth Century', in Weiner A. B. & J. Schneider (eds) (1987).

—— (1997). *Colonialism and Its Forms of Knowledge: the British in India*, Delhi, Oxford University Press.

Collard, A. (1989). 'Investigating "Social Memory" in a Greek Context', in Tonkin, E. et al. (eds) (1989).

Collingwood, R. G. (1946). *The Idea of History*, Oxford, Clarendon Press.

Comaroff, J. & J. Comaroff (1992). *Ethnography and the Historical Imagination*, Boulder, Westview Press.

Connerton, P. (1989). *How Societies Remember*, Cambridge, Cambridge University Press.

Dalrymple, W. (1999). 'Nirvana, by Way of Ancient Greece', *The Independent*, 6 November, London.

Das, V. (1995). *Critical Events: an Anthropological Perspective on Contemporary India*, Delhi, Oxford University Press.

Davis, J. (1977). *People of the Mediterrenean*, London, Routledge & Kegan Paul.

—— (1980). 'Social Anthropology and the Consumption of History', *Theory and Society* 9: 519–37.

—— (1989). 'The Social Relations of the Production of History', in Tonkin, E. et al. (eds) (1989).

Desai, M. (1935). *Two Servants of God*, Delhi, Hindustan Times Press.

Dirks, N. B. (ed.) (1995). *Colonialism and Culture*, Ann Arbor, University of Michigan Press.

—— (1997). 'Foreword', in Cohn, B. (1997).

Donham, D. & W. James (eds) (1986). *The Southern Marches of Imperial Ethiopia: Essays in History and Social Anthropology*, Cambridge, Cambridge University Press.

Donnan, H. & T. M. Wilson (eds) (1994). *Border Approaches: Anthropological Perspectives on Frontiers*, Lanham, New York & London, University Press of America.

—— & —— (1998). *Border Identities: Nation and State at International Frontiers*, Cambridge, Cambridge University Press.

Dresch, P. (1986). 'The Significance of the Course of Events in Segmentary Systems', *American Ethnologist* 13(2): 309–24.

—— (1989). *Tribes, Government and History in Yemen*, Oxford, Clarendon Press.

Easwaran, E. (1985). *Badshah Khan, a Man to Match his Mountains*, Tomales California, Nilgiri Press.

Edgerton, W. (1993). *Memoirs of Peasant Tolstoyans in Soviet Russia*, Bloomington & Indianapolis, Indiana University Press.

Edwards, D. (1986). 'Pretexts of Rebellion: the Cultural Origins of Pakhtun Resistance to the Afghan State', unpublished PhD thesis, University of Michigan.

—— (1996). *Heroes of the Age: Moral Fault Lines on the Afghan Frontier*, Berkeley, California University Press.

Elias, N. (1978) [1939] *The Civilizing Process: History of Manners*, trans. E. Jephcott, Oxford, Basil Blackwell.

Elphinstone, M. 1839 [1815]. *An Account of the Kingdom of Caubul*, Karachi, Indus Publications.

Engineer, A. A. (1995). 'Islam and Non-violence', in Kumar, R. (ed.) (1995).

Erikson, E. H. (1969). *Gandhi's Truth: on the Origins of Militant Nonviolence*, New York, W.W. Norton & Co.

Escobar, A. (1992). 'Culture, Practice and Politics: Anthropology and the Study of Social Movements', *Critique of Anthropology* 12(4): 395–432.

Evans-Pritchard, E. E. (1940). *The Nuer: a Description of the Modes of Livelihood and Political Institutions of a Nilotic People*, Oxford, Clarendon Press.

—— (1949). *The Sanusi of Cyrenaica*, Oxford, Clarendon Press.

Feierman, S. (1974). *Shambaai Kingdom*, Madison, University of Wisconsin Press.

—— (1992). *Peasant Intellectuals: Anthropology and History in Tanzania*, Madison, University of Wisconsin Press.

Feldman, A. (1991). *Formations of Violence: the Narrative of the Body and Political Terror in Northern Ireland*, Chicago, University of Chicago Press.

Femia, J. V. (ed.) (1987). *Gramsci's Political Thought: Hegemony, Consciousness and Revolutionary Process*, Oxford, Clarendon Press.

Finnegan, R. (1992). *Oral Tradition and the Verbal Arts: a Guide to Research Practices*, London & New York, Routledge.

Fox, R. G. (1985). *Lions of the Punjab: Culture in the Making*, Berkeley, University of California Press.

Friedman, S. L. A. J. (ed.) (1992). *Modernity and Identity*, Oxford, Basil Blackwell.

Gandhi, R. (1993). 'Sages of Modern India: Gandhi', lecture at Temenos Academy, London.

Gellner, E. (1969). *Saints of the Atlas*, London, Weidenfeld & Nicholson.

—— (1979). *Spectacles and Predicaments*, Cambridge, Cambridge University Press.

—— (1981). *Muslim Society*, Cambridge, Cambridge University Press.

—— (1983). *Nations and Nationalism*, Oxford, Basil Blackwell.

Ghani, A. (1988). 'Pakhtun', in *Encyclopaedia of Asian History*, New York, Charles Scribner's Sons.

Gilmore, D. (ed.) (1987). *Honor and Shame and the Unity of the Mediterranean*, Special Publication of American Anthropologist No. 22.

Gilsenan, M. (1982). *Recognising Islam: an Anthropologist's Introduction*, London & Sydney, Croom Helm.

—— (1987). 'Sacred Words, unpublished article, University of Oxford.

—— (1996). *Lords of the Lebanese Marches*, London & New York, I. B. Tauris.

Girard, R. (1977). *Violence and the Sacred*, trans. Patrick Gregory, Baltimore, MD & London, Johns Hopkins University Press.

Gooptu, N. (1991). 'The Political Culture of the Urban Poor: the United Provinces between the Two World Wars', PhD thesis, University of Cambridge.

Guha, R. (1982). *Subaltern Studies*, Volume I, Delhi, Oxford University Press.

—— (1999). *Savaging the Civilized*, Delhi, Oxford University Press.

Gutman, M. (1993). 'Rituals of Resistance', *Latin American Perspectives* 20(2): 74–92.

Halbwachs, M. (1945). *The Collective Memory*, New York, Harper & Row.

Hameed, S. S. (1995). 'Non-violence in Islam', in Kumar, R. (ed.) (1995).

Henige, D. (1982). *Oral Historiography*, London, Longman.

Hobsbawm, E. (1959). *Primitive Rebels: Studies in Archaic Forms of Social Movement in the Nineteenth and Twentieth Centuries*, Manchester, Manchester University Press.

—— (1994). 'User's Guide to Barbarism', Oxford, Amnesty Lecture.

Hobsbawm, E. & T. Ranger (eds) (1988). *The Invention of Tradition*, Cambridge, Cambridge University Press.

Holy, L. (1997). 'Martyrdom, Czech National Identity, and Politics', in Pettigrew, J. (ed.) (1997).

Hoskins, J. (1998). *Biographical Objects: How Things Tell the Stories of People's Lives*, New York & London, Routledge.

Hunt, R. & J. Harrison (1980). *The District Officer in India 1930–1947*, London, Scolar Press.

Hyam, R. (1990). *Empire and Sexuality: the British Experience*, Manchester & New York, Manchester University Press.

James, W. (1988). *The Listening Ebony: Moral Knowledge, Religion, and Power among the Uduk of Sudan*, Oxford, Clarendon Press.

James, W. & D. H. Johnson (eds) (1988). *Vernacular Christianity: Essays in the Social Anthropology of Religion*, JASO Occasional Papers, Oxford, JASO.

Jamous, R. (1981). *Honneur et baraka: les structures sociales traditionnelles dans le Rif*, Cambridge, Cambridge University Press.

Jansson, E. (1988). *India, Pakistan or Pakhtunistan*, Uppsala, Acta Universitatis Upsaliensis.

Jeffery, K. (1981). 'An English Barrack in the Oriental Seas? India in the Aftermath of the First World War', *Modern Asian Studies* 15(3): 369–86.

Johnson, D. H. (1981). 'The Fighting Nuer: Primary Sources and the Origins of a Stereotype', *Africa* 51(1): 508–27.

—— (1982). 'Ngundeng and the "Turuk": Two Narratives Compared', *History in Africa* 9: 119–39.

—— (1994). *Nuer Prophets: a History of Prophecy from the Upper Nile in the Nineteenth and Twentieth Centuries*, Oxford, Clarendon Press.

Juergensmeyer, M. (ed.) (1992). *Violence and the Sacred in the Modern World*, London, Frank Cass.

Kelly, J. D. (1991). *A Politics of Virtue: Hinduism, Sexuality, and Countercolonial Discourse in Fiji*, Chicago, Chicago University Press.

Keppley-Mahmood, C. (1997). 'Playing the Games of Love: Passion and Martyrdom Among Khalistani Sikhs', in Pettigrew, J. (ed.) (1997).

Khan, K. A. G. (1969). *My Life and Struggle: Autobiography of Badshah Khan as Narrated to K. B. Narang*, trans. Helen H. Bouman, Delhi, Hind Pocket Book.

—— (1983). *Zama Zindagi o Jiddo Jihad*, Kabul, Pashtu Academy.

Klauss, R. (ed.) (1987). *Afghanistan: the Great Game Revisited*, New York, Freedom House.

Korejo, M. S. (1994). *Frontier Gandhi: His Place in History*, Karachi, Oxford University Press.

Kramer, M. (1992). 'Sacrifice and Fratricide in Shiite Lebanon', in Juergensmeyer, M. (ed.) (1992).

Krishnaswamy, R. (1998). *Effeminism: the Economy of Colonial Desire*, Ann Arbor, University of Michigan Press.

Kumar, R. (ed.) (1995). *Khan Abdul Gaffar Khan: a Centennial Tribute*, New Delhi, Nehru Memorial Museum & Library, Har-Anand Publications.

Lambek, M. (1996). 'The Past Imperfect: Remembering as Moral Practice', in Antze, P. & M. Lambek (eds) (1996).

Last, M. (1997). 'The Colonial Caliphate in Northern Nigeria', in *Les Temps des marabouts: Itinéraires et stratégies islamiques en Afrique occidentale française v. 1880–1960*, Robinson, D. and J.-L. Triaud (eds), Paris, Karthala.

Lindholm, C. (1981). 'History and the Heroic Pakhtun', *Man* 16(3): 463–67.

—— (1982). *Generosity and Jealousy: the Swat Pukhtun of North Pakistan*, New York, Columbia University Press.

—— (1993). 'Review of Ahmed's *Resistance and Control in Pakistan*', *Man* 28(4): 825–26.

—— (1996). *Frontier Perspectives*, Karachi, Oxford University Press.

Lutz, R. (1989). *'Kodeks chesti Pushtunov'*, in *Afghanistan: Istoriya, Ekonomika, Kultura*, Moscow, Science Publishers.

MacDonald, R. H. (1993). *Sons of the Empire – the Frontier and the Boy Scout Movement 1890–1918*, Toronto, Buffalo & London, University of Toronto Press.

Meeker, M. (1979). *Literature and Violence in North Arabia*, Cambridge Studies in Cultural Systems, Cambridge, Cambridge University Press.

—— (1980). 'The Twilight of a Heroic Age: a Rereading of Barth's Study of Swat', *Man* 15(4): 682–701.

Metcalf, B. (1982). *Islamic Revival in British India 1860–1900*, Princeton, Princeton University Press.

Miller, J. (ed.) (1980). *The African Past Speaks*, Hamden, CT & Folkestone, Archon & Dawson.

Mills, M. (1991). *Rhetoric and Politics in Afghan Traditional Storytelling*, Philadelphia, University of Pennsylvania Press.

Mitchell, W. J. T. (ed.) (1980). *On Narrative*, Chicago, Chicago University Press.

Moorhouse, G. (1983). *India Britannica*, London, Book Club Associates.

Nandy, A. (1983). *The Intimate Enemy: Loss and Recovery of Self Under Colonialism*, Delhi, Oxford University Press.

Nehru, J. (1985) [1946]. *The Discovery of India*, New Delhi, Jawaharlal Nehru Memorial Fund/Oxford University Press.

Noble, F. (1997). *Something in India: a Memoir of Service in the Frontier Province*, Edinburgh, Cambridge & Durham, USA: Pentland Press Ltd.

O'Hanlon, P. & D. Washbrook (1992). 'After Orientalism: Culture, Criticism and Politics in the Third World', *Comparative Studies in Society and History* 34(1): 141–67.

Pennel, T. L. (1909). *Among the Wild Tribes of the Afghan Frontier: A Record of Sixteen Years of Close Intercourse with the Natives of the Indian Marches*, London, Shelley & Co.

Perelli, C. (1994). *'Memoria de Sangre*: Fear, Hope and Disenchantment in Argentina', in Boyarin J. (ed.) (1994).

Peters, E. (1967). 'Some Structural Aspects of the Feud Among the Camel-Herding Bedouin of Cyrenaica', *Africa* 3: 261–82.

Pettigrew, J. (1994). 'Reflections on the Place of the Border in Contemporary Sikh Affairs', in Donnan, H. & T. M. Wilson (eds) (1994).

—— (ed.) (1997). *Martyrdom and Political Resistance: Essays from Asia and Europe*, Amsterdam, VU University Press.

Piggott, T. (1930). *Outlaws I Have Known and Other Reminiscences of an Indian Judge*, Edinburgh & London, Blackwood.

Portelli, A. (1990). 'Uchronic Dreams: Working-class Memory and Possible Worlds', in *The Myths We Live By*, London, Routledge & Kegan Paul.

Prakash, G. (1990). 'Writing Post-Orientalist Histories of the Third World: Perspectives from Indian History', *Comparative Studies in Society and History* 32(2): 383–408.

—— (1992). 'Can the "Sub-altern" Ride? A Reply to O'Hanlon and Washbrook', *Comparative Studies in Society and History* 34(1): 168–84.

Pratt, C. (1978). *The Critical Phase in Tanzania, 1945–1986: Nyerere and the Emergence of a Socialist Strategy*, Nairobi, Oxford University Press.

Radtke, B. and John O'Kane (1996). *The Concept of Sainthood in Early Islamic Mysticism: Two Works by Al-Hakim Al-Tirmidhi*, London, Curzon Press.

Ramana Murti, V. V. (ed.) (1970). *Gandhi: Essential Writings*, New Delhi, Gandhi Peace Foundation.

Ramu, P.S. (1992). *Khudai Khidmatgar and National Movement: Momentous Speeches of Badshah Khan*, Delhi, S. S. Publishers.

Richards, F. (1983). *Old Soldier Sahib*, London, Anthony Mott Ltd.

Rittenberg, S. (1977). 'The Independence Movement in India's North West Frontier Province 1901–1947', PhD thesis, Columbia University.

—— (1992). *Ethnicity, Nationalism and the Pukhtuns: the Independence Movement in Indian NWFP*, North Carolina, Carolina Academic Press.

Rosaldo, R. (1989). *Culture and Truth: the Remaking of Social Analysis*, Boston, Beacon Press.

Said, E. (1978). *Orientalism*, New York, Random House.

Salvation Army (1923). *Salvation Army Year Book*, London, S P & S.

Samuel, R. & P. Thompson (eds) (1990). *The Myths We Live By*, London, Routledge & Kegan Paul.

Scott, J. (1985). *Weapons of the Weak: Everyday Forms of Peasant Resistance*, London, Yale University Press.

—— (1990). *Domination and the Arts of Ambiguity*, New Haven, Yale University Press.

Shah, S. W. A. (1999). *Ethnicity, Islam and Nationalism: Muslim Politics in the North West Frontier Province 1937–47*, Karachi, Oxford University Press.

Shariati, A. (1986) 'Jihad and Shahadat', in Taleqani, A. M. & A. Shariati (eds) (1986).

Singer, A. (1984). *Lords of the Khyber: the Story of the North-West Frontier*, London & Boston, Faber & Faber.

Sinha, M. (1995). *Colonial Masculinity: the 'Manly Englishman' and the 'Effeminate Bengali' in the Late Nineteenth Century*, Manchester, Manchester University Press.

Spencer, J. (1997). 'Post-colonialism and the Political Imagination', *Journal of the Royal Anthropological Institute* 3(1): 1–19.

Stokes, E. (1986). *The Peasant Armed: the Indian Revolt of 1857*, Oxford, Clarendon Press.

Taleqani, A. M. & A. Shariati (eds) (1986). *Jihad and Shahadat: Struggle and Martyrdom in Islam*, trans. Mehdi Abedi & Gary Legenhausen, Houston, TX, Institute of Research & Islamic Studies.

Tarlo, E. (1996). *Clothing Matters: Dress and Identity in India*, London, Hurst & Company.

Taussig, M. (1995). 'Culture of Terror – Space of Death: Roger Casement's Putumayo Report and the Explanation of Torture', in Dirks, N. B. (ed.) (1995).

Tendulkar, D. G. (1963). *Mahatma*, Delhi, Publications Division, 8 vols.

—— (1967). *Khan Abdul Gaffar Khan: Faith Is a Battle*, Varanasi, Sarvodaya Sahitya Prakashan.

Thomas, N. (1994). *Colonialism's Culture: Anthropology, Travel and Government*, Cambridge, Polity Press.

—— (1996). 'Colonialism', in Barnard, A. & J. Spencer (eds) (1996).

Thompson, P. (1988). *The Voice of the Past*, Oxford, Clarendon Press.

Tilly, C. (1984). 'Social Movements and National Politics', in *State Making and Social Movements: Essays in History and Theory*, Tilly, C. (ed.), Ann Arbor, University of Michigan Press.

—— (1994). 'Afterword: Political Memories in Space and Time', in Boyarin, J. (ed.) (1994).

Tolen, R. (1991). 'Colonizing and Transforming the Criminal Tribesman: the Salvation Army in British India', *American Ethnologist* 18(1): 106–25.

Tonkin, E. (1994). *Narrating our Pasts: the Social Construction of Oral History*, Cambridge, Cambridge University Press.

Tonkin, E. et al. (eds) (1989). *History and Ethnicity*, ASA Monographs 27, London & New York, Routledge.

Toynbee, A. (1961). *Travels between the Oxus and the Indus*, Oxford, Oxford University Press.

Tsing, A. L. (1993) *In the Realm of the Diamond Queen: Marginality in an Out-of-the-way Place*, Princeton, Princeton University Press.

Uberoi, J. P. S. (1978). 'The Structural Concept of the Asian Frontier', in Chattopadhyay, D. (ed.), *History and Society (Essays in Honour of Niharanjan Ray)*. Calcutta, K. P. Bagchi.

—— (1994). *Religion, Civil Society and the State*, Delhi, Oxford University Press.

Van der Veer, P. (1994). *Religious Nationalism: Hindus and Muslims in India*, Berkeley, Los Angeles & London, University of California Press.

Vansina, J. (1966). *Oral Tradition*, London, Penguin.

—— (1980). 'Memory and Oral Tradition', in Miller J. (ed.) (1980).

—— (1985). *Oral Tradition as History*, London, James Currey.

Weber, M. (1946) 'Politics as a Vocation', Gerth H. H. & C. Wright Mills (eds), *From Max Weber: Essays in Sociology*, New York, Oxford University Press.

—— (1948). 'The Sociology of Charismatic Authority', Gerth H. H. and C. Wright Mills (eds), *Max Weber: Selected Writings*, London, Routledge & Kegan Paul.

Weiner, A. B. & J. Schneider (eds) (1987). *Cloth and Human Experience*, Washington, DC, Smithsonian Institution Press.

Wolf, E. (1994). 'Perilous Ideas: Race, Culture, People', *Current Anthropology* 35(1): 1–24.

Appendix I
List of informants

Date	Name	Age	Place	Year of birth
1) 19.XII.91, 27.XII.91, 8.II.92, 9.II.92, 11.II.92	Haji Sarfaraz Nazim Sahib	86 yrs	Peshawar	b. 1908
2) 27.XII.91	Waris Khan	90 yrs	Sardaryab, Peshawar Dist.	b. 1901
3) 8.I.92	Jarnail Abdul Rahim	70 yrs	Charpariza, Daudzai	b. 1922
4) 15.I.92	Hidayatullah Khan	?	Peshawar	?
5) 20.I.92	Deran Shah	92 yrs	Khatkale, Nowshera	b. 1900
6) 20.I.92	Kudrat Shah	72 yrs	Manga, Mardan	b. 1920
7) 20.I.92	Keramat Shah	62 yrs		b. 1930
8) 20.I.92	Tur Lali	?	Bajaur	?
9) 2.II.92	Ghazi Khan	78 yrs	Pabbi	b. 1914
10) 2.II.92	Fazle Karim	83/84 yrs	Pabbi	b. 1908
11) 12.II.92	Mir Rahman Jarnail	90 yrs	Doaba	b. 1902
12) 12.II.92	Maulana Hamdullah Jan	80 yrs	Matta	b. 1912
13) 16.II.92	Haji Awal Khan	?	Matta	?
14) 16.II.92	Noor Akbar	?	Matta	?
15) 17.II.92	Haji Mohammed Hussain Khan	?	Matta	?
16) 18.II.92	Haji Abdul Wadood	95/96 yrs	District Naib Sadar Matta	b. 1896
17) 18.II.92	Grana	90 yrs	Matta Palangzai	b. 1902
18) 19.II.92	Nabad Khan s/o Sardar Khan	?	Yar Hussain, Swabi	?
19) 19.II.92	Lt. Mohammed Wali	75 yrs	Yar Hussain, Swabi	b. 1917
20) 19.II.92	Muffariq Shah (b/o Firdaus Khan)	79 yrs		b. 1913
21) 20.II.92	Jarnail Mohammed Umar	?	Manerai, Swabi	?
22) 20.II.92	Secretary Amir Nawaz Khan	78 yrs	Shah Mansur	b.1914
23) 22.II.92	Sadar Musa Khan	82 yrs	Chamkani, Peshawar District	b. 1910

Date	Name	Age	Place	Year of birth
24) 23.II.92	Jarnail Hazrat Gul	?	Addezai, Mohmand	?
25) 25.II.92	Jarnail Abdul Aziz	75/76 yrs	Shava	b. 1916
26) 25.II.92	Secretary Wahidullah	77 yrs	Shava	b. 1919
27) 25.II.92	Haroon Kaka	80 yrs		b. 1912
28) 26.II.92	Salar Khaist Amir	?	Parmuli	?
29) 26.II.92	Sher Khan	80 yrs	Baja	b. 1912
30) 26.II.92	Hurmat Khan	90 yrs	?	b. 1902
31) 27.II.92	Haji Saifur Khan	90 yrs	?	b. 1902
32) 27.II.92	Raghibullah Khan	74 yrs	?	b. 1918
33) 28.II.92	Haji Mohammed Sher	?	?	?
34) 28.II.92	Shah Jahan Khan	80 yrs	Swabi	b. 1912
35) 1.III.92	Akram Khan	?	?	?
36) 1.III.92	Haji Chairman Meherban Shah	80/85 yrs	Dagai	b. 1910
37) 2.III.92	Abdul Ahad s/o Abdul Sumad	96 yrs	Mohalla Garugram	b. 1896
38) 2.III.92	Haji Inayatullah	90 yrs	Mardan	b. 1902
39) 2.III.92	Sayyid Mohammed Fasi Badshah	79 yrs	Babda	b. 1913
40) 2.III.92	Gul Rahman	72 yrs	Pdang	b. 1920
41) 2.III.92	Mohammed Roshan	80 yrs	?	b. 1912
42) 3.III.92	Sayid Karamat Shah	?	?	?
43) 2.III.92	Ajab Khan	70 yrs (approx.)	Mirakhel, Charsadda	b. 1922
44) 3.III.92	Colonel Mohammed Sayid	74 yrs	?	b. 1918
45) 3.III.92	Sarfaraz Khan s/o Mohammed Sardar Khan	?	Pdang	?
46) 3.III.92	Derai Khan	80 yrs (approx.)	Manikhela	b. 1912
47) 3.III.92	Muhammadi Shah	85 yrs	Manikhel	b. 1907
48) 5.III.92	Kalam Khan s/o Munawar Khan	?	Navakhali, Nowshera	?
49) 11.III.92	Haji Zamir Gul	90 yrs	Charsadda	b. 1902
50) 11.III.92	Haji Lal Mohammed	72 yrs	?	b. 1920
51) 11.III.92	Hama Gul	75/80 yrs	Pdang	b. 1912
52) 11.III.92	Turab	75 yrs	Utmanzai	b. 1917
53) 16.III.92	Fazle Rahim Saqi	90 yrs	Wardaga	b. 1902

Date	Name	Age	Place	Year of birth
54) 16.III.92	Deputy Tamash	96 yrs	Charsadda	b. 1896
55) 22.III.92	Gul Samand Khan s/o Arabistan Khan	92 yrs	Kakki, Bannu dist.	b. 1900
56) 22.III.92	Mira Khan s/o Bauta Khan	110 yrs	Kakki	b. 1882
57) 22.III.92	Captain Mazullah Khan	100 yrs	?	b. 1892
58) 22.III.92	Janan Khalifa	97 yrs	?	b. 1895
59) 22.III.92	Mohammed Pir Sher Shah	80 yrs	Pir Ram Daud Shah	b. 1912
60) 22.III.92	Sadar Mohammed	120/130 yrs	Daraz Khan	b. 1872
61) 23.III.92	Mohammed Yakub Khan s/o Khadim Shah	75/80 yrs	Wazir Hathi Khel, Lapdi Kala. P.S.Domel Bannu	b. 1912
62) 23.III.92	Mohammed Badshah, Sadar ANP	78 yrs	Mardan	b. 1914
63) 23.III.92	Wazir Mohammed	86 yrs	Mardan Mohalla Badichum	b. 1906
64) 29.III.92	Ghulam Gilani	72 yrs	Mardan	b. 1920
65) 29.III.92	Maulavi Inayatullah s/o Maulana Hafiz Abdul Jamil	82 yrs	Toru, Marda	b. 1910
66) 1.IV.92	Dr Waris Gharader	78 yrs	Mardan	b. 1914
67) 10.IX.93	Mohammed Gul	90 yrs	Tahkal, Peshawar	b. 1903
68) 12.IX.93	Mir Mohammed	80 yrs	Tahkal, Peshawar	b. 1913
69) 15.IX.93	Gurfaraz Khan	95 yrs	Landay Kanday	b. 1898
70) 25.IX.93	Mukarram Khan	85/86 yrs	Spina Vare	b. 1907

Appendix II
Glossary

Alim Learned man
Anjuman Islah ul Afaghina Society for the reforms of Afghans
Arbab Honorific title bestowed by British
Ashram Hindu monastery
Azad Independent
Badla Revenge
Badmash Scoundrel
Bhiga Measure of land
Bhishti Carrier of water
Biraderi Network and community; usually formed by kin
Buzurg Holy man
Chaddar Shawl; one of the distinctive items of clothing for Pukhtun men
Charkha Spinning wheel
Charpoy Four-legged rope cot
Chowkirdari Lit. guard; also revenue tax imposed by British
Cummerband Broad belt worn around the waist
Dua Supplication; prayer
Faqir, Faqiri Poor, world renouncer devoid of material possessions; poverty; also
    landless peasant
Fatwa Authoritative injunction of Islamic law
Ghazi Warrior who fought in a battle alongside the Prophet Mohammed
Ghee Clarified butter
Ghulam Bonded
Gujjars Tribe of nomads found in northern and western parts of South Asia
Gur Mandi Wholesale store for unrefined sugar
Halal Meat that has been slaughtered according to proper Islamic injunction
Hamsaya Tenant
Hujra Men's guest house
Hukumat Government
Islah Reform
Jannat Heaven
Jarnail General; one of the ranks in the KK movement
Jehnaza Funeral
Jihad Holy war
Jirga Council for decision making
Jumna Jamuna; north Indian river
Kafans Funeral shroud
Kafir Infidel

Kaunda Lit., stone; institution of peace making by placing a stone between feuding parties

Khadi Hand-spun cloth; mark of *swadeshi* movement

Khamosh Silence; to silence

Khan Landlord

Khel Clan

Khidmat, Khidmatgari Service; ability to serve

Khilafat Nationalist movement in the Indian subcontinent involving both Hindus and Muslim leaders in defence of the authority of the Caliphate in Turkey

Khudai Khidmatgar Servants of God

Kissa Khani Place for story telling; name of a famous bazaar in Peshawar

Lambardar Village revenue official

Lashkar Irregular army

Madrasah Religious seminary

Malik One of the titles bestowed by the Mughals, Sikhs and British rulers on landlords for allegiance and loyalty

Masjid Mosque

Maulana Islamic scholar trained in a *madrasah*

Melmastia Hospitality

Mian Local religious leader

Mujahiddin Warrior in a religious war

Mullah Local Islamic religious leader

Mushar Respected elder

Nabi Prophet

Parajamba Factionalism

Purna Swaraj Complete freedom

Sahib Suffix added to name as mark of respect; also used to refer to British officers

Salar-e-Azam Commander-in-chief

Shahid Martyr

Shah khel Category of people who provided music at weddings

Swadeshi Home-made

Swaraj Self-rule

Tappa 1 Sub-district

Tappa 2 Couplet

Tehsil District

Ulema Muslim clergy

Wali Wise man

Wesh Obsolete system of periodic land redistribution

Zakat Ten per cent of earnings to be paid to the community

Zalme Pukhtun Lit. young Pukhtuns; organisation formed by Ghani Khan, Badshah Khan's oldest son, in 1946, to protect, if necessary through violent means, the safety of Khudai Khidmatgars and their supporters from the communal riots instigated by the Muslim League

Zilla District

Zulm Oppression

Index

Islam: anti-Islamic colonial laws 65; fundamentalism 7; 'in danger' 184; liberationist interpretations 75, 109; martyrdom 150–2; non-violent elements in 146–52, 165–6, 209; and Pathan culture 29, 152–4, 160–1, 163–5, 208–10; revivalist movements 161–2; Shi'ia 150–1; Sufism 127, 148; Sunni 29, 150; vernacular nature of 152–4
Iqbal 73

Jails (KK experience of) 59, 96, 100, 111–14, 136, 149, 197, 199
Jama'at-i-Islami 161
James, Wendy 26, 27ff, 153ff
Jansson, Eric 9, 17, 18, 31, 42, 44, 186, 189
Jatha 54; see also Akali
Jihad 14, 34–5, 48–9, 67, 110, 133, 140, 146–52, 160, 166, 177, 189, 196
Jinnah, Mohammed Ali 8, 175, 182, 187, 189–90, 208
Jirga (tribal councils): British changes 33, 42, 61; KK adaptations 132–3, 137–8, 156; Pathan traditions 29–30, 35, 69–70, 77, 82–3, 93,160, 185
Johnson, Douglas 17–18, 82, 129, 142, 153ff
June 3rd Plan (1947) 187–8

Kabul 3, 8
Kabuliwallah 2–3
Kafirs see Infidels
Khadi 6, 56–57, 64, 87, 89–90, 98, 127; see also *Charkha*
Khan Abdul Gaffar Khan see Badshah Khan
Khan, Ghani 121, 185–7
Khan Sahib (Dr.) 47, 71, 106–8, 115, 167–72, 181–3, 185
Khans 10, 30, 67, 78, 83, 113, 126–7, 140, 153, 177, 182; 'Big khans': definition 31; honours and medals 33, 63–4, 67, 167; influence 31–2; 126, 134–5, 173, 175, 182, 194, 195; 'Small khans': definition 31; influence 31–2, 63, 67, 106, 134–5, 169
Kelly, John 162–3
Khidmat see Service
Khilafat movement 49–50, 53, 55, 57ff, 68, 162

Khudai Khidmatgar (Servants of God) movement: Activities of KK: anti-liquor campaigns 57, 65; boycotts 57, 93–6, 113, 207; cleanliness drives 64, 75, 77, 199, 207; parade and drill 59, 75, 84–5, 92, 105, 133, 199, 207; picketing 57, 59, 65, 92–94, 111, 133, 174, 197, 199; political and philosophical instruction 51–53, 67, 76; public meetings 76, 92, 139, 186; spinning 75–7, 199, 207; tax strikes 64, 94, 174; training camps 56, 67, 75–81, 85–7; Alliance of KK with Indian National Congress 162, 167–72, 175, 177–91; Badshah Khan's leadership of KK 125–32; British portrayals of KK: as Bolsheviks 18, 121, 179, 182, 209, 121; as Fascists 105–7; as Hindus 110–11, 176–7, 181, 184; as hooligans 104, 209; as infidels 49, 100, 110, 184, 196; as Sikhs 110; Growth of KK 56, 59–60, 73; Ideology of KK see Anti-communalism, Austerity, Bravery, Discipline, Humility, Martyrdom, Non-violence, Patience, Self-reform, Self-restraint, Self-sacrifice, Service, Unity; Launch of KK 56; Motivations for joining KK 4, 10, 11, 60–8, 164, 177, 204, 209; Oath of induction 73–4, 81; Organisation of KK: administration 134, 139, 142–3; civil wing 132–5; communications 139–40; leadership criteria 136–8, 208; military wing 84, 85, 88, 132, 136–8; social support structure 96–7; structure 13, 59, 69–70, 73, 142–3, 170–1, 175, 202, 208, 209: Repression of KK by British: attacks on villages 115–17; beatings and torture 58–9, 114, 116, 119, 135, 137, 175, 177, 196; castration 112, 118; coerced nudity 111, 117–18; collective fines 135; concentration camps 114; exclusion from Tribal Areas 180–3, 185; forced counter-Quranic oaths 117, 119; forced labour 112, 114; homo-erotic punishments 41, 212 (see also Homosexuality); imprisonment 59, 96, 100, 111–14, 136, 149, 197, 199; massacres 57, 59, 70, 103, 114; poisoning of KK camps 115; psychological warfare 116, 118–19; sexual threats 115, 118; Repression of KK activists by